BOROUGH & PAROCHIAL STATISTICS.

	Inhabited Houses.	Families.	Houses Building.	Houses Uninhabited.	Males.	Females.	Total.	Statute.
St MARYLEBONE	11,608	28,918	756	921	53,201	69,005	122,206	1490
PADDINGTON	1,933	3,498	93	104	6,278	8,262	14,540	122
St PANCRAS	12,369	25,392	517	787	46,058	57,490	103,548	260

	Male Servants above 20 Yrs.	under 20 Yrs.	Female Servants.	Annual Value of Property assessed April 1815.	March 1828.	Comparative Population 1801.	1811.	1821.	1831.	Numbers in 1835
St MARYLEBONE	4,785	638	12,925	509,244	692,085	63,982	75,624	96,048	122,206	
PADDINGTON	308	129	1,237	24,712	92,436	1,881	4,609	6,476	14,540	
St PANCRAS	750	470	7,228	238,661	371,376	31,179	46,333	71,838	103,548	8251

Boundary of the Borough
_____ Parishes
_____ Estates

Scale 9⅓ Inches to a mile — Extent 4¼ miles from Highgate to Oxford Street, by 4 miles from Bagnigge Wells to the Boundary in the

ECCLESIASTICAL GOVERNMENT:— CHURCHES, CHAPELS, &c

The Three Parishes of the Borough are within the Holborn Division of the Hundred of Ossulstone, diocese of London: County
and out of the Bills of Mortality: St Pancras is a peculiar, under the jurisdiction of the Dean & Chapter of St Pau..

St Marylebone :— Perpetual Curacy :— Church of All Souls, a Rectory — Parish Chapel, built 1741 :— Parish Church of St P...
6th February, 1818, cost above 60,000 £ :— Oxford Chapel 1739 :— Portland Chapel, 1766 :— Bentinck Chap...
Welbeck Chapel 1774 :— Portman Chapel 1779 :— Quebeck Chapel, 1788 :— Margaret Chap. 1789 :— Brunswick...
St John's Wood Chapel, 1814 :— St Mary's Church, Bryanstone Square, cons.d 1825 :— Christ Church, consecrated...
Trinity Church, (a district Rectory) cons.d 1828 :— Christ Chapel, Northwick Terrace, 1834.

Paddington :—(A perpetual Curacy) St Mary's Church, cons.d 27 April, 1791 :— St John's Church, fin.d 1831 :— Bayswater Ch...

St Pancras :—(Vicarage) Parochial Chapel, Service only once a month in 1789 :— Parish Church consecrated 7 May, 1822, co...
Kentish Town Chapel, rebuilt & opened 1785 :— Woburn Chapel, Tavistock Place, (private property) opened 1802 :—
Camden Town Chap. cons.d 15 July, 1824 :— Somer's Chap. cons.d 11 May, 1826 :— Regent Square Chap. cons.d 8 Ma...
St Michael's Highgate (seperate Chapelry formed of parts of the Parishes of Hornsey & Islington):— Percy Chape...
Fitzroy Chapel, 1776 :— Foundling Chapel, 1748 :—

Chapels belonging to other Parishes :— St James's (with burial ground) Hampstead Road, built 1792 :— St Martin's (with b...

SCALE.

1 Mile
8 Furlongs

The London Square

The London Square

Gardens in the Midst of Town

Todd Longstaffe-Gowan

Published for The Paul Mellon Centre for Studies in British Art
by Yale University Press, New Haven and London

Designed by Sarah Faulks

Printed in China

Library of Congress Cataloging-in-Publication Data

Longstaffe-Gowan, Todd, 1960–
The London Square : gardens in the midst of town / Todd
Longstaffe-Gowan.
    p. cm.
Includes bibliographical references and index.
ISBN 978-0-300-15201-2 (cloth : alk. paper)
1. Garden squares–England–London. I. Title. II. Title: Gardens in
the midst of town.
SB466.G75L645 2012
712'.5094212–DC23
                                            2011045171
A catalogue record for this book is available from
The British Library

Front endpaper: *Topographical Survey of the Borough of St
Marylebone, as Incorporated & Defined by Act of Parliament
1832 . . . Engraved by B. R. Davies from Surveys & Drawings by
F. A. Bartlett under the Direction of John Britton FSA*, 1834,
detail, engraving. Private collection.

Back endpaper: Aerial view of the Ladbroke Estate in
Kensington, 6 September 2006, photograph. English Heritage
Photo Library. © English Heritage, National Monuments
Record.

Frontispiece: Adrian Paul Allinson, *The A.F.S. 'Dig for Victory'
in St James's Square*, 1942, detail, oil on canvas. Westminster
City Archives. © City of Westminster Archives Centre,
London, UK / The Bridgeman Art Library.

Pg. iv: The remains of the equestrian statue of George 1 in
Leicester Square, c.1869, photograph. English Heritage Photo
Library. © English Heritage, National Monuments Record.

Pg. vi: John Mackay, map of the Grosvenor Estate, 1723, detail,
pen and ink with watercolour wash. Private collection / The
Bridgeman Art Library.

To my grandparents Moyra and Ted ('Pliny the Elder') Longstaffe

Contents

Acknowledgements

I am grateful to many friends, colleagues, scholars who over the years have to some degree informed my work, including Adriano Aimonino, Mark Aston, Joyce Bellamy, Michael Berlin, Sarah Blandy, Richard Bowden, Roger Bowdler, Pippa Brill, Patricia Carr, Jonathan Cha, Charlotte Chastel-Rousseau, Edward Cheney, Bridget Cherry, Richard Clarke, Sue Clifford, Anna Costa Novillo, Carrie Cowan, Graham Deacon, Helen Dorey, Bill Drummond, Brent Elliot, Jesús Escobar, Kate Eustace, Terry Friedman, 'Frontager 26 Budden' (Fitzroy Square), Liz Gilbert, Terry Gough, John Goulden, Sarah Green, Peter Guillery, David Hale, Eileen Harris, John Harris, Clare Hastings, Anna Haward, Benjamin Heller, Gordon Higgott, Tess Hines, Chris Hoad, Niall Hobhouse, Justin Hobson, Nigel Hughes, Ralph Hyde, Susan Jenkins, Pauline Karpidas, Marcus Koehler, Jarl Kremeier, Rory Lalwan, David Lambert, Ian Leith, Jill Lever, Nick Llewellyn, Elizabeth McKellar, Rosemarie MacQueen, Lorna McRobie, Kieran Mahon, Jonathan Makepeace, Jonathan Marsden, Anna Maude, James Miller, Ann Mitchell, Sheila O'Connell, Trenton Oldfield, Leonee Ormond, Susan Palmer, Pamela Paterson, Nicholas Penny, Adam Petitt, Henrietta Phipps, Katrina Presedo, Mark de Rivaz, Chris Rolfe, Esther Sanz Murillo, Otto Saumarez-Smith, Richard Sennett, Barbara Simms, Holly Smith, Jeremy Smith, Gavin Stamp, Lucia Strnadova, Laura Summerton, Chris Sumner, Lucy Waitt, Philip Ward Jackson, Nick Wates, Gayne Wells, Anne Wheeldon, Andy Wimble, Catherine Wright and Frank Wu. I am also indebted to the staff at the Lindley Library, London; staff at the Getty Research Institute and the Office of Scholars, Interns, and Professionals, as well as fellow scholars at the Getty Museum and Research Institute, Los Angeles; and staff at the Center for Advanced Study in the Visual Arts at the National Gallery, Washington, DC.

Several people have made special contributions to my work: Simon Bradley made available research carried out by his team on the London volumes of *The Buildings of England* series; Diane Duggan kindly shared her research into the early history of the Bedford Estate; Andrew Saint pored over my manuscript, and has made numerous helpful and insightful recommendations; Brian Allen, Director of the Paul Mellon Centre for Studies in British Art, has over the past two decades been exceedingly supportive of my work; as has Amy Meyers, Director of the Yale Center for British Art in New Haven, who has shown an unstinting interest in my research.

It would have been impossible to complete this book without two splendid periods of American exile. As a practising gardener, this meant abandoning my London office for several months at a time. My very able and congenial colleague, James Fox, allowed me to do so, and kept our small but very busy landscape enterprise on the straight and narrow. My first American sabbatical took place in Santa Monica, California, where I spent three months as a Museum Guest Scholar at the Getty Museum in the spring of 2009. David Bomford, now Acting Director, invited me to this extraordinary Parnassus. My stay was made very comfortable by Antonia Bostrom, Carol Casey, Angie Donougher, Daniela Ferrari, Jay Gam, Meagan Miller, Sabine Schlosser, George Weinberg and Katya Zelljadt, and I was privileged to have the friendship and advice of my fellow scholars, including Sussan Babaie, Carolin Behrmann, Hartmut Dorgerloh, Boris Hars-Tschachotin, Mary Louise Roberts, Andy Schulz and Avinoam Shalem. My second American peregrination took me to the National Gallery of Art in Washington, DC. This great honour I owe to Therese O'Malley, who encouraged me to apply for a visiting fellowship at the Center for Advanced Study in the Visual Arts (CASVA), where as an Ailsa Mellon Bruce Visiting Senior Fellow I was privileged to spend two months in the autumn of 2010. Here I completed my manuscript. Sue Cohn, Elizabeth Cropper, Elizabeth Kielpinski, Alison Luchs, Peter Lukehart, Laura Plaisted and Helen Tangiers all made my stay very memorable and enjoyable. In Washington I also made use of the library of Dumbarton Oaks, and am thankful to Sarah Burke, Linda Lott and Barbara Mersereux for assisting me there.

Beatrice Perry aided me in my research between 2008 and 2010; together we cheerfully and assiduously pored over manuscripts and published material at countless archives. Chloe Chard has been no less helpful: she has, in fact, been my muse since I began my research in the late 1980s. Her sparkling intellect and generous spirit have enriched my appreciation of my subject matter, and have complemented and encouraged my own sometimes eccentric interests. Marlee Busching has, likewise, played a part in the final preparation of my manuscript, and in particular with the procurement of images. I am indebted, too, to my anonymous readers, whose careful assessment of my manuscript has sharpened my narrative and my conclusions.

Judith Menes has created, with characteristic skill, a remarkable index, catering to my rather whimsical demands. David Lambert has cast his eyes over some of my work, and given me wise counsel. Sally Williams, Keeper of the London Parks and Gardens Trust's *London Inventory of Historic Green Spaces* has been characteristically generous in providing me with information on numerous squares contained within it, much of which has been compiled by an array of volunteers too numerous here to mention. Verena McCaig, who possesses a tireless enthusiasm for London squares, and who has carried out extensive original research on their recent history, has been extraordinarily helpful to me in my own research. Philip Davies has very kindly shared with me his intimate knowledge of London's squares, and has read parts of my manuscript. He has for almost four decades been at the forefront of English Heritage's sustained campaign to protect and improve the capital's squares. His former colleague Drew Bennellick, now at the Heritage Lottery Fund, was also involved in English Heritage's *Campaign for London's Squares* (2000). He has been a great ally, and has for several years been very helpful in supplying me with updates on the campaign, and pointing me in the direction of useful material on the subject.

The Marc Fitch Fund has very generously underwritten the cost of many of the book's photographs. The Paul Mellon Centre, too, has contributed considerably to the procurement of images.

I owe a very special debt to Paul Christianson, whose enduring enthusiasm for the subject and good sense have encouraged me throughout the course of my writing. His very generous and careful reading of my manuscript has improved my book immeasurably. My copy-editor, Rosemary Roberts, has combed my text for a range of infelicities, and has rendered the whole more coherent, for which I am truly grateful. Sarah Faulks has designed and produced this very handsome book It has also been a great privilege to work once again with Gillian Malpass, my editor, who has encouraged me over the years to write this book, and has done so with the greatest affection and enthusiasm.

Finally, I would like to thank Tim Knox, who has lived with and, indeed, abetted my square obsession for many years.

Todd Longstaffe-Gowan
London, 2012

Prologue

The communal garden of a residential square is a London speciality with no counterpart abroad. No group has ever understood comfort so well as the English middle class – certainly not the French, with their spindly furniture, nor the Americans, with their hazardous gadgets – and the London square, essentially an upper-middle-class perquisite, is one of the most comfortable garden ideas since the arbour with a turf seat.

Anne Scott-James, 'The London Square', *The Pleasure Garden* (1977)

Anne Scott-James, in her brief essay 'The London Square', waxes both wistful and sentimental when she notes 'there is no middle-class, middle-aged Londoner who has not some poignant memory of the London squares of his youth'. Here 'children could safely play and be watched from the windows of the house. Elderly people could sit in peace and privacy a few yards from home. And the house-holder was relieved of the cares of garden upkeep, for he paid a subscription into a common fund and the garden was run by a residents' committee.'[1]

The former journalist also makes specific reference to 'the jewels of London Square design' – the mid-Victorian communal gardens of Notting Hill. Her essay, produced to accompany one of a set of drawings by her husband, the cartoonist Osbert Lancaster (fig. 1), gives verbal identity to Lancaster's pen-and-ink sketch of the community idyll of such a garden.[2] Recollecting her youth in Bayswater, Scott-James refers to the square as

perhaps the most desirable place in London to bring up a middle-class family. Here small children made pram friendships, which were more satisfactory than the friendships of the park, where

Facing page: A foggy day in New Square, Lincoln's Inn, 1932, photograph. Charles Dickens remarks in *Bleak House* (1852) that the fog around Lincoln's Inn Hall was 'like a soft black drizzle, with flakes of soot in it as big as full-grown snowflakes – gone into mourning, one might imagine for the death of the sun.'

1 (*right*) Osbert Lancaster, *The London Square*, pen and ink, from Anne Scott-James and Osbert Lancaster, *The Pleasure Garden* (1977).

GOLDEN SQUARE.

every game had to be broken up and the prams
wheeled their separate ways at tea-time. Here a
mother who had sacked or been given notice by
her nursery-maid could deposit her children and
continue her own life in the house. Here all could
enjoy fine trees, reasonably long walks and neat if
sooty shrubberies and flower-beds. Children who
lived in these squares and who went to one of
the many good schools nearby were the envy of
their fellows, whom they could patronize with
invitations to Sunday tea.[3]

Scott-James's prose and Lancaster's sketch encapsulate, with almost trite esteem, the essence of the
traditional London square, which is the subject of
her essay. The square was an open space surrounded
by houses with an enclosed central communal

garden, which was kept in what John Loudon described in 1838 as 'perfect order at the expense of
the inhabitants of the squares, who alone have the
use of them' (fig. 2).[4]

Scott-James is right also when she remarks that
the residential or garden square is a uniquely English
device. It is, in fact, pre-eminent among England's
contributions to the development of European town
planning and urban form, as it introduced the classical notion of *rus in urbe* – the visual encroachment
of nature and rural associations into the urban
fabric – that continues to shape our cities to this
day (fig. 3).

Indeed, the idea of the residential or garden square
has been much admired and copied since its incep-
tion in London in the mid-seventeenth century,
when the planners of what were to become Lon-

4   Sir John Soane's key to the central garden at Lincoln's Inn Fields. Sir John Soane's Museum, London. The gates of many London squares remain locked to this day; keys have been replaced with swipe-cards at a number of squares in South Kensington.

5 (*facing page*)   Aerial view of South Kensington, 27 August 2001, showing a variety of squares, including Brompton, Ovington and Cadogan squares, Lennox Gardens, Egerton Crescent, Hans Place and Cadogan Place. English Heritage.

don's earliest squares appropriated the Italian concept of the piazza to create large open places at the centres of the city's new residential neighbourhoods. Most important, however, is the culminatory stage of the transmutation of these bald open spaces into garden squares, which took place from the early eighteenth century onwards, and was contingent on their secure enclosure (fig. 4). Since this time, squares, in their various permutations, have always remained important and ubiquitous constituents in most improvements and enlargements to the capital. As John Timbs remarked in *Curiosities of London, Exhibiting the Most Rare and Remarkable Objects of Interest in the Metropolis* (1855), 'the garden-spaces or planted Squares are the most recreative features of our metropolis; in comparison with which the *piazze*, *plazas* and *places* of continental cities are wayworn and dusty areas, with none of the refreshing beauty of a garden or a green field'.[5] London squares are also distinguished from their continental counterparts, as John Weale recognised with great insight in *London Exhibited in 1851*, in generally not being 'appended to any public buildings'; nor do they make 'any pretension to more adornment than the ordinary dwellings' that surround them.[6]

Of even greater importance is that squares have been appreciated not merely as garden oases or open figures in the dense city fabric but as the purveyors of light and air, whose evolution is closely tied to the provision of spacious residential development

and the improvement of the city's streets. The London Society quite rightly described squares in 1927 as the 'pride of London's planning' (fig. 5). They have been desiderata of urban improvers since the reign of James I, have promoted novelty of design, elegance and spaciousness in the urban plan, and, through a combination of unique local circumstances – including land ownership, management agreements, legislation and the English love of nature – have come to represent what Elain Harwood and Andrew Saint described in 1991 as 'the special strain of civilisation which Britain has bequeathed to the world'.[7] The London square, moreover, has proved a resilient concept, one that has developed incrementally, imperceptibly and occasionally dramatically over the centuries. Thus, while surrounding buildings have been refaced or replaced, and while trees, shrubs, paths, lighting, garden buildings and railings have come and gone, squares almost invariably have stubbornly retained their spatial integrity (fig. 6).

My enduring fascination with squares has been sustained by a number of their physical, conceptual and symbolic features. First, the practice of enclosure, introduced in the early eighteenth century, constituted a dynamic intervention that strongly expressed social changes in physical terms – the transformation of the open, unelaborated spaces in the centre of the city's seventeenth-century piazzas into planted gardens. Squares were enclosed not only with a view to their physical 'improvement' but also as an act of social control. Enclosure was, as James Ralph quipped in 1734, invoked to protect the spaces from the 'rudeness of the populace', or as John Clare would later remark, to create a 'wider space / between the genteel and the vulgar race'.[8]

The advent of secure enclosure, moreover, swiftly led to the creation of codes of behaviour to govern the use of these spaces, and such regimens in turn guided the layout and cultivation of the central areas (figs 7 and 8). As an anonymous commentator remarked in 1866, 'open spaces that, formerly, were the scenes of riot and confusion, are no longer so, since they have been become planted and placed under guardianship';[9] or as a contributor to the *Sanitary Record* observed in 1878, 'a square without railings would always be under the eye of the police'.[10] The nature of the boundary treatment and gates, which define the enclosure, is, of course, no less socially

6 The garden pavilion in
Soho Square, 1939, photograph
by Felix Man. The
building – part toolshed and
part arbour – was erected in
the mid-1870s, when the
central garden was reordered.

7 (*facing page*) Unknown
draughtsman, plan of Fitzroy
Square gardens and environs,
*c.*1818, pen and pencil with
watercolour wash. Private
collection. The drawing shows
the gardens before (1815–16,
above) and after (1818, *below*)
improvements. The central
garden and its surroundings
were enclosed and planted to
discourage the assembly of the
'idle and the profligate'.
Smoking and dogs were also
banned from the garden.

interesting: they have invariably been seen as both defensive and conspicuous, with the aim of offering both protection and privacy.

Because of this evolution of enclosure, I am also intrigued by the social dynamics of squares – not least because they provide tangible evidence for singular and well-developed social organisms. Squares, in fact, take on a kind of life dynamic: they are uniquely complex communities made up of interdependent individuals and groups more or less closely connected with one another, for whom health is dependent on the harmonious interworking of the communities' culture, politics and economics. This social dynamic extends both to the relationship among the inhabitants themselves (how they see themselves), and to the relationship between the inhabitants and the outside world (how they are perceived by others) (figs 9 and 10).

In historical terms, both inhabitants and outsiders were quick to register their awareness of the symbolic elaboration of the squares' central gardens. Regardless of their insular nature (they were separated from surrounding houses by public footpaths and public roads), the gardens were nonetheless per-

ceived as extensions of the house. This unusual, sometimes awkward, and always visible relationship demanded a special approach to the treatment of the central gardens in terms of accessibility and transparency. Osbert Lancaster's illustration of a square, with its scene of idealised outdoor home life, neatly makes the point that domesticity may encapsulate internal tensions: the pointed sprightliness with which all the occupants of the square are delineated, with the possible exception of the nanny, is in ironic contrast to the extreme orderliness of the garden setting, with its proliferation of railings, edgings and fencing.

That having been said, however, the enclosed gardens had – ironically – a contrastingly louche reputation as the scene of illicit assignations and disreputable antics (fig. 11). Squares became commonly defined in the eighteenth and nineteenth centuries as a setting for amorous dalliance; more recently A. A. Gill's *Sap Rising* (1996) and Alan Hollinghurst's *The Line of Beauty* (2004), have used the central garden as the setting for clandestine sexual encounters. Transgressive behaviour is sometimes portrayed as springing, disturbingly but almost inexorably, from the very rituals of decorous domesticity that it throws

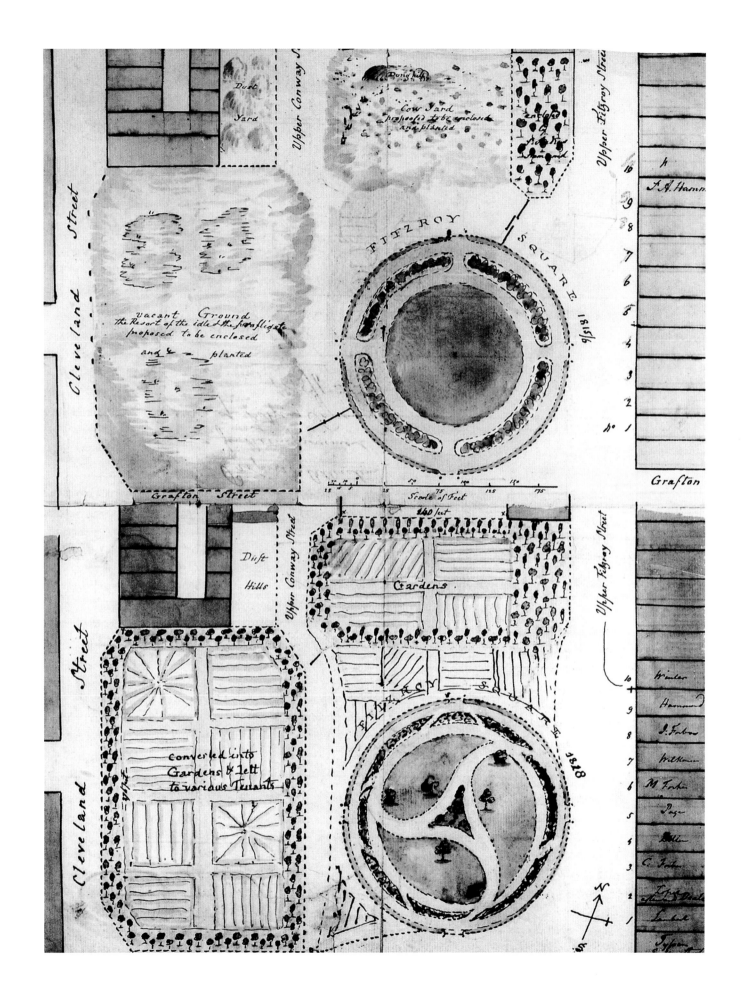

Dust Yard

Upper Conway Street

Dunghills

Cow Yard
proposed to be enclosed
and planted

Cleveland Street

Upper Fitzroy Street

FITZROY SQUARE

vacant Ground
the Resort of the idle & the profligate
proposed to be enclosed
and planted

1818/9

Grafton Street

Scale of Feet

Grafton

h

F. A. Hamm

Dust

Hills

Upper Conway Street

Gardens

140 feet

Upper Fitzroy Street

Cleveland Street

Converted into
Gardens & lett
to various Tenants

FITZROY SQUARE

1828

10 Winter
9 Hammond
8 J. Foster
7 Wilkinson
6 M Foster
5 Page
4 Allen
3 C. Foster
2
1

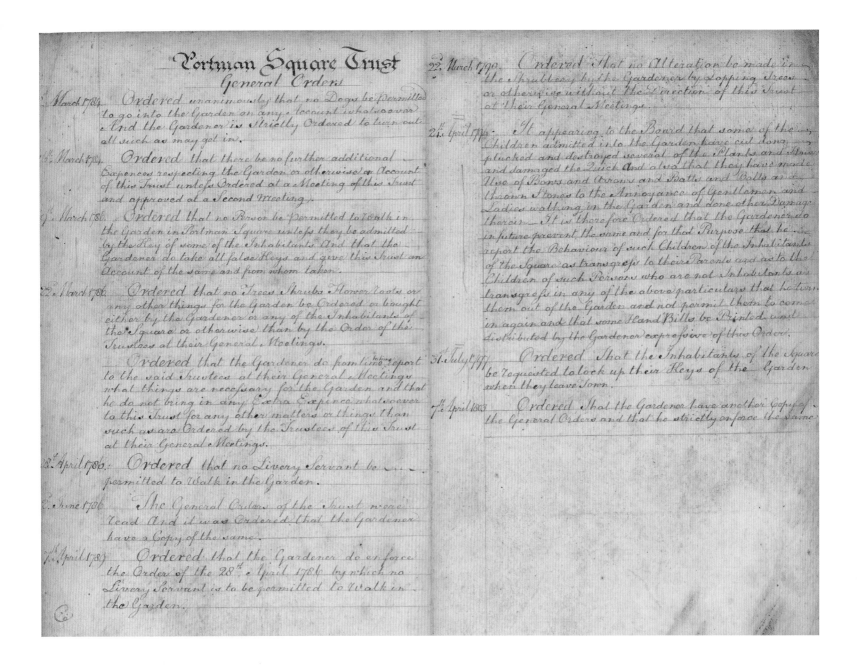

8 This manuscript list of regulations was prepared by the Trustees of Portman Square between 1784 and 1803. Every square had its own code of conduct to govern the behaviour of the key-holders of the central garden. These rules were frequently posted on painted placards within the gardens. Portman Estate Archives.

into disarray (as though enclosure were there to supply a space of privacy for a multitude of sins). One extreme example may be found in Havelock Ellis's *Studies in the Psychology of Sex* of 1906: 'I know of a case in which a nurse in a fashionable London Square used to collect all the boys and girls (gentlemen's children) in a summerhouse when it grew dark, and, turning up her petticoats, invited all the boys to look and feel her vulva, and also incite the older boys of 12 or 14 to have coitus with her'.[11]

My research reflects the increased interest in the development of London's historic urban landscape, but also owes a considerable debt to the efforts of a number of scholars who have studied the London

squares from a variety of points of view. The Scottish barrister and journalist William Weir was among the first to compile a socio-geographical study of the subject, which he published in 'The Squares of London' (1844) (fig. 12); this was followed by Beresford Chancellor's authoritative *The History of the Squares of London: Topographical and Historical* (1907), which remains the most detailed social history of the squares. The writings of Steen Eiler Rasmussen and latterly Sir John Summerson have also had a lasting impact on our appreciation of the square.

Rasmussen's *London: The Unique City* (1937) laid the foundations for the scholarly study of the subject. Like a number of foreign topographers of London

9 (*right*) Lady Caroline Lamb walking her dogs in Cavendish Square, 27 March 1803, pen and ink with watercolour wash. Hertfordshire Archives and Local Studies, DE/LB/F66/1. Although dogs were not generally welcome in London's squares, this self-portrait of the unhappy and eccentric wife of Lord Melbourne, Queen Victoria's first Prime Minister, suggests otherwise.

10 (*below*) George Scharf, *In Bloomsbury Square, June*, 1828, pencil, showing a group of watercarts round the pump in the square. British Museum, London.

tion than the compact and studiously planned continental cities. The main aim of the book is to supply a complete picture of the development of London, and of the ways in which it differs organically from cities on the Continent. The London square is, he remarks, 'very different' from the grand continental squares of the Baroque period:

> The architecture of the Baroque square is generally united into a grand crescendo. It leads the vision of the spectator from one place to the other, the whole lay-out has a distinct tendency and an architectural climax, a monument or a monumental building. Each square is a subordinate element in a great composition. The English square or crescent, on the contrary, is a restricted whole as complete as the courtyard of a convent. They form fine geometrical figures in the town plan, they are regular and completely uniform on all sides, and a series of such squares may be linked together in any order.[14]

before him, the Danish architect and town planner recognised the importance of the residential garden square in this great 'scattered city', and dedicated a chapter of his architectural and planning treatise to it.[12] Rasmussen's view was, at the time, 'shocking' to English readers,[13] as he vaunted the domestic virtues of London – its multitude of small gardens and squares – which he found more worthy of admira-

In Rasmussen's view, London squares 'belong to the town. It is as if the traditions of the Middle Ages had been handed down to the present day in squares, these domestic quarters' (fig. 13).[15]

Rasmussen's research, in turn, informed Summerson's own architectural histories, which were first published in *Georgian London* (1945) and latterly in his

11 (*right*) Thomas Sandby,
A Sceen in the Park, *c.*1780,
engraving. British Museum,
London.

12 (*below*) J. B. Papworth,
Berkeley Square, 1813, pen and
pencil with watercolour wash.
British Museum, London.

book *Architecture in Britain, 1530 to 1830* (1977).[16] Summerson's pioneering work on the great London estates
supplies us with the first original and informed view
of how squares – originally hard paved and later with
planted gardens – became the 'principal features of
attraction' of new residential development.

These studies have been supplemented by exami-
nations of squares in terms of their contribution to
the building process, including Donald Olsen's *Town
Planning in London: The Eighteenth and Nineteenth
Centuries* (1964), *Rural Change and Urban Growth,
1500–1800*, edited by C. W. Chalklin and M. A. Havinden (1974), Dan Cruickshank and Neil Burton's
Life in the Georgian City (1990), and Elain Harwood
and Andrew Saint's essay 'Squares' (in their *London*,
1991). Jules Lubbock has also re-examined the early
origins of the square in *The Tyranny of Taste: The
Politics of Architecture and Design in Britain, 1550–1960*
(1995). Countless new histories of individual or
groups of squares have also been published over the
past few decades, which have made a great contribution to our understanding of the subject, including
Mary Cosh's *The Squares of Islington* (2 vols, 1990,
1993) and the many volumes of the magisterial
Survey of London.

13 Berkeley Square looking north over the central garden, *c.*1927, photograph. Country Life Picture Library.

My analysis has also been informed by the work of scholars such as Paul Zucker, who in his book *Town and Square: From the Agora to the Village Green* (1959) examines the history and aesthetics of squares as artistically shaped 'voids'. Using this 'space–void' approach, the author develops the role of the square as the focal point of organisation of the town, and describes how these spaces, and their relationship between form and surrounding buildings, their relative proportions, their uniformity and variety, sequence and procession, and their elaboration with monuments and other 'three-dimensional accents' create a 'genuine emotional experience comparable to the impact of any other work of art', and played an important role in the development of community spirit. Peter Borsay in *The English Urban Renaissance: Culture and Society in the Provincial Town, 1660–1770* (1989) and Mark Girouard in *The English Town* (1990) discuss how advances in street design and the planting of residential squares 'went a good way towards ordering and "civilizing" the vernacular

landscape'.[17] Further, they explore how these new forms of private urban open space provided an arena for new types of social interaction that shaped contemporary polite society. Since the 1970s a particular school of architectural history has evolved that also has some bearing on square studies. For instance, Elizabeth McKellar in *The Birth of Modern London: The Development and Design of the City, 1660–1720* (1999) examines early squares within the context of the development of other forms of urban open space, and charts the social and spatial evolution of the metropolis's early modern squares.[18]

Henry W. Lawrence, too, addresses the evolving social and aesthetic functions of the London square's central garden, and discusses its 'pivotal role' in the introduction of nature into the urban fabric. In 'The Greening of the Squares of London: Transformation of Urban Landscapes and Ideals' (1993), he affirms that 'the residential squares in London developed in the seventeenth and eighteenth centuries into a unique urban landscape form that introduced rural

14 Albert Square, the fictional location of the BBC soap opera EastEnders, c.2009, photograph. Private collection. The square, given the mythical London postcode of E20, is based on Fassett Square, Hackney.

landscape values into the urban fabric in ways that continue to shape urban landscape ideals today'.[19] He takes the viewpoint of a cultural geographer by looking at physical and social landscapes as cultural processes: the gardens in squares are, in his view, 'symbolic statements expressing social values in a critical period in the history of European cities, as property and social relations were in transition from late feudal to early capitalist modes'. Squares, he continues, not only introduced nature into the town, but their deployment and elaboration reflected the evolving social values of the aristocracy and the gentry, and their efforts to negotiate a new form of social relationship in the context of the city (fig. 14). Squares and their surrounding residential districts were, in fact, among the first expressions of the desire for class segregation, domestic isolation and private open space – aspirations that would later form the basis for suburban living both in Britain and abroad. Squares were, moreover, a 'major arena playing out the tension between classes over access to open space and they influenced the development of early public parks'.[20]

Throughout this book, it should be noted, I employ the term 'square' as it has been used historically to describe not only rectangular open figures and their surrounding houses, but also crescents, circuses and polygons, which possess 'practically the same character'.[21] The gardens of all such squares were invariably provided as part of a building layout for the amenity of the houses adjacent to or overlooking them, from which they are generally (with exception of the 'paddock' enclosures of the Ladbroke Estate in Notting Hill and many mid- to late nineteenth-century communal gardens of Kensington and Chelsea) separated by public roads (fig. 15). So-called 'street squares' and civic or ceremonial squares (including Trafalgar and Parliament Squares) receive scant attention in my narrative as they were not designed to be the centres of residential units.

The geographical limits of my study extend to the edges of Greater London, but most of the capital's squares are situated within inner London, and it is with these squares that I am primarily concerned. If in my narrative I have given a great deal of atten-

tion to some of the older, established squares of central London and the West End, it is largely because they were often in the vanguard of taste and innovation, and as such were remarkably influential.

My book makes no claims to being a comprehensive survey of the London square: the subject is too immense to cover in a single volume, nor has it been my wish to do so. I nevertheless explore many of the major themes and issues that have had a bearing on the make-up and development of the squares over the past four centuries, ranging from the provision of open space for children to play in, to the passing of model improvement acts, and the negative effect of motorised traffic (figs 16 and 17). I have generally followed a practice of mentioning specific squares when they illustrate a point raised in the narrative. It should also be noted that my treatment of some of the major themes addressed

across the period covered in the following pages – including traffic access and circulation, the relationship of squares to other forms of urban open space, views and prospects, the relationship of the central space to the surrounding architecture, *rus in urbe*, health issues, and representations of squares in art – is sometimes uneven, and may appear to some readers as haphazard. It may well be, but it reflects the issues that were perceived and reported at different times in the last four hundred years as having a bearing on the development of this unique urban phenomenon.

Lastly, given the hundreds of squares in London, it has been impossible to mention them all, so readers who hope to find a potted history of their square within these pages will be disappointed. I must, however, here declare that I do not subscribe to the common belief that there are over six

16 (*right*) Lonsdale Square, Islington, *c.*1950, photograph. Country Life Picture Library. This quiet corner shows how most London squares looked before the advent of car parking and the trappings associated with it.

17 (*below*) A group of local residents sitting in Walcot Square, Kennington, on the occasion of King George V's Silver Jubilee celebrations in 1935, photograph. Minet Library, Lambeth. The square was one of many that lost its railings during the Second World War.

hundred squares in Greater London.[22] The total number is, in my view, closer to three hundred: the number has been inflated since the late 1920s by the addition of 'enclosures' – or 'common gardens in the front or rear of houses, shrubberies, roadside strips, and triangles at the junction[s] of roads' – to the *Royal Commission on London Squares Site List* (1928), which later formed the basis for the London Squares Preservation Act of 1931. My interpretation should not, however, in any way diminish the importance of the green spaces included on the 1931 inventory.

I began my research into London squares in the late 1980s, when I was a doctoral student in the Department of Geography at University College London. This interest was piqued by my supervisor, Hugh Prince, who recommended that I include squares within the scope of my analysis of London's vernacular gardening tradition for the period 1700 to 1840. During the course of this research I had the benefit of the wisdom of numerous academics at UCL, including Richard Dennis and Peter Jackson, and Derek Keene at the Centre for Metropolitan History. I also had regular informal tutorials with the late Sir John Summerson, and towards the end of my doctoral research sustained contact with the late Donald Olsen. I published some of my initial findings in my book *The London Town Garden, 1700– 1840* (2001).[23]

My interest was rekindled in 1995 with the advent of the London Parks and Gardens Trust's London Squares Conference, and by my role in co-ordinating, and in part compiling, the trust's *London Inventory of Historic Green Spaces* (then the *Inventory of Public Parks, Gardens, Squares, Cemeteries, and Churchyards of Local Historic Interest in Greater London*), now London Gardens Online – a modern-day Domesday book of small but important urban green spaces that make a contribution to the public health and public amenity of the metropolis. This I did with a very able team, including Hazel Conway, James Edgar, Ruth Guilding and David Lambert.

That it has taken me so long to get down to writing this book has worked, unexpectedly, to my advantage: for nothing short of a 'square renaissance' has taken place since the mid-1990s, the like of which has never been seen before. All over London, squares have been recognised and recorded, their railings restored, and their gardens and surroundings improved. Had I written this book, as I intended to, about ten years ago, I would have missed the impact of this remarkable efflorescence.

I

A New Attribute of 'the Seat Imperiall of this Kingdom'[1]

The London square developed slowly and idiosyncratically, as access to open space in the rapidly growing metropolis became a matter of public concern.[2] It was neither an 'accidental invention',[3] nor the spontaneous creation of public-spirited aristocrats in an 'Age of Taste', but a hybrid of various different antecedents, including cloister gardens, college quadrangles, closes, sheep walks, paddocks and waste common fields.[4]

Early Development of the Square

Two significant traditions contributed to the development of the square: the first was the regular enclosure of waste fields in an effort to protect these public grounds from private interests; and the second was the initiative to create a form of unified residential set-piece, focused on a large 'opening' encompassed by a reasonably uniform architectural framework.[5] The first tradition possibly contributed to the notion that the area in the middle of these large openings should be green, while the second promoted the surrounding of the central space with regular ranges of domestic premises. What the two traditions had in common was that they were intended to safeguard open space within and around the metropolis at a time of decreasing public amenity.

Both traditions, likewise, developed in response to long-standing and sometimes thorny disputes between the monarch, the citizens of London and

Westminster, and the cities' building speculators. The sovereign had, since the sixteenth century, sought to contain the physical growth of the capital and to promote the creation of dignified and ornamental buildings and public spaces within it; the citizens wished to preserve common fields within or adjacent to the city, where they enjoyed rights of way and the use of open spaces for recreation, drying clothes or pasturing cattle; and the developers wished to make as much money as possible by building streets of houses for 'persons of estate of value' (fig. 18). A compromise of a sort was reached in the first quarter of the seventeenth century, when James I and then Charles I took measures to preserve some of the citizens' rights to common land by insisting that, when development took place in open waste fields, 'openings' were set aside to preserve or modestly enhance the rural character of the setting; this often meant little more than keeping a portion the former fields in grass, inscribing it with gravelled paths, and enclosing the resultant patchwork of 'Grass Platts' with post-and-rail fences. They furthermore insisted that the new buildings encompassing these handsome new open places were to be 'clothed in the grand Renaissance style which accorded with their ambition for a magnificent capital to impress foreign ambassadors and make a "memorable work of our time to all posterity"'.[6]

From the late sixteenth century numerous royal proclamations were issued and acts of parliament

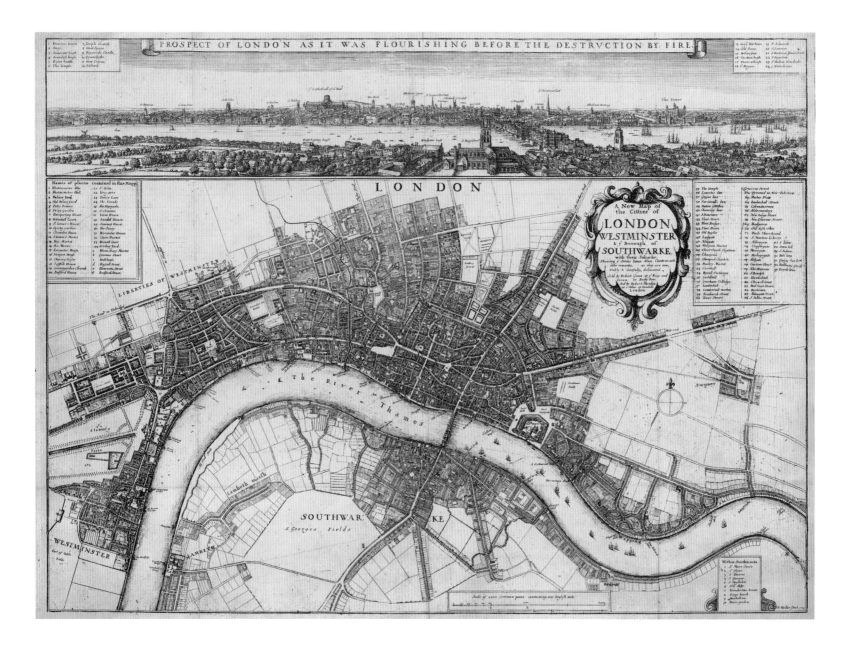

18 Wenceslaus Hollar, *Prospect of London as it was Flourishing before the Destruction by Fire*, 1675, etching. British Museum, London.

passed to prohibit the building of new houses in London, except for redevelopments on old foundations. These restrictions were imposed by the Crown and Privy Council at the request of the Lord Mayor and aldermen of the City of London to control the expansion of London, and latterly to give the sovereign control over the character of the development of his capital. The initial aim was to stop further population growth by immigration, particularly of the rural poor, whose presence posed a threat to public health, public order, the economy and food supply, and the quality of the built environment. But from the accession of James I in 1603, there developed a secondary objective: to exercise control over the appearance of new buildings with a view to

encouraging public magnificence. This in turn led to the appointment in 1615 of a special commission, which consisted of the entire Privy Council and others including Sir Henry Wotton, whose role was to better enforce the proclamations and legislation. The commission's first proclamation was issued in 1615 and affirmed the king's policy of transforming London into a 'truly magnificent city comparable to the Rome of the Emperor Augustus'.[7] Subsequent proclamations, at least until the mid-1620s, set out design guidelines to ensure that new and redeveloped buildings would be uniform in appearance.

In the event the proclamations had little effect on restraining London's overall growth: it was impossible to staunch the flow of migrants to the city, the

19 Richard Newcourt and William Faithorne, *An Exact Delineation of the Cities of London and Westminster and the Suburbs thereof, together wth ye Burrough of Southwark*, 1658, engraving (detail), showing 'Moore Feilds'. British Museum, London. Public works such as the planting of Moorfields were cited at the time as models of good practice.

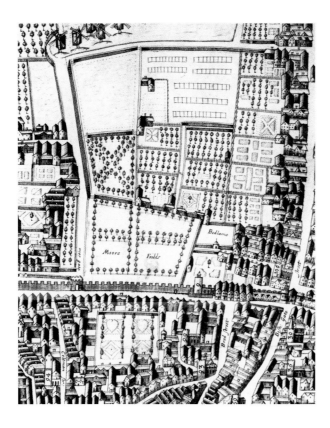

were recast several times at the personal expense of rich public-spirited merchants to render them more commodious and pleasant for the citizens to 'walke in to take the ayre and for Merchants maides to dry clothes in'.[9]

In 1607 the fields were, however, improved in a more comprehensive and coherent manner and much to the benefit of the local inhabitants. Galvanised by the royal proclamations against new building within a 3-mile radius of the City of London, the Corporation of the City of London transformed the still marshy and insalubrious area into what Richard Johnson described in *The Pleasant Walkes of Moore-fields* (1607) as a 'pleasurable place of sweet ayres for Cittizens [including 'the poore and succourlesse'] to walke in'. The 10-acre field was drained, laid out 'in the fashion of a crosse', furnished with 'sweet walkes', fences and benches, and planted with over three hundred trees subscribed by and named after individual citizens.[10]

The example of the improvement of Moorfields was not lost on those citizens who were opposed to the development of the open land at the centre of what is now known as Lincoln's Inn Fields.[11] In the wake of Sir Charles Cornwallis's unsuccessful application of 1613 for a licence to build in the fields 'wth an intent to convert the whole feild into new buildinges, contrary to His Ma'tie's Proclamacion', a second petition was presented to James I in 1617 from the gentlemen of the Inns of Court and Chancery and the four parishes adjoining the fields (fig. 20).[12] The petitioners requested 'that the feildes commonly called Lincolnes Inn Feildes, being parcell of His Ma'ties inheritance, might for their generall Commoditie and health be converted into walkes after the same manner as Morefeildes are now made to the greate pleasure and benefite of that Citty'.[13]

The king, who endorsed the 'special benefits and ornamental value' of Moorfields, was eager to encourage a similar initiative at Lincoln's Inn Fields. Accordingly, the Privy Council circulated a letter to the Lord Mayor, the City aldermen, the justices of the peace for Middlesex and the members of Gray's Inn, Lincoln's Inn, Middle Temple and Inner Temple, urging them to solicit subscriptions to meet the cost of 'soe worthie and comendable a worke'. In 1618 a Commission on Buildings was established (reformed and enlarged in 1620), which included the Earl of

system of building licences was subject to various abuses, and it was difficult to police effectively the large area under the Crown's jurisdiction. The regulation of the general form and appearance of new building was, on the other hand, a great success, for it determined the typical façade of the London terrace, which made up the architectural framework that enclosed and defined the open places in the centre.

The Improvement of Common Fields

Not long after his accession to the throne, James I wrote to the Lord Mayor and aldermen of the City of London 'congratulating them upon the care bestowed upon the walks of Morefields, [and] the re-edifying of Aldgate', and commending the citizens for their energy and generosity 'in things that doe concern the ornament of that our Cittie in the walks of Moorefields a matter both of grace and great use for the recreation of our people' (fig. 19).[8] Moorfields, which lay north of the city walls, had been given in trust to the City of London 'for the ease of the citizens' before the Norman Conquest, and was described as a site of public recreation as early as 1173. Over the ensuing centuries the fields

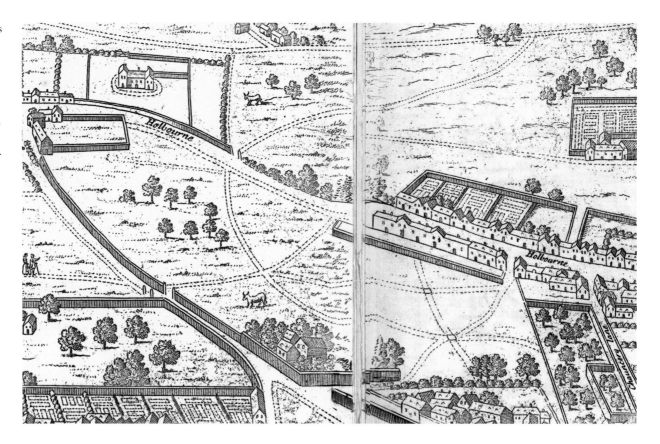

Pembroke, the Earl of Arundel and Inigo Jones, who was instructed to prepare a design for building in the fields.[14]

The aim of the commission was to ensure that the fields were set out with 'faire and goodlye walkes, [which] would be a matter of great ornament to the Citie, pleasure and freshnes for the health and recreation of the Inhabitantes thereabout, and for the sight and delight of Embassadors and Strangers coming to our Court and Cittie, and a memorable worke of our tyme to all posteritie'.[15] To achieve this objective entailed clearing the fields 'and repressing all nuisances and inconvenient buildinges which confine upon the same' so that they could be 'framed and reduced both for sweetnes, uniformitie and comlines into such walkes, partitions or other plottes and in such sorte, manner and forme both for publique health and pleasure'.[16]

The commission was empowered only to lay out the grounds that now constitute the open space of Lincoln's Inn Fields. They could not – as they had at Moorfields – exercise any authority or influence over development around the periphery of the enclosure. Consequently the inner area of the fields was protected but the environs were not. One William Newton of Bedfordshire was therefore able to petition Charles I in 1636 for a licence to build fourteen large houses (each with a 40-foot frontage)

Prospect of Lincolns Fields.
from E.N.E.

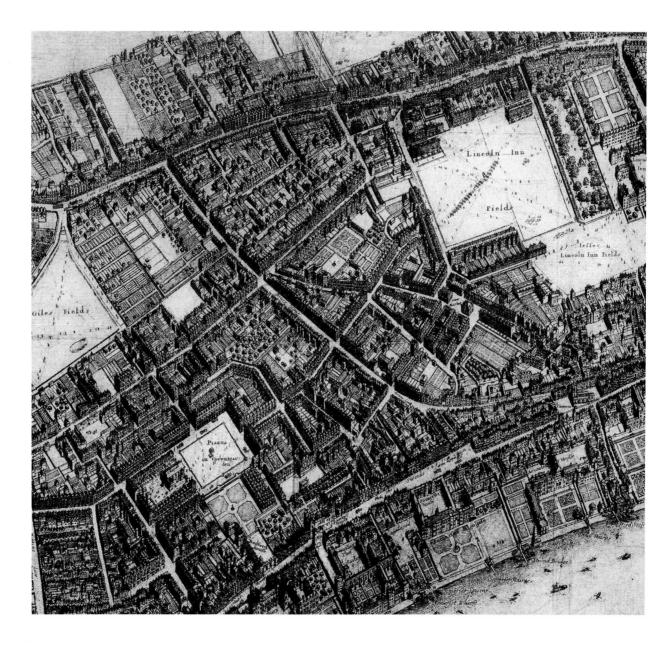

on the western side of the square, which he was immediately granted. In 1638 he obtained another licence, to build a further thirty-two houses thereabouts, most of which were complete by 1641. Newton envisaged a bold, symmetrical, classical composition for his scheme, replicating the pattern established in Covent Garden in the 1630s.

Wenceslaus Hollar's *Prospect of Lincolns Inn Fields from E.N.E.* (*c*.1641–53) gives us a glimpse of what the area must have looked like during the course of the Civil War (fig. 21).[17] The fields are surrounded on three sides by buildings, and the large central area is enclosed with a low railing. They are, furthermore, teeming with troops (some drilling behind a tent at the centre of the space), cavalry

and what would appear to be people going about their daily business. A second etching by the same artist, executed *c*.1658, shows the fields in a similar state and being used in the same manner (fig. 22). Hollar's bird's-eye view also, however, shows the central area as criss-crossed by an irregular web of broad and well-trodden footpaths; these are presumably the scars of the fields' war-time use. Perhaps unsurprisingly, the area was described during this period as being in a filthy state, having been disfigured by the dumping of many thousands of loads of dung and dirt and the digging of a common horse pool. Their appropriation for such purposes annoyed the inhabitants, who affirmed in a petition that they were 'almost quite deprived of their former

23 William Lodge, *Lincoln's Inn, London*, c.1649–89, pen and brown ink. British Museum, London. The view looks east from the centre of Lincoln's Inn Fields, where the two paths crossing the area intersect; among the features visible are Newman's Row (on the north side), Old Southampton Buildings (on the south side), and Lincoln's Inn and its garden and the tower of St Sepulchre (to the east).

liberty of Walking, Training, drying of Cloathes, and recreating themselves in the said fields'.[18]

Robert Morden and Philip Lea's *Actuall Survey of London, Westminster, & Southwark* of 1700 and two near contemporary views – a drawing by the topographical draughtsman and etcher William Lodge, and a panoramic painting by an anonymous artist[19] – portray the fields after they had been 'levelled, plained and cast into grass plots and gravel walks of convenient breadth, railed all along on each side, and set with rows of trees' (fig. 23).[20] The central area is shown as inscribed by two diagonal paths; the southwest leg of the cross splits to form a spur, which appears to be a relict path from the sixteenth century. Lodge's drawing, like a sketch of c.1683–1703 attributed to François Gasselin, also indicates how the fields were laid out with the intention of framing and making the most of the views eastwards to the mature gardens of Lincoln's Inn, and the City beyond (fig. 24).

In the neighbouring parish of St Martin-in-the-Fields, Leicester Fields (afterwards Leicester Square) experienced similar improvements.[21] Formerly the common fields of St Martin's, where the parishioners enjoyed rights of way and the use of the held for drying clothes and pasturing cattle after Lammas Day (12 August), Leicester Fields were described in 1549 as meadow land. In c.1616 the fields were partially enclosed by the Military Company for an

exercise yard (fig. 25). Then in 1630 Robert Sydney, second Earl of Leicester, negotiated the lease of the fields, where he proposed to build his own private house. Before enclosing part of the land for building he was, however, obliged to compensate the parishioners for their loss of rights. Lord Leicester therefore pledged, at the behest of three members of the Privy Council appointed by the king to act as arbiters between himself and the parishioners, to improve 'the nether part' of the field (which later became known as Leicester Fields) by casting it into tree-lined walks and leaving 'fitt spaces . . . for the Inhabitantes to drye their Clothes there as they were wont, and to have free use of the place, but not to despasture it, and all the foote wayes through that Close to bee used as now they are'.[22] Leicester House was raised on the northern half of the fields in 1631–5, and by 1670 the earl had begun to develop houses around the periphery of the fields; through agreements entered into with contractors, who undertook to build houses in the square, the centre of the fields were enclosed with posts and rails and planted with 'young trees of Elm'.[23] John Ogilby and William Morgan's map of 1676 shows the fields enclosed and bisected by two paths (fig. 26).

The desire to improve some of London's common fields was doubtless to some extent encouraged by the success of the large, well-appointed and then

uiul de Jt paul

le coin qui Enure En oborne du jardin dif a uorcat

24 François Gasselin(?), drawing of the view east from the garden of Lincoln's Inn, *c.*1683–1703, pen and brown ink, with grey wash, over graphite. British Museum, London. The gardens, consisting of closely planted trees, are seen from the other side of a low wall; the gable (*centre*) is probably that of the hall of Lincoln's Inn, and at the right is the dome of St Paul's Cathedral.

well-established gardens at the Inns of Court, situated on the banks of the River Thames. The Inns of Court is the collective name given to the four legal societies – Gray's Inn, the Inner and Middle Temples, and Lincoln's Inn – that occupied groups of medieval buildings and operated as both hostels and workplaces for London's legal community. William Noy, treasurer of Lincoln's Inn, remarked in 1632 that 'every inn of the court was a university in itself', or, as the historian Geoffrey Tyack has affirmed, 'a place of legal learning, focusing (unlike Oxford and Cambridge) on common law, and providing a practical training for barristers as well as an agreeable place in which the aristocratic *jeunesse dorée* could prolong their adolescence'.[24]

Although the inns came into being before the fourteenth century, there are no accounts of the gardens until 1510, when the Inner Temple is recorded as possessing a number of garden courts, possibly reflecting earlier monastic planting, including the 'nutgardeyne' and Fig Tree Court.[25] Garden building

appears to have accelerated at all the inns from the 1550s to the 1620s, when the estate began to erect expensive halls and chapels, and to transform their erstwhile rough surroundings of marshy open fields, rubbish dumps, rabbit warrens and irregular cultivated spaces into costly gardens (fig. 27). These gardens were cast into quarters, crossed by walks, and littered with an array of garden features, including mounts, seats, terraced walks and banqueting houses – attributes typical of high-status gardens of the time.[26] The purpose of the new gardens was, unlike the great openings at Moorfields, Leicester Fields and Lincoln's Inn Fields, to provide a dignified setting for a select few to pursue cultivated discourse, entertainment and leisure, as well as sport, including archery and bowling.

Nor was this the only difference between the inns' gardens and the city's improved fields. Although the former were semi-public spaces, used by residents, clients, servants, tradesmen and visitors since at least the late sixteenth century, the inns had put

25 (*right*) Leicester Fields as depicted in the 'Agas Map' of early modern London, *c.*1560, engraving, *c.*1750. British Museum, London.

26 (*far right*) John Ogilby and William Morgan, *A Large and Accurate Map of the City of London*, 1676, engraving (detail), showing Leicester Fields. Private collection.

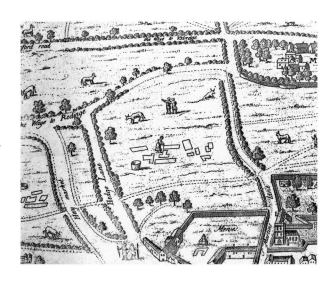

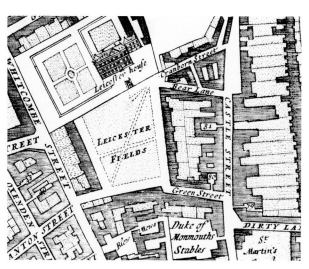

23

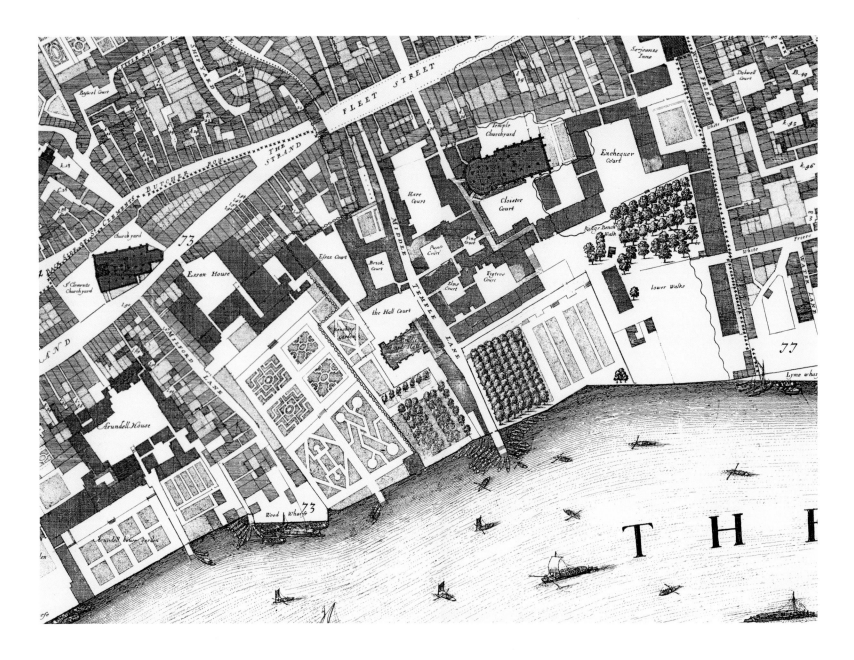

27 John Ogilby and William Morgan, *A Large and Accurate Map of the City of London*, 1676, engraving (detail), showing the Inns of Court and their gardens. London Metropolitan Archives.

in place a range of measures to protect their precincts from 'rogues and beggars', which they considered 'very dangerous both in respect of health as for robbing chambers'.[27] Most importantly, the gardens were enclosed with high brick walls with strong gates fitted with keys.[28] Furthermore, from the early 1580s gardeners at the Inner Temple were given responsibility for security, including 'protecting the garden gate'; and in winter 1581 they were charged with making 'privy searches' within the precincts for 'rogues, and . . . help[ing] carry them to Bridewell or to other places of punishment'. At Gray's Inn there were similar prescriptions: one of the gardener's duties in 1631 was to make sure that 'not boyes gerles rude or beggarly people [were permit-

ted] to pester the walkes nor laundresses nor others to dry clothes on the bouling Greene or rayles and hedges thereof'.[29]

Given the precautions taken by the inns to safeguard their precincts, it is perhaps not surprising that the unguarded and flimsily railed fields at Lincoln's Inn and the open space of Moorfields were prey to a great variety of nuisances. For instance, the use to which the central area at Lincoln's Inn Fields was put proved a great annoyance to the inhabitants. From the 1650s the rails bounding the western edge of the fields were daily torn up, stolen and conveyed away;[30] and in 1664 Thomas Newton erected 'severall wooden houses or shedds and digged gravell pitts in the middle of ye said feild neere ye common ways

and passages there, and employed ye said house for puppet playes, dancing on ye ropes, mountebanks, and other like uses, whereby multitudes of loose disorderlie people are daylie drawne together'.[31] Great crowds of disorderly people also thronged the fields in July 1683 for the execution there of William, Lord Russell; and George Bower's design for a medallion of 1688 depicts a rabble at the centre of the 'Great Square' burning papal emblems removed from the Franciscan monastery attached to no. 54 Lincoln's Inn Fields (fig. 28). The fact that the fields were ill kept and unguarded was also a source of danger to the public. The preamble to the act passed in 1735 to improve the fields provides the most detailed account of the disorders committed there, reporting that:

the Great Square . . . hath for some Years past lain in waste and in great Disorder, whereby the same has become a Receptacle for Rubbish, Dirt and Nastiness of all Sorts . . . but also for want of proper Fences to enclose the same great Mischiefs have happened to many of His Majesty's subjects going about their lawful Occasions, several of whom have been killed, and others maimed and hurt, by Horses which have been from Time to Time aired and rode in the said Fields; and by reason of the said Fields being kept open many wicked and disorderly Persons have frequented and met together therein, using unlawful Sports

and Games, and drawing in and enticing young Persons into Gaming, Idleness and other vicious Courses; and Vagabonds, common Beggars, and other disorderly Persons resort therein, where many Robberies, Assaults, Outrages and Enormities have been and continually are committed.[32]

While at Lincoln's Inn Fields there does not appear to have been a mechanism to deal with the aforementioned nuisances, at Moorfields, soon after the fields were reordered in 1607, the corporation erected stocks with a huge iron chain. They were set up with a view to punishing those that 'lay any filthy thing within these fields, or make water within the same to the annoyance of those who walke therein, which evill famous in times past has much corrupted mans senses, and supposed to be a great nourisher of diseases'.[33]

It was not, in fact, until the early eighteenth century that the inhabitants of London's common fields would begin to tackle effectively the management and protection of their shared amenity. The developers of the city's earliest purpose-built squares were, as we shall see, to experience similar difficulties.

Enclosures Formed by Regular Buildings

The tradition of forming large openings at the centres of new residential precincts, encompassed by rows of regular houses, developed at the same time as the desire to protect some areas of common land threatened by new development. These new openings were referred to variously as 'places' and occasionally 'piazzas', and they were generally formed on open land over which the local parishioners exercised few if any rights of use.[34]

The principal aims behind their creation were the provision of convenient houses for persons of quality, and greater access to light, ventilation and views than could be found in the houses of ordinary streets in the metropolis. There was initially little interest on the part of the developer in elaborating the central areas with any form of amenity, nor an express desire to exclude non-residents from crossing or using these open places, as they were often perceived at the time as a form of street widening.

The first exercise in this new form of suburban residential development took place on the Earl of

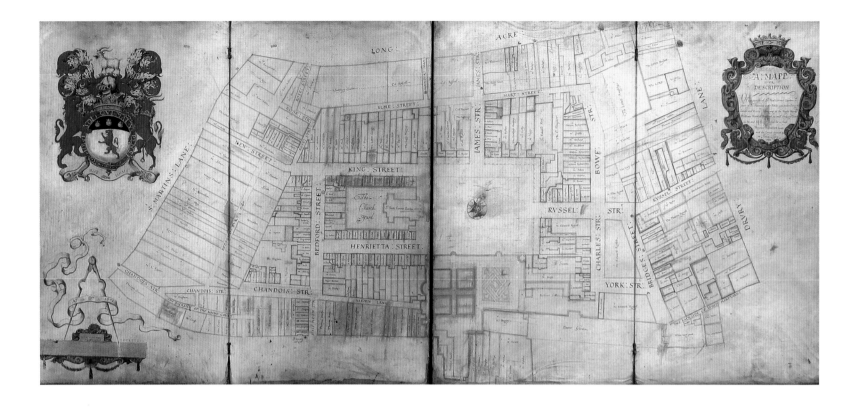

29 John Lacy, *A Map or Description of the Parish of St Paul Covent Garden*, 1673, pen and ink with watercolour wash. Bedford Estate Archive, BL-P73, Woburn Abbey.

Bedford's 'great pasture' at Covent Garden – a 20-acre field enclosed by brick walls, nestled between the Inns of Court and the City to the east and Westminster to the west. The area in which Covent Garden piazza now stands – circumscribed by Long Acre, St Martin's Lane, Drury Lane and an irregular parallel line with Strand – was once pastureland belonging to the Abbey (or Convent) of St Peter at Westminster, which had been confiscated by the Crown during the dissolution of the monasteries and was granted in 1552 to John Russell, first Earl of Bedford. While the second and third earls made considerable improvements to the family's London estate over the succeeding decades, it was Francis, the fourth earl, who initiated the building works that culminated in the creation of the piazza (fig. 29). This revolutionary design was almost certainly the work of Inigo Jones, who was at the time Surveyor-General of the Kings Works, and a key figure in the commission established in 1625 to control new building in London.[35] From the early 1630s a large rectangular piazza was formed: the north and east sides were lined with 'howses and buildings for the habitacons [*sic*] of Gentlemen and men of ability' – brick and stone 'portico buildings' or 'piatzo houses' of strictly uniform and classical character, graced with iron 'pergulas' or balconies.[36] The

houses, which were completed by 1639, had front doors opening into a vaulted arcade, and gardens with coach houses and stabling at the back: indeed, this was the first instance of mews streets in London.[37] The western side of the piazza was enclosed by the symmetrical composition of the imposing Tuscan Doric façade of the Church of St Paul, flanked by two dwelling houses;[38] and the southern side was bounded by the high brick walls that concealed the extensive pleasure ground of Bedford House.[39] This house, although adjacent to the piazza, did not bear any relation to it. The centre of the piazza is shown in an anonymous painted view of the late 1640s as a capacious space enclosed by timber hurdles, and cast into geometrical divisions by a network of broad paths.[40] The rails surrounding the piazza were presumably erected to dissuade people from riding or exercising horses within it (fig. 30).

The Place Royale (now known as the Place des Vosges) in Paris – a grand arcaded square of terraced houses – is generally accepted as one of the principal sources for the layout of Bedford's new residential quarter (fig. 31). The *grande place* was begun around 1605, and would have been seen by Inigo Jones between 1609 and 1612. Jones, moreover, travelled through Provence and visited Bordeaux in 1609, and

toured Italy in 1613–14, during which time he would have seen a number of 'bastide' towns with arcaded central squares and formally designed Italian *piazze*.[41] No less influential was the piazza in Livorno, which was dominated by a church flanked by two smaller buildings. It is, however, also conceivable that, given Charles I's keen and active interest in Bedford's new development, the layout of Covent Garden owes something to the Plaza Mayor in Madrid (completed 1622; fig. 32). The king spent six months in Madrid in 1623, where he was fêted by Philip IV in the plaza,[42] so it is possible that the memory of this magnificent urban space influenced his views on the layout of his courtier's 'newe town'.[43]

32 (*right*) Juan de la Corte, *Horse Tournament in the Plaza Mayor, Held to Honour the Arrival of Charles Stuart, Prince of Wales, in Madrid in 1623*, *c*.1630, oil on canvas. Museo de Historia, Madrid.

33 (*below*) Unknown artist, *Covent Garden Piazza*, *c*.1660, oil on canvas. Collection of the Earl of Pembroke, Wilton House, Wiltshire. The tree on the so-called 'Mount' at the centre of the piazza was replaced in 1668–9 by a 'Doricke columne of polished marble' supporting a sundial.

The architectural uniformity and social segregation of Covent Garden signalled a dramatic departure from past building practice, and were to become the model for a number of squares laid out in the eighteenth and nineteenth centuries. Covent Garden's street plan, devised before development began, further emphasised the area's peculiarity. Instead of forming connecting thoroughfares, like Strand, streets were laid out in concentric squares around the open piazza, creating a reasonably self-contained and isolated enclave. Access to the piazza from its immediate environs was, in fact, very limited. 'Traffic moving to and from the court therefore tended to flow around, rather than through inner Covent Garden, whose layout violated the normal logic of London development, implicitly demanding a new kind of

social geography, based on the demands of residential comfort rather than artisan manufacturing and retail trade.'[44]

As its Italianate name suggests, the piazza at Covent Garden was intended to vie with a handful of well-known continental squares. However, by all accounts Bedford's piazza, which was more or less complete by the 1640s, was not a great success. Various factors, including the outbreak of the Civil War, contributed to the social decline of this fleetingly fashionable neighbourhood. For instance, the early inhabitants of the piazza suffered on account of the inadequacy of its common sewers. The unacceptable problems caused by the main Covent Garden sewer, in fact, resulted in Bedford's prosecution in 1635 for causing a 'public nuisance'.[45] The gentility of the new development was also doubtless compromised by the arrival of the market: the inner area of the piazza, which was initially occupied by reasonably affluent residents, had by 1654 suffered the first incursions of mercantile premises in the 'portico walks'. The square rapidly became a resort of popular concourse, and was by 1667 afflicted with 'great ffylth' caused by the volume of business transacted within the market on the south side of the

piazza.[46] The market, however, was here to stay (at least until it was finally removed to Nine Elms in 1974), as from 1670 it was legally established by the authority of the royal prerogative.[47]

The unsatisfactory character of the central opening of the piazza was not helped by the fact that it lacked the degree of finish it was originally intended to have: it was not paved but laid to gravel (and remained thus until at least 1720), nor was it for many years given its promised central eye-catcher.[48] The 'broad place' instead boasted a single tree at its centre, the root of which was dug up in about 1667 (fig. 33); it was replaced in 1668–9 by a stone sundial column (fig. 34).[49] Bedford proposed to build a 'beautiful Structure' surmounted by a brass statue of Charles I, enclosed with a 'faire Iron gate' at the centre of the piazza.[50] His decision to raise a statue of the reigning monarch was probably informed by his knowledge of the *places royales* in France – most of which featured royal or princely statuary (fig. 35).[51] Bedford also presumably intended the statue to be a mark of his gratitude for the king's efforts on his behalf in obtaining a building licence for his new development, and he possibly saw the statue as an attraction, which would add to its success.[52]

29

35 Unknown artist, *The Exact Portraiture of Charles the First of Blessed Memory*, seventeenth century, engraving of Hubert Le Sueur's equestrian statue of Charles I. British Museum, London. Francis, fourth Earl of Bedford, proposed in 1629 to commission an equestrian statue of Charles I for the centre of his piazza at Covent Garden. Although this commission did not materialise, efforts were made in the 1660s to carry out Bedford's original proposition by erecting Le Sueur's contemporary statue of the same monarch (now in Trafalgar Square).

Although the earl's commission was not realised, his intention to embellish the centre of his large 'piatzo' with a statue of a British monarch set a precedent, prefiguring the pattern of the development of subsequent London squares. Indeed, following this lead, for almost two centuries the projectors and sometimes the inhabitants of several of the city's most distinguished squares commissioned – or, more frequently, let it be known that they intended to erect – statues to adorn the hubs of their new and exclusive residential precincts.

While Covent Garden may not in itself have been a total success, it demonstrated by example how residential development could be done. As Francis Sheppard remarks in *London* (1998), 'the concept of the central square, the church, and the uniform ranges of houses in the surrounding streets became in later Stuart, Georgian, and even Victorian times the standard dress of very many of London's residential estates, particularly in socially self-conscious West London'.[53]

From about 1661 plans began to take shape for two more 'new towns' elsewhere on the suburban fringes: one of these pioneering post-Restoration developments was destined for the open fields south of Bedford House in Bloomsbury, and the other for the area south of Pall Mall and west of the Palace of Westminster in the Parish of St James's Piccadilly. Both were contrived on distinctive models and developed independently of each other.

Bloomsbury – formerly Southampton – Square appears to have been conceived around 1647, at the time of the rebuilding of Bedford House for Thomas Wriothesley, fourth Earl of Southampton (fig. 36). Southampton was then Lord Treasurer to Charles II, and his proposal to build in 'Long Field' a mansion for his own occupation, the walled and paved forecourt of which opened into a square opening surrounded by rows of terraced houses, was doubtless based on the example of Covent Garden. The development was given a market, but not, however, a church. The 'noble square or piazza, a little town' was still incomplete in February 1665, when John Evelyn paid a visit to Lord Southampton.[54]

The courtier Henry Jermyn, Earl of St Albans, began, from 1661, to develop proposals for the court suburb of St James's on land he then owned jointly with Charles II.[55] He was a well-travelled and cultured man. He followed his father into royal service, and in the course of his colourful career attended Lord Bristol's embassy to Madrid in 1622–3, and in 1624–5 was a member of a mission to Paris to negotiate the marriage of Charles I and Henrietta Maria. He subsequently spent protracted spells in France, culminating in his appointment as ambassador to that country in 1661.[56] This sustained and intimate interaction with the French court, and his familiarity with contemporary French building and gardening, doubtless influenced St Albans in the development of his Westminster estate, the centrepiece of which is what we now know as St James's Square (fig. 37).[57] The aim of the scheme was to create a spacious place 'for the conveniency of the Nobility and Gentry who were to attend upon his Majestie's Person, and in Parliament',[58] because, in St Albans's view, 'ye beauty of this great Towne and ye convenience of your Court are defective in point of houses fitt for ye dwellings of Noble men and other Persons of quality, and . . . your Majesty hath thought fitt for some Remedy hereof to appoint yt ye Place in St. James Field should be built in great and good houses'.[59]

The original intention was that the new development should consist of thirteen or fourteen houses of the greatest size, clustered around a central 'place', and should include a separate market place. In the event, St Albans was forced by financial constraints

36   Sutton Nicholls,
*Southampton or Bloomsbury
Square*, 1720–28, engraving.
British Museum, London.

to modify his scheme and to parcel the land around the central area into more than half as many lots again as he had initially planned. The resulting square took the shape of what John Evelyn called 'a little town', suggesting it was, like Covent Garden, more than just a residential quarter formed around a large central opening surrounded by uniform ranges of 'Pyatza Houses' for aristocrats and gentlemen (fig. 38).[60] The scheme also made provision of meaner streets, leading into or adjacent to the square, for shopkeepers and the tradesmen who served them, and in particular for mews. The new neighbourhood was not, therefore, socially uniform. St Albans provided a site for a church on axis with the square, as well as a separate market square west of his new residential square. The market square may possibly

have been formed with a view to obviating the incursion of market traders into the residential square, a circumstance that, as we noted earlier, had contributed to the social decline of Covent Garden.

The French travellers Balthasar de Monconys and Samuel Sorbière were among the first to comment on the ambitious scale of St Albans's new 'place': the former described the site of the square in May 1663 as a 'grandissime place qui peut estre quatre fois la place Royale, et deux fois Bellecour [in Lyons]', and his fellow countryman exclaimed in 1664 that it was 'pas moindre que celle de Belle-Cour à Lyon'.[61] English observers, on the other hand, referred to the square as the 'square place', and, perhaps not surprisingly given their familiarity with Covent Garden, as the 'piatzo' or piazza. Evelyn, who was doubtless

31

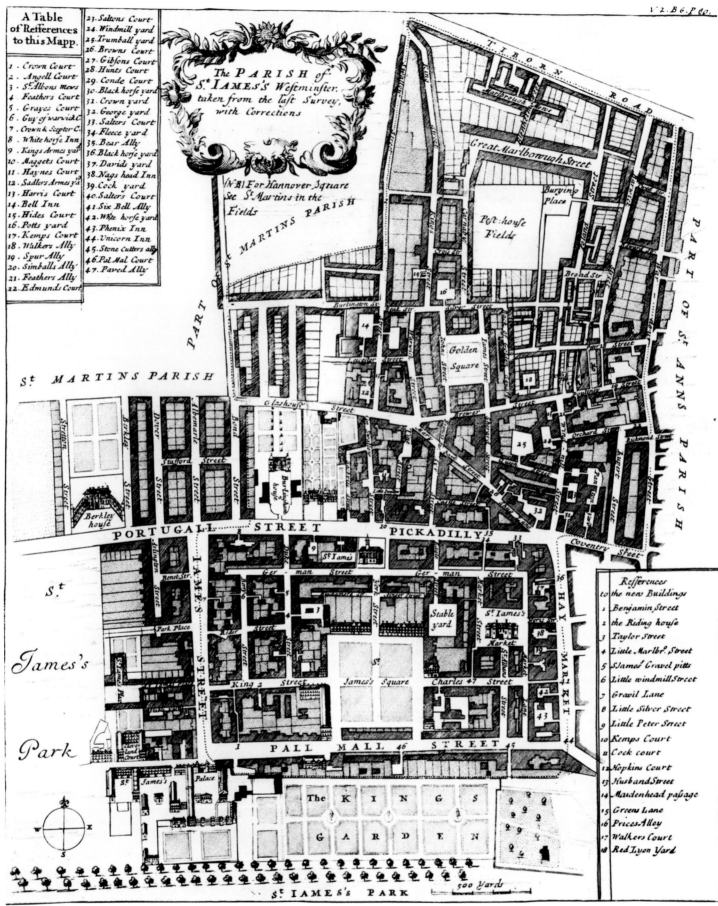

38 Unknown artist, *St James's Square*, c.1720, engraving. British Museum, London. The view is taken looking north towards York Street and St James's Church, with King Street (*left*) and Charles Street (*right*) opening into the square.

37 (*facing page*) John Ogilby and William Morgan, *A Large and Accurate Map of the City of London*, 1676, engraving (detail), showing St James's Square. Author's collection. The central area was often referred to in the 1660s and 1670s as the 'piatzo'.

familiar with the square's continental prototypes, remarked on its 'large and magnificent Structures', which under royal encouragement were introducing a 'renascence' of architecture.[62]

The great building schemes at Bloomsbury and St James's squares established what John Summerson identified in *Georgian London* as the three 'clear principles of development' that determined the shape of London's post-Restoration squares: the first was the principle of an aristocratic lead, where the landowner built and lived in his own house on his square; the second was the principle of a complete unit of development, comprising square, secondary streets, a market and sometimes a church; and the third principle was the role of the speculative builder, who operated as a middleman in these enterprises.[63]

Late Seventeenth-century Squares

Squares were neither restricted solely to the West End nor formed exclusively for the aristocracy and citizens of higher status: from the 1670s they also began to appear in the City and the suburbs, and were built to attract the professional and mercantile classes.[64] Social aspiration played a part in this migration to the fringes of town, but the desire for space, air and the prospect of open fields (such as many aristocratic townhouses had enjoyed for centuries) was also important.[65] Crosby Square, off Bishopsgate in the City, was laid out from c.1671, and neighbouring Devonshire Square from about 1680; Heydon Square, New Square, Lincoln's Inn and Bridgewater Square were formed between 1682 and 1697. Although generally smaller in scale, and less grand in

33

39 Jan Kip, *Templum Dano-Norvegicum*, view of the Danish church in Wellclose Square, 1696–1700, etching. British Museum, London. Here, as at Smith Square (c.1716) in Westminster, the central area of the square was given over to a church.

conception than their West End forebears, these City squares were reasonably regular in outline and their central areas were paved. A clutch of suburban squares was also projected north of the City in the neighbourhood of Shoreditch, including Hoxton Square (1683), Webb's Square (1684) and Charles Square, Hoxton (1685). The building of Kensington Square was begun some time in the mid-1680s, and Nicholas Barbon, the notorious MP, economist, builder and projector, developed Red Lion Fields (later Square) to the north of Holborn from the early 1680s, and Marine or Wellclose Square, off the Ratcliffe Highway in east London from 1683, in collaboration with his fellow MP Felix Calvert (fig. 39).[66]

While some of these post-Restoration squares were little more than street widenings, capacious courts or yards,[67] a few must have borne some resemblance to their former rustic complexion. One wonders, for instance, what the interior of Red Lion Square looked like in the late 1680s. Were the fields' elm trees integrated in the new scheme?[68] According to the bibliophile and horticulturist Narcissus Lut-

trell, writing in June 1684, 'Dr. Barebone, the great builder' originally intended to build over the whole area of the fields. Barbon was, however, compelled to 'break his design and model', and leave a square opening at the centre of his new development: the gentlemen of Gray's Inn 'took notice' of the new building, and 'thinking it an injury to them' confronted Barbon's workmen. An unseemly skirmish ensued, and Barbon was forced to alter his proposals.[69] It is unclear from surviving accounts what factors precipitated the rebellion by the aggrieved gentlemen of Gray's Inn against the developer's plans, but they presumably, like the petitioners at Lincoln's Inn Fields before them, asserted that the new building would deprive them of fresh air, spoil their open prospects, annoy them 'with offensive and unhealthful savours' and cause many other inconveniences, to their 'great discouragement and the disquieting of their studies'.[70] Regardless of the cause, Barbon's revised scheme owes a debt to Moorfields, Lincoln's Inn, Leicester Fields and even the Inns of Court, as he agreed to create 'fair large houses for persons of

34

40   John Ogilby and William Morgan, *A Large and Accurate Map of the City of London*, 1676, engraving (detail), showing Charterhouse Square and the surrounding area. London Metropolitan Archives.

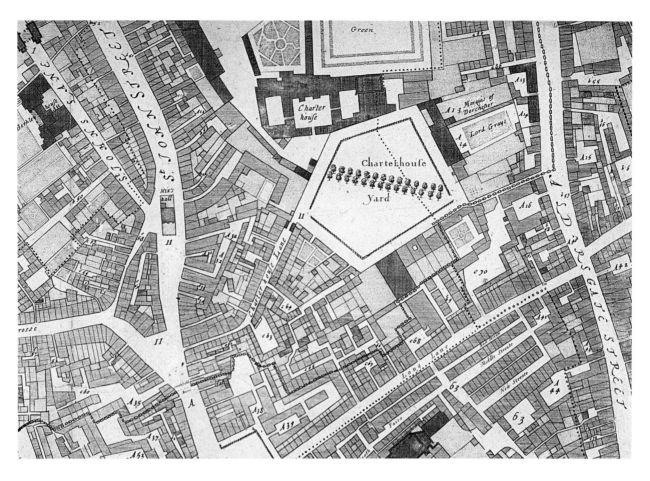

estate and value, before which this defendent [*sic*] intends to leave a very large square unbuilt with pleasant walks therein in which the gentlemen of the said Society or any the persons of quality that visit them may walk and take the air if they please'.[71]

What is now known as Charterhouse Square began to take its present shape in the third quarter of the seventeenth century.[72] The irregular pentagonal garden, which has its origins in the Carthusian priory formed in 1371, belonged to the priory's outer precinct. For several centuries it remained open ground, having served in the mid-fourteenth century as a burial place for victims of the Black Death. The freehold of the area, known variously before the eighteenth century as Charterhouse Churchyard, Charterhouse Precinct or Charterhouse Close, passed, along with the Charterhouse itself, to Lord North in 1538, soon after the dissolution, and then to the Duke of Norfolk in 1565. The priory therefore became a private mansion, and its precincts a verdant forecourt to the same.[73] The so-called 'Agas Map' of London, made in the 1560s, indicates that by this time the area now occupied by Char-

terhouse Square was dotted with a few trees, graced with a chapel, and enclosed on two sides by buildings and on the remaining sides by walls.[74]

From the mid-sixteenth century the former precinct was inhabited by residents of high status on account of its protected seclusion, its proximity to the Charterhouse and its immediate adjacency to the City. It retained this social pre-eminence for almost 150 years, being described by James Howell in 1657 as containing 'many handsome Palaces, as Rutland House, and one where the Venetian Ambassadors were used to lodge'.[75] The square's central area appears to have been improved by 1676, as it is depicted on Ogilby and Morgan's map of that year as enclosed by a post-and-rail fence, and bisected diagonally by an alley of trees (fig. 40).

It is difficult to describe with any certainty the layout of many of the early squares, as the earliest reliable written accounts and visual documents generally date from the early eighteenth century, by which time many of these places had been improved by tree planting and the introduction of paved road surfaces; the squares, moreover, displayed greater

41 (*right*) John Ogilby and William Morgan, *A Large and Accurate Map of the City of London*, 1676, engraving (detail), showing King's (later Soho) Square. Author's collection.

42 (*below*) Sutton Nicholls, *Sohoe or Kings Square*, c.1720–8, engraving. British Museum, London.

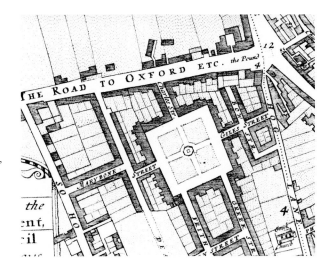

newly built, elegant townhouses and bright and airy enclaves with views to open fields, created for persons of higher status.

At Soho Square we get a reasonably detailed account of an early post-Restoration layout: known originally as Frith's Square, and later King's Square in honour of Charles II, it was built around a purposefully laid-out and enclosed garden with a sculptural group 'in its midst' (fig. 41).[76] The site of the square formed part of Kemp's Field, or Soho Fields, which were leased by the Earl of St Albans and his trustees to the brewer Joseph Girle of Marylebone. In November 1676 Girle obtained letters of patent granting him 'full and free lycence, power and authority' to build in Soho Fields 'such and soe many' houses and other buildings as he should 'from time to time thinke fitt'.[77] The grant stipulated that the houses should be built of brick or stone, and that proper drainage should be provided, but no conditions were imposed on the layout of the development.

architectural coherence as the continuous rows of building that framed the central openings were more or less completed. The fact that the word 'square' was employed to describe such a wide variety of settings – from humble courts and spacious thoroughfares to pleasant walks – suggests, however, that it evoked a desirable environment, associated with

The plan of the new precinct and the surrounding streets was projected in the 1670s by the map

engraver Gregory King, and building entrepreneurs Richard Frith and Cadogan Thomas are credited with having taken a decisive part in the square's layout. Development began in 1677, and leases of houses granted from January 1681 contained clauses charging lessees with garden rents of 10s. per annum 'towards the makeing and keeping in repaire the Rayles, Payles, Fountaine and Garden in the middle of the said Square'.[78]

The neighbourhood almost instantly became one of the most fashionable places of residence in London, and was very well inhabited by aristocrats and prominent Whigs (fig. 42). The Italian historian Gregorio Leti, writing in *Del teatro brittanico* (1682), was impressed by the size of the square, its surrounding houses and, in particular, its spacious central garden surrounded by open railings, which he said was laid out for 'Spasseggiata a piede', or promenading.[79] He was, moreover, impressed by the array of spacious squares in London, which when combined with the city's superb palaces and straight streets made London, in his view, one of the most remarkable cities in Europe.[80] He contended that if squares continued to be formed in London at the present rate, and to such

a high standard, the capital would soon be as large and impressive as Babylon.[81]

One of the greatest novelties of King's Square was its carved fountain by the Danish sculptor Caius Gabriel Cibber, which was projected – and possibly in place – by 1676, and formed the central ornament of the large rectangular opening in the middle of the square (fig. 43).[82] Its design owed a debt to Gian Lorenzo Bernini's Fountain of the Four Rivers (1647–51) in the Piazza Navona in Rome,[83] which might possibly explain why, although puny in comparison, it was warmly received by Leti, who referred to '*Kin[g]squaire*' as a 'Nobilissima Piazza che porta con giustitia il nome di Piazza Reale', describing its handsome fountain made of the finest marble, and commending the place as 'la più bella del Mondo' (fig. 44).[84]

It is not known how or why Cibber's sumptuous, if somewhat ungainly, lapidary confection was set up in the garden, or who commissioned it.[85] It is possible that the fountain was originally made for another location and introduced to the square's central garden; it is, likewise, probable that it was created by the marriage of disparate sculptural ele-

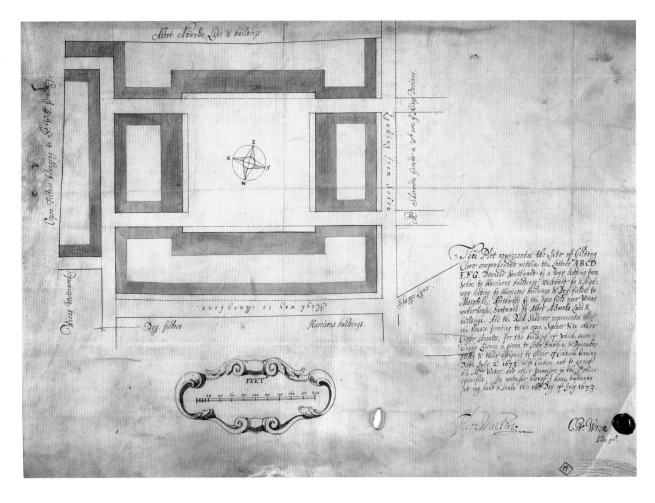

ments. Regardless of its origins, the erection of so grand a water-work in the midst of a square in one of the city's more fashionable quarters was an important innovation. Edward Hatton was impressed by the ensemble, praising the 'Fountain with 4 Streams', the 'Figure of King Charles the 2d in Armour, curiously carved in Stone' and the 'Inscriptions representing the 4 principal Rivers of this Kingdom, *viz. Thames, Severn, Tine* and *Humber*';[86] and John Strype reported in 1720 that the garden was in 'a very large and open Place, enclosed with a high Pallisado Pale, the Square within being neatly kept, with Walks and Grass-plots, and in the Midst is the Effigies of King Charles the Second, neatly cut in Stone, to the Life, standing on a Pedestal'.[87]

If the creation of a securely enclosed communal 'Garden', complete with a central statue, in the square was in itself an innovation, so too was the imposition on the part of the developer of a rate for its maintenance.[88] Only at Golden Square did the developers adopt the Soho Square model.[89] Although Sir Christopher Wren's plan of July 1673 for the 'open Square', which formed part of the royal licence to build Gelding Close (later Golden Square), did not provide for a central garden enclosure, a lease assignment of 1684 indicates that a householder was obliged 'to pay his share towards railing in the said Quadrangle . . . when thereunto requested' (fig. 45).[90] The rails and posts were to be made of good oak 'as large as the rail of the Quadrangle in Leicester feilds'. A similar covenant was engrossed the following year, where a lessee bound himself 'to pay the rates and proportions with others interested in any other building fronting the place, for all charges in posts, rayls and other ornaments or materials fixed, or employed . . . for dividing, distinguishing and adorning the same'.[91]

By the late seventeenth century it had become standard practice for all new buildings in the fashionable squares to be provided with piped fresh water and linked to a main sewer provided by the ground landlord, and for the builders to supply paved footways in front of new houses.[92] However, little consideration was given to the elaboration of the interior

areas of the square; nor was provision made for their subsequent upkeep. Sewers and fresh water were essential for the health and amenity of the new residential quarters, while the embellishment and maintenance of the central areas were not. At St James's Square, the Earl of St Albans exacted covenants from the developers respecting the paving of the square with stone, and the provision of broad footways before each house.[93] He, however, owned neither the central open place nor the streets around it, which remained Crown land. St Albans, therefore, had little right to dictate their use or elaboration. While he desired that 'to the End it [the central area] may never bee built upon', there was no formal means of protecting it from encroachments and other nuisances until this deficiency was remedied by a private act of parliament in 1726 (fig. 46).[94]

Similar circumstances pertained at other West End and smaller suburban squares. For instance, the inner areas of Leicester Fields and Lincoln's Inn Fields were not converted from grass to gardens until the early eighteenth century: Lincoln's Inn Fields was enclosed and planted by 1700, and Leicester Fields remained unfinished and unplanted – with the exception of its several trees – until it was enclosed with 'pallisadoes and fence', and planted in *c*.1720– 5.[95] In some places, such as Covent Garden, paving never gave way to planting.

Despite its shortcomings, Covent Garden established the basis for a pattern of residential development that took place after the Restoration, and which promoted the creation in the West End and the suburbs of regular street layouts, a more uniform standard of building, improved hygiene and comfort, and the preservation of open space within developed areas. The piazza, however, neither precipitated the redevelopment in a similar manner of the neighbouring poor and older districts of Westminster, as Charles I had doubtless hoped, nor did it become a feature of the new City that rose from the ashes of the Great Fire in 1666 (figs 47 and 48).[96] It was Charles II's wish that his formerly congested

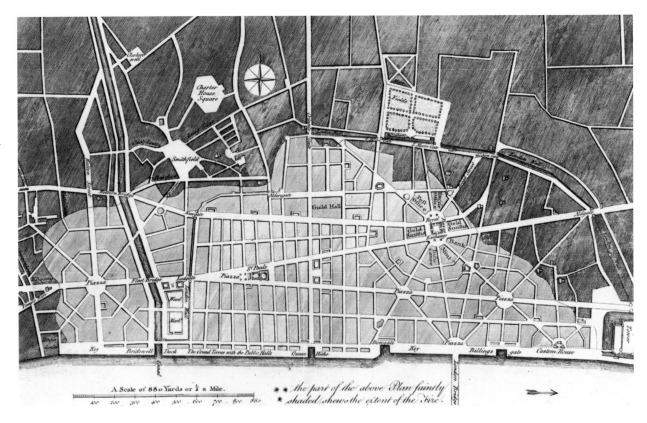

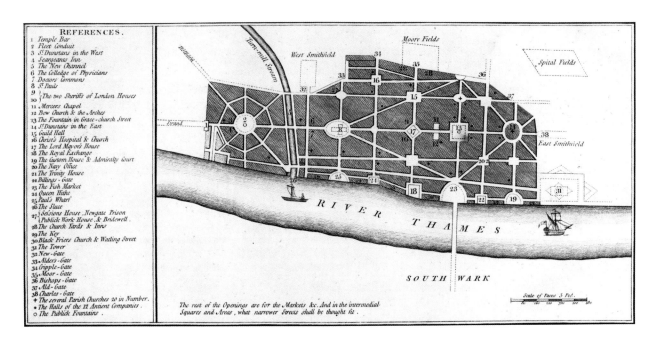

capital should be recast on a magnificent, geometrical plan – criss-crossed with broad boulevards and punctuated with airy piazzas, with a view to health, comfort and convenience (the desire to improve London's coal-smoke-polluted atmosphere being of particular importance to the development and enjoyment of the city's squares and gardens).[97] These aims,

however, were thwarted by the eagerness of his citizens to rebuild and to re-establish their livelihoods. In the event, the City was rebuilt piecemeal, and raised upon the foundations of its streets and alleys established in the Middle Ages.

While the piazza or the 'place' proved a desirable model for the introduction of open space within both old and new developments, it was its union with the waste common field that ultimately established the basis for the London square. The product of this union was, however, on the eve of the eighteenth century, a very imperfect organism. It was neither a piazza in the traditional sense nor a relic of open pasture. If one accepts the premise that in a residential or commercial district the political space of a traditional square is especially important, then the post-Restoration London square was an ambivalent space. Pre-seventeenth century squares and other such informal openings in the city were not merely self-contained open spaces, but were integral to larger street plans: where lesser streets were intended purely as thoroughfares, the openings were used as places to stop, to conduct business or to hold meetings. But as the modern city began to adapt itself to more wheeled traffic, streets began to be designed for transport rather than meeting, and squares increasingly evolved into retired oases in a city relentlessly on the move.

Augustin-Charles d'Aviler, writing in *Cours d'architecture* (1696), identified two distinct types of square, implicitly consonant with the different activities that took place within them: the place of residence, and the market.[98] By combining both public streets and semi-private enclosures in a single space, some of London's post-Restoration squares were something of a compromise between public function and private usage. This tension increased in the first few decades of the eighteenth century, as squares became increasingly exclusive and securely enclosed resorts for private residents, and places of limited – and diminishing – public assembly.

Hamstead

Highgate

Rawbone
Place

Tiborn Road

Charles
Street

W · E

S

2

Adorning Squares in the 'Rural Manner'

Daniel Defoe, struck by the prodigious growth of the metropolis, exclaimed in his *Tour thro' the Whole Island of Great Britain* (1725): 'How much further it may spread, who knows? New Squares, and new streets rising up every Day to such a prodigy of Buildings, that nothing in the World does or ever did, equal it, except Old Rome in Trajan's Time, when the Walls were Fifty Miles in Compass, and the Number of Inhabitants Six Millions Eight hundred thousand souls.'[1] Other commentators, too, were astonished by the 'amazing scene of new foundations, not of houses only, but . . . of new cities, new towns, new squares, and fine buildings, the like of which no city, no town, nay, no place in the world, can show'.[2]

New Squares in the 'Out-part of the Town'

Accounts of the expansion of the capital in the eighteenth century chart the sustained migration of the city's courtiers and professional and landed classes from Old Westminster to the western suburbs, 'the itch of building, that prevails much among our tribe that dabble in mortar', and more particularly the wave of square-building that took place before and immediately after the South Sea Bubble in 1720, which saw the creation of Queen, Hanover, Cavendish and Grosvenor squares in open fields north and west of the metropolis (fig. 49).[3] 'Mr Ambler' in *The New London Spy* (1771) reports that these 'distant

squares' and their complement of regular, spacious streets and elegant piles of buildings had a profound and ennobling effect on the erstwhile scruffy margins of the capital: most notably, Tyburn Road was, on account of its association with the eponymous gallows, renamed Oxford Road when it was 'accommodated with a new pavement; having several squares on either side, which fifty years ago, was mere dunghills'.[4]

London's creation of 'Beautiful Squares',[5] however, had even by the turn of the eighteenth century already achieved a degree of social pre-eminence; as the lexicographer Guy Miège reported in *The New State of England Under Their Majesties K[ing] William and Q[ueen] Mary* (1694), no 'foreign City' could show 'so many *Piazzas* or fine Squares, such as *Lincolns-Inn Fields*, *Lincolns-Inn Square*, *Grays-Inn*, *Red-Lyon*, and *Southampton Squares*, the *Golden Square*, *King's Square* in Sohoe, *S. James's Square*, *Leicester-Fields*, and *Covent-Garden*. The first of which is chiefly noted for its Spaciousness, and *King's Square* for its Stateliness'. Writing again in 1707, he remarked 'The Nobility, and chief among the Gentry, are at this time much better accommodated in fine *Squares*, or Streets; where they breath[e] a good Air, and have Houses built after the modern Way . . . In short, London is remarkable for its Multitude of fine *Squares*.'[6]

What was particularly innovative and therefore noteworthy about many of the squares built from

Facing page: Sutton Nicholls, *Soho Square*, 1754, detail of fig. 72.

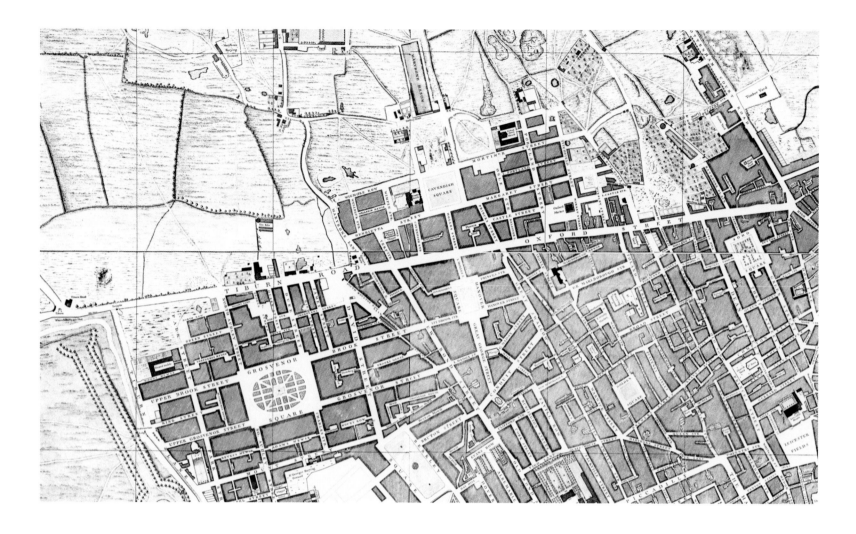

49 John Rocque, *Plan of the
Cities of London and
Westminster, and Borough of
Southwark*, 1746, engraving
(detail), showing the squares of
Soho, Mayfair and
Marylebone. Private collection.

the early eighteenth century was that they were
often 'pleasantly situated on the Out-part of the
Town', with fine open views to the country;[7] that
is, they were contrived to benefit from an affiliation
with both town and country, having at least one side
which opened onto neighbouring fields. This double
aspect was a deliberate conceit, designed to funnel
views from the countryside into the city. The effect
of drawing the country into the town in this way
is a uniquely English phenomenon.

Queen Square was built from about 1708 on the
site of a medieval reservoir a few hundred yards to
the east of Bloomsbury Square (fig. 50).[8] It was a
pioneering effort in the design of such open places
insofar as it was deliberately arranged to take advantage of views northwards to the hills of Hampstead
and Highgate. The result was a curious hybrid – part
piazza and part square: the southernmost section of
the open space was paved, while the remainder was
simply laid to grass. The narrowness, baldness and
diminutive size of the enclosure served to emphasise

its north–south axis, and to strengthen the suggestion that the garden was an extension of the neighbouring countryside. This allusion was enhanced by
the absence of the proposed statue of Queen Anne
at the northern end of the garden.[9]

The precedent of focusing the view beyond the
square itself presumably influenced the design of
Hanover and Cavendish squares, which were laid out
in quick succession from *c.*1714 and 1719 respectively,
and were 'connected by the ligature of a small street',
forming what Humphry Repton later called 'a fine
Enfilade thro' the two squares'.[10] These squares, too,
broke new ground: prior to their creation there had
been no efforts to co-ordinate street patterns or the
layout of squares between neighbouring estates,
thereby acknowledging their mutuality.

Hanover Square – named in honour of King
George I, and trumpeted soon after its creation as
'first of the [city's] new-built Squares'[11] – was the
first to take shape, built on the 13-acre Millfield
Estate situated south of the Oxford Road (fig. 51).

50 (*right*) John Rocque, *Exact Survey of the Cities of London and Westminster*, 1746, engraving (detail), showing Queen's (or Queen) Square. Author's collection.

51 (*below*) Sutton Nicholls, *Hanover Square*, *c.*1720–8, engraving, looking north to Cavendish Square and beyond. British Museum, London.

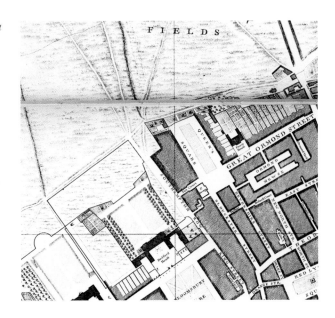

Developed by the Whig magnate Richard Lumley, first Earl of Scarbrough, the square, according to Henry Fielding, quickly became home to the 'circle of people of fascination' who, eager to 'preserve their circle safe and inviolate', and 'jealous . . . against any intrusion of those whom they are pleased to call vulgar', took flight from the older and now less reputable Golden and Leicester squares.[12] The street design associated with the new square was ingenious and appears to have derived from French or Italian civic planning – possibly on account of Lumley's travels in northern Italy in 1706 and 1707:[13] the great open place was bisected by a broad street providing a north–south visual orientation, the roadway gradually narrowing as it descended southwards from Oxford Road to Conduit Street, at which point it encountered the projecting portico of the Church of St George (fig. 52). Such a 'vista', as it became known, was 'calculated to give a nobler view of the square itself' from the south, and a 'better prospect down the street' from the north.[14] The author of this handsome scenographic gesture remains unknown.

No less important in the initial development of the square was the proposal to raise a statue of the reigning monarch in its interior. It was announced in the *Post Boy* in June 1719 that 'they are taking the Dimensions of the Horse at Charing Cross, for his Majesty's statue on Horseback to be put up in Hanover Square'.[15] In light of the fact that this

52 Elias Martin, *View of
Hanover Square*, 1769, oil on
canvas. Private collection. The
view is looking south, with the
tower and portico of St
George's Church on the left.
The Swedish artist's impression
of a London square is among
the most original and
compelling of the period,
conveying the vitality of the
great open space.

'publick ornament' was never built, and that the
square was to remain an arid and featureless field
throughout much of the century, it would appear
that the announcement in the press was merely a
proclamation of intent, if not a blatant sales promotion, and that it, like the regular published notices
charting the arrival and settlement in the square of
people of quality or great riches, was intended to
puff the new development and attract would-be
purchasers.

Cavendish Square, on the other hand, was more
grandly planned on a regular grid as a grandiose
enclave for prominent Tory politicians by Edward
Harley, second Earl of Oxford, in collaboration with
his agent the 'measurer and surveyor' John Prince
(fig. 53). This boastful and 'projecting Prince', who
was criticised in the press in 1718 for drawing 'raw
and inexperienced workmen' – referred to as 'Cas-
tle-builders' – to 'build in and about Hanover-square,
till they have built themselves quite out of doors in

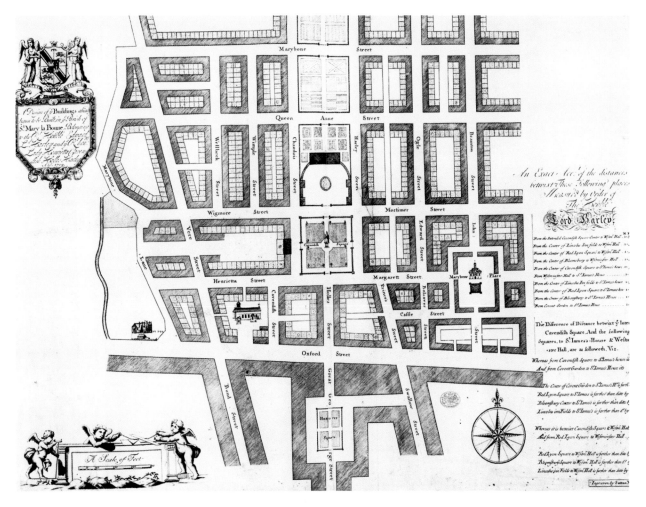

53 John Prince, *A Design of the Buildings already Begun to be Built in the Parish of St Mary la Bonne*, 1719, engraving. British Library, London. Cavendish Square was among the first to be laid out with a view to creating an axial link with an existing square.

this part of the world', may have been responsible for the extension of the Hanover Square vista northwards across the centre of Cavendish Square and even beyond to the open fields of Marylebone.[16] The success of this gesture was praised by James Ralph, who, writing in 1734, commended it as 'one of the most entertaining in the whole city',[17] regardless of the fact that the buildings around the square were not completed until some time after 1745. Here, too, the projectors proposed to erect a free-standing statue – an effigy in white marble of Queen Anne at the centre of a basin in the middle of the square; and here, too, as in Hanover Square, the scheme did not materialise. The vista remained unencumbered, with the reservoir of the York Buildings Waterworks as its northern terminus,[18] until a hard metal statue of William, Duke of Cumberland, was raised in the centre of Cavendish Square in 1766.

Although in the early 1720s this triumvirate of well-inhabited squares possessed some fine buildings and agreeable prospects, their interior spaces were,

on the whole, like so many of the city's openings, bald and characterless places. The Swiss traveller Béat Louis de Muralt remarked in his *Letters* (1726) that several such squares 'are very fine . . . but they are generally far short of what they might be made. They are not much adorn'd, and few People stop to amuse themselves about them, which would be very proper for this great City, and would shew the Number, Wealth, and the leisure Time of the inhabitants.'[19] He was, in fact, rehearsing a criticism put forward by the London nurseryman Thomas Fairchild, who in 1722 affirmed that this 'plain way of laying out Squares in Grass Platts and Gravel Walks' did not 'sufficiently give our Thoughts an Opportunity of Country Amusements'. Why, he asked, 'may we not in many Places, that are airy in the Body of *London*, make such Gardens as may be dress'd in a Country manner? There is St *James's* Square, *Lincoln's Inn* Fields, and *Bloomsbury* Square, besides others which might be brought into delightful Gardens.'[20]

Thomas Fairchild and Laying Out Squares in the 'Rural Manner'

Fairchild, whose nursery lay off Hoxton Square in Shoreditch, remarks in *The City Gardener* (1722): 'I think some sort of Wilderness-Work will do much better, and divert the Gentry better than looking out of their Windows upon an open Figure.' St James's Park was 'as much oppress'd with the *London* Smoke, as almost any of our great Squares; yet the wild Fowl, such as Ducks and Geese, are conformable to it, and breed there; and there is an agreeable Beauty in the Whole, which is wanting in many Country Places'.[21]

The author dedicated a substantial section of his little treatise to the layout of the centres of London squares in 'the Rural Manner'. His first chapter entitled 'Of Squares, and Large Open Places in London and Westminster: The Plants Proper to Adorn Them', charts a course for the improvement of the city's 'plain Squares'. He outlines in five steps how to improve the quality of the areas by listing the useful functions that they might fulfil:

In the *first* place; If a Square was planted in the Manner of a Wilderness, it would be a Harbour for Birds. *2dly*, The Variety of Trees would be delightful to the Eye. *3dly*, Groves and Wildernesses would be new and pleasant in a *London* Prospect. *4thly*, The Walks, tho' regular as the Walks in the common Squares, would be more shady and more private, and the Hedges and the Groves of Trees in every Quarter would hide the Prospect of the Houses from us; every House would command a Prospect of the Whole, as well as if it was lay'd out in plain Grass Platts and Walks. And *5thly* Every Fountain made in such Places, would have double the Beauty it would have in plain Squares, as is now the Fashion; and notwithstanding what may be objected to Fountains in this Wilderness-Work, that a Fountain cannot be discover'd in the Prospect of every House; I say, that it may be done with Ease, to make it appear or shew it self as well to one House as another, as my Draught will show.[22]

As a 'small Example of what may be done', Fairchild then supplies a 'Draught' plan, which 'may be varied by those who make or fit up such Squares', proceeding to list plants that he professes would make the garden 'look well in the Winter, and that Part of the Spring, when Persons of Distinction are in Town' (fig. 54).[23] This outline provides us with an invaluable inventory of early eighteenth-century 'smoke-tolerant' plants, most of which he may have stocked in his own nursery. The common holly, ivy, English box, Italian 'Ever-green Privet', evergreen oak and common bay, for example, are commended for their handsome, agreeable and ornamental qualities. Fairchild remarks that these six sorts 'will afford good Variety, and dress out a Garden for Winter very well; but for the Sake of the Spring, when the Company is generally in Town, we should intermix with them some Flowers, Shrubs, and such Trees as will yield a Beauty in their tender opening Buds'.[24] The 'flowering Shrubs' he then proposes so fulsomely include lilac, laburnum, Spanish broom, the 'Scorpion', bladder senna, 'citisus', jasmine, guelder rose, 'Province Rose', 'Passion-Tree', 'Syringe', apple, pear, grapevine, 'Virginian Acacia', elm, lime, mulberry, fig, whitethorn, plane, horse chestnut, morello cherry, almond, currant and honeysuckle (fig. 55).[25] His final category – '*Flowers that will grow well in London fit for the adorning of Squares*' – also lists plants that would flower from the early spring to the late autumn. He recommends scarlet thrift for the 'Edging of the Borders'; and 'within this Edging' he proposes planting lilies (white, 'intermix'd with the Orange-Lilly, and five Sorts of Martagons', and some with variegated foliage), 'Perennial Sun-flower', Sweet-William, 'Primrose-Tree', Asters, scarlet lychnis, campanula, French honeysuckle, dwarf iris, day lily, monkshood, colchicum, valerian, feverfew, pinks and carnations (fig. 56).[26]

54 Plan of a garden square, from Thomas Fairchild, *The City Gardener* (1722), engraving. Author's collection. Fairchild's design was the first published plan for the improvement of a London square.

55 (*right*) William Curtis, 'Lonicera periclymenum', watercolour, from *Flora londinensis*, vol. 2 (1799), opposite p. 96. Royal Horticultural Society, Lindley Library, London. Honeysuckle is one of the flowering shrubs Fairchild recommends for planting in the gardens of squares.

56 (*below*) William Curtis, 'Primula acaulis', watercolour, from *Flora londinensis*, vol. 2 (1799), opposite p. 103. Royal Horticultural Society, Lindley Library, London. The native primrose (also known as *Primula vulgaris*) is recorded as having been grown in the 'open places' of some of London's early squares.

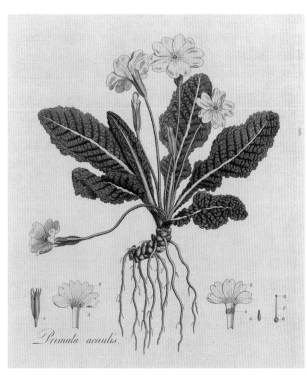

The second chapter of *The City Gardener* described the process of '*making and adorning Squares; and how to dispose the Several Plants in them*'. Having 'treated of such Ever-Greens, Trees for Shade, flowering Shrubs and Flowers proper to adorn a Square', and mindful of the aridity of the city's 'large Places', he suggests various ways to dispose them 'in such a manner as will afford the best Appearance'.[27] His 'Draught' plan shows an elaborate rectangular wilderness crossed by transverse and diagonal paths which form eight planted 'Quarters'; the plan is symmetrical on two axes. The transverse paths terminate in broad semi-circular apses, while each of the four diagonal paths is intersected by a small open *rond-point*. At the centre of the square there is a 'Mount'.

Fairchild also provides alternative layouts for the semi-circular apses of the square. The first option proposes 'Grass Platt[s] encompass'd with Bed[s] for Flowers; and in the middle of the Grass may be placed a Statue, or Urn, which will give good Ornament: Between this and the Grass and the Border, should be a Water-Table about eighteen Inches, or two Foot wide, to be laid with red Sand, or Cockle-Shells, and the Border . . . to be planted with Flowers'. These 'Open Borders', which are lined with 'durable Edging . . . of Scarlet-Thrift, or Dutch-Box', contain an array of bulbs and annual and perennial flowers – 'properly intermix't' – which are intended to give 'an agreeable Show' from early spring to late autumn. The second option for the layout of the apses prescribes a fountain at the centre of each one; the third puts forward the creation of 'some large Basons of Water . . . [which] might be useful, if any Neighbours should be disturb'd by Fire'.[28]

The borders 'under the Hedges', which bind together the several divisions of wilderness, are also edged with thrift (B on the plan; see fig. 54). The borders themselves, like the apsidal parterres, are to be planted with tall ephemeral and 'durable flowers', including tulips, starworts, African marigolds, 'Female-Balsams', 'Great Purple Amaranths' and 'Twisters' (climbers) such as 'Great Convolvulus' and 'the Scarlet-Bean'. Lime or Dutch or English Elm hedges are meant to form the backdrop for the tall borders and define the perimeters of the large 'Quarters' (C), which are filled with graduated displays of deciduous and evergreen trees, contrived to give a good 'Winter Prospect'. The proposed trees within these areas are to be kept 2–4 feet above the top of the hedges so as not to 'incumber the Prospect'. The 'middle Walk' (D) 'may be planted with Horse-Chestnuts, which will grow regular, and rise above the rest of the Wilderness-Plants; and between the Stems of these Trees, the Quarters of the Wilderness-Work would be look'd into'. Finally, the 'Mount' at the centre (E) is to be 'cover'd with Trees very close set together'.[29]

Fairchild's design was, indeed, a bold exercise: while the plan and its range of 'proper Embellishments' was comparable to other early schemes for contemporary wilderness gardens,[30] its specific application to the urban context was probably an innovation of his own.[31] From a horticultural standpoint, the garden he envisioned was remarkable for its extensive, formal, planted infrastructure, as well as its diversity and profusion of flowers and curious plants – all of which were known to the author, cultivated in his nursery in Hoxton, and proven to 'thrive best in the *London* Gardens'.[32]

But again, it is important to note Fairchild's sense of the urban setting of these gardens. His design, in his own words, would 'yield a new Variety of Prospect'. Knowing that residents would be required to pay for the embellishment of the central garden, and that these 'Persons of Distinction . . . will not pay for a Thing that they have no Benefit of, or Pleasure in', he was determined to enhance the view from houses that framed a garden square by introducing shrubs and trees. To that end, he was emphatic that 'by no Means on the Outside of such a Square, should be planted any Trees that rise higher than the Wall or Pale-side, because they will break the Prospect; which by no Means should be interrupt'd next to the Houses, by which the whole is maintained'. Nothing, he insisted, 'must stand in our Way, and resist out Sight, and so rob the Gentleman of that View which they have by their Expence endeavour'd to gain'.[33]

Putting into order such 'large Pieces of Ground, such as are in the Squares' would, he affirmed, 'contribute to the Pleasure and Happiness of those Gentlemen who have Habitations in them'. Fairchild always wanted to appeal to their delight in prospect – and in particular what he called a 'rural' prospect. Observing that 'most People love a Country Prospect, and are even pleased with the most narrow View of it', he resolved that 'the adorning of Squares

in the Rural Manner [as] I propose, will contribute much to the Ease of those, who by their being Great and Noble, are Inhabitants of such Places'.[34]

Grosvenor Square

In light of his vision and enthusiasm, it is paradoxical that Fairchild should have recommended the creation of extensive 'Wilderness-Works', a concept that, in an urban environment, could take on a very different meaning. 'Wilderness-Works', indeed, were to prove to be places in whose leafy depths every proclivity towards licentiousness and transgression could be freely indulged. At a time when the Covent Garden piazza was cluttered with shops, sheds, temporary stands and excavations for wells and boghouses, Bloomsbury Square and the openings at Lincoln's Inn and Leicester Fields were sites of 'great mischiefs' and the resort of 'many wicked and disorderly persons', and the 'Great Square Place' of St James's Square was a 'rude waste in an uncleanly state'.[35] Even the gardens of Soho and Golden squares had begun to suffer for want of regular maintenance.[36]

Given these circumstances it is remarkable that Fairchild's proposals appealed to Sir Richard Grosvenor, fourth Baronet, and the undertakers of the houses built speculatively round Grosvenor Square, who entered into an agreement in *c*.1725 to form a 'Wilderness worke' at the centre of what was destined to become one of London's largest and most fashionable squares.[37] The 8-acre garden, built 'at the farthest Extent of the Town, upon a rising Ground, with the Fields on all Sides',[38] was planned (*c*.1723–5) as the centre, both geographical and symbolic, of the 100-acre Grosvenor Estate in Mayfair (fig. 57); it was also clearly intended to make the new square desirable.

The estate itself was laid out in a functional and socially conscious manner, whereby the square was set within a grid of regular streets. Among the more interesting aspects of the new development was its planning: mews ran parallel to the main streets and contained the stables and the outbuildings of the houses. Mark Girouard (writing in 1990) remarks that such a 'system of back access had appeared in embryo in other London developments, but it was first comprehensively applied on the Grosvenor estate and soon became the standard plan for London'.[39]

57 John Mackay, map of the Grosvenor Estate, 1723, pen and ink with watercolour wash (detail), showing Mayfair, with the Grosvenor Estate shaded in pink. Private collection.

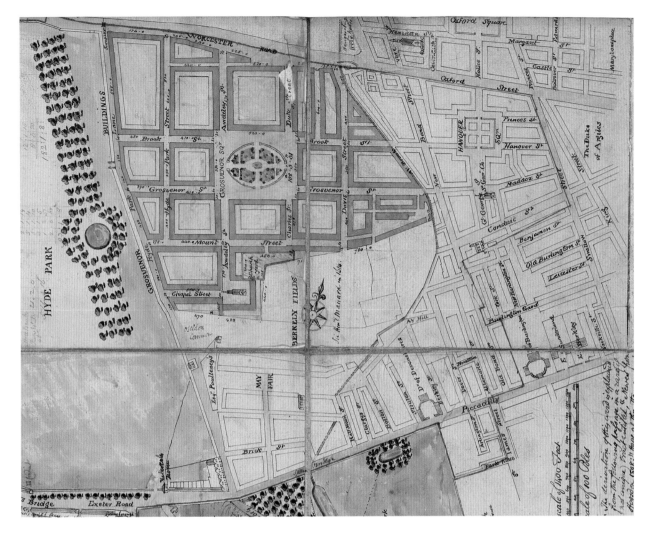

The novel layout of the square's entrant streets was not, on the other hand, entirely successful: 'the architectural will to achieve uniform terraces was not there, and the corners remained practically awkward, giving a sense of the architecture leaking away'.[40] In social terms, however, the square achieved its objective: the neighbourhood radiated in concentric rings of decreasing social pre-eminence from the 'Garden Oval'. The square was thus to be the pinnacle of social prestige, and the garden the exclusive sanctuary of the 'key-holding' inhabitants who lived round it.[41] Moreover, because it bore the family name of its aristocratic landlord, the square was to bring glory upon Sir Richard Grosvenor and enhance the aesthetic character of his new estate. In this grandiose scheme, the gardener and surveyor John Alston provided the layout for the central garden, and was later retained for its maintenance (fig. 58).[42] By 1729 the large sum of £2,871 had been put towards the embellishment of the central

pleasance, which was planted with just under 1 mile of elm hedging, 4,100 turfs, 2,635 small mixed 'shrubs, plants and evergreens' and 3,000 flowering shrubs: the garden had more planting material than most of the other great London squares combined.[43] The magnificence of the garden, in fact, far outshone the square's surrounding buildings, some of which were condemned in 1734 by James Ralph – whose views reflected informed taste – as 'little better than a Collection of Whims, and Frolicks in Building, without any Thing like Order or Beauty'.[44]

Although doubtless inspired by Fairchild's proposals, Alston's garden plan varies in a significant way from its predecessor. The centre is given over not to a 'Mount, cover'd with Trees very close set together', including 'the Elm, the Lime, and others of the tallest Growth', but to a rather puny 'statue of his present Majesty [George I] on horseback'. Whereas Fairchild recommended consigning statuary to the margins of his design, Alston placed the royal effigy

58 (*right*) John Alston,
The Garden Ovall, plan of
Grosvenor Square, *c.*1725–6,
pen with watercolour wash.
Westminster City Archives.

59 (*below*) Unknown artist,
Grosvenor Square, *c.*1730
(reprinted 1754), engraving,
showing the wilderness
garden with its gilt statue of
George I. British Museum,
London.

in the 'middle of the . . . Garden or Ovall'.[45] This
location was presumably dictated by Sir Richard
Grosvenor, who had made a grand tour of the continent between 1706 and 1709, and was probably
familiar with the convention of erecting royal statues
at the centres of great squares. Fairchild's particularised view on the placing of statues was, as we shall
see, to be taken up only by Humphry Repton at
the turn of the nineteenth century.

Grosvenor Square's equestrian statue was, nonetheless, a great novelty, set in a very ambitiously
planted and then wholly original garden layout. Sir
Richard's brazen proclamation of royal loyalty, 'double Gilt with Gold', to the designs of John Nost II,
was in fact the first equestrian composition to be
designed for, and successfully raised in, a garden
square (fig. 59).[46] This statue was also among the first
'publick statues' to provoke an angry response from
members of the public; in March 1727 'some villainous Persons' dismembered the unfinished statue 'in a
most shameful manner, and affixed a traiterous [*sic*]
paper to the pedestal'.[47] The *British Journal* reports
that 'the left leg had been torn off at the Thigh, and

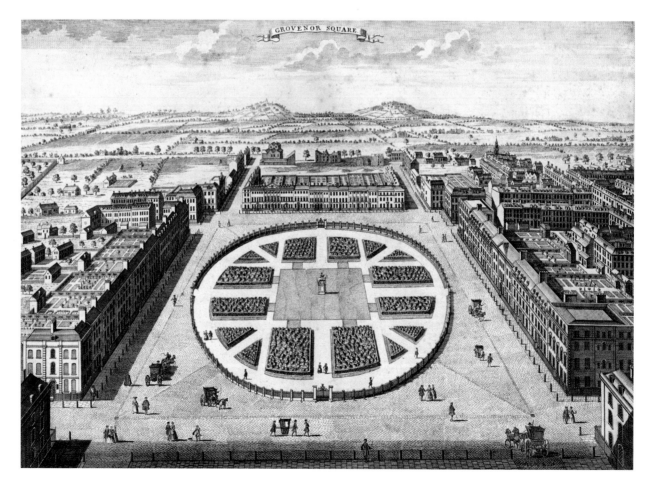

laid upon the Pedestal; one Rein of the Bridle almost cut through; the Sword or Truncheon wrenched off, and carried away; the Neck also hack'd, as if they design'd to cut off the Head'.[48] This 'villainous Action' did not dissuade Grosvenor from completing what he had begun, but it appears to have dampened temporarily the enthusiasm for raising conspicuous statues in the city's squares, for no further statues were put up for over two decades.

The general character of Grosvenor Square was described by some at the time of its creation as 'decent and orderly', and the estate, in spite of its shortcomings, achieved its implicit aim of providing what a recent commentator has called 'exclusive residential housing of moderate size and at reasonable cost in what was currently considered a fashionable quarter in a healthy district with easy access to the main centers of upper-class business and pleasure'.[49] From the outset the central garden was one of the principal attractions of the new development: its broad walks were well turned and rolled, the fence was secure, the garden mould was good and

well hoed (excavated from the basements of the surrounding houses), and the plantations were kept clipped to a maximum height of 8 feet to keep the views across the square unencumbered when looking from the first-floor level of the surrounding houses.[50] An account of 1740 reported, with obvious approval, that 'the inside is surrounded with Rails in an Octagonal Form, different from all the Squares in *London*; and agreeably planted with Dwarf-Trees, intermixed with fine Walks. In the Middle stands the Equestrian statue of King George I, finely gilt; which together with the noble Houses that are building, and those already finished, makes this the most magnificent Square in the whole Town.'[51]

Some commentators were less enthusiastic. One critic, James Ralph, remarked in 1734 that 'as to the Area in the Midst: 'Tis certainly laid out in a very expensive Taste, and hitherto kept with great Decency and Neatness: The making it circular is new in Design, and happy in Effect: the Statue in the Centre makes a very good Appearance in Prospect, and is a fine Decoration: But, in itself, is no Way admirable, or deserving much Applause.'[52] Other contemporary critics, however, reported that the 'Wilderness worke' was perhaps a greater achievement than the surrounding houses: while attempts had been made to give the square architectural uniformity, they were ineffectual, and formality and regularity prevailed only in the central garden.[53] Such limitations notwithstanding, the total effect of the square was, at the time of its creation, pleasing in its moderate architectural variety; but the overall impression must have been of its spaciousness, which derived from the lowness of the buildings in relation to the expansive formal garden they surrounded.

Model Improvement Acts

There can be little doubt that the patrician residents of St James's Square were vexed by the lavish embellishment of Grosvenor Square: for decades their efforts to improve their 'Great Square Place' had been hindered by the fact that they did not own the freehold. Most notably, in 1697 they had proposed to 'erect the king's [William III's] statue in brasse . . . with several devices and mottos trampling down popery, breaking the chains of bondage, slavery, etc.' (fig. 60).[54] The scheme was presumably intended to galvanise the improvement of the 'Great Square Place',[55]

53

and insofar as the residents at the time were among William III's most influential adherents they might well have wished to pay a compliment to the king, while also adorning their place of residence. The gesture, arguably, was made in imitation of the Place des Victoires in Paris (1686), where Martin Desjardin's *monument pédestre* to the glory of Louis XIV had been raised by the Duc de la Feuillade in the centre of his new residential quarter.[56] The St James's Square scheme, however, came to nothing.

The inhabitants, who had ready access to parliament, eventually decided instead to adopt a more practical course of action to clean and adorn the interior of the square, which 'hath lain, and does lie, in a filthy condition and as a common Dung hill':[57] in 1725 they petitioned for leave to present a bill for the square's better maintenance.[58] This private act was the most powerful legal instrument for their purposes, but as a precedent it meant much more. It was the first legislation to provide a formal framework for the management of a London square, empowering residents, who were said to be 'desirous to clean repair adorn and beautify the same, in a becoming and graceful Manner', and who were observed to be in general both occupiers and owners of their houses, to levy a rate on themselves (at 10s. per foot frontage) for this purpose.

Once this urban enclosure act was passed, all the residents on the east, north and west sides, with the exception of one, were thereby made trustees to put the act into effect, and were authorised to raise £6,000 from the residents on the three main sides of the square, by the sale of annuities, to pay for the initial work of cleaning and embellishment.[59] The trustees were given the right to 'fine anyone laying filth in the square 20s. and anyone guilty of an encroachment £50: the seclusion of the square was to be further ensured by the imposition of a fine on hackney coachmen plying for hire'.[60] An annual meeting was to be held in the parish vestry room; the first meeting took place in June 1726, at which time the trustees appointed a clerk, who was also to collect the rates, at a salary of £30 per annum.[61] Two day and two night watchmen, or constables, were subsequently appointed, and provided with two movable watch houses. The night watchman was to cry the hours from 10 p.m. to 6 a.m. These servants of the trustees were to prevent encroachment and the deposit of rubbish, as provided for in the act; they were also to keep beggars and disorderly persons out of the square.[62]

As for the remaking of the square itself, the layout and construction of its inner part were entrusted to Charles Bridgeman, who contracted with the York Buildings Company for a 'large [round] Reservoir or Bason of Water, with a Jet d'eau in the Middle' (fig. 61).[63] The basin was encompassed by an 'Inner Walk' of gravel, which was in turn enclosed by a 5-foot-high iron railing, 'to be joyned to 8 stone Obelisks to carry lamps'.[64] Outside the railings the square was paved with Purbeck stone with 'Square Cubick Stones, commonly called French Paving'.[65]

54

62 Samuel Rawle, *The Equestrian Statue in Bronze of King William the Third, now Erecting in St James's Square,* engraving, from *European Magazine,* 54 (1808). British Museum, London. John Bacon's bronze statue portrays the king as a Roman general on horseback.

EUROPEAN   MAGAZINE. Vol. 54.

J. BACON JUN.ᵗ Sculptor

GVLIELMVS III.

Drawn & Engraved by S. Rawle

The Equestrian Statue in Bronze of
KING WILLIAM THE THIRD,
now Erecting in Sᵗ James's Square.

Published by J. Asperne, at the Bible, Crown & Constitution, Cornhill August 1, 1808.

The decision to introduce a basin, rather than a garden, may have been influenced by James Brydges, first Duke of Chandos, a resident of the square with an amateur interest in hydraulics, who was a shareholder in the water company.[66] It was, in any regard, a very practical conceit as it served as a reservoir from which water could be drawn in the event of fire.[67] It is interesting to note that between 1710 and 1724 there had been at least three attempts to revive the proposal to erect what the MP and royal servant Samuel Travers described in his will of the latter year as a 'Statue of my Dear Master King William on Horseback in Brass'.[68] That these initiatives failed may reflect the fact that many of the square's residents were ambassadors to the Court of St James, or foreign noblemen who had no long-term interest in the place, and even the resident English aristocrats were probably sceptical as to how such an extravagance would improve significantly the character of the central area of their square (fig. 62).[69]

The layout of the enclosure won instant and universal approbation, and was celebrated in panegyrics that exalted the grandeur of the area, which was to a large measure due to 'the neatness of the pavement and the beauty of the bason'.[70] The plaudits also precipitated a spate of square improvements, as one by one resident groups of other squares petitioned for, and were granted, their own acts: Lincoln's Inn Fields (1734), Red Lion Square (1737), Cavendish Square (1737), Charterhouse Square (1742), Golden Square (1750), Berkeley Square (1766), Grosvenor Square (1774) and Hoxton Square (1776). Doubtless the appeal of these acts was that the inhabitants saw the central areas of the city's squares transformed from rude wastes into handsome private enclosures for the enjoyment and assembly of polite metropolitan society. These often dramatic metamorphoses were, furthermore, documented in popular contemporary topographical prints, which began to appear from the mid-1720s, showing the city's principal squares and their newly formed garden enclosures in bird's-eye or perspective views.[71]

'Lincoln's Inn Great Fields' was among the earlier squares to be enclosed by private act of parliament. The residents had attempted to introduce a bill as early as 1707 'for beautifying and preserving the Square'.[72] At the time, the fields were infamous for the 'outrages of every kind' perpetrated within them – from duels to riots and state-sanctioned executions. Prior to the square's enclosure an effort was made to improve the character of the interior of the square by erecting a large sculptural group. In 1714 the architect and connoisseur John Talman proposed to raise a 10-foot-high gilt-bronze statue of Queen Anne, to the designs of the Florentine sculptor Giovanni Battista Foggini (fig. 63). He boasted that the ensemble would be 'y[e] finest figure in Europe', and 'woud render ye town so beautifull, yt. it wou'd be worth a Travellers while to come to London on purpose to see' it.[73] It is unclear whether Talman's scheme had the blessing of the Society of Lincoln's Inn.[74]

Several sketch designs survive for the opulent set-piece scheme, which document a range of proposals: most are towering confections, criss-crossed with steps, strewn with fountains and allegorical figures, and dedicated with fulsome inscriptions (figs 64 and 65). They draw heavily on the Italian Baroque and, in particular, the Porta della Ripetta and the projects for the Spanish Steps, both in Rome, and Foggini's own contemporary designs. Talman, in fact, associated

63 (*right*) Giovanni Battista Foggini, design for a statue of Queen Anne to be erected in Lincoln's Inn Fields, *c.*1714–17, pen and ink with watercolour wash. Gabinetto Fotografico, Florence.

64 (*far right*) Giovanni Battista Foggini, design for a fountain to be erected in Lincoln's Inn Fields, *c.*1714–17, pen and ink with watercolour wash. Gabinetto Fotografico, Florence.

65 (*below*) Giovanni Battista Foggini, alternative design for a fountain to be erected in Lincoln's Inn Fields, *c.*1714–17, pen and ink with watercolour wash (detail). Gabinetto Fotografico, Florence.

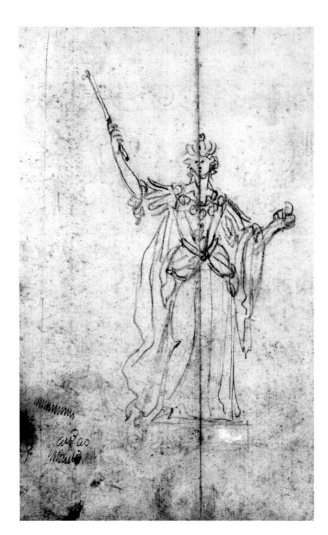

his designs with Desjardin's group of 'Lowis XIV' in the Place des Victoires, which he admired on account of its abundant use of 'water gold' and sumptuous materials; and he hoped that Foggini's statue of 'so pious a Souvreign . . . may stand at least in compitition w: yt. of Lowis y XIV'.[75]

Notwithstanding Talman's efforts, the commission was abandoned in 1717, and Lincoln's Inn Fields did not in the end receive a statue. The inhabitants, however, who were presumably more interested in creating a sense of order within their central open place than raising a monument, eventually succeeded in obtaining a private act of parliament (1734) to 'enclose, clean and adorn the said fields', like the residents of St James's Square before them (fig. 66). The trustees, because of the fields' proximity to Lincoln's Inn, comprised some of the most distinguished lawyers in the country, including the Lord Chancellor, the Master of the Rolls, the Lord Chief Justice of the King's Bench and a handful of leading Tory judges. Still preserved, the meticulous minutes of their frequent meetings provide a remarkably clear and entertaining account of the building and governance of the square.

Upon the passing of the act, the trustees placed a notice for one week in the *Daily Advertiser* 'to forewarn all Persons from rideing Horses in the Fields or laying therein any Rubbish &c. or Assembling there – contrary to the Act of Parliament'. A copy of the same was also 'Printed and Stuck up in proper places in the said Fields'.[76] Additionally, they appointed scavengers, a watch force of six men, and a 'permanent Beadle'. Other plans were forthwith drawn up by the surveyor Thomas Wright, to 'Pave the Ways and Passages of the said Fields, and to

inclose the middle of the fields with [a] Stone Plinth and Iron Rail thereon'. There were to be no 'Plantations of Trees', but a broad 'Inward Walk', a well and a central reservoir for 'extinguishing any Fires';[77] twenty 'Globular' oil lamps were set up on the iron rails beside the footway to light the square, and watch houses were soon duly erected.[78] A mortgage of £3,000 was raised to pay for the improvements, and an annual rate, or 'field tax', was levied on the inhabitants – thenceforth designated as the 'keyholders', as they were given keys to access the garden – to fund the improvements and the co-ordinated provision of services. In 1736 another unsuccessful attempt was made to resuscitate the scheme to erect a statue; this time, however, the royal effigy was to be placed in the middle of the ornamental pond and was to represent William III and not Queen Anne.[79]

The square's new enclosure appears to have been designed for the purpose of promenading. The approaches to the four gates leading into the central area were paved with 'Purbeck squares' for the 'more commodious walking into the said inclosure'; and these in turn gave onto narrow grass and gravel walks.[80] Most of the central area was originally laid to grass. Inhabitants were forbidden from 'running wheels', or from walking 'within the rail part of the fields' with 'pattens' (clogs).[81] When children were admitted they were to be supervised by nursery maids, or occasionally schoolmasters (a school was established in a house in the fields in the early nineteenth century), and they were not permitted to play with bats or balls, or to engage in any 'sort of sport or play'; they were certainly rebuked for playing cricket, running over the beds, destroying the shrubs, or 'being otherwise disorderly'.[82] The lack of garden rules for much of the eighteenth century inevitably led to abuses of the central enclosure: the great lawn was apparently irresistible for 'riding horses [and] airing them in the fields', and the garden's iron railings were likewise convenient for carpet beating.[83] Only in 1798 did the trustees appoint a committee to regulate the fields, and oval notice boards bearing the garden rules were put up in 1805.[84]

The minutes also paint a vivid picture of the operatives who were employed to maintain the square, all of whom wore livery as a mark of authority, and to distinguish them from the visitors and inhabitants of the square. The beadle, whose beat was

67 (*right*) Johan Fredrik Martin, after Elias Martin, *The Gardener*, 1778, stipple engraving. British Museum, London.

68 (*below*) John Augustus Atkinson, *A Watchman in a Square*, late eighteenth century, pen and ink with watercolour wash. British Museum, London.

the 'base, centre, and the four right angles' of the square – or 'in a word, the Beadle is the Square'[85] – was to be bedizened in a 'blew great Coat faced with red and brass gilt Buttons with a red Cape laced with Gold' and a 'Hat with broad Gold Lace, and a Staff with a Silver head'. His mission was to patrol the fields, and to embody the public face of the trustees.[86] The watchmen assisted the beadle, and were instructed to 'call the time of the night every half hour', and to keep the enormous expanse of the fields and the entrant streets and alleys clear of 'beggars and other vagrant persons'.[87] As for the gardener, he was charged with keeping the interior of the square clean and in good order, while the scavengers, dustmen and rakers were to be duly employed to cleanse the areas lying without the garden pale (fig. 67). All of the outdoor servants, with the exception of the lamplighters (who were contracted from a local 'lamp company'), were also expected to assist in extraordinary activities, such as breaking ice on the reservoir in wintertime in order to prevent 'disorderly persons' or 'the mob' from 'Skeeting – or Sliding' upon it,[88] removing dead dogs and unwanted livestock (including goats), maintaining the reservoir (and on one occasion fishing out a person who had drowned in it), and putting sheep into the enclosure 'to mend the Grass and verdure thereof'.[89]

No job was more burdensome than that of the watchmen. It is not, therefore, surprising that these men were often reproved or discharged by the trustees for failing in their duty to preserve the peace of the square, thereby putting the inhabitants in 'great danger by such neglect' (fig. 68).[90] While some watchmen were occasionally rewarded for their 'extraordinary trouble' in detecting and prosecuting malefactors,[91] these guardians of the square were more often accused of laziness, drunkenness, conniving with 'disorderly persons' and dereliction of duty.[92]

Despite its many imperfections, the model for 'regulating the fields,' once established at Lincoln's Inn Fields, was soon to inspire the inhabitants of Leicester Fields, who in April 1737 announced in the *Country Journal* that 'the inclosure in the middle, which alone affords the inhabitants round about it, something like the prospect of a garden', was going to be 'fitted up in a very elegant Manner . . . after the Manner of Lincoln's Inn Fields' (figs 69 and 70).[93] Golden Square, too, was soon thereafter recast

58

69 (*right*) Sutton Nicholls, *Leicester Square*, 1731, engraving. Author's collection. One of the most interesting aspects of Nicholls's plates of the London squares is their focus on the open space of the square itself, and occasionally the views beyond, rather than the surrounding buildings. By adopting a bird's-eye perspective, Nicholls was also able to represent the context of the squares within their larger setting, and convey the airiness of these new great 'open places'.

70 (*below*) Sutton Nicholls, *Leicester Square as it Will Be when the Bason is Made*, *c.*1737, pen and pencil with watercolour wash. British Library, London. It was announced in 1737 that the square was going to be fitted up 'in a very elegant Manner' like Lincoln's Inn Fields, but the central reservoir was never built.

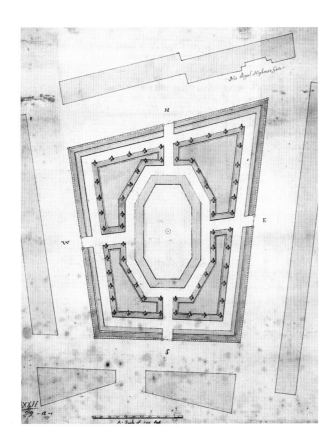

to great effect, its improvement possibly hastened by the square's declining social and political prestige:[94] the outline of the enclosure was reconfigured from a square to an octagon, its earlier layout was swept away in favour of grass plots and gravel walks arranged around a statue of George II, and it was surrounded by an iron railing (fig. 71).[95] And nearby, the 'little, contemptible garden' in the middle of Soho Square, which according to James Ralph, writing in 1734, was 'not so intirely neglected, as many others of the same sort about Town', was energetically reformed, possibly for the same motives as had inspired the changes at Golden Square, the design of which it imitated.[96] The earlier *plates-bandes* were erased and the four quarters of the garden were sown with Dutch clover; the whole was enclosed with iron gates and rails surmounted by eight lanterns (fig. 72).

The improvements to the aforementioned squares would have been unthinkable without – in each case – a strong, unified system of governance within a legally binding framework set out in a private act

71 (*right*) Sutton Nicholls,
Golden Square, 1754, engraving.
Author's collection.

72 (*below*) Sutton Nicholls,
Soho Square, 1754, engraving.
Author's collection. The artist's
original plate of the 1720s (fig.
42) was reworked for the
publication of the sixth
edition of Stow's *Survey of
London* to show the garden's
new layout of 1748–9.

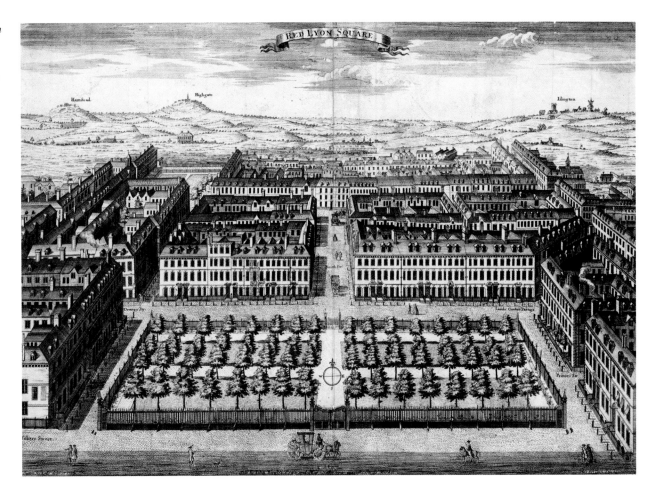

73 Sutton Nicholls, *Red Lyon Square*, c.1725, engraving. British Museum, London. The square lies south of Theobald's Road, Holborn, and the view looks over fields towards Highgate and Islington.

RED LYON SQUARE

of parliament. Given the important role of these acts in the transformation of so many metropolitan open spaces to private pleasure grounds it is worth having a closer look at a typical piece of private legislation.

The aim of the Red Lion Square Act of 1737 was, quite simply, to 'enable the present and future Proprietors and Inhabitants of the Houses . . . to make a Rate on themselves, for raising Money sufficient to enclose, pave, watch, clean, and adorn the said Square' (fig. 73).[97] The rationale for this aim – which was rehearsed in almost identical terms in every London square enclosure act of the eighteenth-century – was that the open space 'hath for some Time past, lain in great Disorder, and the Pales which inclose the Area thereof, are so ruinous, that the said Area, is become a Receptacle for Rubbish, Dirt, and Nastiness, of all Kinds, and an Encouragement to common Beggars, Vagabonds, and other disorderly Persons, to resort thither for the Exercise of their idle Diversions, and other unwarrantable Purposes'. To prevent 'all [such] Mischiefs', and to keep the

square in 'clean, and in good Order', the owners, proprietors and inhabitants protested that they desired to have their square 'inclosed, or otherwise made commodious, paved, watched, and properly adorned, and kept in good repair for the future'. The act also maps out the responsibilities of the new governing body, as well as the nature and extent of the improvements and activities that the proprietors and inhabitants could lawfully execute, all of which were 'necessary or conducive to the accomplishing the End Design' – from carting away rubbish to cutting down trees, dismantling and replacing fences, removing encroachments, and preventing 'all manner of Annoyances'.

Such acts, very importantly, whenever applied, established a legal framework that gave the officers of a square powers to issue precepts to the office of the County Sheriff, who was required and empowered to execute the same, which meant, in effect, that the civic authority was legally bound to issue penalties on persons 'annoying the Square'. This meant, furthermore, that the trustees, their servants

or their agents were duly authorised to present offenders before the Justice of the Peace, who was empowered to levy a penalty payable to the trustees. These penalty fees were in most cases distributed among the watchmen (presumably to encourage them in their duties),[98] and convictions were occasionally published in the local press to dissuade others from offending.[99]

While it is easy to see how the enclosure of squares built on private estates or Crown land inevitably became increasingly secure and the squares themselves more exclusive, it is not altogether clear how some of the city's more prominent 'common Squares', including Lincoln's Inn and Leicester Fields, which in the seventeenth century were improved for 'publique health and pleasure', came to be converted into private recreation grounds. Reading between the lines, one might make the case that, in the absence of co-ordinated enforcement of social regulation, the inhabitants of these squares – many of whom had political connections, were familiar with the running of rural estates, and were eager to safeguard their persons and property in the relatively anonymous and highly mobile environment of the metropolis – simply took it upon themselves to invigilate and maintain the fields.[100] These new squares were, therefore, nothing more than a form of pre-

parliamentary enclosure, whereby so-called 'wastes', or land of marginal productivity, within or on the edges of the city were taken over and forcibly improved.[101]

It is striking, nonetheless, that given the strength of local opposition to similar enclosure schemes in the late sixteenth and early seventeenth centuries, there does not appear, in the eighteenth century, to have been an instant backlash against the regulation of these former public open spaces, as might have been expected. This may be attributable to the fact that the citizenry who earlier might have objected had now been displaced to the margins of the new developments, and were thus less inclined to protest or were less organised than they had formerly been. What is certainly true is that the demography of parishes such as St Martin-in-the-Fields and St Giles-in-the-Fields had changed considerably: their populations of the poorer classes were more heterogeneous and transient as a consequence of steady and significant in-migration.[102]

There appears, in any event, to have been a widespread and genuine confusion about access to these fine open spaces. This uncertainty was probably due to the enduring memory of their former use, the great variability in their management, and the novelty of their enclosure. It was, moreover, perpetuated by guidebooks to the metropolis, which on account of infrequent revision often contained misleading reports as to the status of open spaces. For example, *The Foreigner's Guide* (1740) affirmed that 'those who take delight in the Walking-Exercise' would find 'some satisfaction' in the 'many publick squares inclosed and laid out in Gardens . . . free for every Person above the inferior Rank, and . . . constantly full of Company'.[103] This was not, of course, true: by this time at least four of the 'most stately' squares had been enclosed by act of parliament, and the use of their gardens was restricted to rate-paying key-holders.

Finally, one must note the paradox that while the enclosure of many a square's central garden was calculated to 'preserve it from the rudeness of the populace',[104] these measures in many ways made the spaces more attractive to determined trespassers, who took pleasure in 'getting over the rails', whether for exercising horses, playing cricket, stealing fruit or picking flowers. However, in this regard squares were not very different from the city's other green spaces, which were equally susceptible to nuisances and crime. The general view is well expressed in *St James's Park: A Comedy* (1733), where the '2nd Gentleman' reflects rather sourly that while gardens abet the 'Preservation of Health' and give 'the appearance of Innocence' they present at the same time 'all the opportunities of Vice' (fig. 74).[105] This was certainly the case with many of the new garden enclosures in the city's squares: they were not only a temptation to non-residents of improper dispositions, but they provided a secluded setting for less salubrious rate-paying inhabitants, or degenerate household servants who, like the dispossessed beggars, were inclined to resort to the enclosures for the exercise of their idle diversions.

3

'Squares that Court the Breeze'[1]

Samuel Johnson recounts in *The Rambler* in 1750 that when Frolick, 'a tall boy, with lank hair', remarkable for nothing in his youth but stealing eggs and sucking them, returned to the hamlet of his birth after a London education, 'his dress, his language, his ideas were all new; and he did not much endeavour to conceal his contempt of every thing that differed from the opinions, or practice, of the modish world'. When this haughty urban 'disseminator' deigned to entertain his rustic hearers with stories of his rollicking adventures, he thus took care to 'crowd into it the names of streets, squares and buildings, with which he knew they were unacquainted'.[2]

'Our So-much-vaunted Squares'

By the second quarter of the eighteenth century, streets, squares and their conterminous buildings were, indeed, the unmistakable defining features of urban London: even to the uninitiated, these elements conjured up potent images of the capital's prosperity, opulence and resplendence. The poet James Thomson, who like many of his contemporaries compared modern London to ancient Rome, and considered the cultivation of architecture and the building and adornment of cities as of primary – and political – importance, sums up the excitement of the period, exclaiming in *Liberty* (1736), 'what public works I see! / Lo! Stately street, lo! Squares that Court the Breeze' (fig. 75).[3]

Squares were, in fact, becoming so numerous that William Maitland remarks in *The History of London* (1756) that, in addition to 'The remarkables' – his term for the 'spacious and magnificent Squares' or 'stately Quadrate[s]' of the West End – there were no fewer than forty-nine 'minor squares', including such tantalising spots as Goulston, Jeffreys and Cold Bath squares.[4] Many of these now forgotten places were probably courts that took their names from adjacent thoroughfares on which they abutted, such as Old Street, Petticoat and Plumb Tree squares; others presumably took the names of their builders, such as Baldwin's, Cowper's, Nixon's, Warren's and Webb's squares. Such a plethora of squares, however, corroborates Louis-Sébastien Mercier's observation in 1781 that 'in London one would not consider building a new residential quarter without including a square enclosed by four rows of houses'.[5]

As Mercier's observations suggest, the city's squares were as famous abroad as they were in England. Another Frenchman, Pierre-Jean Grosley, writing in 1765, expressed genuine delight that 'the new quarters of London are both divided and linked by square places, most of which are very expansive; the English call these places "squarres". Most are enclosed like the Place Royale in Paris, and have at their centres open lawns or pieces of water. Grosvenor Square has a garden laid out in alleys. Others have equestrian statues commemorating late sovereigns.'[6] In a similar fashion, his fellow countryman François

La Combe, writing in *Tableau de Londres* in 1777, compared the city to Babylon, praising its 'twenty, spacious squares surrounded by beautiful houses', whose centres were 'embellished with equestrian and *pédestre* statues, obelisks, basins or little woods enclosed by iron railings'.[7]

'Great streets and squares' did not, however, in themselves give a 'just notion of the magnitude of this city'. According to Samuel Johnson, one had also to survey the innumerable little lanes and courts, as it was not in the 'showy evolutions of buildings, but in the multiplicity of human habitations which are crowded together, that the wonderful immensity of London exists'.[8] Thus, while the great lexicographer admired architecture, appreciated landscape and took a profound interest in the development of London,[9] he relished all the more the chaotic spontaneity of the city's post-Fire evolution, and his prose celebrates insistently the social diversity and unpredictably formless energy of the metropolis.[10] London was, in his estimation, above all the concentration of what is true everywhere, and is therefore the appropriate stage for

the complete articulation of human nature. A 'great city', he said, 'is the school for studying life'.[11]

In light of his strong views on the virtues of the organic growth of the metropolis, it might appear surprising that Johnson would write the dedication to the king for John Gwynn's *London and Westminster Improved* (1766), a pamphlet that projects the systematic improvement of the metropolis through the adoption of a 'general plan' – a proposal that has been disparaged by a recent biographer of Johnson as 'breathtakingly iconoclastic, even ludicrous'.[12] While Johnson offered the author friendly support and encouragement in respect of those improvements that were 'conducive to health as well as publick convenience', he did not, nor could he, share his dream of rebuilding London as a grandiose monument to 'elegance' and royal power.[13]

Gwynn, whom Boswell called a 'fine, lively, rattling fellow',[14] had since the late 1740s nurtured an ardent desire to rid London of its 'glaring absurdities' and 'inconvenient and inelegant deformities', and to encourage 'men of sound judgement, taste and activ-

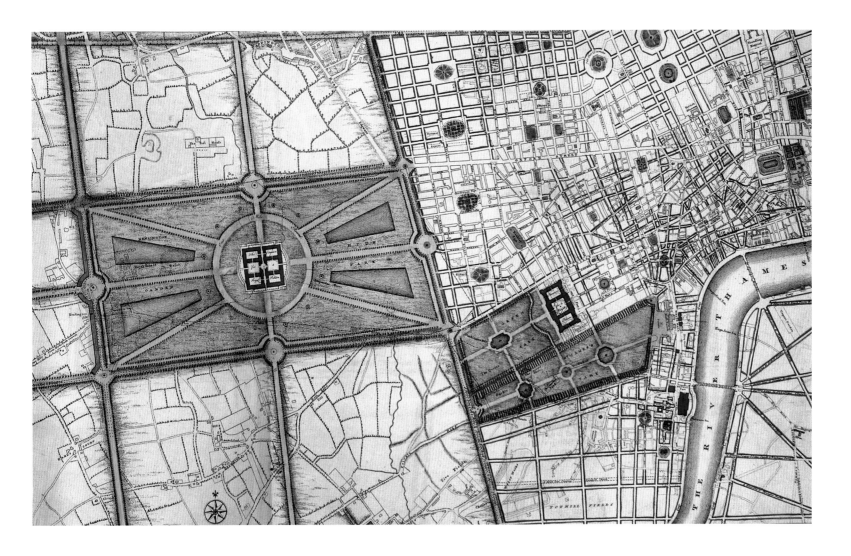

ity' to adopt a 'general well regulated limited plan'
for the capital. His visionary proposals were eventually projected in *London and Westminster Improved*, the
publication of which coincided with the centenary
of the Great Fire. What concerns us here, among the
author's many sweeping civic improvements, is his
proposal that new quarters of town should be
planned with regular buildings, intermingled with
open squares, octagons and circuses, which in his
own words promoted 'novelty of design, elegance
and spaciousness'.

Gwynn expressed special regret that a 'range of
squares' had not been built many years earlier to link
the West End with neighbouring parts of town (fig.
76). Had these squares been formed 'each of the
same size with Grosvenor-Square, with streets cor-
responding from the new road to Piccadilly one way,
others at right angles with them, instead of that heap
of absurdity and confusion . . . it would certainly
have been more profitable, as well as more elegant

and convenient'.[15] It is, he continues, 'a little surpriz-
ing that among the great number of squares in
London, not one is to be found that is regularly
built, on the contrary it is hardly possible to conceive any thing more confused and irregular than
the generality of them are'.[16]

With a view to remedying such a 'great defect',
he proposed to create new squares, surrounded by
regular streets, in Marylebone, Mayfair, Westminster,
the City of London and Bloomsbury. The most
capacious of these was to be a great 'circular area'
off Tottenham Court Road, which at 700 feet in
diameter, was to be over twice the size of the Circus
at Bath. The circle was to have four broad entrant
streets, and the central area was to be divided into
four segments – each possessing a 'grand principal
building'. At the centre of this huge area Gwynn
proposed to place a large basin with a fountain, 'suitable to the magnificence of the whole', surrounded
with verdure encompassed by a gravel walk, the

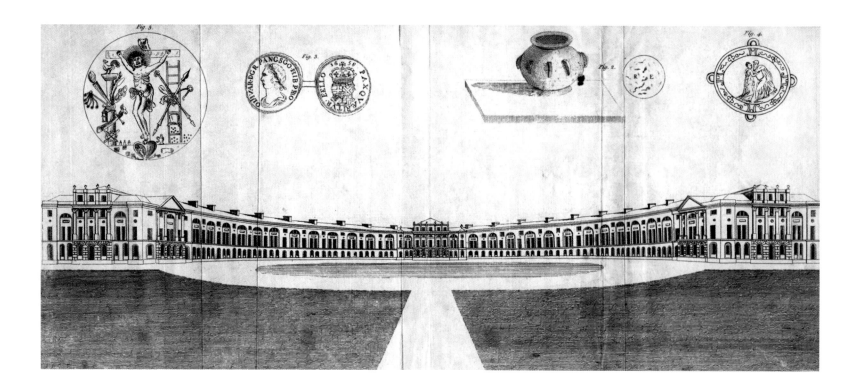

whole enclosed with iron rails. 'The novelty of the design, the elegance and spaciousness of the area itself, and above all, its magnificent appearance, would combine to render it the most desirable situation for persons of rank and distinction, that can possibly be imagined.'[17]

In such grandiose schemes, Gwynn's primary aim was to deploy civic magnificence to exalt the power of the king, in much the same manner as Wren, Evelyn and Boyle had sought to do before him. To achieve this he advocated what he saw as an ambience of urban beauty, which he describes as 'elegance', a quality that would educate people in the properly polite values of the educated classes. The author's choice of word is in itself revealing, showing first that the quality of the built environment cannot help but serve as an instrument of social ordering: 'In the same proportion as publick magnificence increases, in the same proportion will a love of elegance increase among the ranks and degrees of people, and that refinement of taste, which in a nobleman produces true magnificence and elegance, will in a mechanic produce at least cleanliness.'[18] Such a utopian dream of civic perfection was, however, completely out of step with the then prevailing public sentiment, which, much like Johnson's, rejected abstract social planning in favour of a largely unrestricted and haphazard growth for the metropolis.

While Gwynn's 'generall plan' remained, understandably, unrealised, some of its more palatable recommendations were nonetheless adopted piecemeal by individual landowners and speculators, who were, in fact, giving Georgian London uncoordinated yet imposing grandeur. Such ambitions doubtless contributed to the creation of London as a cleaner, brighter and more convenient place, even as it led to the making of squares as a more important element of improved street design from the mid-eighteenth century onwards. Indeed, Gwynn's plan was arguably at least partly responsible for the development of the square to its full potential in English urbanism, in which the square and its derivative forms (crescents, circuses and polygons) formed sequences of planned open spaces and residential developments.[19]

We can, for example, discern Gwynn's improving spirit in some new civic works of his contemporaries, as well as the next generations of town planners, including George Dance the younger, who in 1768 introduced a circus into his proposal for roads in Southwark and Lambeth linking the bridges across the Thames; he also planned a crescent in St George's Fields in 1786 (fig. 77). Dance was personally responsible for laying out the ensemble of America Square, the Crescent and the Circus, just off the Minories in the City (1768), Finsbury Square (1777; fig. 78), Finsbury Circus (proposed as 'The

68

London Amphitheatre', and designed in 1802), and subsequently Alfred Place, off Tottenham Court Road, while his contemporary Robert Mylne designed the monumental *rond-point* in the French manner at St George's Circus (complete with a giant obelisk), which foreshadowed the building of Piccadilly and Oxford circuses.[20] Charles Bacon, by contrast, projected a string of small squares and *rond-points* arranged along a new thoroughfare in Marylebone as an alternative to John Nash's scheme for the development of Regent Street (1815). To be sure, many of these spaces were not in themselves conceived as garden squares, but instead were 'places', or open figures, that recollected – however modestly – the great openings of Rome, Vienna and Paris. Their practical function was to provide open space and air (fig. 79).

Regardless of their location, 'The Squares' were, as the clergyman and author John Trusler implied in 1790, rapidly becoming a special and very distinctive type of neighbourhood in their own right.[21] They were truly now London's urban phenomenon. As fine, open, geometrical figures providing versatile links and pivots in the town plan, squares could no longer be perceived solely in isolation, but had become central as elements that, when deployed in combination, formed what John Britton referred to in the early years of the next century as an 'immense mass of streets and squares';[22] they also forged a framework that informally integrated new and existing street patterns and estate developments to create order and spaciousness in the ever expanding and hitherto largely unstructured mosaic of the city.[23]

Squares and the Great Estates

While mid-eighteenth-century London was not laid out to Gwynn's 'general well regulated limited plan', its component parts were in most instances carefully designed as self-contained developments, though initially with little reference to those that might happen to adjoin. From the late seventeenth century onwards countless ground landlords, their agents or building speculators imposed rationally conceived albeit independent patterns of growth and development in London.[24]

Prior to the establishment of the Metropolitan Board of Works in 1855, and to a great extent there-

after, the landed estate was the primary planning unit in London. These estates were large landholdings vested in the hands of a small number of families and corporate bodies, whose land was disposed on long leases; ownership of properties built on the land reverted to the ground landlord when a lease expired.[25] The concentration of so much land in the hands of so few enabled these 'great estates', as they became known, to exert immense control over the fortunes of the metropolis: the landlord could guide the social, architectural and economic character of a particular neighbourhood by determining everything from its street plan to the nature of the leases. Many of these estates, and those in the West End in particular, took shape after Henry VIII's suppression of the religious houses in 1536, at which time lands previously in the hands of the religious institutions, notably the Abbey of Westminster, the London Charterhouse and St Giles's Hospital, were acquired by purchase or expropriation and redistributed in large parcels either for financial gain or to reward court favourites. We have seen in Chapter 1 how the Bedford Estate in Covent Garden pioneered planned estate development in the late 1620s, and how with

the advent of the building boom in the 1660s the earls of St Albans and Southampton began to follow suit, with the development of their respective estates in St James's and Bloomsbury. And again, after the Treaty of Utrecht of 1713 put an end to more than a decade of warfare and the economy started to recover, the great estates led the westward expansion of London: first among them were the Grosvenor and Cavendish-Harley estates, south and north of 'the Oxford Road' (later Oxford Street), which in John Summerson's words became 'large units with tolerably well-built-up squares and streets'.[26]

On the typical London estate, building ordinarily began before all the features of the general plan had been decided, and modifications were frequently introduced into the original scheme while building was going on. One should not, however, conclude that estates were commonly developed in a piecemeal manner. Indeed, most were planned, but insofar as these developments were very often long and drawn-out affairs, they had to be sufficiently fluid to adapt to unforeseen circumstances.

In order to put an estate plan into effect the landowner had first to enter negotiations with one or more large-scale builders. The aim of these negotiations was to agree contractual terms for the development of the property, which included the design of, and provision for, housing, stabling, streets, paving, lighting, water, drainage and sewers, and sometimes markets and churches. The landowner or his surveyor generally proposed the overall architectural pattern for the estate plan, and from the mid-eighteenth century many landlords, estate surveyors and speculative builders alike appreciated that laying out squares as imposing architectural units was beneficial in promoting both the quick sale and long-term value of residential property. While some of the more important building contractors played a part in drafting overall estate plans, and were occasionally wholly responsible for them, ultimately it remained the landowner's decision to set aside large open spaces on his estate for the development of squares. Builders did not, of course, object to schemes that devoted space to broad streets and squares, as it was not they who suffered from the sacrifice of valuable building land. Landowners, however, were conscious of the fact that by introducing squares into their estate plans they were more likely to encourage builders to put up larger and more substantial houses than they might otherwise have done.[27]

The development of the Portman Estate in Marylebone provides a good example of how a typical West End estate took shape. On 31 January 1765 the *Public Advertiser* announced: 'it is said that Portman-Square now building between Portland Chapel and Marylebone, will be much larger than Grosvenor Square; and that handsome Walks, planted with Elm-Trees, will be made to it, with a grand Reservoir, in the Middle'. The square was in fact only the first of five (including Manchester, Dorset, Bryanston and Montagu squares) to be built on the then semi-rural Portman Estate on high ground north of the Oxford Road, and took its name from Henry William Portman of Orchard Portman, Somerset, who owned and began to develop it from 1761. The estate was among the earliest West End speculations to apply the principled town planning so esteemed by Gwynn, in which a square with a garden at its heart formed the centrepiece of a planned residential unit, and had a direct link with an adjacent development – in this case with Grosvenor Square to the south.[28]

Portman did not play an active role in the development of his estate: the speculative builders Abraham and Samuel Adams took many of the earliest leases and were chiefly responsible for the erection of the square's well-proportioned houses. It is, however, assumed that Portman – possibly in collaboration with his surveyor, Mr Buck – proposed that a capacious pleasure ground should form the centrepiece for the new and extensive grid-iron development, as it was he who allocated the space for the eventual central garden. The central garden or 'inclosure' seems to have been laid out by the speculative builder William Baker, and first appears on *The Plan of Portman Square Drawn by Samuel Donne from a Plan taken by Mr Buck A.D. 1771* (fig. 80).[29]

The square, which, as Sir John Soane was later to note, had 'some houses which would have done honour to Grosvenor Square',[30] was not, however, like Cavendish Square before it, conceived on grand architectural lines, whereby the development was to be dedicated to noblemen's palaces. Instead the frontages here were more modest and offered only in the speculative market, and therefore taken up slowly, not to be completed until after the passing of the Building Act of 1774. Portman Square garden was not formally laid out until the mid-1780s, and only then with the advice of the landscape gardener and surveyor Nathaniel Richmond and latterly the nurseryman Henry Hewitt (fig. 81). It was reported in 1773, that 'There are but 3 sides of [the square] yet Compleated & one House only on ye 4th from wich you have a Prospect of Mary bone Gardens Hemstead & High Gate. The Centre of it is fenc[e]d in in ye Form of an Amphitheatre'.[31] Yet, notwithstanding its slow development, the square was already a commercial success – so much so that by 1773 the Portman Estate would grant the speculative developers Messrs J. Pearson and Samuel Adams the first building leases in nearby Manchester Square (known originally as 'Bentin[c]k Square').[32]

Just under a mile to the east of the Portman Estate a greater building campaign was soon to get under way on the Duke of Bedford's estate in Bloomsbury. Here, as on the Portman Estate, there had been talk of building soon after the Peace of Paris of 1763: the fourth duke had proposed the creation of 'Bedford Circus' in imitation of the King's Circus in Bath.[33] The duke died in 1771, and it was left to Robert Palmer, principal agent to the estate, to carry

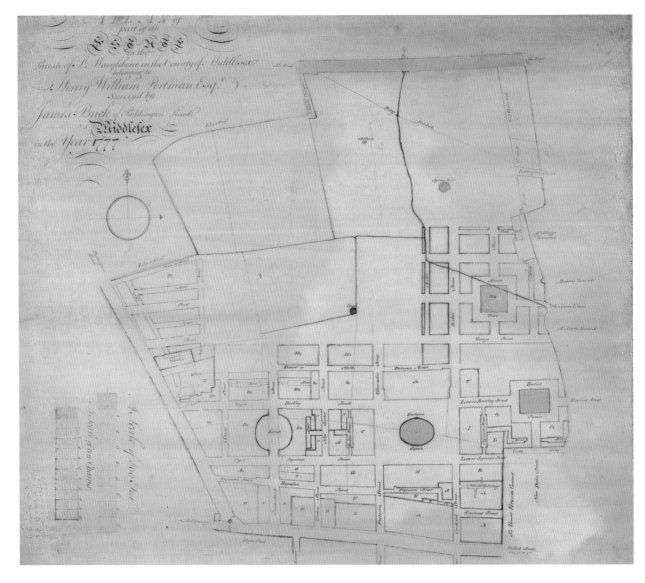

80 James Buck, *A Plan of Part of the Estate in the Parish of St Marylebone . . . belonging to Henry William Portman Esqr . . . in the Year 1777*, pencil and ink. Portman Estate Archives. Buck's plan, an elaboration of Samuel Donne's plan of 1771, shows the oval garden Portman Square shortly after it was laid out, but before it was enclosed and planted. Manchester Square and Great Cumberland Place (then projected as a circus) are also shown.

out the speculation in association with the builder Thomas Leverton. The first square to be developed on the estate was Bedford Square, begun in 1776, and distinguished as being one of the first squares to be enclosed on all sides by uniform ranges of palace fronts (fig. 82). Even today the original integrity of the square's uniform buildings remains a potent witness to the past. Although many landlords and developers have since striven to achieve such a degree of symmetry and homogeneity in the surrounding architecture, absolute uniformity has never been either practicable or desirable. According to Harwood and Saint, 'Bedford Square is a golden example of what the classical ideal and an authoritarian London landlord could achieve together. But the diversity of St James's Square is equally agreeable; even so chaotic an agglomeration of buildings as

Golden Square can give pleasure. In the end it is the old formula of variety and uniformity that suits the London square best.'[34]

The success of the Bedford Estate's salient feature doubtless encouraged the development of the neighbouring Southampton and Foundling estates: by the late 1780s Fitzroy Square began to take shape on the former, within a grid of streets north of Oxford Street, to the designs of the architects James and Robert Adam; and from the early 1790s Mecklenburgh and Brunswick squares were raised on the Foundling Estate. The latter large open spaces originated as the 'principal features of attraction' in a strategic development plan prepared by the architect Samuel Pepys Cockerell for the Foundling Estate in 1790 (fig. 83). Their design had two objects: in Cockerell's own words, first to retain for the Foundling

Hospital (the charitable organisation that owned the estate) 'the advantages of its present open situation'; and second to provide an architectural setting so as 'rather to raise than depress the Character of this Hospital itself'.[35] Very importantly, the architect suggested not only that the new squares should be focus points of the estate, but also that they should be wedded to neighbouring built-up areas by a network of subsidiary streets; this condition ensured that the squares played a critical role in determining the layout and character of the surrounding neighbourhood. He also recommended that the plan for the new estate should be capable of gradual execution, so that each part might be complete in itself and not depend for its success upon the execution of the others.

Much of the building that took place on the Foundling Estate was undertaken by James Burton, who was then practising as an architect but in the ensuing years was to become the most powerful and important London builder since the early seventeenth century. It was on the Bedford Estate in Bloomsbury that Burton established his reputation, and it was his collaboration with the fourth Duke of Bedford and the latter's surveyor James Gubbins that precipitated the transformation of the estate

into what the historian Hermione Hobhouse has called a *quartier des carrés* and William Weir referred to in 1851 as 'the Bedford Square group': 'a whole nucleus of squares, all comely, and some elegant, but all modern and middle-class . . . all new, spruce, and uninteresting' (fig. 84).[36] Indeed, this flurry of building caused the antiquary Francis Douce to grumble in *c.*1796, from his house in Upper Gower Street, that 'we have too many squares. At this time 4 new squares had started up in the course of a year in my neighbourhood.'[37]

Burton's work commenced with the razing of Bedford House on the north side of Bloomsbury Square, which in turn facilitated the development of Russell Square from 1800.[38] The initial plan for the latter is credited to Gubbins, although the design of the building façades was probably initiated by Burton. Here, as in other squares on the estate, the estate surveyor generally recommended the actual garden layout, which could be accepted at face value or modified at the discretion of the speculator. So long as the garden was enclosed and planted, and the scheme was completed within its budget, it generally met with the estate's approval. Nevertheless, some landowners, who were more attuned to the advan-

83 (*right*) Unknown
draughtsman, plan of
Brunswick and Mecklenburgh
squares, April 1811, pen and
ink with watercolour wash.
Thomas Coram Foundation
for Children, London. The
plan records the squares some
time after they were built.

84 (*below*) Unknown
draughtsman, plan of the
Bloomsbury Estate, *c.*1815,
pen and ink with watercolour
wash. Thomas Coram
Foundation for Children,
London.

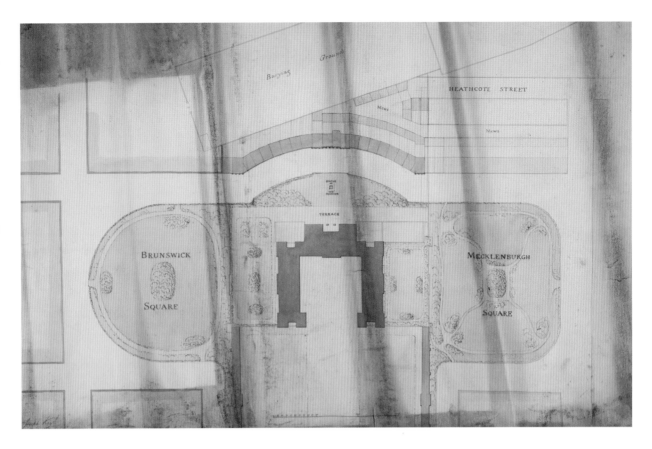

82 (*facing page*) Unknown
draughtsman, plan of the
Bedford Estate, *c.*1795, pen and
ink with watercolour wash.
Bedford Estate Archive,
BL-PXI, Woburn Abbey. The
plan shows Bedford and
Bloomsbury squares and the
gardens of the British
Museum and Bedford House
(parts of which were
developed from *c.*1800 as
Russell Square).

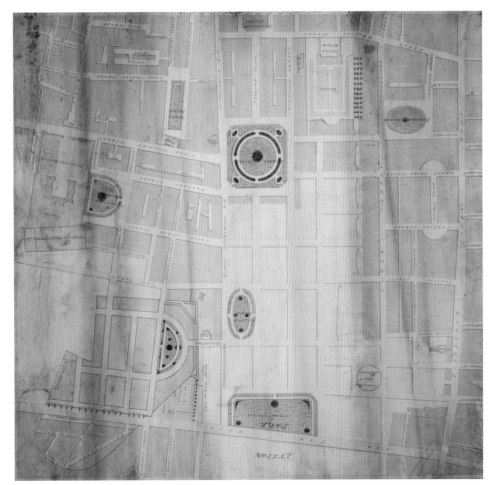

tages of imaginative and modern garden design, were quick to recognise the inadequacies of the speculators' garden schemes. Although invariably cheaper than those proposed by their respective surveyors, the speculators' layouts were often uninspired, and unresponsive to the new demands inhabitants placed on the squares to provide for both private and public enjoyment.[39]

A genuine concern for the development of handsome central gardens prompted both the Duke of Bedford and his neighbouring landowner, the former Surveyor of the King's Gardens Charles Sloane, first Earl Cadogan, to engage the professional services of the celebrated landscape gardener and writer Humphry Repton.[40] Repton's *Observations on the Theory and Practice of Landscape Gardening* (1803) proposed the seamless integration of landscape and architecture, and at the turn of the century he was, in his own words, at the 'pinnacle of my ambition';[41] he planned the gardens of Russell Square (before 1806) and Bloomsbury Square (c.1807) for the fifth and sixth dukes of Bedford respectively, and Sloane Square for Lord Cadogan (c.1806).[42] At Bloomsbury Square, however, the trustees rejected Repton's proposals. The commission was instead given to Thomas Barr, who nevertheless was asked by the inhabitants to adopt part of Repton's plan.[43]

The fact that many estate offices or landowners from the early nineteenth century onwards were compelled to consult qualified or experienced landscape improvers to assist them with the layout of their garden squares underscores a fundamental change in the public perception of these urban spaces. As the design of London squares increasingly became a matter of public debate and a serious consideration for garden writers and eminent landscape improvers, there developed a desire on the part of would-be occupants of these new residential quarters for better design that was both attuned to contemporary landscape taste and responsive to new and evolving domestic social arrangements.

The Impulse to Enclose and Improve

If the welcome promise of spacious living in salubrious, respectable and convenient quarters played an important part in the increasing popularity of London squares, real crime and the fear of it continued to be the driving force behind what now was

to become a common feature, the enclosure of the central space. For example, the enclosure with iron railings of Grosvenor and Berkeley squares may have been precipitated by a spate of crimes of violence from the mid-1750s, which were reported to be taking place in 'Hanover, Cavendish, Bloomsbury and other Squares'.[44] Robberies, too, it was alleged, 'often happen in the Squares of this metropolis', given that 'the inhabitants of Squares are generally persons of distinction and property'.[45]

A tried and tested defence against such criminal activities was the enclosure of the garden, but other remedies were the provision of improved street lighting, the exclusion of undesirables, and the establishment of patrols of guards (fig. 85).[46] One correspondent to the *Gazette and New Daily Advertiser* helpfully proposed in 1767 that a square's inhabitants 'should concur to appoint and pay four extraordinary watchmen, that one may be placed at each corner of a square with handsome watch-houses, and every watchman well cloathed and armed, as in Germany'.[47]

The weakest link in a square's defences was its gates, of which there were usually two to four in every square; and the most vulnerable point of a gate was its lock.[48] Garden gate locks and their keys feature regularly and prominently in most Trustees' Minute Books because keys were frequently 'forged & in use', which necessitated changing the locks.[49] Although the distribution of keys was scrupulously controlled – households were given one (and occasionally a second for 'family use'), and the owner was required to sign a declaration that prescribed its proper use – it was difficult to staunch the flow of so-called 'false' or 'spurious' keys, which all too frequently were made and circulated without the authority of the trustees. For example, household servants occasionally stole, bartered or sold keys,[50] and some inhabitants freely circulated them among their friends and relatives without realising that they were contravening the rules. Even the most trusted authority of the square, the beadle, was sometimes susceptible to a bribe in exchange for unfettered access to the central garden.[51] To combat such abuse, residents were frequently urged to take special care 'that keys are kept out of reach of servants (except where necessary) as gt. Mischiefs & inconveniences have arisen for want of such caution more particularly when the families are out of town'.[52] In an

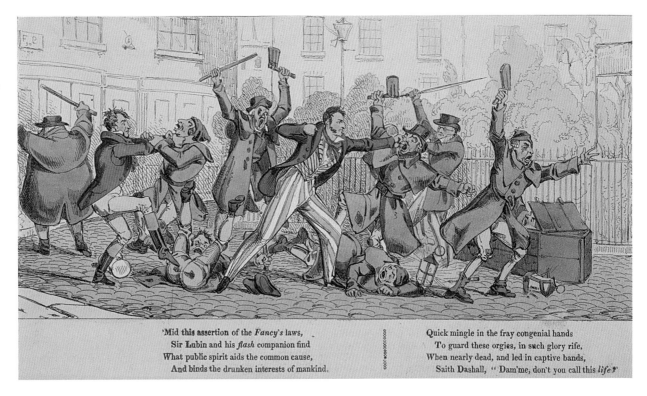

'Mid this assertion of the *Fancy's* laws,
Sir Lubin and his *flash* companion find
What public spirit aids the common cause,
And binds the drunken interests of mankind.

Quick mingle in the fray congenial hands
To guard these orgies, in such glory rife,
When nearly dead, and led in captive bands,
Saith Dashall, " Dam'me, don't you call this *life?'*

attempt to control the misuse of garden privileges, beadles and gardeners were also given orders to examine keys used by people not known to them, and to confiscate false keys.

Regardless of these stringent and costly precautions, it was difficult to exclude all strangers or improper people from breaching a garden's defences. At Portman Square, for example, in the 1790s many female residents complained that they could not walk in the gardens without 'the Danger of being insulted nor could they permit their children to walk therein lest they should catch some Disorder' because 'many Children of Strangers are frequently walking in the Garden who have just had small Pox and that Great Boys and Men are also almost daily playing in the Garden with Bats and Balls and destroying the Turf and Gravel Walks – That the Shrubs are continually broke and the flowers taken and various other Depredation are daily committed'.[53]

Costly security measures were not, it should be noted, intended solely to obviate infrequent and unorganised acts of antisocial behaviour; they also were attempts to ensure that large intrusions or disturbances would not take place. Squares, like large public open spaces, were seen as potential sites for gatherings of 'massive, disruptive, fiercely acute or wickedly capricious, crowds' (fig. 86).[54] Records sur-

vive, for example, noting destructive mobs in Leicester Fields and bonfires in Lincoln's Inn Fields, while the 'principal inhabitants about Hanover and Oxford Squares' were regularly inconvenienced by the assemblage of large crowds on their way to 'their old Neighbour the Gallows' at Tyburn (fig. 87).[55] In April 1802 the Trustees of Portman Square made special arrangements to protect the square in anticipation of celebrations to mark the Treaty of Amiens, and in particular, the house of Monsieur L. G. Otto, the French Ambassador to the Court of St James (fig. 88). They resolved, moreover, that it would be 'expedient to procure a Guard of able Men' to protect and preserve the square, such a force 'to consist of some Beadles in this Parish (and who are Constables) The Gardener and his Men, and as many others as will amount to Thirty two in the whole. And that they come upon Duty at Seven o'Clock and continue to patrole the Garden and protect the same from Depredations so long during the Night as any Throng or Mob of People are assembled in the Square or Streets adjoining and likely to commit any Depredations in the Garden'. As it turned out, the unruly mob was able to smash 'all of the ambassador's windows', but even so did not breach the garden's defences.[56] Later, in February 1808, several gentlemen of Lincoln's Inn Fields assisted the square's

86 (*right*) R. Banks, *The Manner in which the Queen Proceeded Daily from Lady Francis's House, St James's Square, to the House of Lords*, 1810, etching. Private collection.

87 (*below*) John Hamilton, *A Back View or Sketch of Tybourn*, at an execution on 14 October 1767, pen and ink with watercolour wash. British Museum, London.

beadle and constables to combat a 'mob . . . eager to get over the rails as inside were stones, mould [soil], turf & trees' with which they could 'pelt' a malefactor in a pillory at the corner of the fields.[57]

While throngs assembled at elections, civic events, royal and military celebrations, political meetings and demonstrations were, quite understandably, considered destructive and anti-social, they were in fact less threatening than those who at times perpetrated spontaneous, inchoate protests. The inhabitants of London's squares were finally inured to such sporadic disorders, most of which resulted in nominal damage to their personal property.[58] For example, during the Corn Law riots in 1815 a rabble 'speedily demolished with missiles of every sort' the lower windows of Lord Ellenborough's house in St James's Square; they then proceeded to Lord Eldon's in Bedford Square, where they 'instantly tore up the railings before his door, and these were used as weapons to force an entrance through the doors and windows'; then the mob, its numbers augmented to roughly 800, made its way to Lord Darnley's house in Berkeley Square, where they smashed all the windows, before the approach of the military intimi-

78

88 A. C. Pugin, *An Illumination / The Night of an Illumination*, 1806, etching and aquatint from two plates, joined. British Museum, London. The house of Monsieur L. G. Otto, the French ambassador, on the south side of Portman Square, is shown illuminated after the Peace of Amiens in 1802.

dated them and induced them to desist from any further violence.[59] All of the men whose houses were targeted by the mob were members of the government of the day.

These events could not, however, compare with the earlier disturbances of June 1780, when the city was at the mercy of a rampaging mob, which in the course of a few days burnt down several prisons and damaged over a hundred houses (two of the insurgents – Charles Kent and John Gray – were executed in Bloomsbury Square for their part in these events).[60] The riots began as demonstrations in support of the anti-Catholic bigot Lord George Gordon, after whom they are now named, but degenerated into a confused revolt (fig. 89). Over 11,000 militia and 1,000 officers were drafted in to quell the disturbances, most of whom were stationed in the City, in St James's and Hyde parks, and in the gardens of the British Museum.[61] The West End, however – with a few notable exceptions – appears to have emerged relatively unscathed. A map drawn up after the riots were over, marking in coloured ink the disposition of troops and strategic points within the capital, goes

some way to explaining this anomaly. Foot patrols were stationed in Red Lion, Bloomsbury and Queen squares, as well as in Lincoln's Inn Fields; horse patrols encircled the immediate precincts of Cavendish, Portman, Hanover, Leicester, Soho and Manchester squares; and the neighbourhoods of St James's, Grosvenor, Berkeley and Golden squares were surrounded by lines of troops (fig. 90). What such evidence serves to document, of course, is how difficult it was to defend squares and their inhabitants from such large-scale and exceptional depredations without invoking emergency measures. Clearly, London squares had become integrated, for good or ill, into the urban fabric itself, and were no longer a marginal phenomenon in the city's growth.

'Beguiled into the Country, in the very Centre of Business and Care'[62]

The unmistakably urban quality of the garden in a mid-eighteenth-century London square is affirmed in a novel of the period: Samuel Richardson's *History of Sir Charles Grandison* (1753). In it, Reeves, the

89 (*right*) Fielding and Walker, *The Mob Destroying & Setting Fire to the King's Bench Prison & House of Correction in St George's Fields, c.*1780–5, etching. British Museum, London.

90 (*below*) Unknown draughtsman, *Disposition of the Troops and Patrols in and Adjoining London during the Gordon Riots the beginning of June 1780*, engraving with annotations. London Metropolitan Archives. The solid black lines show how the city was carved into precincts for the purposes of protecting the metropolis during the disturbances.

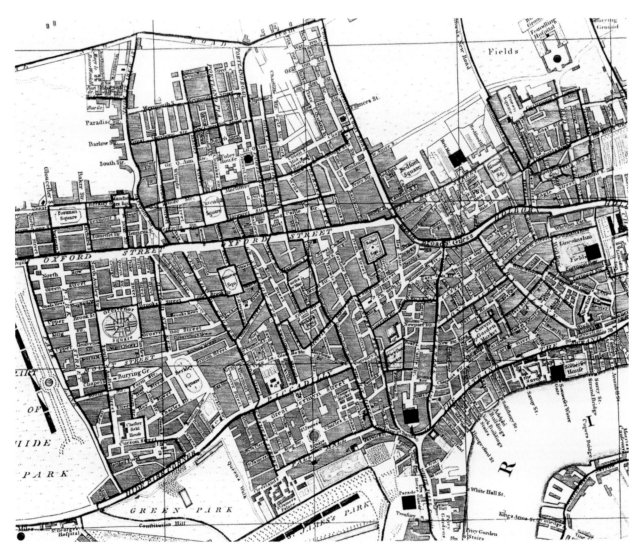

cousin of the heroine, gives an account of Grosvenor Square, which assumes that the reader is aware of the discrepancies between the garden of the square itself, as an evocation of *rus in urbe*, and the authentic rurality of the countryside outside town. This assumption is endorsed, moreover, by a more general sense of the impossibility of the *ci-devant* dream of urban pastoral: the knowledge that the cosy orderliness of a London square could never be mistaken for the rural or semi-rural terrain that lay beyond the boundaries of the city imprints itself on the dialogue between the heroine and her abductor in a grimly ironic manner. Miss Harriet Byron is intercepted by the agents of her villanous ravisher, Sir Hargrave Pollexfen, as she attempts to make her way to Grosvenor Street after a masquerade in town. She soon finds herself captive in a sedan chair and is spirited off to the countryside. The young lady only realises her plight after some time, when she draws aside the window curtain of her carriage, and sees that she is 'in the midst of fields'. She is, in fact, in Lisson Green.

After screaming for succour, she composes herself sufficiently to beg to be carried home:

> She asked for Grosvenor Street. She was to be carried, she said, to Grosvenor Street.
>
> She was just there, that fellow [the chairman] said.
>
> – It can't be, sir! It can't be! – Don't I see fields all about me? – I am in the midst of fields, sir.
>
> Grosvenor-square, madam, replied the villain; the trees and garden of Grosvenor-square.[63]

As the reader is all too poignantly aware, poor Harriet could hardly have been deceived. There could clearly have been no mistaking the open and bucolic surroundings of suburban Lisson Green for the suave formality of Grosvenor Square garden (fig. 91).

The interior of Grosvenor Square was, nonetheless, perceived by some contemporaries as little more than a vast, flat, open field surrounded by a 'clumsey' brick wall, which was condemned by one author as 'not only superfluous, but a blemish to the view it was intended to preserve and adorn'.[64] Writing in 1765 the author and politician Thomas Whately remarked that such 'dead flat' areas raise 'no other idea than of satiety: the eye finds no amusement, no repose, on such a level; it is fatigued'.[65] Although his criticism was not levelled at any particular square, it was clearly intended as generally applicable to small, flat, confined gardens. Whately's remarks were in fact accurate, coming at a time when many of the city's squares were little more than rustic paddocks hemmed in by buildings, with interiors occasionally 'filled up with bushes and dwarf trees' and invariably criss-crossed or encompassed by conspicuous gravel walks. They were, on the whole, neither convincingly rural nor wholly urban. The author clearly found small, regular gardens, regardless of their geographical position or their relationship to their architectural setting, incapable of admitting sufficient variety or contrast to amuse the eye. These sentiments were shared by his contemporary and fellow Member of Parliament John Stewart, whose anonymously published and widely circulated pamphlet of 1771, entitled *Critical Observations on the Buildings and Improvements of London*, focuses almost entirely on the design and layout of squares and private houses in the West End, in particular those in the Cavendish-Harley Estate and Oxford Street.[66] Stewart, like John Gwynn before him (whose *London and Westminster Improved* Stewart commended as 'the most judicious and well-digested plan that has been yet proposed'), applauds the fact that a variety of recent public improvements and private undertakings had promoted the advancement of taste, elegance, utility and the conspicuous display of civic grandeur, and that these factors had, in turn, introduced a series of material changes that had raised standards of order and decency in the capital.

Stewart's pamphlet merits an extended review as his ideas had a profound and lasting influence on the subsequent evolution of the square. The principal object of his work was to introduce 'a greater correctness of taste for the future', the prime constituent of which he saw as propriety.[67] He remarks: 'we have indeed in the new buildings avoided many of the palpable inconveniences of old London; which precaution, has perhaps bestowed collateral ornament without any primary intention on our parts. But have we succeeded in displaying a more refined taste, wherever beauty and elegance were the principal objectives to view? To be satisfied in this, let us examine our so-much-vaunted squares.'[68]

Stewart's particularised notion of the 'perfect square, or public *place* in a city' is then made clear:

a large opening, free and unincumbered, where not only carriages have room to turn and pass, but even where the people are able to assemble occasionally without confusion. It should appear to open naturally out of the street, for which reason all the avenues should form *radii* to the centre of the place. The sides or circumference should be built in a stile above the common; and churches and other public edifices ought to be properly introduced. In the middle there ought to be some fountain, groupe, or statue, railed in within a small compass, or perhaps only a bason of water, which, if not so ornamental, still, by its utility in cases of fire, &c., makes ample amends.[69]

To illustrate this 'in some degree' he refers to St James's Square, which 'though far from perfect in that stile, and altogether uncompleted on one side, still strikes the mind (I judge from my own feelings) with something of more ease and propriety than any square in London. You are not confined in your space; your eye takes in the whole compass at one glance, and the water in the middle seems placed there for ornament and use.'[70] But 'almost every other square in London', he declares, 'seems formed on a quite different plan; they are gardens, they are parks, they are sheep-walks, in short they are everything but what they should be. The *rus in urbe* is a preposterous idea at best; a garden in a street is not less absurd than a street in a garden; and he that wishes to have a row of trees before his door in town, betrays almost as false a taste as he that would build a row of houses for an avenue to his seat in the country.'[71]

Stewart's attack on *rus in urbe* illustrates how far the context of many squares had changed since the idea's heyday in the early eighteenth century, and the extent to which, by the early 1770s, some squares, conceived upon the grandest lines, were now struggling to reconcile the layout and function of their central areas with their new built-up surroundings.

CRITICAL OBSERVATIONS

ON THE

BUILDINGS

AND

IMPROVEMENTS

OF

LONDON.

———— Nil fuit unquam
Sic impar.   Hor.

LONDON:
Printed for J. DODSLEY. in Pall-Mall.
MDCCLXXI.

For example, Hanover, Cavendish, Queen and Gros-venor squares had by this time been absorbed into the dense urban fabric, and their strong visual links with the countryside were substantially diminished.[72] This retreat of the open countryside appears to have precipitated what Stewart condemned as 'preposter-ous' country-in-town scenes, such as the introduc-tion of meadow grass and sheep into the 'butcher's pen' of Cavendish Square (fig. 92).[73] His satirical descriptions of the intrusion of animals and other 'rural appurtenances' into urban settings voiced the perception that the function of the squares was ill resolved, and that this form of urban garden was now, in fact, to be seen as quite distinct from the countryside.[74]

Having set out his general observations, the author then proceeds to particulars, observing in what manner the absurdity of this taste is aggravated or extenuated in current practice. He begins with Grosvenor Square, which, he remarks, is

generally held out as a pattern of perfection in its kind. It is doubtless spacious, regular, and well-built; but how is this spaciousness occupied? A clumsy rail, with lumps of bricks for piers, to support it, at the distance of every two or three yards, incloses nearly the whole area, intercepting almost entirely the view of the sides, and leaving the passage as narrow as most streets, with the disadvantage at night of being totally dark on one hand. The middle is filled up with bushes and dwarf trees, through which a statue peeps, like a piece of gilt gingerbread in a green-grocer's stall.[75]

Cavendish Square next provokes his disdain; 'the apparent intention here was to excite pastoral ideas in the mind; and this is endeavoured by cooping up a few frightened sheep within a wooden pailing; which, were it not for their sooty fleeces and meagre carcases, would be more apt to give the idea of a butcher's pen'. He compares this bathetic scene to Virgil's description of Aeneas's visit to Evander on the very spot where Rome was destined to be built, where at the time herds of cattle were wandering over what was later to become the Forum.[76] After this digression, he continues to describe the scene at Cavendish Square, remarking that 'to see the poor things starting at every coach, and hurrying round and round their narrow bounds, requires a warm imagination indeed, to convert the scene into that of flocks ranging the fields, with all the concomitant ideas of innocence and a pastoral life'.[77]

Stewart proclaims that '"some silly swain, more silly than his sheep, Which on the flow'ry plains he used to keep" must have first conceived the design'.[78] He affirms, moreover, that this metaphor 'might yet have been improved, by a thought taken from one of the most flagrant perversions of taste that was ever exhibited to publick view'. He refers here to the gardens of the deposed King Stanislaus of Poland, at Luneville ('one of the richest and most delightful countries in Europe, full of real pastoral objects and rustick images'), where the true qualities of the place were degraded by 'sticking up clock-work mills, wooden cows, and canvas milk-maids, all over his grounds'. This 'ridiculous scene' is a 'precious thought' for Cavendish Square: 'imitation here would appear with greater propriety than nature itself. I would therefore recommend it to the next designer

of country-in-town, to let all his sheep be painted. And I think if a paste-board mill, and tin cascade, were to be added it would compleat the rural scene.'[79]

The spectacle at Hanover Square (fig. 93) is, to him, no less preposterous:

It is neither open nor inclosed. Every convenience is railed out, and every nuisance railed in. Carriages have a narrow, ill-paved street to pass round in, and the middle has the air of a cow-yard, where blackguards assemble in the winter, to play at hussle-cap, up to the ancles in dirt. This is the more to be regretted, as the square in question is susceptible of improvement at a small expence. The buildings are neat and uniform. The street from Oxford road falls with a gentle descent into the middle of the upper side, while, right opposite, George street retires, converging to a point, which has a very picturesque effect; and the portico of St. George's church seen in profile, enriches and beautifies the whole.[80]

And Red Lion Square, 'elegantly so called, doubtless from some alehouse formerly at the corner', has, he remarks, a 'very different effect on the mind':

It does not make us laugh; but it makes us cry. I am sure, I never go into it without thinking of my latter end. The rough sod that 'heaves in many a mouldering heap', the dreary length of the sides, with the four watch-houses, like so many family vaults, at the corners, and the naked obelisk that springs from amidst the rank grass, like the sad monument of a disconsolate widow for the loss of her first husband, form, all together, a *memento mori*, more powerful to me than a death's head and cross marrow bones: and were but the parson's bull to be seen bellowing at the gate, the idea of a country-church-yard would be compleat.[81]

Despite the sharpness of his criticism, Stewart was hopeful that with his encouragement the residents of the city's squares would bestow 'every embellishment' on the areas that the places would admit, remarking 'our squares are in general inhabited by the great and opulent, who are surely in a condition to finish them as they ought to be, for their own convenience, and the honour of the metropolis'.[82] Indeed, despite their shortcomings, the capital's squares were, in his estimation, conspicuous and outstanding displays of grandeur in the metropolis, which demonstrated the superior advantages in

England of private enterprise – of 'public improvements that spring originally from the spirit of the people, and not from the will of the prince'.[83] They could, if properly improved and adorned, be 'superior to what can be met with in any other city in Europe. If this were once effected, London could boast of fifteen elegant squares (besides marketplaces and inns of court), while Paris, her proud rival, cannot shew half so many that deserve the name. The *Place de Louis Quinze* is not yet finished, and probably never will; and the *Place Royale*, the next in size and grandeur, may be compared to one of our second rate squares, with many of the defects in the worst.'[84]

In sum, then, Stewart derides the central areas of the city's squares for their failure to succeed in their purported objective of evoking *rus in urbe*: they are 'all, more or less, tinctured with the same absurdity, an awkward imitation of the country, amid the smoke and bustle of the town'.[85] To underscore this point of criticism he turns to the royal parks, which he remarks, 'by no means fall under this censure. These, with the many delightful fields which skirt this capital, render it unrivalled in situation; and, what is peculiar, they are all within the reach, and open to the health and amusement, of the inhabitants; a circumstance which renders the mock-parks in the middle of the town still more unnecessary and absurd'.[86]

Such derision of the notion of *rus in urbe* was soon echoed in Charles Jenner's energetic satires on contemporary poetical expositions of this concept, in his *Town Eclogues* of 1772:

In vain, alas, shall city bards resort.
For past'ral images, to *Tottenham-court*;
Fat droves of sheep, consign'd from *Lincoln* fens,
That swearing drovers beat to *Smithfield* penns,
Give faint ideas of *Arcadian* plains,
With bleating lambkins, and with piping swains.[87]

William Mason, too, cheekily remarked in 1773 that 'a perfect garden must contain within itself all the amusements of a great city' and that '*Urbs in Rure*, not *Rus in Urbe*, is the thing which an improver ought to aim at'.[88]

All such pointed criticism, it would seem, shared a common idea – the belief that the large central expanses of squares were still only sites of conflicting desires, ideals and aims – and as a result commentators could define the 'areas in the midst' at best simply as scenes of absurdity and impropriety. Yet such easy criticism failed to see that there were, in fact, numerous practical and symbolic obstacles to creating large gardens in town: gardens perforce had to jostle with buildings, barriers and public rights of way, each attempting to assert its supremacy.[89] Despite his abhorrence for the concept of *rus in urbe*, and for these diminutive gardens in general, Stewart was truly prophetic when he acknowledged the status of the open ground at the centre of the square as an intermediate category bound for change, though he defined only tentatively what that change might be. But what was clear was that this intermediate status rendered the garden a discomfiting category for any critic who insisted on the need to establish a sharp distinction between the urban and the rural.

The Disposition of 'Superficial Embellishments' and Statuary

The evocation of *rus in urbe* was a difficult objective to achieve within the confines of a square, insofar as the notion itself of what constituted 'country in town' remained intangible and unquantifiable. Statuary, and commemorative sculpture in particular, were a much more powerful and practical organising motif for these small enclosures – one that was capable of readily unifying the space, and projecting the aspirations of the square's inhabitants in a durable and tangible manner.

Although from the late seventeenth century there had been occasional mutterings in the press about the possibility that statuary in squares would invite popish idolatry,[90] there was little public discourse on the propriety, character and disposition of 'publick' sculpture until the anonymous publication of James Ralph's *A Critical Review of the Publick Buildings, Statues and Ornaments, in and about London and Westminster* (1734).[91] Although the author advertised the usefulness of his work to tourists, his real aim was to 'stir up the publick', and to reform the taste of his age by demonstrating the defects and merits of public buildings, statues and ornaments.[92] Possessed of an informed lay interest in gardens, and susceptible to the scenographic qualities of landscape and buildings, Ralph registered disappointment with the layout and character of all but one of the eleven

94 Sutton Nicholls, *St James's Square*, 1754, engraving (detail), showing the central basin and *jet d'eau*. Author's collection. On draining the basin for the purpose of erecting the statue of William III, the workmen found 'many curious articles, which villany to conceal its guilt had committed to the place. The most singular of these were, the keys of Newgate, together with a quantity of fetters, which it is well known were stolen, at the time that prison was burnt down during the riots in 1780.'

squares he surveyed, opining that the only reason that they claimed 'any regard' was because they were called squares.[93]

The gardens and their embellishments, in particular, were, he said, affected adversely by their surrounding buildings, but were nonetheless 'capable of great improvements'. He was not, for instance, impressed by the stately piece of water in St James's Square, remarking, 'I can never thoroughly applaud the bason itself, till 'tis finish'd as it ought, with a statue or an obelisk in the middle, worthy of the place it was to appear in, and the neighbourhood it was to adorn' (fig. 94). He also condemned Soho Square, purporting that 'it has, beside, a little, contemptible garden in the middle of the area, and a worse statue, if it be possible, in the middle of that.' He was, as we have seen in Chapter 2, no less uncharitable in respect of the garden at Grosvenor Square.

Ralph's views may not have been shared by all observers, but they did, nonetheless, attest to a shift

in taste in the deployment of 'superficial Embellishments' in a garden, and to a change in the manner in which statuary in squares was perceived. For him, with the rise of gardening in the 'Modern style', and in the picturesque taste in particular, statuary was sadly demoted from its status as principal ornament to that of mere garden accessory: as the once open central areas of the city's squares were slowly transmuted into lush gardens, the statues that adorned them became less noteworthy, and subsidiary in interest to the planting that surrounded them.

This tendency to treat statuary as subsidiary ornament began to take effect as early as 1748 when the inhabitants of Leicester Fields set up an equestrian statue of George I to mark the improvement of their central garden (fig. 95).[94] They had acquired the statue from Canons – the home of the dukes of Chandos at Little Stanmore, Middlesex – when the house was demolished and its contents dispersed in the same year. It is tantalising to equate the rede-

ployment of John Nost II's effigy of the late monarch (*c.*1723) with Pope Paul III's gesture to re-erect the antique statue of Marcus Aurelius in the Piazza del Campidoglio in Rome[95] – especially given the fact that between 1717 and 1760 Leicester House on the north side of the square, was the home of the princes of Wales (first Prince George Augustus, later George II, followed by Prince Frederick Lewis, and then Prince George William Frederick, later George III). What is surprising is that residents chose to adorn the central area of their new garden not with a bespoke sculpture, but with a second-hand lead statue, which was 'gilt with all Expedition' upon being put up in the square.[96]

The success of this venture appears, nonetheless, to have encouraged the residents of Golden and (later) Berkeley squares to erect similar royal effigies to mark the receipt of private acts that empowered them to embellish, adorn and protect their central areas. Golden Square, which had originally been laid out by 1688, was in 1753 fitted with 'a fine Statue of his Majesty in Stone';[97] and although at Berkeley Square the act of 1766 decreed that there was to be 'no statue or bason in the middle', a lead statue of George III, a gift of the king's sister Princess Amelia, was erected in the garden (fig. 96).[98] The garden was

'laid out and planted after the manner of Grosvenor-square', with a large 'grass-plat in the middle, a gravel walk round, and iron palisadoes'.[99] Red Lion Square was rare among its neighbours in rejecting a royal monument for the embellishment of the central

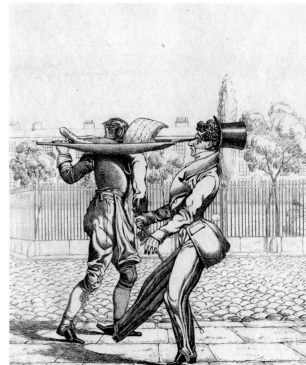

garden; in *c.*1750 an obelisk was 'built by subscription of the inhabitants, which was pretended to cover the bones of Oliver Cromwell'.[100] And in Devonshire Square the central feature was a statue not of the king but of the naked figure of Mercury (fig. 97).

While from the mid-eighteenth century statues in various London squares became 'nearly obumbrated by the neighbouring foliage', 'bosomed in trees', or 'invisible', the taste for raising statues in the central areas of squares did not wither.[101] The French visitors Pierre-Jean Grosley and François La Combe noted in their travel journals of 1765 and 1777 respectively that several 'superbes places' were embellished with 'equestrian statues or *pédestres*, or obelisks, or by basins or bosquets enclosed by iron palings', and that statues were commonly gilt.[102]

'Country and Town in the Same Spot is a Charming Idea'

Topographical views by the early to mid-eighteenth-century engravers and artists Sutton Nicholls, Nathaniel Parr, John Maurer and Thomas Bowles project the first popular images of the new London squares and those that, like St James's Square, had been recently reordered after private acts of parliament for their enclosure and improvement had been obtained. Timothy Clayton in *The English Print, 1688–1802* remarks that the primary purpose of such prints was to convey information and quality of design, and their tone, like other contemporary topographical views, was one of 'celebration of England's growing power and wealth'.[103]

These bird's-eye views – and those of Sutton Nicholls in particular – are still very popular, and give the impression that London's Georgian squares and their central enclosures were bare, rational and sometimes austere places: the pavements are sprinkled with knots of polite staffage, and a statue occasionally makes a very good appearance in prospect at the centre of a field laid out in simple but expensive taste. The city's topographers, like the squares' inhabitants themselves, were eager to promote the novelty, excitement and magnificence of these architectural set-pieces, and the airy splendour, freshness and repose of their new enclosures.[104] These generalised views, however, convey few of the squares' idiosyncrasies, peculiarities or inadequacies at the time: they were less accurate reflections of the true character of the spaces they would commemorate than idealised evocations of what were at the time novel and uncommon residential precincts, generally built for and inhabited by 'people of fashion' or 'the better class of merchant'.

99   J. B. Papworth, *Soho Square*, 1816, aquatint, from his *Select Views of London: With Historical and Descriptive Sketches of Some of the Most Interesting of its Public Buildings* (1816). London Metropolitan Archives.

The next generation of topographers, on the other hand, who adopted a lower, pedestrian viewpoint, were better able to capture the dramatic change in taste that swept through the metropolis in the third quarter of the eighteenth century, which saw many of the earlier enclosed fields transformed into leafy gardens. This observable shift was in part precipitated by a redefinition of the ever evolving idea of *rus in urbe*: 'rus' is no longer seen as a view of untamed countryside; instead it becomes a reference to the rural rusticity of the picturesque gardens of the country estate. The aim to bring the country into town thus takes on an entirely new meaning.

These new views of the city's squares tend to emphasise the much vaunted verdant foliage of these agreeable retreats, and the extent to which this new planting could serve as a deliberate contrast and complement to the surrounding buildings. Some artists, moreover, begin to portray more truthfully the robust vitality of some of the city's squares, and

the inhabitants and visitors that animated them: Richard Dighton portrays a street vendor in a London square as 'A London Nuisance' (1821), John Buonarotti Papworth shows sheep and cattle being shepherded through Soho Square (1816), George Scharf records the workaday world of Bloomsbury Square (*c.*1826) and Jacques-Laurent Agasse shows a jobbing gardener selling his wares in Soho Square (1822) (figs 98–101).

These views, however, illustrate day-to-day activity on the public carriageways surrounding squares, and not in their enclosed central areas. The open expanses in the middle of the central area are, in these views, invisible, concealed behind the dense screens of verdure of their newly formed gardens. The foliage serves to underscore the exclusivity of the central gardens and their physical separation from the street: the gardens were reserved for private residents, and were spatial luxuries in the sense that they were destined to be used neither for actual

100 (*above*) George Scharf, *View Taken from N[o]. 19 Bloomsbury Sqr*, *c*.1826, pencil drawing. British Museum, London.

101 (*right*) Jacques–Laurent Agasse, *The Flower Seller*, 1822, oil on canvas. Stiftung Oskar Reinhart, Winterthur.

residence nor for trade but for pleasure. John Wood the elder, who modelled the design of Queen Square, Bath, on Grosvenor Square in London, remarked in 1742 that 'the Spot whereon [the residents] meet, ought to be separated from the Ground common to Men and Beasts, and even Mankind in general, if Decency and good Order are necessary to be observ'd in such Places of Assembly'.[105] The historian Simon Varey has recently observed that the inhabitants of the city's squares, in fact, derived 'negative pleasure' from seeing their central spaces empty of people who had no right to use them, and that as such they were expressions of social division.[106]

The increasing physical separation of the central garden of the city square from its encircling streets was to a large extent abetted by the advent of 'modern' garden design, and we must once more look to Grosvenor Square for pioneering innovations in this respect. The refurbishment of the central area corresponded with the passing of their act to enclose and adorn their square in 1774,[107] and entailed adopting a plan, attributed to the draughtsman and writer George Richardson,[108] which reduced Thomas Alston's earlier geometrical wilderness work to four divisions, arranged around a central raised grass platform, crowned with the existing equestrian statue (fig. 102). Each quarter was appointed with eight clumps of shrubs set in ovals of variable size arranged symmetrically on the longitudinal axis of the square.[109] This was among the earliest instances of the creation of shrubberies in a London square.

In 1785 Abigail Adams, wife of the American ambassador, described the new sense of the rural character of Grosvenor Square garden, conveying the wonder typical of the response of newcomers to the metropolis: 'in the middle of the square which is very spacious is a circuleer [*sic*] inclosure in which clumps of trees are planted which look like shrubbery as the trees are small and close together. Round them is the hedge which when cut has a very rural appearance. In the middle is the King on horse back. The whole is laid out into walks and those who live in the square have a key to one of the gates which you may make use of for to walk.'[110] The striking layout also prompted the German clergyman Carl Philipp Moritz – who compared London to Berlin, and praised the 'real magnificence, and beautiful symmetry' of the former's 'quadrangular places' – to remark in 1782 that 'in Grosvenor square, instead of the green plot, or area, there is a little circular wood, intended, no doubt, to give one the idea of *rus in urbe*', again looking to the phrase's new meaning (fig. 103).[111]

At another 'pleasing inclosed grass plat on the side of an hill', not half a mile away, a similar remodelling took place a few years later. In 1790 the gravel walks and grass plots of Leicester Square were banished, and the kite-shaped pleasure ground was circumscribed by a broad gravel walk, and embellished with eight crescent and wedge-shaped shrub clumps that radiated from the central statue like the petals of a flower. Although at first glance the geometrical scheme would appear to derive from the flower gardens of earlier pleasure grounds, William Hodges's painted view of *c.*1790 suggests that it was not dissimilar to some contemporary gardens being formed in country house pleasure grounds (fig. 104).[112] The beds appear to be planted with flowering shrubs marshalled in ascending ranks – the most floriferous set on the perimeters of the beds. The beds also appear to have contained a considerable number of fastigiate trees. An engraved view of 1801 portrays the semi-mature shrub clumps dotted with stately Lombardy poplars, and a sketch done some fifteen years later shows the garden at the acme of its picturesqueness (fig. 105).[113]

Such picturesque planting was not unique to these squares: from 1790 major replanting also took

92

104 (*right*) William Hodges, *Design for a Proposed New Opera House in Leicester Square*, *c*.1790, oil on canvas. Museum of London.

105 (*below*) Alexander Nasmyth, *Leicester Square, June 10 1816*, pencil. Museum of London. Nasmyth's view captures the central garden at the period when it was described as 'a neglected and dirty place'. The garden looks forlorn, and its giant poplar 'peristyle' brings to mind Pope's fantasy of creating an 'old Roman temple in trees'. Lombardy poplars abounded in London's squares.

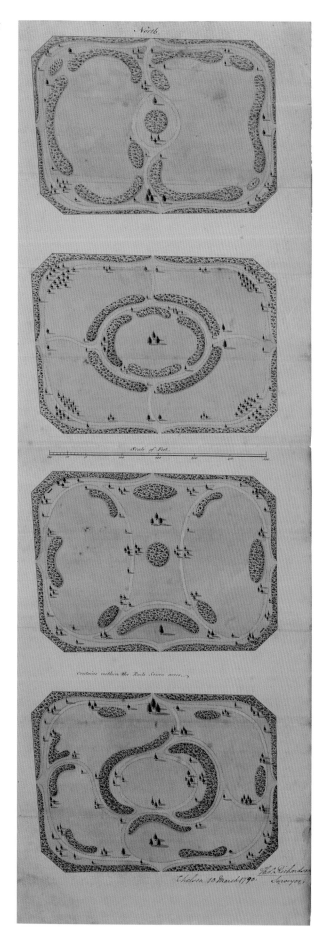

place at both Soho Square and Lincoln's Inn Fields. The residents' committee at Soho Square embarked upon an 'improvement' of the central garden, which entailed 'trenching the Borders, the clumps, altering the Walks, [setting] two Rows of Quick Setts within the Iron railing, [and planting] Trees and Shrubs'. William Malcolm & Son, nurserymen from Stockwell, supplied and planted the garden in early 1791. Among the trees and shrubs placed in the garden were laurel, *Viburnum tinus*, phillyrea, dogwood, honeysuckle, lilac, box, euonymus, peach, cherry, laburnum, yew, almond, azaleas, sweet briars and roses. The choice of plants was doubtless influenced by Sir Joseph Banks, who was a member of the Garden Committee.[114] The new, naturalistic planting pleased Sir Charles Bell at No. 34, who reported in 1811 that he was very pleased with his house, and especially 'the walk in the drawing-room looking down on the green and trees of the square'; and in 1815 John Britton praised the 'very pleasing and somewhat rural appearance' of the new garden.[115]

At Lincoln's Inn Fields the basin was filled in 'after much debate and opposition among the inhabitants', and the gardens were restructured into a naturalistic scene: 'a double row of Quick Set [hedging]' was set 'inside the railings', and a great quantity of elm, almond, laburnum, balsam poplar, Siberian crab, double-blossomed cherry, birch, service tree, lilac, ash, acacia, plane and lime were planted throughout (figs 106 and 107).[116] The rationale for the square's impenetrable hawthorn hedge was to prevent trespass; this measure was, in fact, part of a larger strategy considered by Sir John Soane to put in place the 'most effectual mode of fencing it [the square] in as to prevent nuisances'.[117]

The gardens of Berkeley Square were also remodelled. Whereas 'the area of this quadrangle was till very lately an uninteresting slope of grass', in *c.*1800 'the inhabitants, sated with the sameness of the scene, entered into a resolution of planting shrubs and trees around the enormous pedestal which supports the equally enormous equestrian statue of his present Majesty'.[118]

Such was the enthusiasm for well-planted gardens at the centre of squares that in some cases early attention was given to the enclosing and planting of the areas even before the surrounding houses were erected. Tavistock Square (begun 1803), for example, was planted three years prior to the commencement

107 Robert Chantrell, view of London from the top of No. 13 Lincoln's Inn Fields (Sir John Soane's house), 1813, watercolour. Sir John Soane's Museum, London. The view faces south-east towards the garden of Lincoln's Inn and St Paul's Cathedral.

of building works, so as to enable the garden to 'become at once pleasant, healthy, and desirable'. This formula became more widely copied about two decades later: both Euston (from 1811) and Belgrave squares (begun 1826) were 'dressed as nursery grounds' before the surrounding houses were thrown up; and the topographer David Hughson remarks that at Russell Square 'much pains have been used, and expence incurred, in laying out and planting the area . . . which, when the trees and plants shall have arrived at a greater degree of maturity, will render it one of the most agreeable in London'.[119]

Insofar as squares were often seen as capable of improving the 'dignity of character' of their surroundings, we should not be surprised to find that the promise of central openings or gardens, and views over, or direct access to, them often succeeded in connecting the actual architectural image of

squares with their immediate precincts. The effect was symbiotic, for gardens were also generally perceived to be neater, more convenient, more orderly and more beautiful when the surroundings beyond the circumference of the garden rails were improved through the introduction of regulated improvements such as artificial lighting, paving and policing, all of which were enforced both by the trustees of the squares and the parochial authorities. To these criteria of respectability should be added the character of the buildings that surrounded the central area: squares that received the highest commendations were often those that were surrounded by elegant houses.[120] Indeed, the character of a square was now seldom to be described without reference to its context.

Inspired by these examples, the planting in the centres of many other squares became increasingly

naturalistic, and there was a new emphasis placed on landscaping (fig. 108). Many of the metropolis's immured and orderly gardens were, as the artist Jean Claude Nattes shows us in his various views of the period, dramatically metamorphosed into informal, naturalistic scenes: straight paths were serpentinised, and walls and wooden palisades were replaced by open iron railings through which passers-by could catch glimpses of velvet lawns, luxuriant shrubberies and clumps of foliage and flowers. The gardens in the centres of squares were henceforth perceived as able to compete with their immediate and neighbouring built surroundings in terms of the bulk and stature of their planting.

Open iron railings – a relatively new form of fencing for squares – did much to reveal the scenery of 'shrubbery-walks and grass-plats', which 'afforded very seasonable relief, the eye being wearied of the sameness of colossal piles of bricks and mortar'.[121] Or as William Weir would later remark, 'the verdant foliage and evergreen turf on earth, and the ever-varying features of our rarely cloudless sky, freely revealed by the opening amid a forest of houses, lend a charm to every square; and simple as these elements be, they are susceptible to an infinite multiplicity of *nuances* of character' (fig. 109).[122]

Designers of the new gardens in fact drew on various theories of the picturesque, using them as a means of confronting, in aesthetic terms, the problem of creating country gardens in town. They supported their arguments by proposing theories that reconciled aesthetic categories that previously had been opposed to one another: the sublime versus the beautiful; the wild versus the cultivated and the ordered; and the general versus the particular. As a result, the unchecked growth of garden plants and trees was no longer perceived as a potential threat to the harmony, grandeur and uniformity of the surrounding buildings, but vaunted as a necessary complement to architectural urbanity and sophistication. Indeed, to be urbane and sophisticated in garden design clearly marks how closely London squares had become woven into the townscape. The imitation of a 'rural prospect' was, as we have seen,

109 Unknown artist, *View of Queen Square, Holborn*, 1812, aquatint. Author's collection. Rudolph Ackermann, writing in *The Repository of Arts* in 1812, praised the 'open iron railing' at Queen Square, though he regretted that the 'fine views' from the square northwards to Hampstead and Highgate were 'now shut out by Guildford-street' (*foreground*).

a long-standing objective of the designers of garden squares. It was not, however, until the last decade of the eighteenth century that it was no longer always considered important to have clear distant vistas beyond the garden, or even across the gardens to the opposite side of the square – the view could be embowered by foliage. Inhabitants and observers alike desired the gardens to express 'a degree of maturity'.[123]

Hermann von Pückler-Muskau remarks in 1814 that the city's 'beautiful squares' are a 'great ornament to London'.

Country and town in the same spot is a charming idea. Fancy yourself in an extensive quadrangular area surrounded by the finest houses, and in the midst of its delightful plantations, with walks, shrubberies, and parterres of fragrant flowers, inclosed with an elegant iron railing, where ladies arranged in all the splendour of fashion are taking the air; where children sweet as Loves chase one another; and growing beauties, with che-

quered silk cords in their showy hands, skip like Zephyrs among the roses, by plying the string over head and under foot, straight and cross-wise, with a grace and pliancy you have no conception of; then you will have a faint representation of those private promenades. Private, because they are constantly locked up for exclusive use of a number of families who have keys to their entrances. Thus the inhabitant of the square has a rural prospect before his eye, without having to leave his house.[124]

The French visitor François Philippar, who visited the capital in the late 1820s, declares that *places publiques* or *Squarres* are 'all ornamented in the centre with gardens encircled by railings; a method which presents the advantage of attenuating the severity which is inherent in the regular layout of the enclosure' (fig. 110).[125] And the American topographical artist James Peller Malcolm notes the change in character of many of the city's squares, which he attributes to new railings and more luxuriant plant-

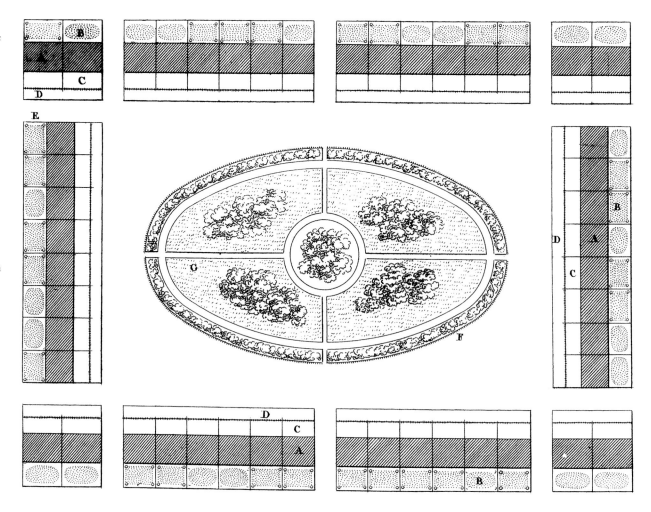

110 François Philippar, *Plan d'une place de la ville de Londres (Squarre)*, engraving, from his *Voyage agronomique en Angleterre, fait en 1829* (1830), pl. III. Private collection. The French traveller's reconstruction of a typical London square is somewhat idealised. Legend:
A: surrounding houses;
B: town gardens; C: house façades opening to the square and courtyard gardens;
D: pavements; E: the street;
F: the square; G: the centre of the square enclosed by an iron railing.

ing when he remarks in his *Anecdotes* (1808) that 'pure air so essential to the preservation of life, now circulates through the *new* streets; squares calculated for ornament, health and the higher ranks of the community are judiciously dispersed, and their centres converted into beautiful gardens'.[126]

One might pause here to note one unintended consequence of this new, fulsome garden design. Gardens, once graced with excessive plant cover – notwithstanding their secure enclosure – were at times sites of dangerous impropriety, in that shrubberies or well-placed hedges, in particular, offered convenient and sheltered places for indecorous behaviour. It was announced in the *Daily Register* in September 1785, for example, that 'Lady Foley and Mrs Arabin have kindly undertaken to plan the intended *shrubbery* behind Gower-street – can anyone doubt their *capability*, who reflects with what *art* they displayed the *beauties of nature* in their own gardens'. This notice alludes to the criminal trials of these two women, who had been detected *in flagrante* in shrubberies:

Lady Ann Foley had been publicly besmirched for engaging in 'criminal conversation' with the Earl of Peterborough, and Mrs Arabin for her indecorous congress with Thomas Sutton. The historian Sarah Lloyd posits that this news item was 'typical of adultery reporting in its use of innuendo and fabrication, and in its appropriation of discourse, including that of landscape improvement'.[127] Clearly neither woman had an interest in gardening: the shrubbery was appropriated by the press as a setting for their *plein air* sexual transgressions as it was at the time a new, exotic and fashionable accessory of both urban and rural gardens (fig. 111).[128]

The interiors of various other squares were troubled by similar incidents of 'disorderly conduct', and some residents, like those living by Lincoln's Inn Fields, were annoyed by the occasional congregation of 'prostitutes in the Fields in an Evening before the Watch is set'.[129] John Papworth remarked in 1816 that Grosvenor Square 'has of late years . . . been deprived of much of its shrubbery, in consequence

of the cover afforded by it to the servants in the neighbourhood, whose noise disturbed the nobility and gentry during their morning repose'.[130] Loudon observed in 1822 that planting in a square should not preclude surveillance of the central area from the first floor level of the houses surrounding it.[131] In 1829 the Duke of Bedford – for unspecified reasons – personally recommended the thinning of the plantations in Gordon Square.[132] Indeed, the residents of Hanover and Fitzroy squares may have demurred from creating large and dense plantations within their central gardens for fear of potential mischief that could be caused by disorderly intruders

(fig. 112). On the other hand, they might simply have felt that picturesque planting would compromise the grandeur of their surroundings. Such are the vagaries of garden history.

Squares and the 'Perfection of Modern Gardening'

A far more idealistic view of gardens was soon to become another unintended consequence of an enhanced development of London squares. Although Stewart affirmed in 1771 that 'every inhabitant [of the metropolis] participates in the advantage' of the

public improvements – among them the spacious areas in so-called 'public squares' – it was not until December 1803 that the design and treatment of the central areas was addressed as a general public concern: John Loudon elaborated upon the subject in a letter to the editor of the *Literary Journal*. It was the author's first proposal for civic improvements.

Loudon considered that squares should – in fact, not just in theory – make an important contribution to the beauty of the metropolis, to the salubrity of its inhabitants, and even 'to some degree to the honour of the British nation'.[133] Such a role was, for him, contingent on public access to the gardens. This did not entail opening the central areas of the great and established squares to the public; but Loudon suggested that at the very least the residents of private squares could contribute towards the well-being of their fellow citizens by planting their gardens to the 'utmost picturesque advantage', so that everyone, including non-residents, could profit from the experience of viewing natural scenery in town. Ideally, however, he envisaged that garden squares might one day be open to everyone, and laid out to 'interest and relieve the eye and satisfy the mind'; in other words, they should provide

a structured natural setting for passive public recreation and public instruction – particularly the pursuit of botany.

Putting forward his own model for a 'public square', Loudon recommended that such a feature of the urban topography should be fluidly integrated into the community in a way that surpassed the earlier models' fusion of art and nature. These ideas informed a design for a London square that Loudon published in 1812 (fig. 113). The formula 'nature in the midst of art' was transmuted into 'art in the midst of nature', by which he meant that the emphasis on garden boundaries should be diminished, and ungated, sunny and umbrageous garden paths should traverse spacious lawns and large plant beds and dissolve into the mosaic of the surrounding streets. Loudon's engraving of his model square projects this powerful centrifugal thrust, conveying the notion that the garden – full of common sorts of plants, singular for beauty, fragrance and luxuriant growth and planted following the principles of natural scenery – is intended to suffuse its urban architectural environment.

Loudon's ultimate goal was to galvanise ordinary citizens to think about garden squares in terms of

their role in the metropolitan plan – as one of dozens of interactive parts of a whole coherent system. The square, which at the level of planning was simply an unelaborated open green space, was now assigned a complex function and purpose in the structure of the city. For him, however, the square was not to be assigned a fixed visual image. Although Loudon proposed practical ways by which to reform the layout and treatment of squares, his foremost objective was to cultivate in his readers a desire to question, improve and adapt his ideas to their personal requirements. Thus there is no pro-

priety of design for a garden. He comments in the *Encyclopaedia of Gardening* (1822) that 'a small city square might be laid out in terraces, like the Isola Bella, or the gardens of Babylon'. Indeed, the tide of picturesqueness had changed the face of many squares across town: Sloane Square (from 1771) had been formed to approximate a hummocky wood-land, and Edwardes Square, Kensington (1811–19) had been laid out in 1820 with winding vales by Agostino Aglio, 'an eminent landscape painter'.[134]

Humphry Repton also approached the subject of garden square design as a 'Public concern', and took

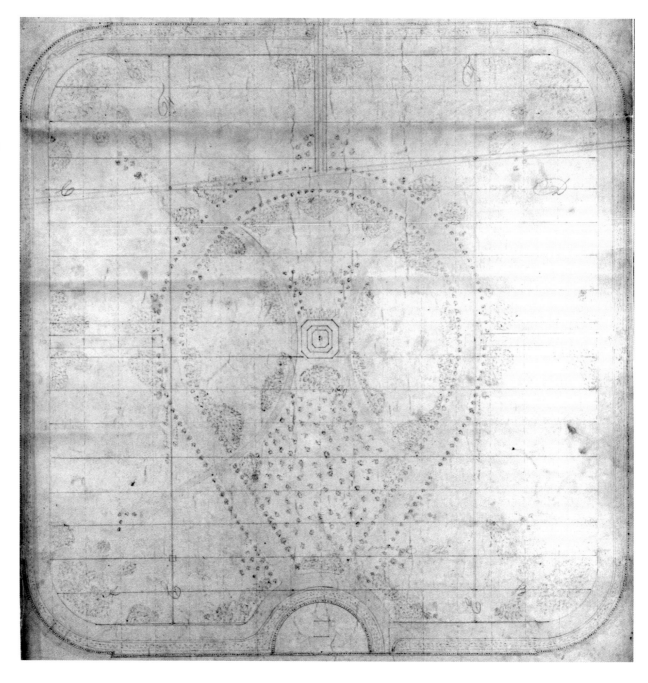

114 Humphry Repton, preliminary design for Russell Square garden, 1804, pencil. Bedford Estate Archive, Woburn Abbey. This drawing documents the celebrated improver's efforts to enhance the original 'insipid' layout proposed by the builder James Burton. Repton was subsequently engaged by Burton to design and plant the square.

'a sort of Pride in contributing to the Embellishment of the Capital'. His views on London squares were, in his own words, based upon 'plain common sense improved by observation & experience', and he remarked that the 'Artist' of a garden 'area' had to treat the square both as a *public* object' and a private garden. The author and landscape improver, who almost certainly was acquainted with Thomas Fairchild's essay on London squares, presumably refined his particularised concept of the propriety of garden squares from *c.*1805 after he was entrusted with the layout of Russell Square (fig. 114).[135]

In *An Enquiry into the Changes of Taste in Landscape Gardening* (1806), Repton remarks that to achieve a degree of 'perfection of Modern Gardening', the design of a square has to satisfy the following requisites:

First, it must display the natural beauties, and hide the natural defects of every situation; *Secondly*, it should give the appearance of extent and freedom, by carefully disguising or hiding the boundary; *Thirdly*, it must studiously conceal every interference of art, however expensive, by which the

natural scenery is improved; making the whole
appear the production of nature only; and *fourthly*,
all objects of mere convenience or comfort, if
incapable of being made ornamental, or of becoming proper parts of the general scenery must be
removed or concealed.[136]

The interior of the place, moreover, 'wants to be
perfectly secluded; somewhere between a garden and
a park'.[137]

Repton also pays a great deal of attention to the
display of statues in squares, setting down his prescriptions for the deployment of these conspicuous
and lofty 'eye-traps'. Referring to his own involvement in proposals in 1807 to raise a statue to Francis,
fifth Duke of Bedford, in Russell Square, he remarks
that while 'equestrian statues have usually been
placed in the centre of public squares, in one of such

large dimensions no common sized object could be
sufficiently distinguished; it was therefore very judiciously determined (by committee) to place the fine
Statue of the late Duke of Bedford, now preparing
by the ingenious Mr Westmacott, on one side of the
square facing Bloomsbury [Square], forming an
appropriate perspective, as seen through the vista of
the two streets crossing the two squares'. The statue
was raised in 1809, and effectively became an element
of the neighbouring streetscape, though one that was
'shaded by a grove of trees of various kinds' within
the square (fig. 115).[138]

Repton opined that all eye-catching ornaments
'tend to lessen the apparent greatness of a place; for
one can seldom lose sight of so conspicuous a land-
mark; we are in a manner tethered to the same
object'. Having recommended banishing statues to
the margins of the square, Repton proposes that

116   Humphry Repton and
John Adey Repton, *Design for
Burlington-Place*, perspective
view looking north, 1808, pen
and ink with watercolour
wash. The Royal Academy of
Arts Library, London,
presented by the Art Fund.

their central position should be usurped by a simple
'Reposoir' – a low seat 'sheltered from rain and
defended from the sun' for the purpose of rest and
contemplation.[139] Looking out from what Loudon
later describes as this open-sided 'centrical covered
seat and retreat', the key-holders could survey the
transitory images that animated their square.[140]

In a letter of March 1807, in which Repton
defended his rejected proposal for Bloomsbury
Square, he elaborates on the 'Reasons upon which
the Plan was founded'. He first explains the public
objectives of his scheme, proposing to create a 'Walk
around the Area for convenience & in compliance
with the general custom of all other Squares'; the
walk is to be 'defended from without & ornamented
on the inside by the margin of Shrubs by which it
is accompanied'. His 'one great object' of the plan
is to 'keep open the View from Holborn thro'
Bedford Place to the statue forming a fine Enfilade
thro' the two squares – such as prevailed from Cavendish Square thro' Hanover Square to the Portico
of St George's'. He considers that the 'two great
private uses of all squares are space for the children
& a Pleasure Ground for the inhabitants of the

Square'. In so far as 'evergreen and winter plants will
not bear the air of a City', he recommends planting
a shaded walk of lime trees 'like that in Russell
Square'. His final recommendation is to introduce
some 'tall trees' to increase the 'apparent dimensions'
of the ground by partial concealment. He remarks,
'that as a small lake appears large, by the Intervention of Islands, so a small area is increased by the
interruptions thrown in the way of viewing the
whole at once'.[141] Repton and his son John Adey
Repton proposed to implement such a planting
strategy at Burlington House in Piccadilly: in 1808
they presented a scheme to the fifth Duke of Devonshire, which entailed sweeping away the family's
seventeenth-century town mansion and replacing it
with a garden square (fig. 116).[142]

That both Loudon and Repton – two of the
greatest landscape improvers of the age – address the
role and character of the London square, and are both
involved in the layout of such public spaces, suggests
that by the early nineteenth century the square had
become a distinctive category of 'landscape gardening' – a branch of the polite arts which, in Repton's
estimation, 'can only be advanced and perfected by

the united powers of the *landscape painter* and the *practical gardener*.[143] Painting and gardening were not, however, the only foundations of the landscape gardener: the artist must also possess 'a competent knowledge of *surveying, mechanics, hydraulics, agriculture, botany*, and the general principles of *architecture*'.

While these circumstances might lead us to conclude that garden square design was henceforth a serious, indeed, almost professional consideration, it does not follow that the efforts of the landscape gardener met with universal public approval, or that there was a consensus on the disposition of the central areas of squares. Indeed, Repton remained sceptical of the ability of his contemporaries to assess the medium- to long-term benefits of laying out squares in the new manner, remarking that Russell Square 'for the first few years of its growth . . . will be liable to some criticism, because few are in the habit of anticipating the future effects of plantation'.[144] He was, therefore, compelled to explain and defend the reasoning behind his design; he likewise reassured his readers that while the benefits of his scheme may not have been immediately apparent, his legacy would be appreciated by succeeding generations of users:

A few years hence, when the present patches of shrubs shall have become thickets, when the present meagre rows of trees shall have become an umbrageous avenue, and the children now in their nurses' arms shall have become the parents or grandsires of future generations, this square may serve to record that the art of Landscape Gardening in the beginning of the 19th century was not directed by whim or caprice, but founded on due considerations of utility as well as beauty, without a bigoted adherence to forms and lines whether straight, crooked, or serpentine.[145]

What Repton could not foresee was that the square as he knew it was about to take a new turn: while it remained essentially what it had earlier been – that is an open space laid out as a garden and surrounded by houses – it was evolving in an unexpected but interesting way into something more problematic and complex. Squares were poised to mutate into a greater number of geometrical figures, including crescents, ovals, triangles and polygons, and the relationship of the houses that encompassed them and their central garden areas was to become more variable and less self-contained.

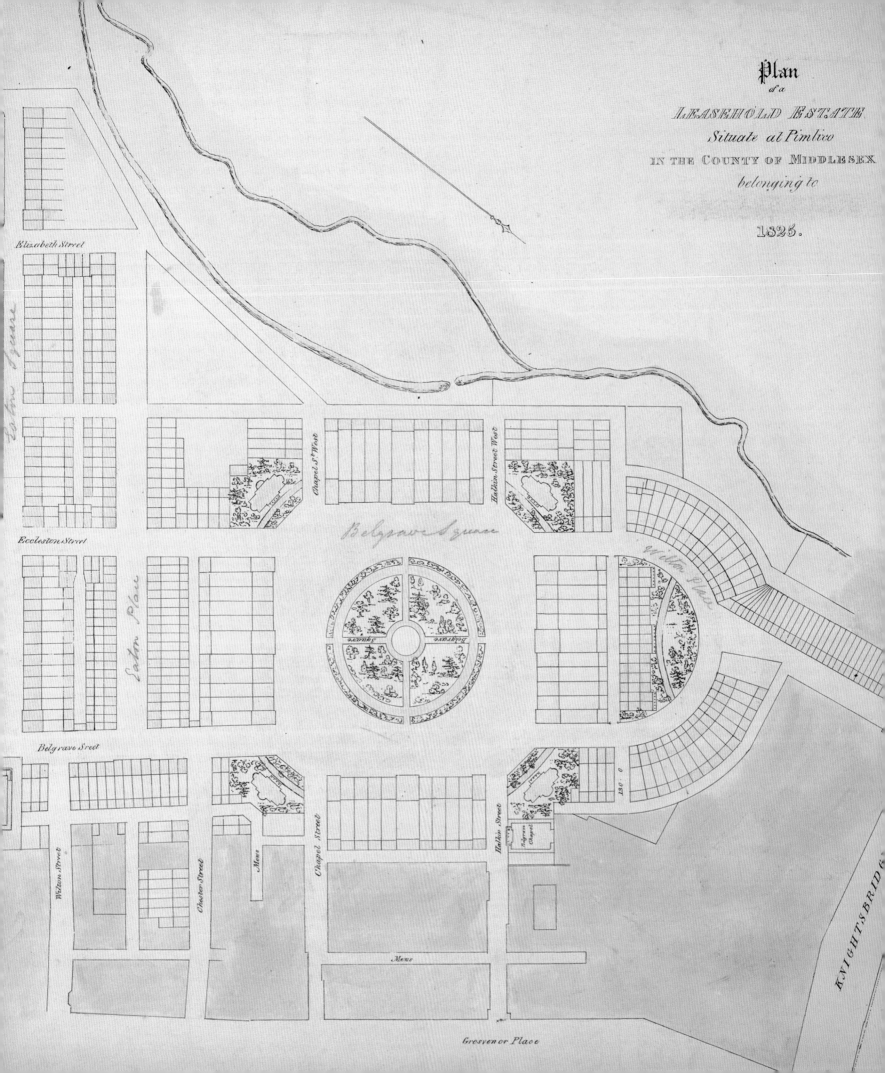

Plan
of a
LEASEHOLD ESTATE
Situate at Pimlico
IN THE COUNTY OF MIDDLESEX
belonging to

1825.

Elizabeth Street

Eccleston Street

Belgrave Street

John Square

Eaton Place

Chapel St West

Halkin Street West

Belgrave Square

Wilton Place

Wilton Street

Chester Street

Mews

Chapel Street

Halkin Street

Belgrave Chapel

KNIGHTSBRIDGE

Mews

Grosvenor Place

4

'Genuine Squares', 'New Squares' and 'Places'

By the early nineteenth century, the success of the London square was guaranteed, and undeniable; indeed, squares were now on the cusp of becoming just as much a feature of the outer suburbs as they had been of the West End in the preceding century.[1] Squares, and even more so squares and crescents, were to become synonymous with privilege, elegance and prosperous metropolitan living. The hero of Waterloo and commentator on French life Alexander Cavalié Mercer contrasted the London square of the early nineteenth century favourably with its counterparts in the French capital:

> [I]f London is inferior to Paris in [one] respect [in having wharfs where Paris has neat quays, giving a hard edge to the Seine], how superior she is in public squares! The costly iron railings, the masterly statues that decorate some, and the pleasant shrubberies, smooth, well-kept turf, and well-rolled walks which characterise most of them, are nowhere to be seen in Paris. The Place Louis Quinze is not what we should call a square in London; it is a sort of esplanade.[2]

'Second-rate' Squares and Early Nineteenth-century Suburban Expansion

A close examination of Richard Horwood's *Plan of the Cities of London & Westminster, with the Borough of Southwark Including their Adjacent Suburbs* (1799) reveals what had become the ubiquity of garden squares and their distribution (fig. 117). Horwood's plan is, in fact, a useful guide to the general growth of London between the years 1799 and 1819; the fourth edition, in particular (1819), charts new and significant developments in the geography of the capital, whose inhabited houses by then numbered about 150,000, reflecting a population approaching 1 million people. This immense survey is, moreover, a snapshot of a city in the midst of an unprecedented building boom, accompanied by one of the most intensive periods of square building, though many projected openings depicted on the plan were never built, or did not assume quite the shape indicated.

For our purposes, however, Horwood's survey charts the widespread and novel deployment of the square as a planning device to create or link new residential developments – from the hesitant beginnings of John Nash's Regent's Park to the tentative building lines of the Bedford Estate's squares in Bloomsbury and the Grosvenor Estate's 'new colonies' in Belgravia.[3]

The plan, for instance, depicts a quite staggering array: in Marylebone, Cumberland Square, Prince of Wales and Princess Charlotte circuses, Regent's Circus (later Park Square and Park Crescent), and Dorset, Montagu, Bryanston, Carmarthen and Rutland squares; in Bloomsbury, the newly created Tavistock, Euston, Russell and Mecklenburgh squares and Burton Crescent; in St Pancras, Seymour, Euston,

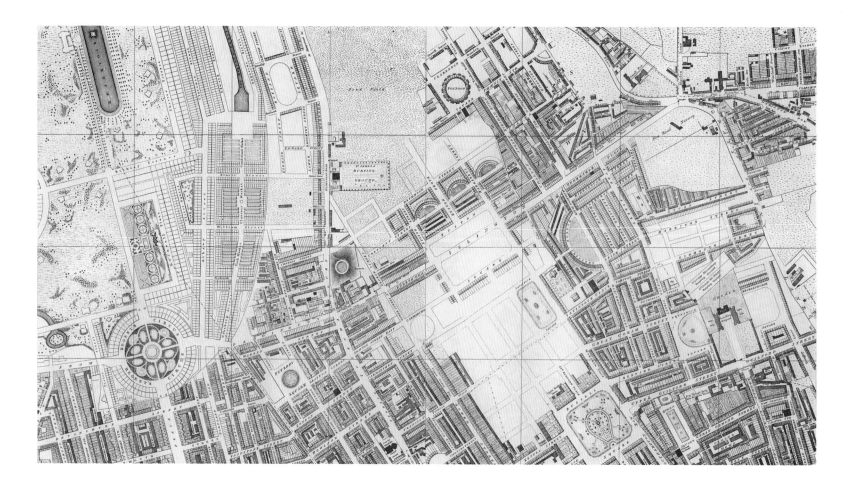

117 Richard Horwood, *Plan of the Cities of London & Westminster* (4th ed., 1819), engraving (detail), showing parts of Marylebone and Bloomsbury. Author's collection.

Southampton and Clarendon crescents; in Clerkenwell, Banner, Cold Bath and Northampton squares; in Knightsbridge, Hans and Cadogan places, and Sloane and Cadogan squares; in Chelsea, Vincent Square; in Bethnal Green, Wilmot and Patriot squares; in Stepney, Trafalgar Square; in Lambeth, Princes (later Cleaver) Square; and in Southwark, Bermondsey, Nelson, Surrey and West squares. For a modern viewer, the survey is a stunning gazetteer (figs 118 and 119).

The new squares, it should be noted, were not generally equal to the earlier great openings of the West End, but were instead what John Stewart described as 'second-rate' squares,[4] spaces that were often more modest in conception, and generally less ambitious in intent, and which were, as a consequence, frequently mere incidents in, rather than the principal objects of, new developments. These new metropolitan streets and squares, moreover, were in many cases laid out for a new type of resident: 'Independent Families who prefer the Air of the Country and Vicinity of London, or Placemen [officers of the Crown], Merchants, or Attornies who have Cham-

bers or Offices therein'.[5] Thus, while the central areas of these new squares might not, in themselves, have offered authentic rurality, their suburban context certainly made them successful exercises in the projection of *urbs in rure*, or town in country. Their appeal is captured by the Reverend John Newton in April 1780, who, when describing the setting of his house in Charles Square, Shoreditch, to his friend William Cowper, observed that while the central area of the square possessed 'handsome trees', the close behind it seemed 'as green as . . . meadows, and the cows that are feeding in it have very much the same look of country cows'.[6]

As the nineteenth century got under way, the margins of London were still an immense and diverse patchwork of pastureland, market gardens, orchards, nurseries and a variety of industries, intermingled with scores of ancient hamlets and villages – small communities which, despite their rural or semi-rural surroundings all existed under the overshadowing influence of the capital. They were, in fact, an expanse of extramural suburbs, linked to the city by a network of highways that, in Horace Walpole's words, shot

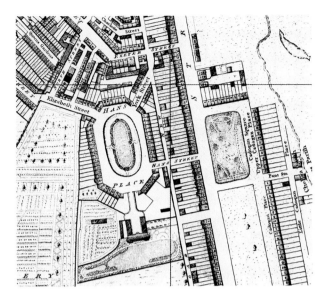

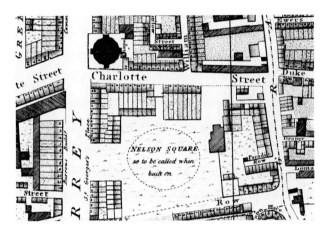

out every way 'like a polypus',[7] each of which was lined with sometimes scruffy ribbon development.

We saw in Chapter 1 that from the 1670s the city's suburbs had become increasingly desirable places for residential settlement, and they were also a popular destination for day-trippers of all classes, who came in great numbers in pursuit of semi-rural pleasures. But, by the early nineteenth century, suburban development was not only desirable, it was also a necessity, to accommodate the thousands of people who, year upon year, flocked to the metropolis in ever increasing numbers. The political, economic and topographical circumstances that favoured and encouraged the growth of London's suburbs have been discussed in great detail elsewhere;[8] suffice it to say that personal security and tranquillity were among the most important factors that led to the rise of suburban development – so much so that many (albeit by no means all) of these new develop-

ments were, in Summerson's words, 'built up solid with streets and squares, set out in a tidy design'.[9]

The estates upon which these new squares were created were initially developed along much the same lines as their West End counterparts, differing only insofar as they did not grow out of the pattern of London proper, but were 'planted between the main roads at points dictated by the watchful opportunism of landowners and builders'.[10] Indeed, from the late eighteenth century many of these suburban estates styled themselves 'new town', or else affixed the word 'town' to the family name or title of the freeholder – hence Somers Town, Camden Town, Mile End New Town, Portland Town, De Beauvoir Town, Kensington New Town and Walworth New Town. The appropriation of the word 'town' also recalled the seventeenth-century convention of labelling the then new developments in St James's and Bloomsbury as 'new towns'. Hans Town, south of Knightsbridge, which originally comprised Sloane Street, Cadogan Place and Hans Place, was among the earliest examples: it was developed by the builder Henry Holland, who in 1771 took a lease on 89 acres from Lord Cadogan.[11] Holland, like Bedford before him, appears to have looked abroad, ambitiously, for the inspiration for Hans Place, as the square's amphitheatrical layout recollects, on a modest scale, the Place Vendôme in Paris or the Colosseum in Rome.

Somers Town soon followed, planned and developed from 1786 by the speculative builder and architect Jacob Leroux on land belonging to the first Lord Somers of Evesham. The streets of the new town, or 'place', were here laid out in a grid pattern, the chief feature being Clarendon Square, within which was built the Polygon, a fifteen-sided block comprising sixteen pairs of semi-detached houses which faced outwards, with gardens at the rear converging on a central point. The scheme was the architect's second attempt at forming a 'polygon',[12] and both looked back to Gwynn's great 'circular area'.

Further east, squares also began to appear in Islington, Clerkenwell and Hackney. From 1775 the enterprising developer John Dawes began to build around Highbury Fields with the intention of forming a large square, and in 1805 the surveyor Robert Mylne projected a small circus at London Spa.[13] Canonbury Square was, however, the earliest

of the Islington squares to be fully realised, and was developed by Henry Leroux[14] in collaboration with Richard Laycock. Henry Leroux also built Compton Terrace (which boasted a communal front garden) by 1805. De Beauvoir Town, stimulated by the opening of the Regent's Canal in 1820, was to be developed by William Rhodes, who initially proposed to build residences for the upper classes in a grid pattern, with four squares on diagonal streets intersecting at an octagon.[15]

Lloyd Square, built on a steep sloping field in Pentonville as the centrepiece of the Lloyd Baker Estate, was one of the more original and bizarre residential developments to be built from the 1820s (fig. 120).[16] The square, largely designed by the surveyor John Booth, is formed of semi-detached pedimented stock-brick villas, which encompass a trapezoidal garden. Granville Square, the estate's second square, was built between 1831 and 1843, and its central enclosure was given over almost entirely

to St Philip's Church. The development of the Lloyd Baker Estate is characteristic of a number of London estates at the time: first on account of the fact that while its squares were not planted with a view to forming direct visual links with nearby enclosures, they were nonetheless planned so as to make the most of 'lines of communication' with streets or neighbourhoods of comparable or higher social character;[17] and second because many squares from the 1830s onwards – particularly in Kensington and Islington – were, like Granville Square, to receive major buildings in the form of churches at the centres or on the margins.[18]

William Fuller Pocock devised plans for the layout of Trevor Square from 1810 on the site of the former Powis House in west London,[19] and south of the Thames, in Southwark, the developer Mr Hedger began from the late 1790s to lay out West Square, near Bethlehem Hospital, on land belonging to the Temple West family, and broke ground in Addington

Square, Camberwell, in *c.*1800 (fig. 121).[20] The ubiquitous Mr Cockerell was probably responsible for the design of Nelson Square, which from *c.*1807 began to take shape on land of the Manor of Paris Garden in Bankside.[21] Speculative building south of the Thames, however, only really began to take off after the building of Vauxhall, Waterloo and Southwark Bridges (1816, 1817 and 1819 respectively).

Squares were not necessarily included in every new development: most notably, Pentonville was built up along the New Road (that is, Marylebone Road) from the 1770s on a plain, rational and orthogonal plan without a single square – perhaps restricted by its narrow, linear estate plan.[22] And, of course, many squares or similar open areas were projected in ambitious estate plans that never saw the light of day. For instance, as early as *c.*1700 Albemarle Square was proposed at the northern ends of Dover and Albemarle Streets (where the Royal Institution now stands);[23] later in the century John Noorthouck reported in his *New History of London* (1773) that 'Northward of Cavendish Square, toward Mary[le]bone, a 'new Square is now compleating called Queen Anne Square', the design of which was

subsequently abandoned;[24] and plans in the Portman Estate archive indicate that in *c.*1775 a 'Circus' was projected east of Portman Square, of which only the eastern segment was built and became known as Cumberland Place. Similarly, in 1789 William Porden, in his capacity as Surveyor of the Grosvenor Estate, launched a campaign to improve the character of the estate through the consolidation of small and disparate properties into larger landholdings, with a view to creating a planned development on a regular street pattern with a 'handsome opening' at its centre. In the event this 'intended square' near Grosvenor Place was not realised.[25]

Two unrealised late eighteenth-century schemes, which proposed the creation of a string of squares on the same estate, stand out for their sheer boldness and inventiveness: the first is George Dance the younger's proposal for the development of the Camden Estate (*c.*1790); and the second is an anonymous scheme for the improvement of the Eyre Estate in St John's Wood (1794) (fig. 122).[26] The first was galvanised by the Kentish Town Act of 1788, which enabled Charles, first Earl Camden, to lay out streets on his north London property. He commis-

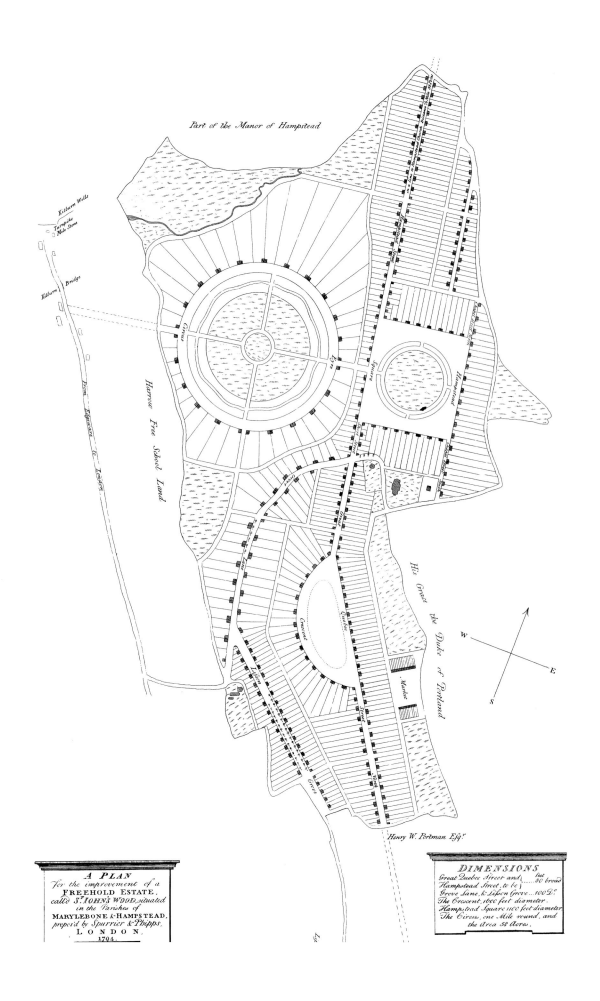

Part of the Manor of Hampstead

Kilburn Wells

Turnpike
Mile Stone

Kilburn Bridge

From Edgeware to London

Harrow Free School Land

His Grace the Duke of Portland

W

E

S

Henry W. Portman Esq.

A PLAN
for the improvement of a
FREEHOLD ESTATE,
call'd St. JOHN'S WOOD, situated
in the Parishes of
MARYLEBONE & HAMPSTEAD,
propos'd by Spurrier & Phipps.
LONDON.
1794.

DIMENSIONS
Great Quebec Street and } feet
Hampstead Street, to be } .....80 broad
Grove Lane, & Lisson Grove...100 Do.
The Crescent, 1800 feet diameter.
Hampstead Square 1100 feet diameter.
The Circus, one Mile round, and
the Area 58 Acres.

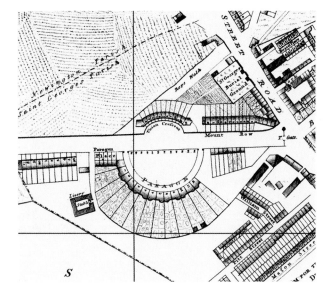

heath. Searles also deployed a variation of this formula in the layout of Surrey Square (fig. 123). This innovation is, however, probably best illustrated in St Peter's Square in Hammersmith (formed from *c.*1825), where the central area was surrounded by tall, three-storey stuccoed houses grouped in threes and linked by low porticos.

John Nash and the 'usual intervention of Squares, Crescents, and Circuses'

The story of the 'metropolitan improvements' that transformed London in the early nineteenth century, and the role of the architect and master scenographer John Nash within this episodic, protracted and fragmented enterprise, are well known.[30] Nash's highly personalised and idiosyncratic picturesque vision transformed London's West End; here he 'demonstrated an ability to compose and group buildings for their scenic effect, and to conceive and carry out large urban planning enterprises, which has rarely been matched before or since'.[31] Few English architects have, in fact, displayed greater imagination and panache in the playful integration of landscape and architecture, and have at the same time satisfied a widespread desire for comfort, individual expression, and conformity to the *genius loci*. What concerns us here is how it came to pass that the square, which since the Great Fire had been among the most popular constituents of new residential development, was marginalised in the Crown Estate's grand strategy for the redevelopment of the fields and pastures of its 500-acre London estate on what was formerly known as Marylebone Park, but is now Regent's Park.

The idea to redevelop Crown land had its origins in the mid-1780s, and grew out of the need to 'maximise revenue at a time of royal extravagance and unprecedented war time expenditure'.[32] The officials behind this initiative were Scottish civil servants John Fordyce and Sylvester Douglas, Lord Glenbervie, who transformed the administration of the Crown Estate into something like a modern government department.[33] It was, however, Fordyce's reports to the Treasury of 1793 and 1809 that formed the guidelines for the resultant scheme, which was to see the formation of Trafalgar Square, Regent's Park and Regent Street – the last a *via triumphalis*, or 'new convenient communication by means of a

sioned his old friend Dance to assist him in this work, and the design focused on The Circus, Camden Coliseum and Bayham Crescent, all of which were formed by rows of semi-detached houses. The second scheme, for St John's Wood, projected an elegant constellation of three openings – Eyre Circus, Hampstead Square and Quebec Crescent – the layout of which owed a great deal to the planning of Bath, as well as to Gwynn and Dance.[27] Although the scheme was not built (possibly blighted by the French Wars), it influenced the young architect John Shaw's 'British Circus near Hampstead', which was exhibited at the Royal Academy in 1803, and was later adopted by Nash in his early proposals for the treatment of the central area of Marylebone (later Regent's) Park in 1811–12.[28]

These schemes are noteworthy as they chart a shift in the morphology of the square: whereas it was formerly an interdependent, inward-looking development, it was henceforth more frequently projected as an element of a larger urban narrative. This shift, furthermore, began to break down the architectural framework of the square: the once impermeable ring of buildings that enclosed the central area would be eroded by the introduction of semi-detached houses, which conveyed a new 'semi-suburban sense of greenery and openness'.[29] The Paragon in Blackheath was among the first essays to be built to this new model: designed by Michael Searles for John Cator, and built between 1795 and 1806, the giant crescent comprised fourteen semi-detached houses that opened directly on to the

124 John Nash, *Plan of an Estate Belonging to the Crown, called Marybone Park Farm* (now Regent's Park), 1812, lithograph. The National Archives, Kew.

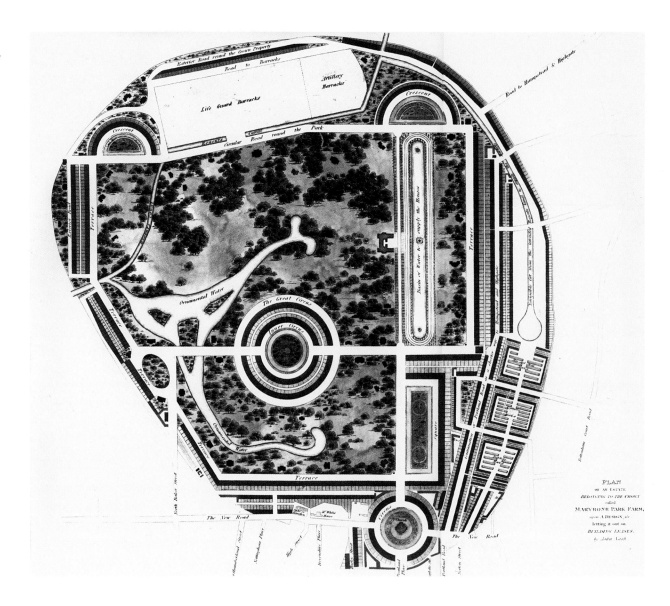

broad street', forming a much needed direct line from Charing Cross to the southern boundary of the park and the northern suburbs.

From 1794 Fordyce sponsored a survey, and subsequently a design competition, the results of which were to inform Nash's ultimate plans for the park layout, among them John White's influential proposal, engraved and published in 1809, and Thomas Leverton and Thomas Chawner's plan of 1811.[34] The latter proposed the redevelopment of the park with the same familiar pattern of streets and squares as had unfolded on the neighbouring Bedford, Portland, Southampton and Portman estates[35] – what the historian J. Mordaunt Crook has described as a 'good scheme, in effect a new Bloomsbury'.[36] Nash, in his capacity as one of the architects and surveyors to the Department of Woods and Forests, also sub-

mitted a proposal at the same time, and his scheme was no less urban: much of the then open parkland was proposed to be laid out on geometrical lines, dominated by a giant circus and a double circus, and inscribed with squares, avenues and crescents, as well as a serpentine stretch of water and a scattering of villas (fig. 124).

None of the above proposals met with the approval of Fordyce and the Commissioners of His Majesty's Woods, Forests and Land Revenues, who were keen to adopt the 'most advantageous and eligible method' of redeveloping the park into 'a handsome, elegant, and commodious addition to the Metropolis of the Empire'. The government of the day was vulnerable to criticism that the initial building proposals, and the Crown's 'virtual enclosure of Marylebone Park', was 'trenching on the comfort of the poor for the

125 Robert Kirkwood, *Plan of the City of Edinburgh and its Environs*, 1817, engraving (detail), showing the geometric layout and the squares of the New Town. National Library of Scotland.

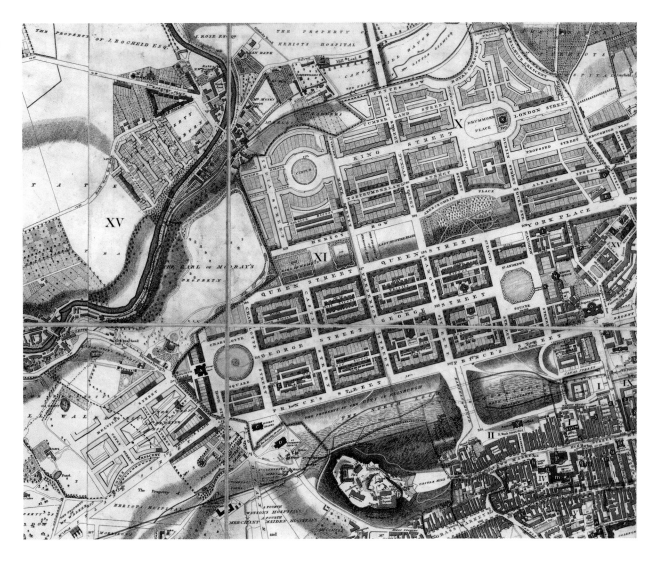

accommodation of the rich'.[37] They were, therefore, compelled to increase the area of the park that was accessible to the public.

In their revised instructions of December 1811, the commissioners instructed Nash 'to procure information, and state the methods which have been pursued with regard to improvements of a like nature by the Dukes of Bedford and Portland, Lord Camden, Lord Southampton, Mr Portman, and others, on whose adjoining property extensive streets and squares have recently been formed; and in the great additions, made forty years ago, to the city of Edinburgh; and, at a more recent period to the city of Bath'. Nash was also requested 'particularly to attend to the improvements already made, and in contemplation, on the adjoining estates of Lord Southampton and Mr Portman; and to concert measures with them, if [he] . . . should think a more advantageous plan could be formed by doing so'

(figs 125 and 126). They furthermore instructed him to include villas set on small allotments of 5 to 10 acres each in the northern part of the park, as they were of the view that this area was possibly 'situated at too great a distance from the present boundary of the town to render it probable that streets and squares, and dwelling-houses, for a considerable length in time, could be established there'.[38]

Nash's second scheme followed closely the aims of the commissioners, and also embraced, in James Elmes's words, 'those beauties of landscape gardening which his friend Humphry Repton so successfully introduced'.[39] In his explanation of his scheme, Nash employed the rhetoric of his political masters infused with his own picturesque vision, remarking that he proposed that the park should be made to contribute to the 'healthfulness, beauty and advantage, of that quarter of the metropolis'; that the houses and buildings should be useful and permanent, and

126 Unknown draughtsman, *A New Plan of the City of Bath, with the Additional Buildings to the Present Time*, 1792, engraving (detail), showing The Circus, Royal Crescent and Queen Square. British Library, London, Maps K.Top.37.19.

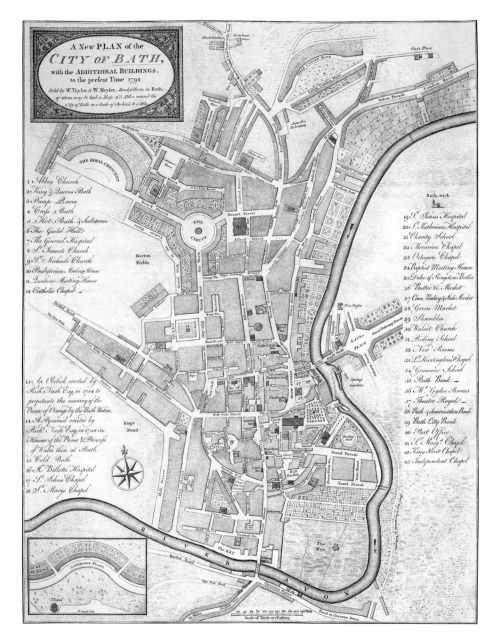

possess 'such local advantages, as shall be likely to assure a great augmentation of Revenue to the Crown at the expiration of the Leases'; and that the 'attraction of open space, free air, and the scenery of Nature . . . shall be preserved or created' in the park as allurements for the 'wealthy part of the public to establish themselves there'. Predicting that within a few years the park would be enclosed on three sides by buildings, and that these would be of 'such mean sort as have been built in Somers Town, and are now building in Lord Southampton's ground', it was, Nash believed, incumbent on the Crown to take measures to preserve the Park from the 'annoyance and disgrace' which threatened it, and to form a

'beautiful termination to that elevated and conspicuous Boundary of the Metropolis'. Whereas conventional speculative builders would, in his view, lay out the ground by resorting to the 'usual intervention of Squares, Crescents, and Circuses', to employ such a means of development on so vast an area was, he observed, both impractical and undesirable.[40]

By rejecting the convention of the square as the principle means of colonising the new park, he secured 'a greater variety of beautiful scenery' as well as a higher level of leasehold value.[41] Nash nonetheless conceded that squares could be planted on the periphery of the open expanse, and in particular at the point where the park joined the town: to 'dis-

116

guise the appearance and to prevent the impression of having crossed the New [Marylebone] Road', he proposed that the field immediately adjoining the end of Portland Place, together with the field adjoining it, beyond the New Road, should be converted into a 'large Circus'. This circus – which was salvaged from his earlier proposals – was to enclose an area 'equal to that of Lincoln's Inn Fields, and be in unison with the magnificent scale of Portland-place'.[42] He proposed that a square be built on the south side of the park, immediately beyond the New Road, 'of the size of Russell-square (the largest in London) with a Street at each end, of the same breadth as Portland-place, leading to it'. The houses on the north side of this square and street would 'enjoy the Scenery of the Park'. He also proposed to admit 'two Crescents of houses' to the perimeter of the park, 'each fronting the most beautiful part of the Scenery, each Crescent having a sort of Park of its own in front'.[43] It should be noted that Nash also planned a string of three modest but dignified market squares – Cumberland, Clarence and York markets – to serve the Regent's Park district. Only Cumberland Market, however, was built as a market; Clarence and York (later Munster) Squares were developed as residential.[44]

While the foundations of Nash's western quadrant of the great circus were laid, the general plan was abandoned. Instead, the lower half of his circus at the top of Portland Place was built to form Park Crescent (1812–23), its broad side left 'open to the park' – a device that had been proposed in 1809 by John White.[45] James Elmes remarks in *Metropolitan Improvements* (1827) that this alteration was a 'manifest improvement of the entire design, and is productive of great benefit to the houses in the crescent and in Portland Place' (fig. 127).[46]

From 1823 Nash embarked on the building of Park Square, consisting of two rows of houses 'elongated upon the extremities of the crescent and in Portland Place, and separated from the New Road, from the park, and from each other, by a spacious quadrangular area laid out with planted pleasure grounds, and enclosed by handsome iron railings'. The square and the crescent were, very unusually, connected by a tunnel that still runs beneath Marylebone Road. Elmes found much to praise in the new square garden, and in particular its picturesque devices, including 'meandering walks', 'ambrosial shrubs', 'velvet turf', 'gay flowers' and 'serpentine walks'. It was, he remarked, important for an 'enclosed garden in the neighbourhood of buildings or other works of art' to possess 'neatness, symmetry and trimness, approaching to elegance . . . characters that should be sought after by the landscape or artist gardener. How refreshingly cool and soft the velvet turf of this smoothly shaven lawn is to the feet, after coming from the arid hardness of the gravelled road; and how delightful to the senses are the fragrancy of those gay flowers, the symmetry of those beauteous dwarf shrubs, and the artfulness of those serpentine walks'.[47]

This smoothness and 'dressed gaiety' was in opposition to the picturesque style of William Gilpin, who according to Elmes would have turned the garden's velvet lawn 'into a piece of broken ground, would plant rugged scrubby oaks instead of flowering shrubs, would break the edges of these walks, would give them the roughness of a new made road, would corrugate them with ruts, would defile the beauty of its whole face by stones and brushwood, and by making all rough and dirty, where all is now fair and smooth'.[48] (It is striking that this rude picturesqueness was much admired by the poet laureate Henry James Pye (d. 1813), who, according to Lou-

128 James Burton, *Design for Planting the Area of the Two Crescents at the End of Portland Place*, *c.*1819, pen with watercolour wash. Westminster City Archives.

don, had 'proposed to lay out a square in imitation of a wild overgrown quarry or gravel-pit, and plant it with thorns, hollies, furze, brambles, ferns, &c. This mode he would adopt on account of the contrast it would produce to suburban garden scenery generally.'[49]

Nash, in fact, held – in strong contrast to Gilpin's views – a very particularised notion of the picturesque, which he invoked to exploit the potential of what Sir John Soane called 'Principles of modern Decorative Landscape Gardening' to improve civic architecture and planning.[50] The practical usefulness of the theory of the picturesque lay, for Nash, partly in his concern with a particular problem posed by the planning of Regent's Park: the problem of how to assimilate domesticity and individual idiosyncrasy within a framework of public magnificence. The role of palatial buildings as private dwellings, Nash assumed, would necessarily determine to some extent, the options and strategies of design available to the planner. In emphasising and exploring the relationship between public and private, Nash developed a series of principles that can be seen as establishing a specific concept of the 'metropolitan picturesque'.[51] This aesthetic, as we shall see, would influence the approach to the development of urban landscape by a number of Nash's contemporaries, and Thomas Cubitt in particular.

Nash distinguished 'architecture in towns' as 'principal and independent'. He therefore set about attempting to distinguish buildings by setting them amid 'considerable bodies of plantation', without subordinating them to the landscape.[52] This was not easily accomplished within the confines of a square, insofar as the perception of the central space, and the effect of the garden setting were often constrained by the nature of its enclosure and overwhelmed by uniform architectural surroundings. As his old friend Uvedale Price remarks on the subject in 1798: 'in a street, or square, hardly anything but the front is considered, for little else is seen . . . the spectator, also being confined to a few stations, and those not distant, has his attention entirely fixed on the architecture, and the architect'.[53] Nash, however, like Cubitt after him, probably succeeded in his aim at Park Square and Park Crescent, for the central areas were sufficiently extensive and the plantations sufficiently dense to diminish the architectural commonality of the surrounding buildings.

Nash was also directly involved in the layout of a number of communal gardens on the perimeter of Regent's Park. He never intended that these openings should be laid out as so-called 'planted squares', but his friend and collaborator the builder James Burton thought otherwise. This inevitably led to several confrontations, the most important of which was the protracted dispute over the correct character for the gardens facing the park at York Terrace. Here Nash was unyielding in his view that the stucco-encased terraces which formed the 'great central entrance to the Park' should be imposing and spacious, and that there should be 'no divisions in the gardens of the houses to denote individuality but the whole should appear as one entire building'.[54] Burton, however, rejected this approach, proposing instead to 'take land within the Park enclosure' to lay out in 'ornamental Plantations and walks . . . for the use of the inhabitants of the several houses opposite – with permission to erect one or two low ornamental Pavilions thereon at once serving the purpose of seats & gardeners tool houses' (fig. 128).[55] This displeased Nash, who observed that such a proposal was 'out of harmony with the Park scenery', and 'would be censured by every person who should possess common sense – much less taste'. Such gardens would, he quipped, resemble 'subscription Tea gardens for genteel subscribers', and the 'plantations would be likened to the Circus in Portland Place, to Russell Square and other ornamentally planted enclosures'. Ornamental plantations, Nash argued, were 'fine on the outer boundary [of the Park] . . . breaking the uniformity and monotony of straight rows of houses, and if Mr Burton would set his houses back and form such quadrangular areas in front there would be no objection to such – but the plantations and walks and rails proposed cannot be compared with the planted squares in the different parts of the Town which are surrounded on all sides by housing, the proprietors of which are bound to keep them up'.[56]

Nash, as has been said, was only incidentally a planner of squares, and promoted an aesthetic of domesticity touched by aspirations to grandeur. One of his more successful small-scale essays in this taste was not, however, in Marylebone, but in Piccadilly, where from 1817 he embarked on the redesign of the central enclosure of St James's Square. Although the square had undergone a series of piecemeal improvements over the preceding century, Nash's scheme was the first general rearrangement of the central area since the early eighteenth century.[57] Under his supervision the central area was enlarged, new lighting was installed, a 'screen of plantations' was set out, and an Ionic garden seat was formed on the south side of the square.[58] One of the most

contentious aspects of this refurbishment was the treatment of the large circular basin at the centre of the enclosure. It was the 'unanimous decision of the Ladies [of the square] that there should be a fence round the water', and that Nash's plan for the 'laying out of the inside of the Square' be submitted to them for approval.[59]

'The City has been all Pulled to Pieces': Bloomsbury, Belgravia, Pimlico and Tyburnia[60]

Despite the ambivalence of Nash and the Commissioners of Woods, Forests and Land Revenues towards the idea of the square, other estate owners and builders continued to embrace the device as one of the key features of new residential development. Squares were, in fact, being formed at a greater rate than at any time in the past, and were generally commended on account of their potential to evoke a degree of desirable rurality within the metropolis. The American essayist Washington Irving – who admired the 'quick sensibility' of the English to the 'beauties of nature' – summed up this sentiment, remarking in 1819 that 'in the most dark and dingy quarters in the city, the drawing-room window resembles frequently a bank of flowers; every spot capable of vegetation has its grass-plot and flower-bed; and every square has its mimic park, laid out with picturesque taste, and gleaming and refreshing verdure'.[61]

John Britton proclaimed in *Illustrations of the Public Buildings of London* (1828):

> large squares, wide streets, good draining, and cleansing are manifestations of the progressive and rapid strides made towards metropolitan happiness . . . By examining the map of London, we perceive that our forefathers, if they imitated the bee in industry, also seemed to think it necessary to crowd and press together like that insect into one hive – narrow street, alley and lanes, were formed to keep out fresh air, and to keep in foul; but an open square was scarcely designed. Now we see squares and crescents and wide streets, formed and given up to public comfort and public beauty.[62]

These remarks were clearly directed towards the spectacular building achievements of the Cubitts:

their 'land-drainage, the sewerage, the road-surfaces, the lighting, the planting, as well as the construction of the houses and mews' were, according to Summerson, 'accurately thought out and superbly constructed'.[63] Britton's encomium serves to remind us that in the wake of Waterloo, and at the outset of a period of financial prosperity, similar operations were appearing in diverse quarters of the city. Some were outward-growing limbs from the main body of the London organism, while others were developed separately on the rural perimeter and in a more suburban spirit. Many of these estate plans, in their efforts to attract would-be purchasers or tenants, employed open figures in the form of squares, crescents or polygons in combination with broad streets to articulate and animate the new developments.

Four major building initiatives had a profound impact on the future development of the metropolis: the Bedford Estate in Bloomsbury, the Grosvenor Estate in Belgravia and Pimlico, and the Bishop of London's Estate in Tyburnia (now Bayswater).

We have seen in Chapter 3 how, by the turn of the nineteenth century, Francis, fifth Duke of Bedford (d. 1802), had begun the orderly development of his Bloomsbury Estate, and that many openings had been formed and planted. The building operations, however, were deferred until the early 1820s because of the Napoleonic Wars, which caused a shortage of building materials. It was left to his successor, John Russell, the sixth Duke, to resume these incomplete building initiatives, and to embark on the development of an even larger portion of his Middlesex Estate that was already laid out for building.

Bedford found an admirable collaborator in Thomas Cubitt. The latter was not only an astute and enterprising local builder, but he like the duke took a great interest in the layout and the planted character of squares. Bedford was knowledgeable about horticulture and botany and, according to the historian Hermione Hobhouse, was in these, as in every other matter concerning the development of his estate 'the final arbiter of taste'.[64] We know, for instance, that from 1829 the duke played an active role in tree planting in Gordon Square and 'decorating the interior'; he was also responsible for the introduction of 'Forest Trees and shrubs of large growth' in Torrington Square, including sycamore, birch, ash, Spanish chestnut, 'Scarlet Flowering' horse chestnut, lime, Eastern and Spanish planes, lilacs,

thorns and flowering cherries (fig. 129).[65] It was, in fact, on Bedford's Bloomsbury Estate that the London plane (*Platanus × acerifolia*) is believed by some to have made its debut: here the trees were planted at the same time as the new squares took shape. Regardless of the veracity of this claim, it is undeniable that from the early nineteenth century these large and vigorous deciduous trees were identified as capable of thriving in the smoky atmosphere of London, and were planted in great numbers in the city's squares.[66]

Although possibly less informed in practical matters of gardening than his aristocratic patron, Cubitt was, on the other hand, attuned to the practical and aesthetic benefits of inserting garden squares within new developments. His first large 'take' was as a developer on the low and swampy Bedford and Southampton estates in Bloomsbury,[67] where from 1824 he undertook, in collaboration with the Duke of Bedford and Lord Southampton, the completion of a 'parcel of bran-new squares' – Gordon, Torrington, Woburn, Tavistock and Euston – all of which were, according to Cubitt, designed to be wide so as to make them appear 'more healthy', and to be attractive to the 'best class of occupiers'; this, he stated, would prove 'most to the advantage of his Grace by giving a superior character to his estate by making the Communication with the New Road better than [that of] the adjoining neighbourhood'.[68] Here, as with many of his subsequent commissions, Cubitt supplied the gardens with trees and shrubs from his own nursery ground of 'several acres' – a commercial concern formed specifically for this purpose.[69]

In 1825 Cubitt and his office entered into a more challenging agreement with Robert Grosvenor, later first Marquess of Westminster, to develop roughly 100 acres of the then 'clayey swamp' of the Five Fields to form Belgravia – the name of which was a sobriquet for Belgrave and Eaton squares and the radiating streets, which Cubitt was to lay out in collaboration with the developers George and William Haldimand and Seth Smith, the architects James Wyatt and George Basevi, and the surveyor Thomas Cundy II (fig. 130).[70] The development of the 'new and elegant town', which was to connect London and Chelsea, and to form an impressive western entrance to the metropolis, was begun under a special act of parliament passed in 1826, empowering

129 (*facing page*) Unknown draughtsman, *Plan* [of the Bedford Estate] *showing Intended Buildings between Russell Square and the New Road*, 1830, engraving. Bedford Estate Archive, Woburn Abbey.

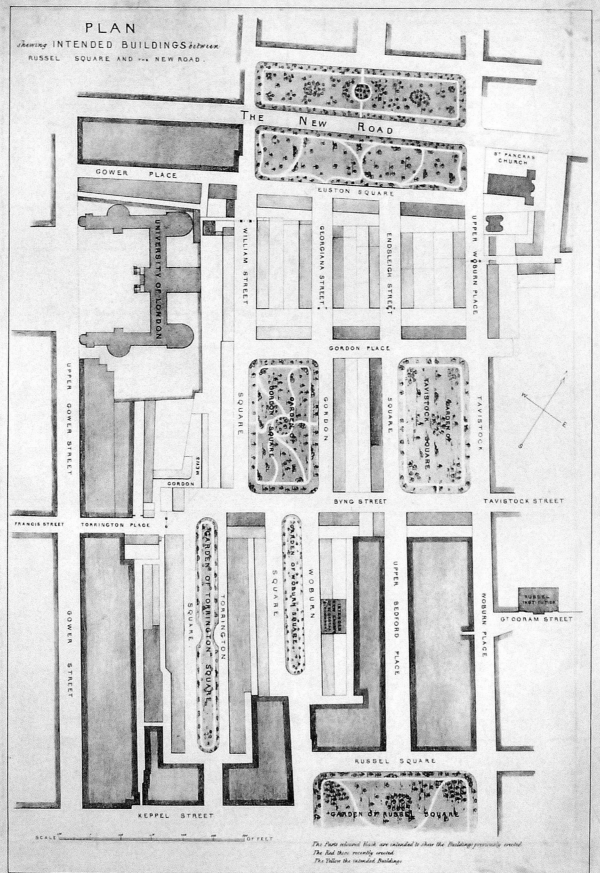

PLAN
shewing INTENDED BUILDINGS *between*
RUSSEL SQUARE AND THE NEW ROAD.

THE NEW ROAD

GOWER PLACE

EUSTON SQUARE

ST PANCRAS CHURCH

UNIVERSITY OF LONDON

WILLIAM STREET

GEORGIANA STREET

ENDSLEIGH STREET

UPPER WOBURN PLACE

UPPER GOWER STREET

GORDON PLACE

MEWS

GORDON

GARDEN OF GORDON SQUARE

GORDON SQUARE

SQUARE

GARDEN OF TAVISTOCK SQUARE

TAVISTOCK SQUARE

BYNG STREET

TAVISTOCK STREET

FRANCIS STREET   TORRINGTON PLACE

GARDEN OF TORRINGTON SQUARE

TORRINGTON SQUARE

GARDEN OF WOBURN SQUARE

WOBURN SQUARE

UPPER BEDFORD PLACE

WOBURN PLACE

RUSSEL INSTITUTION

GT CORAM STREET

GOWER STREET

KEPPEL STREET

RUSSEL SQUARE

GARDEN OF RUSSEL SQUARE

SCALE   OF FEET

The Parts coloured Black are intended to shew the Buildings previously erected.
The Red those recently erected.
The Yellow the intended Buildings.

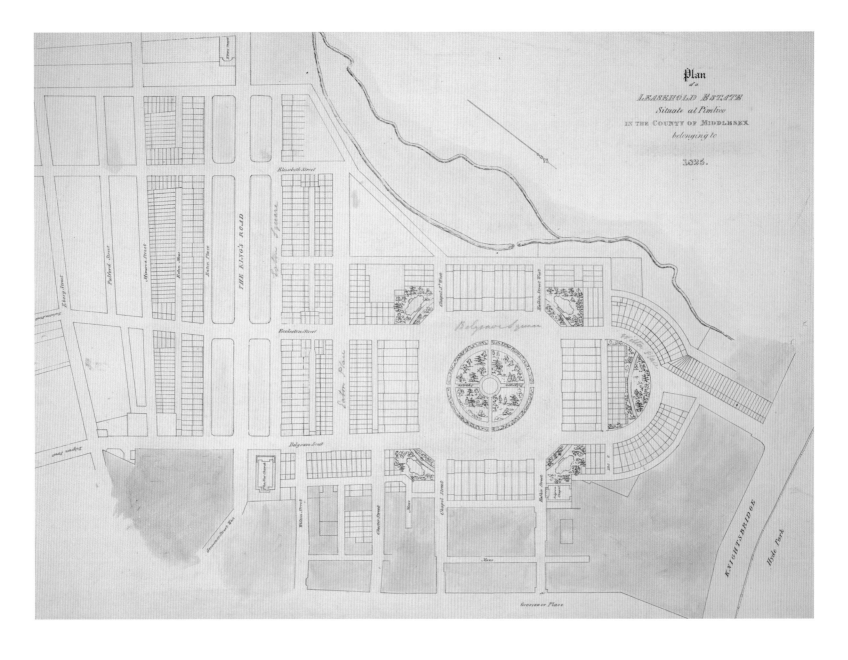

130 Unknown draughtsman, *Plan of a Leasehold Estate Situate at Pimlico, Belonging to the Marquis of Westminster*, 1825, engraving with watercolour wash. British Library, London.

Lord Grosvenor to 'drain the site, raise the level, and erect bars, &c.'.[71] The topographer John Britton recounts how the builders immediately set about forming streets and communications, and intersecting the whole of the estate by 'immense sewers, which are high above the Thames, and the soil being dry gravel serves the lower stories against damps and bad air'.[72]

The original designs for Belgrave and Eaton squares were conceived along innovative lines, although the generous provision of open spaces for gardens shows something of the influence of Nash's Regent's Park development. The bones of Belgrave Square – 'the most prominent feature of this district'[73] – were set out by Wyatt before *c.*1813, and

ultimately enclosed about 10 acres within the front walls of the houses, the centre of which was encompassed by 'lofty and handsome railing' and 'laid out in pleasure gardens, with lawn, walks, shrubberies, &c.' The four nearly equal and uniform sides of the square were lined with spacious stucco-fronted terraces, with porches and balustraded balconies, and each house was connected to its mews by a long garden similar to those of the houses of Grosvenor Square. A fresh approach was taken in the layout of the entrant streets: four 'insulated villas, or mansions' were set at an angle on the four corners of the square, each with 'spacious gardens and shrubberies', and the entrant streets joined the square on the diagonal. These villas, Britton observed, 'will greatly

augment the apparent area, as well as add to the rural beauty of the square'.[74] This feature of the layout moreover enhanced the approaches to the square, and extended the plantations 'beyond the real boundary lines of the four rows of houses' (fig. 131).[75] William Weir later opined that 'the central space is, perhaps, too large to admit even such large houses as are here telling, *en masse*, as a square'. This was possibly, however, an advantage, as the square is

> situated between town and country. The houses are already becoming sensibly less dense, like a London fog, as one approaches the outskirts. Hyde Park behind it: St James's Park intervenes between it and town; the great thoroughfares in the vicinity have more of the road in them than the street. In such a neighbourhood a square confined enough to allow the height of the house being felt in proportion to the extent of the ground-plan would convey a sense of confinement – of oppression to the lungs, though in the heart of town it would feel a relief.[76]

The plan of Eaton Square (formerly Eaton Place) put forward by Alexander and Daniel Robertson in 1813 was no less inventive: although, like Euston Square, it was bisected by a broad east–west thoroughfare, the 15-acre pleasure ground was cast in three pairs of gardens, enclosed by three 'divisions' of large stucco-encased terraced houses, laid out

symmetrically upon the long axis, intersected at equal distances from the two ends of the square, the east end of which was terminated by the Ionic portico of St Peter's Eaton Square.[77] William Weir characterised the square in 1851 as a 'mere bulging out of the highway . . . what geologists would call the transition formation – the structures intermediate between town and suburbs'.[78] The gardens, in fact, owe their innovative 'driveway' layout to economic necessity: when Cubitt took his gardens on the north side of what was then known as the 'King's Road' they were under lease to market gardeners, and 'the Estate may have been compensating the existing leaseholders [by] giving them the Square gardens for the remainder of their term'.[79] A further curiosity in the layout of the square was the addition to the houses of 'square, massive, protruding porches'. While these were considered by some to be 'heavy' and obtrusive, one writer opined that the ingenious inhabitants amply redeemed this 'defect' by transforming them into eye-catching Babylonian hanging gardens.[80]

A third and significant open figure in the Belgravian town plan also merits our attention. At some time after 1821 Thomas Cundy inserted the D-shaped Wilton Crescent into the Wyatt plan to form a northern terminus to Belgrave Square; the apex of the D funnels into Wilton Place, which in turn leads to Knightsbridge.

132 Ebenezer Landells, *Lowndes Square, Knightsbridge*, 1840–50, wood engraving. British Museum, London. The square was described in 1841 as exhibiting 'a better style of street architecture, than has been produced among the new squares and buildings at the West End of Town'.

It is significant that the Grosvenor Estate plan, unlike the Bedford Estate plan in Bloomsbury, was not very strictly laid down: this inherent flexibility gave Cubitt and his fellow builders greater scope to recommend modifications and improvements to the development. The result was the creation of a greater number of squares in the new district than had been initially envisioned by the Estate Office: for instance, both Chester and Victoria squares were formed from the 1830s on the recommendation of developers.[81] At the time, houses in squares were clearly more valuable and desirable than those in streets: all housing was priced by the linear foot of street frontage, but purchasers paid a premium to live on a square.[82] According to the author of 'On the Ridiculous Consequence Assumed from Superiority of Places of Residence' (1803) living in squares conferred 'ideal dignity and precedency'. This social superiority of squares over streets often led to the houses in the cross or entrant streets of squares being 'included' in the square itself, as 'polite situations' not only conferred dignity on the parties residing in them, but also, by the emanation of gentility, in some measure ennobled the vicinity.[83] These 'ridiculous pretensions to pre-eminence' explain the apparently 'irrational' attempts by builders to get their houses in streets adjoining squares to be generally accepted as part of the square. More specifically it accounts for the 'hysterical protest' in 1848 by the tenants of houses on the periphery of Chester Square who were aggrieved by the Grosvenor Estate's proposal to revert their street addresses from Chester Square to Chester Terrace; the residents maintained that it was wrong to change the name since 'the occupants of the greater number of the houses have taken them as in the square'.[84]

Messrs Cubitt's ample, planted Belgravian squares doubtless did much to promote the initial success and continued prosperity of Lord Grosvenor's New Town; they also presumably encouraged the builders to extend their operations westwards from 1826 to encompass the adjoining Lowndes Estate in Knightsbridge, and the vast open and low-lying district of 'South Belgravia', now known as Pimlico. The Lowndes Estate was embellished from *c.*1830 with a single but capacious lozenge-shaped square surrounded by Italianate palace façades, the composition taking the eponymous name of its ground landlord, William Lowndes of Chesham (fig. 132). Pimlico, on the other hand, was built up with a 'mass of fine buildings' laid out on a grid-iron plan of streets and squares, all of which were 'paved, Macadamised and . . . lighted, on the most approved principles'. This new district, extending from Buckingham Palace Road to the Thames, and stretching westwards to Chelsea, was raised within a 'short space of time, beyond all precedent', and was quickly settled by 'noblemen and persons of rank'.[85] Cubitt proposed and built three open spaces within the new district: Eccleston Square was laid out south of Grosvenor Canal from March 1828, and he began the development of Warwick Square in 1842. The largest of the new openings, St George's Square, was, on the other hand, laid out as an afterthought on a site originally intended for a street: both sides were formed in 1839 as thoroughfares to connect the Crown Estate with Belgrave Square, but in the event Cubitt transformed the central area into an oblong square, opening at the south end to the River Thames. When it was laid out and planted in 1844, *The Builder* pointed out that 'every house would have a view of the river', and would be but 'a short mile from the new Houses of Parliament' by the new embankment road.[86]

Not all new residential development was, however, taking place in the south-west corner of the metropolis: from around 1800 rival building operations also began to emerge on the northern frontier of Hyde Park, immediately west of what is now Marble Arch. The development of the south-eastern triangular tip of the rural parish of Paddington into a fashionable residential district of broad streets and squares was precipitated by the Grand Junction Canal Company's being given permission in 1795 to develop part of the Bishop of London's Estate for the Paddington Canal Basin.[87] The bishop's surveyor, Samuel Pepys

124

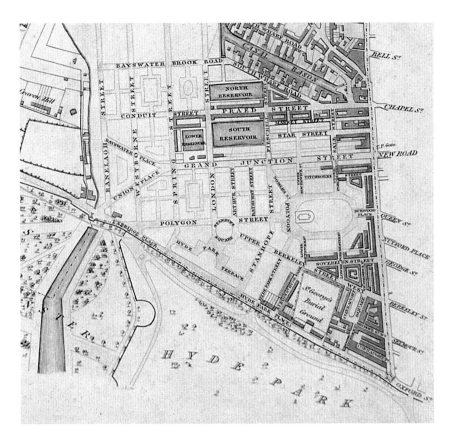

Cockerell, devised the initial plan for the estate in c.1804,[88] a key component of which was the creation of Grand Junction Street (now Sussex Gardens). This tree-lined street was to serve a dual purpose: to unite the New Road (now Marylebone Road) with Uxbridge (now Bayswater) Road further west, so as to complete the north circular route from the City; and to divide the proposed residential area from the canal basin industrial area to the north. The focal points of the new district were to be a large opening known as the 'Polygon', in which it was proposed that the 'Connaught Chapel' be raised, and a capacious hemi-cycle or crescent opening into and facing Hyde Park. The layout skilfully resolved the geometrical problems of the triangular site, and the alignment of the long axis of the Polygon on the north-eastern spoke of the giant *patte d'oie* (goose-foot) of radiating avenues in Kensington Gardens shows the inherent majesty of Cockerell's conception. The link forged between the new town and Charles Bridgeman's Baroque pleasure grounds is a highly imaginative *tour de force*, and unique in contemporary London estate planning.[89]

In contrast to contemporary operations in Blooms-bury and Belgravia where large contractors were employed to develop extensive tracts of land, the estate's policy was to entrust the construction of roads, houses and squares to the relatively small-scale builders who lived locally and who frequently occupied one of the houses they had recently erected. The development of the district's first square did not, in fact, begin until 1821, with the onset of the building boom: Connaught Square was formed in the south-east corner of the estate, and took the form of a traditional late eighteenth-century square.[90] It was a modest echo of Portman Square, with which it was linked by a pair of parallel streets.

After Cockerell's death in 1827 the estate plan was modified by his successor, the surveyor George Gutch, so as to produce a denser development within a more refined layout. His *Design for Letting Ground on Building Leases Opposite to Hyde Park* of 1838 shows how Cockerell's crescent was abandoned in favour of Hyde Park Gardens (begun 1836) with its south-facing back-to-front houses overlooking the park – each house with an elevated terrace garden (fig. 133). It also shows how the angular profile of the Polygon was softened to form an ellipse, whose north and south flanks were to be laid out as Oxford and Cambridge squares, and whose eastern and

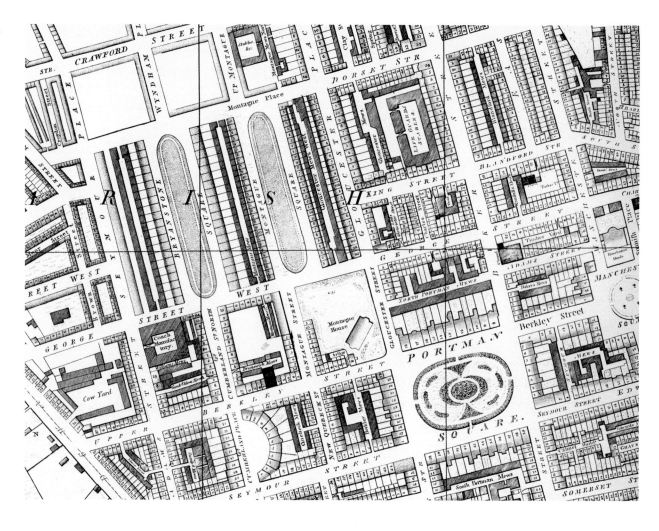

western apsidal ends were to be given over to Norfolk and Southwick Crescents respectively. Southwick Crescent in turn debouched to the west into Gloucester and Sussex squares, while Hyde Park Square was set at an angle off Gloucester Square. Cockerell's idea for a central church was retained, however, so as to add respectability and value to the new district, but the building was reconceived to Charles Fowler's Gothic revival designs and dedicated to St John the Evangelist.[91]

The earliest houses raised in the district were similar to those of neighbouring Marylebone, with stucco ground-floor decoration, and stock brick above; but this reticent style soon gave way to early Victorian stuccoed grandeur, still visible in Hyde Park and Gloucester squares. William Weir disapproved of these 'colossal and somewhat ponderous squares yet unfinished',[92] and the topographer Peter Cunningham observed in his 'carefully compiled, amusing and instructive manual of popular antiquities and street history', *Modern London, or, London as It Is* (1851) that, being 'built at one time, on nearly one principle', Tyburnia 'assumes in consequence a regularity of appearance contrasting strangely with the older portions of the Metropolis. Fine squares, connected by spacious streets, and houses of great altitude, give a certain air of nobility to the district. The sameness, however, caused by endless repetitions of "Compo" decorations, and the prevailing white colour of the houses, distresses the eye, especially after the red brick of Grosvenor, and the older and still great fashionable squares.'[93] John Weale, on the other hand, painted the new district in a more sympathetic light, remarking in *London Exhibited in 1851* that in Tyburnia one found 'that studied symmetry and variety in street planning which the classic taste of Wren and Evelyn vainly endeavoured to introduce into the city after the fire'.[94]

Although very rapidly inhabited by people of great rank and riches – or so-called 'mushroom aristocrats' on account of their new wealth – and celebrated for its healthiness on account of its proximity

126

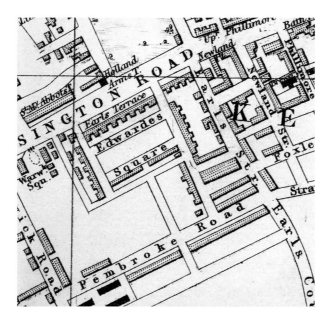

to, and direct integration with, Hyde Park, the district, like so many other contemporary developments, evolved slowly and intermittently.[95] Gamma reports in *Once a Week* (1860) that when he paid a visit to one of the earliest denizens – or 'call birds' – living amid the 'magnificent squares, crescents and places of the modern Tyburnia', he found the surroundings so unfinished that he was prompted to ponder why he had chosen 'this desert for his dwelling place';[96] and the Marylebone resident Wilkie Collins might possibly have been referring to neighbouring Tyburnia in *Basil: A Story of Modern Life* (1852), when he mentions a 'suburb of new houses, intermingled with wretched patches of waste land, half built over. Unfinished streets, unfinished crescents, unfinished squares, unfinished shops, unfinished gardens, surrounded us . . . Its newness and desolateness of appearance revolted me.'[97]

New Suburban Squares

We shall conclude our survey of the new towns with a brief overview of suburban squares 'of very recent growth' elsewhere in the metropolis.[98] Between 1810 and 1815 the axis of Great Cumberland Place on the Portman Estate in Marylebone was thrust northwards over land known as Ward's Fields to form the centre line of Bryanston Square, which was paired with Montagu Square. Both of these narrow, oblong openings, and later the more capacious Dorset Square,[99] were laid out by the architect Joseph Par-

kinson in collaboration with the speculative builder David Porter (fig. 134).[100]

From 1811 Louis Léon Changeur began to lay out Edwardes Square in Kensington, its central garden being formed later by Alexander Paul Sack (afterwards Director of the National Botanic Garden, Buenos Aires) 'from his own plan' (fig. 135).[101] Loudon remarked in 1822 that the garden was laid out in 'groups and winding walks, in a manner different from most other squares';[102] and Weir commented in 1851 that

the houses are all small, yet the central enclosure is more spacious and more tastefully laid out than in many squares that force themselves ostentatiously upon notice. This delicious square, thus stowed away in a corner, must have been designed by one who wished to carry the finest amenities of Patrician life into the domestic habits of the narrowest incomed families of the middle class. We regret to add that so delightful a plan did not originate with an Englishman: Edward Square was a Frenchman's speculation.[103]

As one ventured north-westwards from Belgrave Square, new squares were 'to be found "thick as the leaves in Vallombrosa strewed"',[104] among them Chelsea (created from 1810), Brompton (1823–35), Pembroke (1823–35), Alexander (1827–8), Onslow (1845), Wellington (1830), Carlyle (1836), Markham (1836) and Thurloe (1840) squares, and Hyde Park Gate (from 1838). Pembridge Square was planted on the Hall-Radford Estate, east of the Ladbroke Estate (from 1844); and the illustrious Campden Hill Square (formerly Notting Hill Square, and also nicknamed 'the Dukeries' on account of its exalted tenants) was laid out from 1826 to the designs of George Edward Valintine on land developed by Joshua Flesher Hanson, who had earlier promoted the building of the very similar Regency Square in Brighton (fig. 136).[105] A clustering of squares was also established on the Norland Estate, north of Holland Park Avenue, from c.1839, including Norland Square, St James's Gardens and Royal Crescent, to the plans of Robert Cantwell.[106]

In the East End, along the Mile End Road and towards Stratford were built 'some pretty enough common-place squares', which according to Weir 'have too little of individual character to leave a

lasting impression': these included Albert Square (now Gardens, 1831), York Square (from 1823) and Trafalgar Square (now Gardens, 1820s). An exception to this rule was Tredegar Square in Bow, where from 1828 the local bricklayer Daniel Austin embarked on a development so ambitious and so grand – 'copying all the latest tricks in the Georgian repertory in a simple and crude manner' – that he swiftly went bankrupt.[107]

In Islington, too, the rage for square-building continued unabated with the enclosure of Annett's Crescent (1822) and Canonbury (1805), Tibberton (from 1823), Gibson (mid-1820s) and Barnsbury (1835) squares. The picturesque Elizabethan-style architecture of Lonsdale Square (1838–42), and the yellow-brick canyon of Milner Square (1841) rank among the most original exercises in the development of Barnsbury, and demonstrate how diverse the range of possibilities in square design could be (figs 137 and 138). More tame, but equally curious, is the D-shaped Wilmington Square, with a narrow pedestrian walk on its north side, which was settled in 1817.[108] Percy Circus (1841–53) and its counterpart, the oblong Holford Square (1841–8; now demolished), were raised on the New River Estate between 1841 and

1853; the former was set on a steep hillside, and was conceived by W. C. Mylne, who also laid out Myddelton and Claremont squares from the early 1820s on the same estate. Of these openings, Myddelton Square – with St Mark's Church at its centre – is the largest in Islington; and Claremont Square, atop Islington Hill and adjoining Pentonville Road, is the most curious, the centre of which was originally a sheet of water (the Upper Pond of the New River Company, dug in 1708, and now covered), surrounded by a precipitous grassy embankment dotted with shrubs, and enclosed with an iron railing.[109]

Although seemingly the *sine qua non* of development at this time, squares remained much less popular in new developments south of the river, where only Crescent Grove (1824), Albert Square (from 1846) and Lansdowne Circus (1843, now Lansdowne Gardens) in Lambeth, and Royal Circus in Norwood (from 1826) were built in this period (fig. 139).[110]

The Squares of the Ladbroke Estate

The estate layouts we have examined so far in this chapter were generally devised by surveyors or architects. In northern Kensington, however, the

137 (*right*) C. H. Matthews, *Canonbury Lane, Islington*, *c.*1850, pen and ink with watercolour wash. British Museum, London. Matthews's view probably records the area as it was in his youth in the early nineteenth century. The field on the left later became the site of Canonbury Square.

138 (*below*) Edward Weller, *London*, *c.*1859, engraving (detail), showing some of the squares of Islington. Islington Local History Centre, Finsbury Library.

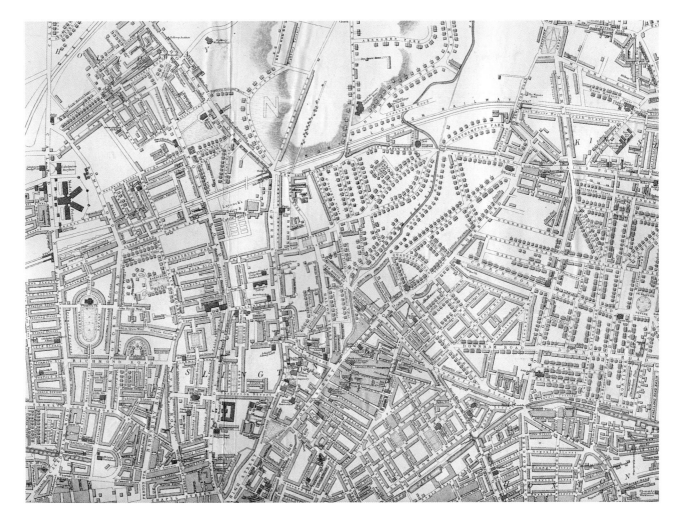

139 Unknown draughtsman, *Stanford's Geological Library Map of London and its Suburbs* (1878), engraving (detail), showing Lansdowne Circus (now Lansdowne Gardens), Lambeth. Private collection.

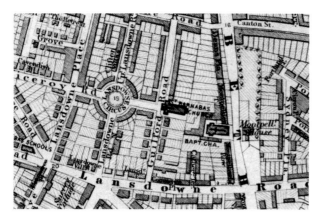

inventive plan of concentric crescents and oblong 'paddocks' that was superimposed on James Weller Ladbroke's vast and undulating estate was in a large part due to the informed and sustained efforts of the surveyor and one-time landscape gardener Thomas Allason. Allason's layout for this 'entirely new neighbourhood . . . [which] has grown up in this quarter "like an exhalation"' is quite unlike anything previously, or indeed subsequently, to be found in London.[111] It ranks, in fact, among the greatest innovations of London landscaping. Realised between 1823 and the mid-1870s, the originality of the plan lies in the fact that it inverted the traditional concept of the square to devise a most innovative and successful form of private enclosure, which in years to come was to lead to the creation of no fewer than fifteen such communal gardens on various parts of the Ladbroke Estate. Allason's garden 'paddocks' or 'shrubberies' were proposed to lie behind the continuous rows of houses of 'Kensington-Park', to complement the provision of small private gardens for the occupants' own exclusive use behind each individual house (fig. 140).[112] This arrangement was attractive, highly practical, and well adapted to the needs of families with young children, as the communal gardens were more easily accessible to the residents than those isolated by roads in the middle of a square. Such a plan, however, made back access and mews stables impossible, suggesting that it was, unlike many earlier squares, 'emphatically designed for modest middle-class families who did not own a carriage'.[113]

Allason's ingenious plan of 1823 responded to the gently undulating contours of the estate, the near-centre of which was occupied by a commanding knoll; it provided for a broad straight road (now

Ladbroke Grove) leading northward from the Uxbridge Road, which bisected an enormous circus, some 560 yards in diameter and about a mile in circumference. The ground on the inner side of the 'great circus', and that on either side of Ladbroke Grove within it, extending to a depth of 200 feet, is marked on Allason's plan as 'building ground', and was probably envisaged to be covered with a ring of large detached or semi-detached houses, possibly in imitation of Nash's early proposals for Regent's Park, or the double circus for the Eyre Estate of 1802–3. The two segmentally shaped areas to be formed by the enclosure of the broad strips of buildings in the circus, and a third triangular area outside the edge of the circus (also entirely surrounded by building ground) were proposed to be laid out as 'paddocks'. That these paddocks were to be encompassed on all sides by housing suggests that they were intended to be private enclosures for the general use of the inhabitants.

Although the landscape improver's grandiose scheme for a great circus was abandoned by 1832, his paddocks were adopted and much amplified by his subsequent collaborators, including the architects James Thomson, John Stevens, and latterly William Reynolds and Thomas Allom.[114] It was, above all, Thomson who put Allason's original idea of shared private enclosures into practical form, and it was he who first put forward the idea of concentric crescents skirting the north-west slopes of the hill. Thomson, like his predecessor, was imbued with a picturesque sensibility, which he presumably developed during his close association with J. B. Papworth and afterwards with John Nash, with whom he collaborated in Regent's Park. His *Plan of Kensington Park, Notting Hill, as Designed and Laid Out for Building with Ornamental Grounds, Public Drives, &c.* (1842), and his subsequent designs of 1843 and *c.*1846, chart the beginnings of Lansdowne Crescent with its centrally placed church of St John the Evangelist, and established the basis for Lansdowne Road, Elgin and Blenheim crescents, Ladbroke Gardens and Ladbroke Square (fig. 141). That most of these immense gardens in this rapidly developing and highly picturesque district, such as the 'large span of ornamental ground, called Ladbroke Square',[115] were formed on uneven terrain increased considerably the picturesque character of the district; this effect was further enhanced by the variety and artic-

140 (*facing page*) Thomas Allason, *A Plan of Notting Hill Estate*, 1823, pen and pencil with watercolour wash. London Metropolitan Archives.

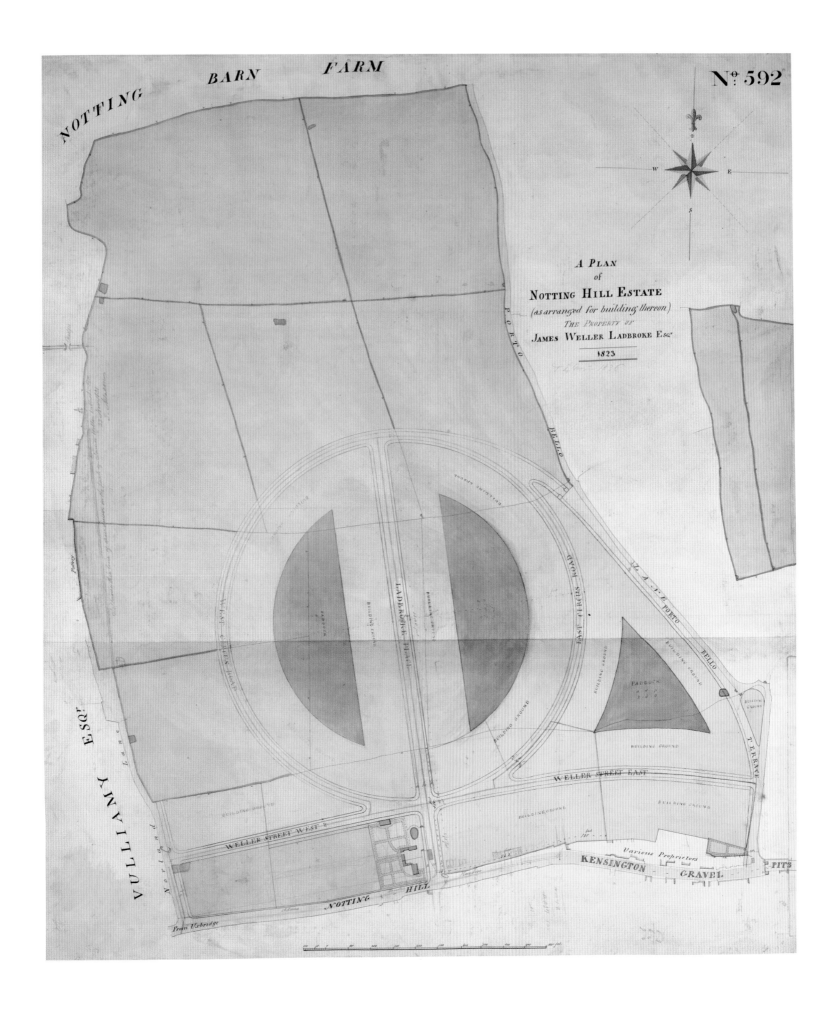

NOTTING BARN FARM

A PLAN
of
NOTTING HILL ESTATE
(as arranged for building thereon)
THE PROPERTY OF
JAMES WELLER LADBROKE Esqr.
1823

VULLIAMY ESQr.

WELLER STREET WEST

WELLER STREET EAST

LADBROKE PLACE

EAST CIRCUS ROAD

PORTO BELLO

PORTO BELLO

TERRACE

Various Proprietors

KENSINGTON GRAVEL PITS

NOTTING HILL

From Uxbridge

PADDOCK

BUILDING GROUND

W E S

141 James Thomson, *Plan of the Kensington Park Estate, Notting Hill*, c.1846, engraving. London Metropolitan Archives.

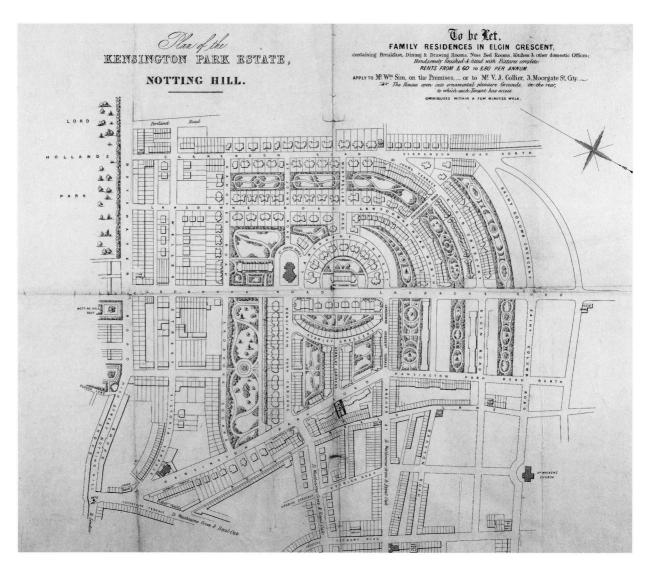

141 James Thomson, *Plan of the Kensington Park Estate, Notting Hill*, c.1846, engraving. London Metropolitan Archives.

ulation of the district's houses, which were, in some instances, like Ladbroke Square, given stucco dressings, and in others, including Norland Square and Royal Crescent, entirely dressed in the same.

The gardens on the rising ground of the so-called 'western lands' of the estate (lying west of Ladbroke Grove) were generally to be laid out in long, narrow bands to follow the natural contours, while those on the more gently sloping eastern lands were – with the exception of Stanley Crescent – to be oblong or polygonal in shape. Thomas Allom was largely responsible for the layout of these eastern lands, and the area south-west of Kensington Park Gardens and Ladbroke Gardens in particular. As a former landscape painter, his compositions were designed with 'scenic effect uppermost in his mind. The design of houses, streets, gardens and tree-planting is seen with a painter's eye, so that each turn and every vista is composed

in a picturesque manner.'[116] The playful grandeur of Stanley Gardens and Stanley Crescent (from 1853) is testimony to his masterful application of scenic display. A contributor to the *Westminster Review* (1845) praised the new district, which he believed had 'more varied and more picturesque squares and crescents' than Belgravia and Tyburnia.[117]

The use of the estate's communal gardens, which were, in fact, enclosed private squares in all but name, is very clearly set out in early leases. These specify that the gardens were 'for the convenience and recreation of the tenants and occupiers', who were permitted to 'walk and demean in and upon the same premises in a manner customary in enclosed pleasure and ornamental garden grounds in Squares and other like places in London', provided that 'none of the Livery or other servants . . . save and except the domestic servants in actual attendance on

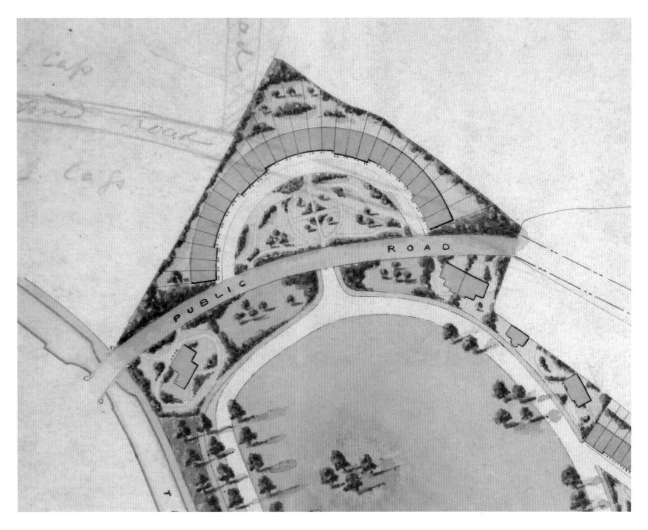

the Children or other members of the family' should be permitted to enter.[118] The paddocks were developed in a variety of manners, although the general arrangement was that the land was leased from the landowner to the builder, who in turn sub-let it to his tenants for an annual garden rent ranging from 1 to 3 guineas for each house, in return for which he would maintain the garden at his own cost for the whole of his leasehold term.[119]

The deployment of communal gardens was not, of course, restricted to the West End. Nash's pupil and successor James Pennethorne proposed a combination of crescents and terraces with front communal gardens in his early plans for the peripheral development around Victoria Park in East London.[120] His scheme of October 1846 draws heavily on Nash's work at Regent's Park (fig. 142). The Ladbroke Estate model, however, was to remain most influential in Kensington, where it continued to inform the layout of new squares well into the 1880s: two out-

standing examples are Harrington Gardens and Collingham Gardens, where the houses, which 'represent the extreme point in late-Victorian architectural individualism', would be given equally large back and front gardens.[121]

Thus far we have considered the perceived benefits of the encroachment of wide streets and squares upon the city's suburbs. While the genteel classes were tantalised by the prospect of an ever increasing stock of fashionable streets and squares, others were critical of these 'sordid speculations', which inevitably resulted in the displacement of the labouring poor.[122] In an article entitled 'The Pioneers of London' (1853), the anonymous author describes the misfortune of being a member of this transitory 'colony', living 'where town and country join', in 'towns of the temporary class . . . unpaved, un-lighted, unwatered clump[s] of temporary tenements', where one sat 'in hourly expectation of being ordered to "move on:" terraces, squares, crescents, and carriage company are

coming' (fig. 143).[123] He describes his experience of having being expelled from the edge of town to a further edge fifteen times in thirty years, and laments the approach of the

Goddess of Building . . . in her brick-layer's apron and mural crown – close at her heels a body-guard of agile Irishmen armed with what at a distance, appear fearful clubs, but which on a nearer approach, we ascertain to be so many hods of mortar. With her comes a pale consumptive creature, neither woman nor man, – fish, flesh, nor good red herring – the Genius of Stucco with plasterer's hammer; precisely like the Indian tomahawk, does this fearful thing seize upon a wood-nymph, chop to pieces her laurel locks, and with his abominable whitewash, change her verdant robes into one dull unmeaning mass of Roman cement – petrifies her, in short, like the Gorgon, into a false pretence of stone.[124]

He then charts in detail how the 'magnificence and independence of wealthy London . . . Magnificence that covers miles upon miles with palaces for the rich, and independence that can afford utterly to *ignore* the habitations of the poor', has made his life and that of his compatriots miserable: how upon the expiry of the leases on their modest premises in the future Belgravia, 'down upon us came Cubitt with a cubic acre of bricks, an ocean of stucco, and a building lease from the Bishop of London'. Nor were they secure in the 'sweet valley by the banks of the Bayswater River' (future Tyburnia), for no sooner had they settled here than 'like another destruction of Pompeii, a flood of lava – *concrete*, I should say – overwhelmed our pastoral abode'. They then migrated a mile further westward, where 'we *should* have settled, but a thing called the Norland Estate, coming down on us, in a whirlwind of squares, crescents, villas, detached and semi-detached, put us to flight'.[125]

'Have we not Inclosed Squares Enough in Westminster Already?'[126]

Samuel Leigh remarked in his *New Picture of London* (1834) that although 'there are nearly 200 areas, bearing the name of square, in this metropolis, the

144 Robert Chantrell, *Perspective View of Burton Crescent* (now Cartwright Gardens), *c.*1817, pen with watercolour wash. Sir John Soane's Museum, London.

greater portion . . . are undeserving [of this] description'. He lists a mere twenty-five as 'remarkable either for historical reminiscences, or, for that peculiar beauty which forms one of the chief characteristics of this imposing city'.[127] There were, however, 'independent of the squares . . . numerous open spots called by the various names of places, circuses, crescents, polygons, &c. which add to the beauty and salubrity of the metropolis' (fig. 144).[128]

Leigh's contemporary W. S. Turner, writing in the *Gardener's Magazine* in April 1835, proposed the establishment of a 'Society for Promoting the Improvement of Public Taste in Architectural and Rural Scenery', commended the 'excellent effect of a few trees judiciously planted . . . in squares and large streets' in the 'western quarter of the metropolis', and expressed the wish to 'render London incomparably more ornamented by trees than at present'.[129] While Turner, like some fellow topographical writers, was content to praise the planting of the new and airy additions to the metropolis, the garden writer the Reverend Prebendary Jonas Dennis was disappointed by both the scenographic qualities and the horticultural character of their central gardens. An advocate of 'pictoresque horticulture', Dennis asserts in *The Landscape Gardener: Comprising the History and Principles of Tasteful Horticulture* (1835) that there prevailed an 'egregiously tasteless disposition of the areas in public squares':[130]

Of all subjects for arrangement of plantations, areas of squares are most perplexing, from the difficulty of commanding an ornamental view from each of the four lines of surrounding houses. The inhabitants should be presented with the refreshing verdure of an open lawn in each direction, terminated by foliage not in one unbroken mass, but admitting through two or three apertures perspective display of the ulterior verdure. Trees should be evergreen and sparingly admitted, the foliage being principally composed of evergreen shrubs, supplying shade and shelter to an included curved walk, furnished with appropriate seats. Against the rail should be planted a hedge of wild holly uninviting to cattle, and including a walk of four feet width surrounded by privet backed by laurel. Viewed from the opposite side of the square, these graduated tints will be displayed, while the walks will be concealed.[131]

John Claudius Loudon likewise deplored the tasteless disposition of plantations in so many of the capital's public parks and gardens, which were full

of the 'common stuffing of the nurseries', or trees and shrubs which 'might as well be under the care of a common woodman'.[132] Loudon's remarks, however, were placed in a broader context of a more democratic approach to the use and distribution of these urban gardens: he believed that 'civilisation . . . in this country, has now nearly arrived at that point, when the higher classes find that while they enjoy the luxuries and indulgences of their station, it is their duty, as well as their interest, to see that the whole mass of society be rendered comfortable'.[133]

Loudon here referred to the fact that the public were 'completely excluded by a close fence, with a locked gate' from some of the city's most attractive gardens. As he later remarked, in *The Suburban Gardener* (1838):

it is partly owing to the taste which the public have shown for botanic gardens adjoining town and suburban residences, that the idea of ornamenting the area of public squares with verdant scenery has been adopted; but, though such squares are very agreeable, and may contain many fine plants, trees, fountains, statues, and other objects, yet they want the peculiar animation of the culti-

vated botanic garden or nursery; which cheerfulness arises from the labours continually going forward there. A public square laid out as a garden, in England, is never so varied and interesting, considered as a scene of public recreation, as a similar scene is on the Continent; because, in England, such squares are only accessible to the occupiers of the surrounding houses; whereas on the Continent they are open to all persons whatever.[134]

Others, too, began to challenge the need to create so many new squares that were destined to be consecrated to the private delectation of the rich and privileged (fig. 145). This sentiment began to be aired in the press from the early 1830s, and particularly in reaction to the proposal to convert the open space of what is now Trafalgar Square into a garden (fig. 146).[135] The space, which had formerly been occupied by the Royal Mews, and which lay adjacent to the infamous Charing Cross pillory,[136] was cleared on John Nash's recommendation in the mid-1820s as part of his major redevelopment scheme for the extension of the east end of Pall Mall and its associated improvements, to make way for a square or crescent.[137] The Street Commissioners then proposed to convert the opening into an enlarged square,

146 T. M. Baynes, after John Goldicutt, *Design for a Naval Monument Proposed to be Erected in Trafalgar Square*, 1835, engraving. London Metropolitan Archives. The view is taken from the south side of the square, looking towards the National Gallery and St Martin-in-the-Fields.

indeed the grandest open public space in London, for which a scheme by Nash was published in 1826.[138]

A contributor to the *Morning Chronicle* on 18 August 1837 remarked on the imminent enclosure of the 'open space' in front of the National Gallery:

Every one, I think, who is interested in the architectural beauty of the metropolis must regret that the finest spot in any city in the world is to be sacrificed in attempting to create a second Golden or Leicester square. All who have observed the fine effect produced by open spaces in a town such as Piazza del Popolo at Rome, the Place Vendome at Paris, and the Wittelsbacher Platz in Munich, and who have remarked the gloomy appearance and dingy vegetation of London squares, will at once decide that good taste had nothing to do with the determination to make Trafalgar-square an inclosure. Indeed, during the last two or three years that the improvements have been going on in that neighbourhood, I have never met with any one acquainted with art who did not express a desire that the square should be left an open space.[139]

It was, he continued, clear that the public health of a densely populated town like London could be 'very much promoted by open spaces, where the air

freely circulates, instead of being impeded by a crowd of stunted streets, introduced to shield aristocratic nurserymaids from the eyes of the mob'. The contributor, furthermore, objected to the erection of a railing around the square, and the forming of gravel paths and plantations within it: 'all this shows that a garden is to be made, in which the children of a very few rich people in the neighbourhood are to be allowed to sun themselves, while the exclusion of all the rest of the world is the means by which so very small an advantage is to be gained'.[140]

Nor was this contributor the only one to voice his dismay that 'we have not one grand open space in all London resembling that before the Tuileries, the Chamber of Deputies, the Court of the Louvre . . . &c., as in Paris and other cities on the Continent'.[141] In the event, the central area of Trafalgar Square was not laid out as a 'very insignificant inclosure', but as a paved piazza to the design of Sir Charles Barry, who drew from earlier proposals put forth by William Wilkins (fig. 147).[142]

The square was not an instant success: no sooner was the hoarding removed 'which for so long has veiled in mystery the works which have been carried on within the enclosure' than it was, like so may earlier large open spaces, 'shamefully disfigured'. *The Times* reported on 8 May 1844 that it was 'polluted by brutes in human shape, and dirty boys besides' who vandalised the reservoirs, filling them with

147 T. Picken, after E. Walker,
Trafalgar Square, 1852,
hand-coloured lithograph.
Victoria and Albert Museum,
London.

'orange-peel, wood, filthy rags and paper'. The pavements and large portions of the stonework throughout the square and at the base of Nelson's column,
were also broken and damaged by the 'practical
experimentalism' of the public, who employed 'sticks,
stones, umbrellas, and in some cases, hammers' to test
the 'solidity of the works'.[143] It was observed at the
time that although the broad terrace at the centre
of the square was intended to be one of the 'greatest
ornaments of the metropolis, and should be thronged
by respectable people, for whom it forms a most
agreeable airy promenade at all hours of the day', if
no pains were taken to keep it in a 'decent and
orderly state, it will assuredly ere long be quite
deserted by all but the lowest and most vagabond
portion of the community, and instead of being the
boast, it will become the disgrace of London'.[144]
Trafalgar Square, perhaps more than any other newly
created open space in the metropolis, became a
political arena, and the setting for a continuous
struggle between the authorities and social activists,
which continues to this day.[145]

While some of the objections to the creation of a
garden in Trafalgar Square had doubtless been fuelled
by the increasing pressure put on the government to
provide more public open space,[146] it was also galvanised in part by the increasing decrepitude of neighbouring Leicester Square, which had been in a poor
state since at least the late eighteenth century, and was
described in 1837 as 'a very pretty dirty looking
place'.[147] The condition of this private enclosure had
not improved by 1843, when a correspondent to
Punch remarked that the 'Woods & Forests have determined upon arranging an expedition to the interior
of Leicester Square. Many surmises are afloat as to
what discoveries will be made in this new world. Its
dead seclusion – the centuries it has remained undis-
turbed – the valuable relics of antiquity with which
it doubtless abounds, all conspire to render the undertaking equal in importance to the exhumation of
Pompeii and Herculaneum.'[148] This was the first of a
series of satires published over a decade that derided
the decay of this 'West-End Wilderness', in which the
abandoned enclosure was compared to 'a sort of min-

138

A WEST-END WILDERNESS.

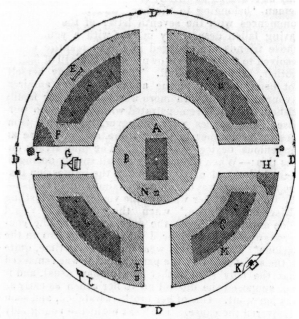

A. Statue of Somebody.	H. A Mysterious Arbou[r]
B. Green Stuff.	I. A Tree.
C. Beds for Flowers.	J. No Dogs Admitted.
D. The Gates.	K. A Pump.
E. A Rustic Seat.	L. Ajax defying the &c.
F. Gothic Arbour.	M. The Hollyhock.
G. Garden Roller.	N. A Sundial.

iature continent, where every thing is going to ruin, and getting into a savage state for want of an established government' (fig. 148).[149]

As we shall see in Chapter 5, the central area of Leicester Square was to remain what Charles Dickens condemned as a 'howling desert enclosed by iron railings' until the early 1870s, and its spectacular social and physical decline were doubtless perceived as a grim portent to the inhabitants of some of the city's squares.[150] Leicester Square, like neighbouring Golden Square, was one of the 'squares that have been; a quarter of town that has gone down in the world'.[151]

The 'Perfect World' of 'Our Square'

By the early 1840s the square had become such an integral part of the city that it became, like so many other topical issues in society and government, the object of numerous genial satires. On 29 July 1842 a notice appeared in the *Morning Chronicle* advertising the commencement of Horace Mayhew's good-humoured and philosophically witty essays entitled 'Our Square' to be published in the *Lady's Newspaper*. The 'series of outlines' was to be based upon a new plan of Social Geography . . . drawn after a recent survey of 'Our Square', forming a map (in neutral colours) of one of the most select features of London, by the Oldest Resident. A key to Our Square will be given to anyone who wishes to explore the interior, with a view of studying the manners, customs, sports, pastimes, and idiosyncrasies of its inhabitants, and of describing, in all their branches, the various rare plants which are cultivated by them. Everyone is admitted [fig. 149].[152]

Mayhew's first 'outline' declared that Our Square was a 'perfect world; and consequently it is a world having a plurality of worlds, and these contain respectively A Little of Fashion, A Little of Politics, A Little of Law, A Little of Literature, A Little of Theatres, [and] a Little of Music; in fact it contains a little of everything, including a little scandal, as a matter of course'. The cicerone then invited his readers to take a turn around the square so that he could point out the different houses and describe in 'true colours' the different people who were in the habit of moving in its ring. While not quite as 'aristocratic' or 'ridiculous' as the city's grandest squares, Our Square was 'no mean, ill-endowed, suburban

150 Unknown artist, *Our Statue*, engraving, from Horace Mayhew, 'Our Square', *Lady's Newspaper*, 7 August 1847. British Library, London.

square, into which all classes are admitted indiscriminately, like a vulgar park'.[153]

The 'Geography of Our Square' is described in the second outline.[154] Here the author pondered its pedigree, and the identity of its founders: 'who was the great man who laid the first bit of turf? [and] who was the Lady who planted the first daisy?'. The origins, he concluded, were a 'most questionable act'. The boundaries and tributaries of Our Square were, on the other hand, more readily determined. He produced a map showing the 'tract of country which is comprised within 3142 railings (fifteen are wanting) which form the iron hoop that keeps Our Square in its circular shape, like that of a butt'. It was said to cover an area scarcely bigger than a German principality; its population, too, was about the same: 'call it Saxe-Golden, or Maida-hill-Sedlitz, or Fitzroybad, or Eustonberg, and it would be entitled to a dot and a separate name on the map of Europe'.[155] He then provided an inventory of Our Square, 'as taken through the railings'. The elements included a 'common compo' (artificial stone) and perishable 'statue of some-one'; 'green stuff'; beds for flowers; gates and a rustic seat; a Gothic arbour; a garden roller; a 'mysterious arbour'; two or three trees including a magnificent chestnut, a willow 'which has nearly wept itself into the grave, and the others mere birchbrooms of trees,

whose only blossoms are caterpillars'; a 'no dogs admitted' sign; a 'mighty pump'; a statue of 'Ajax defying the &c.'; a sundial; and 'some half-dozen flowers which, if there was a floricultural show for the exhibition of plants of London rearing, would certainly obtain the first prizes for being the very best specimens of Cockney botany' (fig. 150). These articles in themselves were not worth very much, but they were 'invested with an ideal value which cannot be estimated'. For instance, 'that Gothic arbour would scarcely produce ten shillings if cut up for firewood, and yet it is so dear, so enriched with histories of flirtations and stolen meetings, and has been made the hiding-place for so many billet-doux, that it would be a calumny on all young gentlemen, and a libel on all the young ladies, of Our Square to say that it would be allowed to be converted into lucifer-matches for the sake of half-a-guinea! No sum in the world would buy that arbour.'

And the third and last of Mayhew's outline sets out the 'laws, management, government, revenue, possessions, and standing army' of Our Square. Its government was republican, insofar as – 'like the United States' – it had a president elected once a year, and a committee chosen among its inhabitants. It also 'resembles America in other respects: for no Yankee could have at heart a more profound love and veneration for any human being labelled with a title than Our Square'. The role of president of the garden square committee was described as honorary and was 'much coveted' as there was a 'great deal of importance' connected with it. It involved a quantity of ordering, and admitted of a little bullying, and was usually held by the most prosperous and meddling inhabitant – one who bribed his constituents, and who was in the habit of bestowing, out of his own pocket, 'nice little presents' on Our Square, from sundials to slips of 'strange trees from the Rocky Mountains' and the 'latest invention in the way of heartsease'. Every inhabitant who pays his subscription is entitled to vote, and the elections of Our Square were 'carried by Universal Suffrage'. The revenue of Our Square was 'not extensive' – limited to a garden rate of 1 guinea per house per annum. Nor was the 'standing army' of Our Square great. It had one regiment, and that regiment had, for general, officers and private, but one man: that man was 'Our Beadle'. In Mayhew's estimation, the 'Beadle is the Square'.[156]

LONDON OUT OF TOWN.

Mayhew's satiric vision was not an isolated case: there are frequent references to squares in the pages of *Punch*, most of which poke fun at the scruples and pomposity of their inhabitants and their efforts to uphold the dignity and respectability of their enclosures.[157] It was for instance, announced in 1843 under the banner of 'Public or Metropolitan Improvements', that 'Punch understands that a new square is about to be built in a fashionable part of the metropolis, and that it is to be called, after himself, Punch Square'. The 'contemplated square' was to be formed of 'edifices adapted for the residence of the superior classes', and at the centre 'will be erected a colossal statue of Mr Punch, for the execution of which the services of an eminent sculptor have been engaged'. Spacious and handsome streets were proposed to open into the square: 'on the north will be Joke street; on the south will be Jibe street; on the east, Banter Street; and in the west, Fun Street'. The scheme promised to be, in Mr Punch's opinion, 'a great improvement in street nomenclature, which has hitherto displayed a great poverty of invention'.[158]

Another article in 1846 mocked the seasonal flight of the *beau monde* from the metropolis to the countryside, remarking that 'the squares, from their probability of being completely deserted, as well as from their being possessed of a few trees', would be a 'most eligible spot' for turning out sheep to graze

'with advantage to themselves, and perhaps with profits to the rate-payers; for a charge might be made for pasture, which would go some way towards the cost of paving on some future occasion' (fig. 151). It was also recommended that their 'beadles might be usefully employed towards tending the flocks, and some lace-coated CORYDON would add to the sylvan beauty of the scene by playing on "the most musical, most melancholy" pipe on the kerbstone'. The proposed arrangement would also have the additional good effect of 'supplying something like a glimpse of country life to those whose pursuits keep them penned up – often by a pen at a desk – all their lives within the metropolis'.[159] (The author may have been referring here to Mecklenburgh Square, which was described in 1857 as 'that bleakest and most inhospitable-looking of squares, in whose road the grass grows all the year round, and where a carriage, or even a pedestrian, is seldom seen'.)[160]

Other journalistic exposés, too, make light of the petty rivalries between squares, especially in regard to their floral displays,[161] or the antics of their beadles and 'square-keepers' – officers 'flourishing in all plenitude' in all the squares – who were regularly taunted by 'boys with a love of mischief', and 'young gamins'.[162] Critics also lampooned the 'tediousness of living on a square': these 'desirable nook[s] in the heart of a busy town like London' were condemned as dreary and desolate backwaters, devoid of all signs of life.[163]

The square was not, however, always the object of satirical scrutiny: it was occasionally praised for its capacity to evoke convincingly the pleasures of country life.[164] 'Old Humphrey' remarked in *The Visitor, or, Monthly Instructor* (1847) that in the 'crowded city . . . every tree in the pleasure-grounds of the crescents and squares, and every bush in the gardens that I pass, reminds me of waving woods, and warbling birds, and nooks and shady lanes';[165] and in 1849 Henry J. Slack, walking about the 'Square part of the "Great Metropolis"', described the 'odd sensation' of coming across Bloomsbury Square in springtime, where he was 'startled, almost affrighted, not out of my propriety, but out of a fit of reverie by the bright green hue of its little grass plot, which looked as smooth as if it had just been shaved by the most expert barber in the parish . . . in the very heart of London I had seen an undoubted proof that

152 John Doyle, *Manners and Customs of ye Englyshe in 1849*, sketch, from *Punch*, 17 (1849): 212. Private collection. This chaotic scene in a square pays homage to Pieter Bruegel the elder's picture *Children's Games*, c.1560.

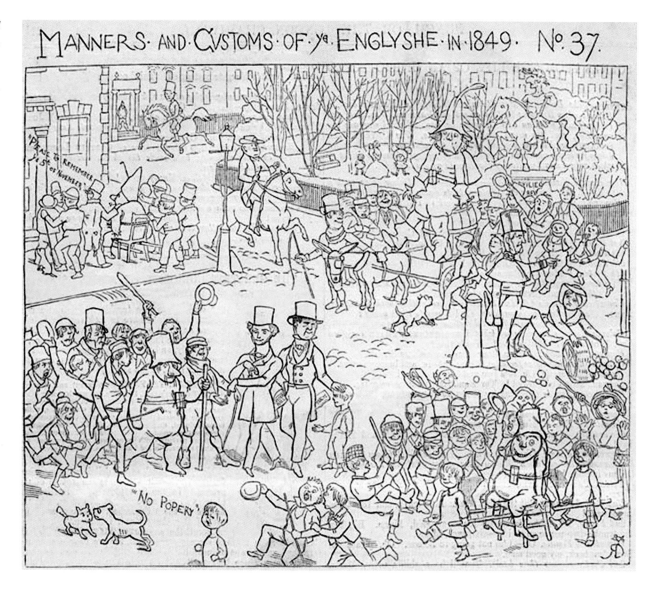

MANNERS·AND·CVSTOMS·OF·Yᵉ·ENGLYSHE·IN·1849. No. 37.

Nature had not entirely forgotten us, but kindly sent a few green leaves to speak glad tidings to the dwellers in dirt and smoke, and tell them what glorious things were doing in wood and field'.[166] John Fisher Murray even went so far as to opine that such metropolitan gardens surpassed their rural counterparts, as 'all the pleasure derivable from the observation of dress, manner, deportment, and the infinite varieties of human character is superadded to the enjoyment of charms of merely natural beauty'.[167]

The 'Grand Divisions' of Squares

In 1849 the editor of *Punch* remarked that 'very lately we took a walk with [Thomas Babington] Macaulay round some of the London squares . . . and our promenade extended as far as Soho and Blooms-

bury'. Macaulay made the following observations: 'foreign princes were carried to see Bloomsbury Square as one of the wonders of England', and Soho Square 'which had just been built was to our ancestors a subject of pride with which their posterity will hardly sympathise'.[168] The essayist, like some of his contemporaries, was interested not only in exploring the origins and history of the streets and squares, but in making social reflections upon them as well (fig. 152).[169] Dickens, for instance, endowed the capital's squares with descriptive adjectives that characterised both their inhabitants and their layouts – thus the melancholy of the 'City-Square', 'the aristocratic gravity of Grosvenor-square and Hanover-square, [and] the dowager barrenness and frigidity of Fitzroy-square'.[170] Few, with the exception of William Weir, examined the square so perceptively in terms of its contribution to the layout and magnificence of the metropolis and the well-being of its inhabitants. Weir opined in his 'desultory remarks' entitled 'The Squares of London' that the square had little to do with the *piazza*, *place* or *platz* of Italy, France and Germany;[171] that 'like many other good things in this world – as, for example, roast-pig (*teste Elia*), the lyre (*vide* the legend of Mercury and the tortoise-shell), and the theory of gravitation (Newton's apple, to wit) – [it] appears to have been in a great measure an accidental invention. Seeking to make something else, men stumbled upon the square, as the alchemists, in trying to make gold, stumbled upon truths compared with which the purest gold is valueless'.[172]

Weir, who remarks that 'in all the suburbs squares are now springing up like mushrooms', devised a typology in an attempt to distinguish the 'great diversity in the character of squares, simple though the elements be that comprise them' (fig. 153). The basis of his nomenclature was broadly social and geographical; it did, however, take account of a square's extent, its natural topography, historical associations, function, airiness and position relative to neighbouring streets and buildings. The author classified squares into four 'grand divisions'. The first embraced all the squares west of Regent Street, which he called 'fashionable squares'; these were, in his view, the 'most perfectly developed' of the metropolitan squares. The second and third divisions included squares situated between Regent Street to the west, and Gray's Inn Lane and Chancery Lane to the east, Holborn and Oxford Street forming a line of demarcation between them; and the fourth division encompassed squares south of Oxford Street, which 'having once been the seats of fashion, and still bearing upon their exterior the traces of faded greatness, have descended to become haunts of busy trading life'. To these grand divisions he appended two 'sub-divisions': squares north of Holborn inhabited by the 'aristocracy of the law, among whom mingle wealthy citizens and the more solid class of *literati*; and the 'obsolete, or purely City squares' – or what Dickens referred to as quiet, ill-frequented, retired spots 'favourable to melancholy and contemplation'.[173] There were, furthermore, 'anomalous squares' within some of the divisions that did not fall into line with their geographical counterparts.

Weir's spirited narrative compares dozens of London squares, ranging from the city's oldest and witheringly ostentatious to the melancholy products of failed speculations. Praise and delight constantly alternate with criticism and condemnation as he jumps about the metropolis in pursuit of squares and their derivatives. However, unlike the authors of earlier commentaries on the subject, Weir places the square in the context of the whole range of metropolitan improvements: they are discussed in terms of their relationship to parks, sewers, building densities, streets and circulation. He also charts the vicissitudes of many squares, from the dusty, deserted and neglected City squares with the 'soot-encumbered semi-vegetation of the trees', which have a 'tolerable sameness about them', to the rise of the 'comfortable squares' north of Holborn and Oxford Street, which contrast with the '*passé*' appearance of Lincoln's Inn Fields or Bridgewater Square, and their respective class-fellows on one hand, or with the imposing appearance of the west-end squares on the other' (fig. 154).[174]

Weir also observes very astutely that many a square is 'worthy of notice rather on account of the inequality of the ground, so much greater than is easily found in London, than for anything remarkable in its buildings'. The openness of the squares preserved the natural contours of the earlier rural landscape, which had otherwise vanished or become imperceptible through the accretion of streets and buildings. Berkeley Square is, therefore, praised owing to its sloping position, and the open wooded space between it and Green Park, as 'one of the most airy and picturesque of our squares'.[175] This topographical anomaly persists in many squares to this day, and merits the inspection of the curious. What is particularly noteworthy, but not perhaps surprising, is how many squares are laid out on gentle south-facing slopes.

Conscious of the fact that the term 'square' was used to describe a wide range of situations, Weir paid particular attention to distinguishing 'genuine squares' from 'new squares', or 'places', and even disused burial-grounds. 'Places' were an early nineteenth-century 'innovation', which were based upon the 'continental vacuums'. The term was used of such features as Waterloo Place and Trafalgar Square but also included the 'twin deformities' of Montagu and Bryanston squares, of which Weir remarked: 'these two oblongs, though dignified with the name of squares, belong rather to the anomalous "places"

153 (*right*) Unknown artist, *Belgrave Square*, engraving, from William Weir's essay 'Squares of London' (1844). Author's collection. Weir considered this large square south of Hyde Park as one of the 'most perfectly developed' and 'fashionable' precincts in his 'grand division' of the metropolitan squares.

154 (*below*) Unknown artist, *Bridgewater Square*, engraving, from William Weir's essay 'Squares of London' (1844). Author's collection. The overgrown gardens and air of neglect of this small square in the City typify Weir's description of an old-fashioned, faded locale.

155 Unknown artist, *Norfolk Square, Hyde Park, near Westbourne Terrace*, c.1850–60, lithograph. London Metropolitan Archives. The houses here were, like those in Saxe-Coburg Square, criticised by some as being gaunt and ugly.

which economical builders contrive to carve out the corners of mews-lanes behind squares, and dispose with a profit for those who wish to live near the great'. Most of the central enclosures of the City of London's squares were, on the other hand, disused graveyards, which Weir compared to 'those minikin open spaces with green turf on them . . . which might delude the stranger with the notion that they were the first attempts at squares – something between the court and the square – child squares, in short, but in reality the fallow churchyards of churches not rebuilt since the great fire'.[176] They were, in fact, innovations in their own right, prefiguring the initiative of the Metropolitan Public Gardens Association by well over half a century.

'We Begin to Grow Impatient of Gardens Desecrated to Semi-public Use'

The narrator in Edmund Hodgson Yates's satirical novel *Broken to Harness: A Story of English Domestic Life* (1864), affirmed that to buy a house in Saxe-

Coburg Square was a 'splendid speculation', though they were all, 'as Mr Thackeray said of the Pyramids, "very big", and very ugly' (fig. 155). The 'great gaunt stuccoed erections' were 'bow-windowed, plate-glassed, and porticoed after the usual prevalent manner', had delightful views '"over the way", in front', and, most importantly, were good investments as they 'let wonderfully'. It was 'the thing to live in that quarter; and hangers-on to the selvage of fashion, clerks in public offices, who have married into aristocratic, poor families, and such like, will be found bargaining for a ghastly little hole in Adalbert Crescent, or Guelph Place, when they could get a capital roomy house at Highgate, or Hampstead with a big garden'.[177]

Squares, crescents and wide streets were, in fact, by the time Yates was writing, no longer the acme of fashion, nor the only 'thing to live in'. Although in the guise of communal gardens hidden from the front street they remained a viable component of suburban development well into the late nineteenth century, in their old form they were increasingly rejected by suburban developers and prospective inhabitants, who

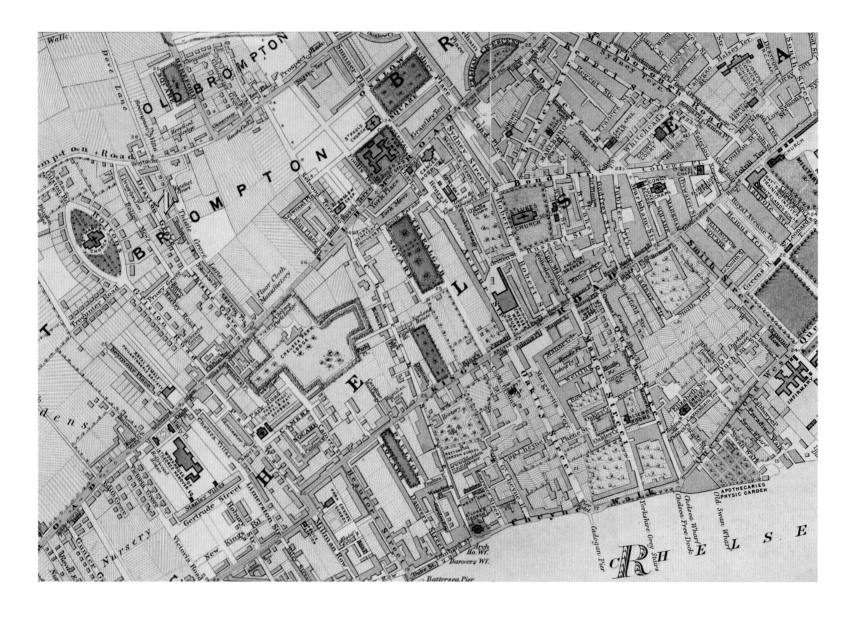

saw their proliferation and application to the suburbs as insidious, objectionable and inappropriate. Squares, it was proclaimed in *Building News* in 1857, wasted space that could have been more usefully and agreeably devoted to individual gardens.[178]

A letter to the editor of the same journal in 1859 typifies such a plea for a code of building propriety:

> Will you allow me to enter my protest against the rage which now prevails among builders for the formation of 'squares' in the suburbs! In the densely-crowded streets and alleys of London we are but too happy to find, here and there, an opening sufficiently expanded to allow a short glance to look at the sky, or a compassionate look at some blackened trees, but after travelling five miles from the Bank, we begin to grow impatient of gardens desecrated to semi-public use, and to demand a plot, however small, for the special delectation of our own family. Surely at places like Highbury, Camberwell, Brompton, and Bayswater, removed so far from either the Strand or Cornhill, we may be spared the infliction of 'rows' of brick-and-mortar walls even in squares, and may be excused for spurning the offer of a common parade-ground, where no plot is left to the private dwelling except the compulsory 10 feet by 10 at the back, well paved with York Stone![179]

Such statements mark the beginning of the end of an era for the London square, and should be duly noted. Indeed, the heyday of the Georgian square and variants of such private-communal gardens was in many ways antithetical to a very different sensibility. Henceforth, the very essence of Victorian middle-class suburban life would glorify the pursuit of innocent amusements, seclusion and comfortable domestic retirement in surroundings that offered picturesque variety and aesthetic diversity.

Squares were still formed in the second half of the nineteenth century, and, indeed, some of them were, like Bolton Gardens (1864), Earls Court Square (1868) and Cadogan Square (1880), quite imaginative in layout and grand in conception, but they were no longer the only residential quarters of consequence (fig. 156).[180] The collapse of new square-building began in the 1880s, and corresponded with the waning prestige of the unified London terrace. London's rich began to prefer to live in serviced mansion flats like those in Whitehall or Kensington Court, while others moved out of the centre altogether to colonise new suburban villas.[181] 'Handsome, spacious' Nevern Square in Earls Court (1880–6), with its 'large gardens, its three well-kept tennis courts, and its fine red-brick dwellings', is typical of what Andrew Saint has characterised as the 'dying' middle-class square, where, the 'architecture and planting alike lack animation and the houses start to give way to flats'.[182]

The uniformity and anonymity of terraced housing had begun to lose its appeal to people now eager to cultivate individuality in spacious suburban surroundings. Squares had imposed social diversity by juxtaposing the classes; they denied the ever growing demand for private gardens; and in their role as visible communal centrepieces to residential units they failed to satisfy the desire for increased social exclusivity and privacy essential to what was now regarded as respectable family living.

Most importantly, squares began to ebb in popularity because they were implicitly understood to exclude spacious informality. The informality of the garden was classified as a quality that could not be reconciled with the indomitable uniform and formal character of the surrounding architecture and the street, just as the animated and ostentatious residents who lived in the squares were averse to the genuine pursuit of the gentle and simple pleasures of inconspicuous rustication.

5

Squares 'Going Down in the World'[1]

In 1858 the anonymous author of the article 'Social Rivalry, or the Dangers of Modern Luxury' censured the desire for 'fashionable position' and 'a dangerous emulation of neighbours', lamenting the fact that

> many live, not for themselves and their families, but in a spirit of absurd social competition, and with the object of dazzling and astonishing the out-door world . . . The growth of luxury in the metropolis creates wants, and custom intrudes with fantastic demands, which tend to make the man of science and genius a slave of his station in society. The sweat of his brain ought to be spent in something better than merely to live in a fashionable square, to dress his family in the newest gauds, to enable them to appear in all places of public resort.[2]

We have noted in previous chapters how the inducements of 'free air, open space, and scenery of nature' made squares among the most desirable places of residence in the metropolis. While such allurements were important motives in the decision of 'families of position and means' to establish themselves in these ubiquitous precincts, they did not in themselves ensure that a square would retain its original enchantment. Few squares were enduringly fashionable: indeed, many plummeted from being at the very acme of fashion to being 'places of very inferior rank' within years or decades of their cre-

ation, and most were, in fact, at some point eclipsed in splendour by 'more modern ones'.[3]

The 'Distinctive Classes . . . of the Squares'[4]

Most squares of all classes whether in the West End or the suburbs, somehow miraculously maintained a degree of social pre-eminence regardless of the vicissitudes of fashion: at best they were, as Thomas Moore remarked of 'Grosvenor's lordly square', impregnable redoubts, where 'guarded, with Patrician care, Primeval Error still holds out', and at worst, 'dreary in the extreme', but 'blooming with verdure, and graced with the branching elegant plane'.[5] Regardless of their complexion, many squares were thus consistently perceived throughout the nineteenth century as conferring material and social advantages, and bestowing social rank, dignity and precedence on their inhabitants, a great number of whom were slavish aspirants to fashion and fortune (known occasionally as 'gentility-mongers'), and some of whom had no other claim to public consideration than that of living within their leafy purlieus (fig. 157).[6]

Although by the mid-nineteenth century there were over one hundred squares, in every 'shape or condition', within what is now Greater London, there was little agreement on what constituted a 'commonplace' square. Indeed, even the nature of a square's use was 'a point not easily determined',[7] and

Facing page: Leicester Square improved, *c.*1880, detail of fig. 168.

though this urban phenomenon was collectively referred to as 'the squares', it was becoming increasingly difficult to generalise. In fact, the astonishing diversity of aspect and use encouraged some writers to formulate what they saw as helpful taxonomies of the square. Yet, in any age, critics are rarely truly prophetic. For example, the social reformers Henry Mayhew and John Binny, who were acutely aware of the social nuances of the metropolis, reworked with admirable, if laborious, aplomb William Weir's earlier analysis of the character and distribution of the city's 'innumerable quantity of Squares, Circuses, and Crescents'.[8] In their introductory essay to *The Criminal Prisons of London* (1862), entitled 'The Great World of London', they chose to examine, among other things, the striking 'physiognomical expression – the different countenance, as it were' of the houses in the 'several localities inhabited by the various grades of society', which meant that 'to him who knows London well, a walk through its divers districts is as peculiar as a geographical excursion through the multiform regions of the globe'.[9]

The physiognomy of the metropolitan thoroughfares is well worthy of the study of some civic Lavater. The finely-chiselled features of an English aristocrat, are not more distinct from the common countenance of a Common Councilman, than is the stately Belgravian square from its vulgar brother in Barbican; and as there exists in society a medium class of people, between the noble and the citizen, who may be regarded as the patterns of ostensible respectability among us, such as bankers, lawyers, and physicians; so have we in London a class of respectable localities, whose architecture is not only as prim as the silver hair, or as cold-looking as the bald head, which is so distinctive of the 'genteel' types above specified; but it is as different from the ornate and stately character of the buildings about the parks as they, on the other hand, differ from the heavy and ruddy look of the City squares; for what the Belgravian districts are in their 'build' to the Bedfordian, and the Bedfordian again to the Towerian, so is there the same ratio in social rank and character among nobles, professional gentry, and citizens.[10]

The London square, in Mayhew's estimation, was 'so purely national – so utterly unlike your foreign "place", or "platz", that bare paved or gravelled space, with nothing but a fountain, a statue, or column, in the centre of it'. Although the trees of the average square 'may grow as black in London as human beings at the tropics', it possessed a 'broad

and Manchester squares, and 'still more stately and gorgeous' at Belgrave and Eaton Squares.[12]

Next to these Mayhew and Binny ranked the 'respectable and genteel squares', such as Montagu, Bryanston, Connaught and Cadogan squares in the West End, and Fitzroy, Russell, Bedford, Bloomsbury, Tavistock, Torrington, Gordon, Euston, Mecklenburgh, Brunswick, Queen and Finsbury squares, all lying in that district east of Tottenham Court Road. The City squares, in marked contrast, were

those intensely quiet places immured in the very centre of London, which seem as still and desolate as cloisters; and where the desire for peace is so strong among the inhabitants that there is generally a liveried street-keeper or beadle maintained to cane off the boys, as well as dispel the flock of organ-grinders and Punch-and-Judy men, and acrobats, who look upon the tranquillity of the place as a mine of wealth to them. To this class belong Devonshire Square, Bishopsgate; Bridgewater Square, Barbican; America Square, Minories; Wellclose Square, London Docks; Trinity Square, Tower; Nelson Square, Blackfriars; Warwick Square, Newgate Street; and Gough and Salisbury Squares, Fleet Street; though many of these are but the mere bald "places" of the continent.[13]

The next category of squares were those that the authors condemned as 'obsolete, or "used up" old squares', all of which lie 'south of Oxford Street and Holborn, and east of Regent Street, and which have mostly passed from fashionable residences into mere quadrangles, full of shops, or hotels, or exhibitions, or chambers; such are the squares of Soho, Leicester, Golden, Lincoln's-Inn-Fields, and even Covent Garden' (fig. 158). And, lastly, Mayhew and Binny looked to the 'pretentious *parvenu*-like suburban squares, such as Thurlow and Trevor, by Brompton; and Sloane, by Chelsea; and Edwardes, by Kensington; and Oakley, by Camden Town; and Holford and Claremont Squares, by Pentonville; and Islington Square; and Green Arbour Square, by Stepney; and Surrey Square, by the Old Kent Road; and the Oval, by Kennington' (fig. 159).[14]

However differentiated, all such squares were still, Mayhew and Binny concluded, 'now . . . generally in such extreme favour among the surrounding inhabitants, that they are regarded as the headquarters of the *élite* of the district by all aspirants for

carpet of green sward in the centre, and occasionally the patches of brightly-coloured flowers that speak of the English love of gardening – the Londoner's craving for country life'.[11]

Mayhew and Binny were right. The squares of the fashionable West End had, indeed, a 'distinctive air'; but how different they were from 'the "genteel" affairs in the northern districts of the Metropolis as well as from the odd and desolate places in the City, or the obsolete and antiquated spots on the south side of Holborn and Oxford Street – like Leicester and Soho'. How strikingly unique, too, were the handsome old mansions around Grosvenor Square, spacious piles with 'their quoins, windows, and door-cases of stone, bordering the sombre "rubbed" brick fronts. In France or Germany such enormous buildings would have a different noble family lodging on every "flat". The inclosure, too, is a small park, or palace garden, rather than the paved court-yard of foreign places.' The houses were 'all but as imposing in appearance' at St James's, Berkeley, Cavendish, Hanover

159 T. H. Shepherd, *Brompton Square*, *c*.1850, watercolour. Kensington and Chelsea Local Studies collection. The elaborate railings and the character of the houses mark out Brompton Square as one of the kind that Mayhew and Binny would class as 'pretentious'.

fashionable distinction; so that the pretentious traders of Gower Street and the like, instead of writing down their address as Gower Street, Tottenham Court Road, love to exaggerate it into Gower Street, Bedford Square'.[15]

'The Earliest Air he Breathed was in a Smoky London Square'[16]

What Mayhew and Binny do not tell their readers is that squares were as much admired by English and foreign visitors to the capital as by Londoners themselves. Every contemporary respectable guidebook to the metropolis included glowing descriptions of the now ubiquitous London squares, which they ranked among the principal attractions and the greatest 'curiosities' of the English metropolis. Squares were praised not only for the fact that outside the capital there were few equivalents to these 'oases

highly kept' surrounded by 'well-built' houses, but because they were widely regarded as epitomising the *beau idéal* of an eminently refined, comfortable and respectable form of metropolitan domesticity.[17]

The desire to live on a square – whether genteel or parvenu – was not, however, simply a reflection of extravagance, personal pride or social ambition: in more immediately practical ways, squares offered tangible benefits that ministered to the health and comfort of their residents. As the American author and clergyman the Reverend Heman Humphrey remarked in 'Publick Squares' in the *Family Magazine* (1836):

The English people, in good circumstances, seem to be more anxious than we are, to secure the luxury of deep front yards, and of large open spaces in the rear of their dwellings. They want room – they want fresh air – they want, when

within doors, to be as much retired as they can from the noise and bustle of the streets . . . [but] in parts of the city, where the luxury of spacious court-yards and gardens cannot be enjoyed by every family, I observed here and there, a charming little park, or square, neatly enclosed by a high iron railing, and apparently belonging to a number of families in the immediate vicinity. These enclosures, tastefully laid out into gravelled walks, and adorned with fine shade-trees, shrubbery, flowers, and ivy-clad summer-houses, are favourite resorts in pleasant weather, and it is especially delightful to see very young children, spending hours together with their nurses, in these miniature Elysian fields, inhaling the fresh breezes, and playing upon the smooth grass-plats, and among the bushes. How very different, I could not help saying to myself, is this young freedom and early exposure to air and sunshine, and soft showers too, if one happens now and then to surprise them in the midst of their sports – from that tender imprisonment, to which the children of wealthy families, are for the most part doomed in our own cities. And how very striking, I may add, is the contrast, too, between the rosy health of the former, and the white, lily complexion and frailty of the latter.[18]

Although the central enclosures of London's squares were in fact used at different times of the day, week or season by virtually all members of the surrounding households, nonetheless they were from the early nineteenth century onwards commonly perceived by the outside world as little more than leafy resorts for the exercise of privileged children (fig. 160).[19] Children and their nurses were indeed among the most frequent and regular users of the garden – so much so, that Theodore Edward Hook observed in 1857 that the only sign of life in the 'bleakest and most inhospitable-looking of squares, in whose road the grass grows all the year round, and where a carriage, or even a pedestrian, is seldom seen', was a 'thick-set servant-maid or two carrying a brace of moon-faced babies in their arms'.[20]

In what became characteristic of nineteenth-century London, children were introduced to the central enclosures from an early age. An anonymous contributor to the *New Monthly Magazine* (1823) gives some indication of the nature and frequency of their admission, remarking that 'it was the fashion to make children hardy . . . they were daily sent out in all weathers to walk for one hour (the canonical duration of a lesson), and to trail their listless limbs round the interior of a fashionable London square for the purpose of air and exercise'.[21] This observation was presumably drawn from the popular writings of the novelist and educational reformer Elizabeth Hamilton, who had earlier implored the residents of the metropolitan squares to adorn their central enclosures with a view to providing places 'where children might be safely let to find amusement for themselves'. Somewhat more critically, Hamilton remarked in *Letters on the Elementary Principles of Education* (1813) that 'at times, indeed, you may see some of the privileged children of the square in this sacred spot [the garden]; but never do you see the poor little beings left to enjoy the liberty of nature. Even in this place of safety their steps must be watched by a train of attendants, or, perhaps, by their wearied arms, dragged in slow and solemn pace round and round the dull, joyless scene. Why torture them with attendants, where no attendance is necessary? What harm could befall them, if left to themselves?'[22]

Hamilton's contemporary Margaret King Moore also addressed the subject of the adaptation of central gardens for the purposes of children's play.[23] In *Advice to Young Mothers on the Physical Education of their Children* (1835) she recommended that children of all ages should be out as much as possible, that playing in the open air was much better for them

than taking long walks, and that those parents who are 'obliged to inhabit large towns, and have no gardens to their houses, should make it a rule to send their children to some square, or open place, every tolerably fine day, either on some errand of amusement, or under some pretext which may induce them to go with pleasure'.[24] It was, according to the surgeon and pioneer of vaccination Charles Rochemont Aikin, writing in 1836, not only desirable, but advisable to confine an infant's daily exercise to the area 'within the privileged rails of a London square . . . anxiously secluded from any intercourse with the crowds who fill the adjacent streets, [the infants] may have a fair chance of escaping this dreaded contagion [smallpox] during all the first months of childhood.'[25]

Although frontagers often compared their central gardens to countryside, and their children doubtless benefited from exercising within them, the enclosures were a poor substitute for real rurality.[26] According to the novelist Catherine Grace Frances Gore,

writing in 1846, one could distinguish town children from their rural counterparts by their play, as the 'little creatures' who lived in the town exhibited a particular 'zest for country pleasures, known only to children whose walks have long been restricted to the dreary, sooty, flowerless monotony of a London square' (fig. 161).[27] The 'monotonous confinement of a London square'[28] was, however, invariably deemed preferable to the city's public parks and gardens. Augustus and Henry Mayhew reported that a square's central garden was not only a place 'where the nurse could let the child roll about, and no harm could possibly come to it', but a considerably safer place than the public resorts such as 'that bothering Regent's Park, where the soldiers, and a parcel of vagabonds, made it quite as dangerous for the nurse as it was for the child'.[29]

The central enclosures of squares in fact provided a rite of passage for many urban children: it was in these 'smoked groves' that some first encountered nature, or experienced the outside world. An author

154

who was probably Arthur Edwin Quekett reminisced in 'In and Out of a London Square (a Chat of a Childhood Passed in Lincoln's Inn Fields)' (1899) that the square's trees, lawns, gravel paths and its flower-beds were 'the background of all my earliest ideas'.[30] When he was a child in the mid-1850s, the enclosure was his 'Eden': he identified the Tree of Knowledge and the Tree of Life with the 'two fine old plane-trees in one part of the garden'; he could picture to himself the deep sleep of Adam on the 'daisy-clad lawn, in the brilliant sunshine'; the gate at the corner farthest from his own entrance was the point where, in the 'dark story of temptation and fall', the guilty pair were driven out of Paradise; the narrow path 'closely bordered with thick lilac bushes' led to the 'very spot where the angel stood with his flaming sword turned every way'; and the serpent itself was to him 'but a magnified copy of one of the long, brown snake-like caterpillars which frequented "the Square" and were known to us in after days by the familiar name of "walking-sticks"'.[31]

In less biblical terms, the author also remarked that the garden in a square served as a means of comprehending the world: 'when we were told that the ground covered by the base of the great pyramid was of about the same area as "the Square", and that the pyramid itself was some fifty or sixty feet higher than St. Paul's, it was easy for us to form some idea of its actual appearance and size'; and when the children were informed that the square comprised about thirteen acres they got 'some notion what an acre was'. The square, moreover, and the many noteworthy events that took place within or around it, also enhanced the author's understanding of local history – from the execution of William, Lord Russell, in 1683 to the 'red glare and the shooting tongues of flame which told the destruction of Covent Garden Theatre' in 1856.[32]

Although under supervision children were encouraged to make regular use of the gardens, they were, in fact, more grudgingly tolerated than openly welcomed by many inhabitants of the squares, who took pleasure in the desolate character of their central openings, 'where all is cheerless, solitary, and, as it were, without the pale of metropolitan civilization'.[33] Children's conduct was strictly prescribed by regulations drafted by trustees or frontagers, who regularly introduced 'fresh rules' to reflect changes in taste or acceptable behaviour, and to combat all forms of potential nuisance and annoyance. These solemn prohibitions were frequently inscribed on small oval notice boards, raised on short iron stalks at the entrances to the squares. Inhabitants only on occasion granted 'special licences' to authorise new or unfamiliar activities in their gardens, as when the Trustees of Lincoln's Inn Fields, in August 1859, granted a frontager's servant permission to push a children's perambulator in the gardens (the exception warranted, it was argued, because such 'Vehicles' were 'admitted into Belgrave Chester Montagu and other squares at the West end of London').[34]

While nursery maids or maidservants were expected to watch over and protect their juvenile charges, the square's complement of outdoor servants – including beadles, watchmen and gardeners – was also expected to assist in their superintendence: they were instructed to protect the gardens from children's depredations, and to report their bad behaviour to their parents or to the trustees. Accounts abound in Trustees' Minute Books of children being admonished for 'playing & making noise', throwing stones,[35] playing sports (making use of 'Bows and Arrows and Batts and Balls'),[36] plucking or destroying flowers, trampling flower-beds, climbing trees and even destroying garden furniture.[37] Such regulations doubtless went some way to maintaining a degree of orderliness in most squares; it was, nonetheless, sometimes difficult to deal with mischievous or unruly children of rate-paying inhabitants, who 'invaded' or 'intruded' upon the central garden. One exasperated resident of Lincoln's Inn Fields, for example, exclaimed in 1868 that the children who were entitled to use the square were 'very little better than the rabble outside the railings whose language is very offensive & whose behaviour is of the roughest and rudest kind'.[38]

We know comparatively little about the manner in which, by adolescence, boys and girls were using the nineteenth-century squares (fig. 162). There were few 'active sports' considered 'at once healthy, pleasant, suitable for girls, and practicable in London'. Skipping and quoits were favourite 'childish games', while shuttlecock and battledore were generally deemed too noisy for the enclosures. Croquet – which became popular in the late 1850s – was, on the other hand, praised by a contributor to the *Museum and Journal of Education* (1867) for its agreeable

162 Unknown artist, *Brunswick Square, c.*1830, pencil and ink wash. Private collection. This unusual drawing, showing the west side of the garden, depicts a young woman reading and drawing within the garden enclosure of the square, which is entirely secluded from the surrounding street.

'domesticity', and was well suited to the smooth grass of the typical enclosure; it had, moreover, the 'cardinal merit of being almost universally popular, and it requires little preparation'.[39] Although boys, in turn, were generally encouraged in most places to engage in robust exercise and athletics to increase their mental happiness and physical prowess, such activity was frowned upon in the typical square.[40] Almost all forms of ball game were prohibited, as were any activities that involved the use of bats.

As for athletics among young adults, garden committee minutes are reliable indicators of the vagaries of fashionable recreation, as they determined what sports could be played within the enclosures. For example, from May 1879 the frontagers of Portman Square engaged in lively debates about the propriety of the 'rather objectionable' practice of 'playing at Lawn Tennis', and later bicycle riding (fig. 163).[41] Lawn tennis became a popular urban sport from the spring of 1878, especially among young men and women, who were given, as the contemporary phraseology had it, to 'hygienic excess'.[42] The advent of tennis, in fact, had an unexpected beneficial impact on the square: it was reported in 1885 that it had become such a 'fashionable recreation' that the enclosures 'are now more frequented by the residents than they used to be'.[43]

The squares' opponents of active sports must have been pleased when, from the mid-1870s, a handful of publications began to appear that encouraged juveniles to engage in the quiet and reflective pursuit of amateur entomology. Articles published in the *Entomologist's Monthly Magazine* and *The Entomologist: An Illustrated Journal of British Entomology* (1878), brought about an interest in the abundant and varied insect life in the city's squares;[44] and Emily Dibbin's 'A London Square and its Inhabitants' (1879) supplied 'instructions in entomology, which may be helpful to attract juvenile readers', and provided 'some clear and interesting descriptions of the characteristics of the habits of caterpillars, moths, beetles, gnats, and other insects as may be observed even in a London square, by those who have eyes trained to watchfulness and a love for the wonders of nature'.[45]

That amateur ornithology failed to catch on in the city's squares can probably be attributed to the

SPORT IN A LONDON SQUARE.

paucity and dismal variety of insectivorous birds in and about the metropolis.[46] The most common denizens were rooks, jackdaws and 'Cockney house sparrows'; the 'dingy bird of a London square' was in some squares so numerous among the leaves in summer that the trees were 'literally alive and black with them'.[47] There were few songbirds. Their scarcity was attributed not to the smoke, or the want of trees and food, but instead to the 'number of bird-catchers, and, in some respect, the cats'.[48] It was suggested that were fewer 'wild birds of any kind to be shot, or otherwise caught or destroyed . . . the result would be a great increase in their numbers, great tameness and familiarity with man, great facilities of studying their habits, and a powerful accession of enjoyment to the lovers of ornithology and natural song. Kensington Gardens, Regent's Park, Greenwich Park, and all the squares and the gardens of suburban cottages, would then resound with the notes of nightingale, the blackbird, the thrush, and probably the canary'.[49] In such ways, it would seem, the London square in many instances defined nature for nineteenth-century citizens of the metropolis.

Squares, Sanitary Improvements and Reform

The promise of 'free ventilation', achieved by setting wide streets around an open figure, was, as we have seen, one of the most attractive inducements of the squares. The fact that squares were occasionally referred to as 'perpetual lungs', 'immense reservoirs of oxygen' or 'ventilators' suggests that they were con-

sidered among the most healthful places of residence in the metropolis.[50] The topographer John Weale even went so far as to say that 'the pure necessity of ventilation' was the sole purpose of the square: 'A garden inclosed by open railing serves to hide the ugliness of sham art, refreshes the eyes wearied with the sombre monotony of our rude dwellings, and, though occupying some of the space, hardly impedes the circulation of air, but, according to modern chemists, actually helps to renew its vital principle.'[51]

From the second quarter of the nineteenth century, however, an awareness had developed that good ventilation was not in itself a guarantee of healthy living, and that some of the 'most airy and cleanly parts of town and country' were just as susceptible to insidious contagions as the less prosperous parts of the metropolis.[52] These perceptions were borne out by new medical discoveries, which posited that public-health hazards, and air-, water- and insect-borne diseases in particular, multiplied as the population increased, the town became more densely settled, industry became more polluting, and disruption, demolition and building became ever more frenzied.

The *London Medical Gazette* reported in July 1842 that Dr Link of Berlin, who had earlier published a paper comparing the salubrity of London to that of other large towns in England and the continental cities, had concluded, seemingly in celebration, that:

[London's] parks and squares, which have been called the *lungs* of the metropolis, play no mean part in contributing to the health of the citizens. In addition to the important use of affording space for relaxation and amusement, they serve as reservoirs of pure and fresh air. This is the especial advantage of squares situated in the middle of the city, which, forming as it were centres from which pure air may radiate into the surrounding districts, purify the neighbourhood in a more effectual manner by their number, than the larger parks situate in the vicinity can do. Many of the most thickly inhabited districts in London enclose open spaces of this sort, and are in no small degree indebted to them for their immunity from fevers and other diseases generated by close dwellings and impure air, which, in so large and populous a city, would almost constantly rage but for these causes.[53]

Link, however, qualified what would have seemed quite a rosy assertion by adding a damning fact – namely, that 'all parts of London are not equally healthy, even independently of the number of squares contained in them . . . for instance, low fevers are very prevalent in the districts situated between Hyde Park and the River, including Belgrave and Eaton Squares, and the surrounding neighbourhood, perhaps as much or more so than in any other part'.[54]

A much better picture of the truth emerges if one considers that, while many squares were in themselves reasonably healthy places, their environs, and often the mews immediately behind them, were not. Indeed, some exhibited a complete neglect of the most common precautions necessary to ensure health. A variety of factors contributed to the unwholesomeness of these areas, not least 'bad sewerage, open stagnant drains, ditches, and waters, in which animal and vegetable substances are allowed to turn putrid . . . undrained marsh-lands . . . accumulations of filth in the streets . . . the situation of slaughter-houses in densely populated districts, and the bad regulation of these establishments . . . [plus the frequent] want of ventilation in narrow streets'.[55]

The fact of the matter was that bad drainage and defective sewers caused foul odours, which came to be seen as, in themselves, prejudicial to health (fig. 164). For instance, in July 1849 the Trustees of Lincoln's Inn Fields complained to the Board of Health that the activities of neighbouring 'slaughter-men, tripe-boilers, tallowing-melters, and other offensive trades' led to the emanation of putrid odours from the 'untrapped gully holes in and about the square', and that the 'whole atmosphere of the Square is infected by them during a still night'.[56] Even earlier, the author of 'The Dirt of London' (1841) had remarked that 'often in summer, in walking along the gay squares and streets of the West End, the olfactory sense is met by streams of fetor at regular intervals. These arise from the dust-holes over which the passenger is treading.'[57]

Some noxious vapours were not only offensive but could be potentially harmful or fatal. In his 'Report on the Prevalence of Certain Physical Causes of Fever in the Metropolis, which Might be Removed by Proper Sanatory [sic] Measures' (1838), Dr Neil Arnott, MD, remarked that the proximity of some of Bloomsbury's squares to open sewers and the 'refuse of extensive cowsheds', which 'used to overflow and stagnate', led to the prevalence of several fatal maladies in the district.[58] And a contemporary and much publicised report that 'typhus fever ran through an entire family residing in a large airy house in a spacious open London square', was a sober reminder of the indiscriminate and unpredictable spread of such diseases.[59]

It was true that, on the whole, the inhabitants of squares in the most fashionable districts were less likely to contract typhus, cholera or other fevers than those in poorer districts. Yet, ironically, if spacious and sanitary living conditions were a deterrent to these diseases, the fact that the houses of the upper and middle classes were drained and sewered and those of the working classes were not (they had no internal plumbing, but privies in the outside yard) meant that the former were more vulnerable to the dangers of sewer gases. Such fatal odours of decomposition generally infiltrated homes equipped with modern sanitary conveniences, and as a result 'the sewer-gas scourge' afflicted the upper and middle classes more seriously than any other social group.[60]

The sanitary conditions of the metropolis began to improve with the passing of the Public Health Act and the Metropolitan Sewers Act, both of 1848, and the efforts of Sir Edwin Chadwick and the Metropolitan Commission of Sewers.[61] This 'concerted cultivation of cleanliness' was an immense and disruptive undertaking, and it would be several decades before the problems of London's sewers were satisfactorily remedied. The social and physical

165 The remains of the equestrian statue of George I in Leicester Square, c.1869, photograph. English Heritage Photo Library.

Labour and the London Poor (1864) that when it came to sewerage, 'the most aristocratic parts of the city of Westminster, and of the fashionable squares, &c., to the north of Oxford-street . . . have not been unduly favoured; that there has been no partiality in the construction of sewerage'. The sewers in the 'Belgrave and Eaton-square districts', he noted further, had many faults, and abounded with 'noxious matter, in many instances stopping up the house drains and "smelling horribly"'. It was 'much the same in the Grosvenor, Hanover, and Berkeley-square localities (the houses in the squares themselves included). Also in the neighbourhood of Covent-garden, Clare Market, Soho and Fitzroy-squares; while north of Oxford-street, in and about Cavendish, Bryanstone, Manchester, and Portman-squares, there is so much rottenness and decay that there is no security for the sewers standing from day to day, and to flush them for removal of their "most loathsome deposit" might be "to bring some of them down altogether"'. One of the subterranean surveys, in fact, reported that the sewers of the notorious rookery of Seven Dials were in a more 'satisfactory state' than those of 'the new Paddington district the neighbourhood of Hyde Park Gardens, and the costly squares and streets adjacent'.[63]

'A West-End Wilderness'[64]

Rottenness and decay were not confined solely to the city's sewers: Leicester Square, the one-time refuge of royalty and Parnassus of Georgian London, was by the mid-nineteenth century a festering wound on the metropolitan topography.[65] The square had begun to decline soon after the maintenance of the garden ceased to be the responsibility of any of the ground landlords of the surrounding houses (fig. 165). Although it was in the inhabitants' best interests to keep the garden in good order and prevent its misuse, collectively they were unable to force successive owners of the central area to put in hand the arrangements that had been made during the late eighteenth century to preserve the character and amenities of the enclosure. Even the Commissioners of Woods, Forests and Land Revenues, the Metropolitan Board of Works (established in 1855) and the government found themselves 'too weak to grapple with the subject with anything like effect'.[66] It was only after a series of tedious and protracted legal

responses to this essentially new urban phenomenon are told elsewhere: suffice it to say here that the advent of sanitary reform brought about new challenges, not only to health but also to the social order, physical geography and cultural identity of a metropolis in the throes of modernisation.

What is of interest here is the extent to which the construction of a great underground system of sewers threatened to erode social distinctions: the upper and middling classes became alarmed by the idea that waste from unhealthy, impoverished districts was infiltrating the 'salubrious districts'.[62] Such anxiety was in part due to the fact that the houses of all classes and districts were now physically connected by an underground labyrinth, which in the eyes of the denizens of the squares had the capacity to convey both physical and moral contamination from one area to another. With sewers – unlike the connecting network at street level – there was no means of distinguishing those of the rich from those of the poor: they were all the same. To articulate such a view, Henry Mayhew remarked in *London*

proceedings that the gardens were finally transformed from a 'depository of refuse into an exquisite public garden'.[67]

The trouble in Leicester Square began in 1788 with its partition into a variety of parcels, whereby the garden was awarded to the Tulk family, subject to the proviso that 'the Owners and Proprietors . . . shall for ever afterwards at their own sole and proper costs and charges keep and maintain the said Square Garden or pleasure Ground and the railing round the same in sufficient and proper repair as a Square Garden or pleasure Ground in like manner as the same now is'.[68] This proviso seemed to hold when, in 1807, the central area was settled by John Augustus Tulk on his son Charles Augustus, who covenanted with his father that he and his heirs and assigns would 'at all times hereafter keep . . . the piece or parcel of ground in Leicester Square now used as a Garden . . . in its present form and in an open state uncovered by any buildings upon the same and shall and will keep . . . the said piece or parcel of ground now used as a Garden in neat and ornamental order'.[69] Charles Augustus Tulk then sold the garden to Charles Elms, a dentist living in the square, to whom the obligation to maintain the gardens free of buildings was transferred. The conveyance also provided that Elms 'should not permit the defacement or removal of the equestrian statue, and that on payment of "a reasonable rent" to him, the Tulk family's tenants in the square should be granted keys and the privilege of admission to the garden'.

Elms's stewardship was not assured, however, and under his ownership the garden began to decline – indeed, so much so that it was described before his death in 1822 as a 'neglected and dirty place'.[70] For the next half a century, in sad fact, the square was to remain a squalid and inhospitable tangle, even while many legal challenges were mounted by the residents and other interested parties to rescue it from being stripped of its railings, denuded of its cover of trees and shrubs, and given over to building land. Dickens described this 'howling desert enclosed by iron railings':

There was no grass, but there was a feculent, colourless vegetation like mildewed thatch upon a half-burnt cottage. There were no gravel-walks, but there were sinuous gravelly channels and patches, as if the cankerous earth had the mange.

There were rank weeds heavy with soot. There were blighted shrubs like beggars' staves or paralytic hop-poles. There were shattered marble vases like bygone chemists' mortars which had lost their pestles, half choked with black slimy mould like preparations for decayed blisters. The earth seemed to bring forth crops, but they were crops of shattered tiles, crumbling bricks, noseless kettles, and soleless boots. The shrubs had on their withered branches, strange fruits – battered hats of antediluvian shape, and oxidised saucepan lids. The very gravel was rusty and mixed with fragments of willow-pattern plates, verdigrised nails, and spectral horseshoes. The surrounding railings, rusty, bent, and twisted as they were, were few and far between. The poor of the neighbourhood tore them out by night, to make pokers of. In the centre, gloomy, grimy, rusty, was the Statue – more hideous (if such a thing may be) than the George the Fourth enormity in Trafalgar Square – more awful than the statue of the Commendatore in Don Giovanni.

There were strange rumours and legends current in Leicesterian circles concerning this enclosure. Men told, holding their breath, of cats run wild in its thickets, and grown as large as leopards. There was no garden, and if any man possessed a key to the enclosure, he was too frightened to use it. People spoke of a dragon, a ghoule, a geni, who watched over the square, and for some fell purpose kept it desolate. Some said, the statue was the geni.[71]

Some notable events in the later history of Leicester Square garden included its sale in 1840 to the builder Edward Moxhay, who immediately began to cut down the trees in the enclosure in preparation to erect a bazaar, and later James Wyld's conversion of the central area into a 'great geographical school' by building a Panopticon of Science and Earth. Wyld's 'Great Globe', completed in 1851, was 'a sort of superior polytechnic', featuring a great circular building of 'somewhat pretentious character' enclosing a globe 60 feet 4 inches in diameter, and lighted by day from the open centre of a dome (as in the Pantheon at Rome); the whole structure was crowned with a pair of minarets nearly 100 feet high, setting off the domed roof and other 'eastern features' (fig. 166).[72] (The statue of George 1 – al-

166 Day & Son, after Edmund Walker, *Leicester Square with Wyld's Great Globe*, c.1855, lithograph, looking south-east, with the spire of St Martin-in-the-Fields in the distance. London Metropolitan Archives.

ready disfigured and dismembered – was apparently 'sunk into a pit' beneath the centre of the globe.)[73] This popular but 'dreadful eyesore' did little to improve the square, which remained 'an arid waste – a cat's paradise, varied by old shoes and oyster-shells'.[74] On the removal of the globe in 1861 the enclosure became, according to the historian Walter Thornbury, 'exposed once more in all its hideous nakedness', and 'a public nuisance, both in an aesthetic and in a sanitary point of view'.[75]

Finally, in 1865 the Metropolitan Board of Works proposed to resort to the Public Gardens Protection Act as a means to 'grapple with the long standing reproach to the Metropolis in the disgraceful state of Leicester Square'.[76] The act, which had earlier received royal assent in May 1863, made provision for the 'better Protection and Charge of enclosed Garden or Ornamental Grounds which have been set apart for the Use of the Inhabitants of any public Square, Crescent, Circus, Street, or other public

Place surrounding or adjoining such Gardens or Grounds in any City or Borough'.[77] The general effect of the legislation was to empower the Metropolitan Board of Works and the corporate authorities to take charge of and improve any neglected enclosed garden or ornamental ground which had been 'set aside other than by the revocable permission of the Owner . . . for the use and enjoyment of the Inhabitants thereof'. This act was based on the earlier Kensington Square Improvement Act (1851), which had come about as a direct result of the inhabitants' dissatisfaction with the vestry's inadequacy in dealing with problems of footpaths and lighting. In both cases, the acts made it possible for a garden square to be placed under the management of a committee of residents, irrespective of the ownership of the central enclosure. The future management and maintenance then became the responsibility of the garden committee, which agreed annually the sum of money required to maintain the garden.

Under the 1851 act, for example, the corporate authority collected (as the local authority does to this day) the garden rate, which it redistributed to the garden committee.

Although the 1863 act of parliament had doubtless been formed with Leicester Square in mind, the 'prolix, complicated, and confused' wording of the legislation, combined with the complex legal status of ownership of the ground, and the fact that Leicester Square had never been irrevocably dedicated by its owners to the use of the inhabitants or the public, meant that the act did not apply.[78] Further wrangling thus ensued, and the square's condition continued to deteriorate: the equestrian statue – the 'one time pride and delight of Londoners', which for so long had been treated with 'treasonable familiarity' – was sold, and a 12-foot high hoarding was thrown up around the garden for the display of advertising placards (fig. 167).[79] Only in 1873 did the tide finally begin to turn, when Henry Webb, the long-time resident and tireless campaigner for the restoration of the garden, successfully filed a bill of complaint in Chancery. The Master of the Rolls resolved that the square's owners were not at liberty to use the ground for any other purpose except as a garden; he also prohibited the erection of any building on the ground, or of any fence around it other than a stone kerb surmounted by an iron railing. This ruling not only paved the way for the reform of Leicester Square, it also established a legal

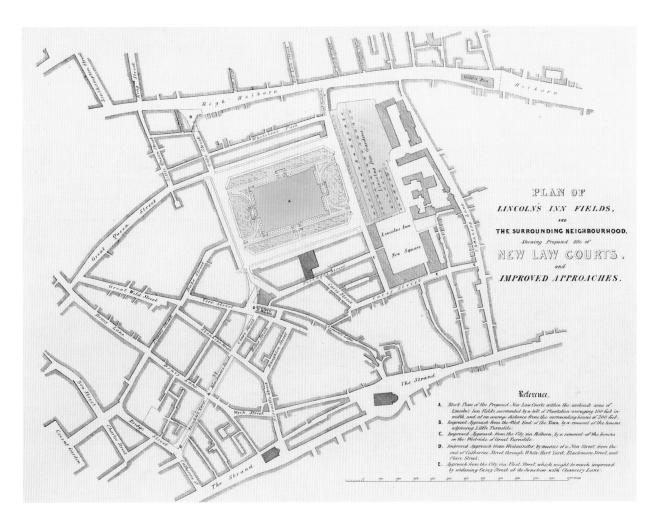

169 Unknown draughtsman, *Plan of Lincoln's Inn Fields, and the Surrounding Neighbourhood, Shewing Proposed Site of New Law Courts, and Improved Approaches, c.*1840, hand-coloured lithograph. British Museum, London.

precedent for the protection of similar open spaces across the country.[80]

In 1874 the ground was acquired by the wealthy entrepreneur and notorious fraudster Baron Grant, whose explicit motive was to lay it out as a 'people's garden' to be handed over to the Board of Works as 'a gift to the Metropolis'. What appeared to be a magnanimous gesture was, in fact, nothing less than a vehicle to win popular support. The redesign of the square was entrusted by Grant to the architect James Thomas Knowles, and the scheme was built at the former's expense. The new ornamental garden, which opened to the public in July of the same year, was created in collaboration with the landscape gardener John Gibson junior, the plan calling for broad paths, flower-beds, statuary and a white marble fountain surmounted by a statue of Shakespeare by Signor Fontana after the eighteenth-century effigy by Peter Scheemakers. In addition, four white marble busts were raised on pedestals in the angles of the enclosure to commemorate famous former denizens of the square – Sir Joshua Reynolds, William Hogarth, Sir Isaac Newton and John Hunter (fig. 168).

The public reaction to the new 'people's garden' was mixed. For some, the 'glorified inclosure, with its busts and fountains' was to be censured for being too much 'cut up', and its layout and planting unimaginative. It was likewise condemned for failing to 'regenerate the Leicester Square that most of us remember', as it became little more than a 'playground for dirty children'.[81] The prevailing view, however, was favourable: indeed, the garden renewed interest in the history and condition of garden enclosures throughout the metropolis (some of which, it was hoped, would be regenerated after the manner of their 'fellow in old Leicester Fields').[82] And it was a victory for those who had been campaigning hard since the early 1840s to protect the square and similar open spaces and gardens – and particularly Lincoln's Inn Fields and Gray's Inn – from building encroachments and redevelopment (fig. 169).[83]

163

What was also undeniable was that Leicester Square's 'swept and garnished' enclosure was a 'boon to the district', especially in light of 'the number of people to be seen in Leicester Square . . . [who] show how glad people are of a seat in the open air'.[84] A contributor to *Chambers's Journal of Popular Literature, Science and Arts* was full of praise, remarking in 1874 that 'what has been so tastefully effected for Leicester Square, is eminently suggestive of transformations in some other squares in London'. Here he presumably was referring to 'experimental open gardens' created in the early 1870s at Ebury Square and Lower Grosvenor Gardens, in neither of which had 'things gone to wreck; on the contrary, considerable care is expended in keeping the inclosures in good order'.[85]

Writing in *Macmillan's Magazine* in 1875, the social reformer Octavia Hill exclaimed that 'a few Baron Grants are wanted!' She likewise appealed to the key-holders of the city's 'sternly secluded' gardens to make them occasionally accessible to the public, and 'lay them out as "people's pleasure-grounds"': 'let them, our small open places, look well cared for. If they are not large enough to be opened to the public without limit, open them under restrictions, lend the key to district-visitors, to the schoolmistress, to the clergyman, to the biblewoman, let them take in small companies of the poorest by turns. But make the most of what small spaces you have, do not close them wholly because you cannot open them wholly'.[86]

Despite such praise and enthusiasm, however, the transformation of Leicester Square from an exclusive pleasure ground to a public square – that is a garden with 'unrestricted dedication to public use' – did not usher in immediate changes to the access or management of other 'moping melancholy' places. The celebrated horticulturist William Robinson, who from 1869 played a leading role in the reform of the London square, declared at the time: 'private interest and public prejudice' were against the 'opening of our squares to the public now, and may long continue so'.[87] It nevertheless remained the earnest desire of some reformers that many of the city's enclosed private gardens might some day become more publicly accessible, or be transformed into 'playing places with crowds of happy children on fine days'.[88]

The Proposed Reform of our 'Painful Mementoes of Exclusiveness'

Reform of London squares, it should be noted, was not merely a parochial interest. As William Church would remind Londoners, a foreign visitor, in this case from Paris, knew whereof he spoke: 'Armed with a huge umbrella and a *Guide de Londres*, he finds his way at once to Leicester Square, in obedience to a mysterious but undeviating law. In Paris, London is celebrated for its squares. If you say "How beautiful they are, the Boulevards!" the polite Parisian responds, "Ah, mon Dieu, but we have them not, your squares."'[89]

Henry B. Wheatley was also to declare, in his review of *Leicester Square: Its Associations and its Worthies* (1874) published in *The Academy*, that 'the inhabitants of London have reason to be proud of their parks and squares, where they can occasionally turn their eyes from dusty bricks to refresh them with the sight of trees and grass. Napoleon III thought so when he introduced the London square into Paris, and now Baron Albert Grant presents us with a Parisian adaptation of the original English model.' It was perhaps not inappropriate, he noted, that the 'French quarter of London should have a slice of Paris set down in its midst.'[90]

By a curious irony, only apparent today, much of the impetus to reform the character of the London squares in the nineteenth century emanated from the French capital. Between 1829 and 1839 the French public health reformer Adolphe Trébuchet endeavoured to put in place a programme of social and structural reforms in Paris, which would 'see established in the centre of every quarter of the town a spacious square, railed in, and planted with trees, in which the children of all classes might, without apprehension, and without the special superintendence of their parents, give themselves up to the exercise suitable to their years, and in which the inhabitants of all ages might enjoy the solar influence, and breathe a purer air than in their dwellings'.[91] England, too – a fact often forgotten – had launched a comparable initiative: a Select Committee for Public Walks was appointed to 1833 to consider the best means of securing open spaces in the vicinity of London and other populous towns as 'Public Walks and Places of Exercise, calculated to promote the Health and Comfort of the Inhabitants'. Such a

In the Square des Batignolles.

committee could, however, only recommend potential open spaces that, in its view, needed to be protected for public recreation, and the places they identified were those where the 'humbler classes have been in the habit of visiting with their families in fine weather'.[92] This initiative ultimately led to the creation and protection of commons, parks and public walks, and yet it had at the time no bearing on the metropolitan squares in London or elsewhere. In France, on the other hand, Trébuchet's recommendations resulted in the creation of a network of new 'squares' in the heart of Paris (fig. 170).

Among early respondents to such French innovation, the Reverend Thomas Milner championed the 'commendable' Parisian initiative in his book *The Elevation of the People, Moral, Instructional and Social* (1846), campaigning for the provision of similar spaces in London for improvements to the comfort, health and moral welfare of the metropolitan poor. The streets and squares of London, he remarked, 'present us with large and stately temples erected for the occupation of congregations some three or four hours per week; but what a contrast frequently in the immediate neighbourhood! Many thousands of permanently occupied dwellings, crammed with men, women, and children, where none of the decencies of life can be observed . . . [mean that] luxury and wretchedness – decency and demoralisation – lie upon the borders of each other; and yet the inhabitants of these territories are as practically unacquainted with their respective domains as if the Atlantic rolled between them.'[93]

In the event, it was not until the early 1860s that a square along the lines of the Parisian model was built in London – and then not in the West End, but in Bethnal Green, where, according to the Reverend Isaac Taylor, writing in 1867, 'between 6,000 and 7,000 human beings are thickly crowded together in poverty and squalor' into an area 'considerably less than that of Russell or of Belgrave square'.[94] Dickens announced in *All the Year Round* in June 1862 that 'in one of the remotest and most impoverished parts of the remote and impoverished districts known generically as Bethnal-green, there exists a certain piece of ground, which together with the buildings that stand upon it, goes by the name of Columbia-square'. The square was a 'substantial oasis of comfort and luxury' that emerged from a tangle of 'sordid wretched alleys'. He referred to a modest and dignified paved square surrounded by model tenements that had just been raised by the philanthropist Angela Burdett-Coutts.[95]

The square was built on the site of Nova Scotia Gardens, a notorious rookery in the East End, which was described by the Medical Officer's report of 1856 as 'pestiferous' with 'mountains of house refuse, road mud, offal and filth'.[96] The 'Nova Scotian proposals' had been commissioned from the architect Philip Hardwick, and had been sent to Dickens for comment, who in turn advised Burdett-Coutts that the 'noble design' would benefit from being shown to Thomas Southwood Smith, MD, of the General Board of Health, and Henry Austin, consulting engineer to the same body, to ensure that it 'would get good sanitary arrangements on the most efficient and simple terms'.[97]

It was, Dickens affirmed, a 'happy day for that miserable district of Bethnal-green, and indirectly, no doubt, for other of the poorer London neighbourhoods, when the abject wretchedness of the inhabitants became known to one whose profound sympathy with human suffering is united in the rare ability to relieve it, and a wonderful discretion in the manner of relief'. He praised the newly completed square – the first model dwellings in London – as a 'silent testimony borne of neat convenient rooms': it improved 'the bearing of the inhabitants whose lives are altered by the self-respect which the place engenders' and was reflected in the 'wholesome faces of the children living in good air and clean and decent human habitations': 'the surrounding neighbourhood is very dwarfish in height; Columbia-square is composed of houses of considerable elevation. The surrounding neighbourhood is very dirty; Columbia-square is spotlessly clean. The surrounding neighbourhood is stuffy and close; Columbia-square is airy and open. The surrounding neighbourhood is highly flavoured as to odour; Columbia-square is as sweet (as the saying goes) as a nut.'[98]

While Columbia Square may have been praised at home as a decent enclave for the working classes in the city's East End, the French press were unimpressed: they alleged in 1861 that it was reprehensible that Londoners did not open their hundreds of existing private squares – that 'the immense and numerous squares of London . . . are rigorously shut against the working classes, and that the rich or aristocratic alone have access to them, for they are cultivated exclusively for them. When these gardens are kept for the happy and privileged few there is much loss of health, morality, and recreation to the people. The square of Lincoln's Inn Fields, six times larger than our Square du Temple, is fresh, blooming, and deserted. The rich, however, disdain it; and the poor can only look into it.'[99]

This opinion prompted a sharp riposte from the editor of *Punch*. Although he cordially concurred with the spirit of the Frenchman's remarks, so far as they advocated opening as many gardens as possible to the people of London, he protested that he was plainly ignorant of the details. There was 'nothing in Paris', he said, 'to equal either in beauty or extent, the series of parks which are open to our people', in light of which London squares are 'simply the private gardens of the houses around, which have no gardens attached to them, and therefore the compensation is given in the area, and it would be as reasonable to ask any dweller in a snug villa to throw his garden gate open, as to claim the squares for others than the house-owners'.[100]

While Mr Punch's antipathy to Parisian gardens may have been current in the early 1860s, by the end of the decade there had been a considerable shift in English public opinion in favour of things French, including the role both of gardens and of open spaces in public health and social reform.[101] For instance, the landscape gardener Alexander McKenzie, writing in *The Parks, Open Spaces and Thoroughfares of London* (1869), devoted considerable attention to the 'best modes of improving the British Metropolis, with a view, first, to the health of its dense population, and next, in order to render it somewhat more worthy of comparison with that of France than it is at present'.[102] He advocated that the English legislature could

> confer no greater benefit on the metropolis than by the abolition of all private rights in London Squares, the use of which is at present restricted to nurserymaids employed by the residents in the houses built round them, and the children under their charge, a rigid lock and an almost exclusive key prohibiting the admission of hundreds of the poor who are always to be found in close proximity to these jealously protected gardens. Lincoln's Inn Fields, Russell Square, Grosvenor Square, and a host of others might with the greatest possible advantage be dedicated to the public.[103]

At the same time, a far more significant writer, William Robinson, had also become fervently Francophile, contending that 'we may learn from the French,' and remarking in *The Parks, Promenades and Gardens of Paris* (1869; 2nd ed., 1878) that Parisian squares were 'far in advance' of our own 'in every way'. Although 'it may be noted that the idea was first taken from London . . . while we Londoners still persist in keeping the squares exclusively for the few overlooking residents, and usually without a trace of any but the poorest plant ornament, the French make them as open as our parks, and decorate them with a charming variety of trees and plants' (fig. 171).[104]

Robinson's expansive views were informed by those of Adolphe Alphand in *Les promenades de Paris* (1867–73) and by the 'judicious' remarks of the Parisian resident Mr Robert Mitchell.[105] Mitchell, who was editor of the journal *Constitutionnel* during the Second Empire, alleged that while the English once carried 'material civilization further than we have', and London had long surpassed Paris in many ways, recent improvements to the French metropolis meant that the latter was now a happier, healthier and more spacious place than its English counterpart: 'Paris need envy London for nothing'.[106] The English, he quipped, 'invent for the sake of privilege, and . . . when their ideas are good we take advantage of them and popularize them'. He cited a single example:

Every one knows how justly the English pride themselves on their gardens called squares, which are the admiration of every foreigner. Our unfortunate public places that a pedestrian cannot cross in summer without being grilled by the sun or blinded by the dust only serve as examples of our inferiority in this respect. The square, that is to say, a little park surrounded by a railing, is the representation at once of a question of health, a question of morality, and perhaps even of national self-respect. We certainly could boast the Place Royale, which, however, much more closely resembled an unsuccessful attempt than the first step in a happy way. At present, however, Paris need envy London for nothing. The squares of St Jacques, La Boucherie, St Clothilde, the Temple, Louvois, des Arts et Métiers, and the Parc Monceau are worthy of our city. These masses of vegetation widely distributed amongst the most populous neighbourhoods, cleanse the air by absorbing miasmatic exhalations, thus enabling everyone to breathe freely.[107]

In tandem with such trenchant remarks, Robinson now declared that 'it would perhaps be difficult to find a greater contrast than that presented by the London and the Paris squares, both as regards their arrangement and management'.[108] Most people were, he affirmed, 'familiar enough with the aspects of squares in London, their ill-keeping, melancholy and deserted air, well though the scraggy hedges of miserable Privet conceal their interior. Indeed they are so carefully locked up that of them might well be written the motto, "Thieves without and nothing to steal within"' (fig. 172). The squares in Paris were, on the other hand, he noted, run on a 'very different system', which was 'infinitely superior to ours': they were open to the public. The 'establishment of public squares in Paris' was, moreover, 'an eminently social idea'.[109]

As an Irish-born gardener, Robinson came to write his horticultural treatise as a result of his protracted travels in France, where for seven months he had studied horticultural practices and visited gardens and nurseries, and had attended the Exposition Universelle in Paris. A belligerent and capricious character with strongly held, sometimes contradictory views, he made his name through the publication of a series of influential books, including *The Wild Garden* (1870), *The Subtropical Garden* (1871) and, most famously, *The English Flower Garden* (1883).

" *Thieves without and nothing to steal within.*"
Margin of a London Square, with Edge of Plantation designed to cut off the View (Park Crescent).

Haussmann, who laid out the city's new architectural framework, and Adolphe Alphand, who resolved the formidable technical problems of creating the new pleasure grounds.[111]

Robinson, who was quick to recognise the value of such ideas, also promoted the benefits of rational recreation, proposing that the ideal square was one that was open to the public and possessed 'wide walks thronged by people' – a place that should be as 'attractive to the passer-by as to those inside'.[112]

What bright refreshing spots would these be in the midst of our huge brick and stone labyrinths, if we saw them crowded on summer evenings with tradespeople and mechanics from the neighbouring streets, and if the poor children who now grow up amid the filth and impurities of the alleys and courts, were allowed to run about these playgrounds, so much healthier both for the body and the mind! We have them all ready, a word may open them. At present the gardens in our squares are painful mementoes of exclusiveness. They who need them the least monopolize them. All the fences and walls by which this exclusiveness bars itself out from the sympathies of common humanity must be cast down.[113]

That the 'High Priest of English flower gardening' alighted on the London square as an object of study, and that he chose to compare it with its Parisian counterparts, is for us fortuitous, but also demands an explanation. Robinson, like many well-travelled Englishmen at the time, was enthralled by Napoleon III's rebuilding of Paris – that is, by the dramatic transformation of a then largely medieval city into a well-ordered metropolis to meet the demands of modern commerce and transportation. One of the great benefits conferred by such an energetic project was the creation of an abundance of small garden spaces, dotted throughout the densely settled quarters of town.[110] The originator of this legacy was the romantic, impulsive and unashamedly Anglophile French emperor, who had *illusions généreuses* about the positive effects that parks and gardens had on the morals and customs of the working classes, and held that access to sunshine and fresh air was a means of preventing the spread of epidemic disease in crowded cities. In the event it was his prefect, Georges-Eugène, Baron

Robinson further advocated that no system of city gardening 'can be good' that does not provide playgrounds for children: 'it is not good enough to have open spaces or beautiful little gardens; we should keep the children from the filth and dangers of the crowded streets. The best way, in the case of large cities, is to have, as far as possible, squares or open spaces arranged as playgrounds alone . . . The smaller class of square would do best as playgrounds . . . The only requirements are hardy trees, gravelled spaces and seats . . . Of course garden-squares are needed as well as playing-squares; but in most districts the playground is the greater want' (fig. 173).[114]

Robinson also persisted in a wish to see the central garden more integrated with its immediate surroundings, so that clumps of 'shrubs of commonplace character cutting it off from view' would be replaced by belts of grass 'of varying width, kept perfectly fresh and green', and on them 'here and there large beds and groups usually distinct from each other'. London squares, he affirmed, lacked the

173 Unknown artist, *Scene in Leicester Square, Illustrated London News*, 10 February 1872. Private collection. Groups of juveniles, for want of proper playgrounds, sometimes congregated in the city's open squares, where they took pleasure in tormenting the square-keepers.

'profuse variety of the very best shrubs', the sparkle, colour and glistening verdure of their Parisian counterparts. The squares of Paris possessed ruins, and exotic and alpine plants.[115]

Quoting his Parisian friend Robert Mitchell, Robinson reports that the 'Parisian Aediles' formed squares 'wherever a too-crowded population threatened to contaminate the atmosphere, and in all the parts of the city farthest from the Tuileries, the Luxembourg, or the Bois de Boulogne, so that those living in the neighbourhood might be able to get to them easily'; the squares in London, however, were found, with few exceptions, in the 'rich and open neighbourhoods' such as in the 'West-End in Belgravia, or at Brompton, that is to say, at the very gates of Hyde Park'.[116] He emphasised that 'it can hardly be necessary to point out the benefits a square confers on the district immediately around it. All, or nearly all, our present expenditure for public gardening is on the vast parks of which London is happily the possessor. As, however, many of the parks are separated by miles from each other, the squares or any open space is of the highest importance. Parks for play and exercise, and garden scenery, let us have by all means; but our great want is the smaller open spaces called squares, and wide roads planted with trees.'[117]

The reality of the day, however, was a different matter. According to Mitchell, London squares were 'useless, and nearly always deserted' (fig. 174). 'In London the squares are private property with which the state cannot meddle. With us, on the contrary, it is the Government that takes the initiative in these municipal improvements. It is to the city of Paris that we owe their construction; they have cost a great deal, and the idea has to be yet further carried out.'[118]

Despite his quibbles over the London squares, Robinson was prescient in his conclusion: 'Whatever the condition of the squares of London now, we should be thankful that we have them. The haunts of disease are weakened by these islets in our desert of slate, brick, and mud. In them the sun shines – dimly, no doubt from our smoke-plague – the air seems to attain a little more freedom, and trees persist in growing, no matter how badly they are treated.' That there were many squares in London was fortunate, but their number was 'assuredly not half so many as its colossal expanse requires. In the suburbs, unhappily, they do not seem fashionable with the cheap builders nowadays.' He then concluded with an idyllic dream:

if matters were arranged as in Paris, the square and the wide airy road would be laid down well before the builder came to arrange the ground as seemed best to him. There they say to him: Here you may build, but do not encroach on the space necessary for public convenience; and thus avoid the tortuous close, and often dirty suburban roads which tend to make many districts round London unvisited by and unknown to all but their inhabitants. A broad and pleasant tree-planted road through such a district would, by opening it up and making it attractive to the inhabitants of London generally, prove as beneficial from a commercial as from a sanitary and aesthetic point of view. And if such roads as convenience and good taste demand existed in a city the size of London, squares would be of less importance. Our Thames Embankment, for example, is better than a score of squares.[119]

174 The Swedish Lutheran Church in Swedenborg Square, 1908, photograph. London Metropolitan Archives. Some squares were condemned for being so deserted that they were described as enclosures 'where only ghosts walk'.

Robinson's words did not fall on deaf ears: they were to galvanise the improvement of countless small gardens across the metropolis; and his view, which he shared with, among others, the London Recreational and Playground Society, that small paved courts and squares could form much needed playgrounds for children of all classes, doubtless encouraged the creation of a great number of working-class gravelled, and later tarmac-surfaced, squares in model housing developments.[120]

'A Struggle between Privet and Lilac'

The Parisian experiment notwithstanding, London's existing squares remained a *fait accompli*, though not to everyone's liking (fig. 175). As a writer in the *Gardeners' Chronicle* noted in 1877: 'A London square, viewed as an example of gardening, may, as a rule, be set down, in general terms, as one of the worst examples of taste and unfitness – to say nothing of

ugliness – that could possibly be found . . . Very few indeed of them fulfil their requirements in even a moderate degree. Too often they are altogether unsightly in their aspect; and the very best examples frequently lack most of the essential requirements of such gardens in such situations.'[121]

There was from the late 1860s considerable debate as to what, in fact, would be the proper expression for square gardens – the arguments often rife with recommendations for their improvement. This controversy was to a large extent fuelled by Robinson's reports published in the popular garden press. While many London squares were, in his opinion, at best 'small dark grimy', or 'badly kept, and unworthy of London',[122] there were some in which the views were 'almost Arcadian in their beauty'. Yet, except from the windows of the houses that surrounded them, passers-by could see 'nothing but a struggle between Privet and Lilac'. Robinson cited the example of Brunswick Square, where 'two of the finest

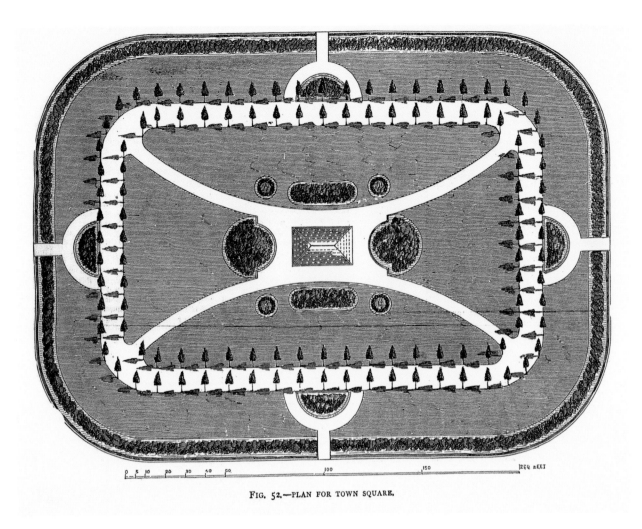

175 Unknown draughtsman, *Plan for Town Square*, engraving, from *Gardeners' Chronicle*, 10 March 1877. Private collection. The layout of the typical London square was condemned by a number of critics who did not enjoy access to the gardens as perpetuating a 'sense of dreariness and seclusion which would not be tolerated by public opinion in any other capital in Europe'.

FIG. 52.—PLAN FOR TOWN SQUARE.

weeping Ash-trees in London are near the margin . . . but they are so surrounded by the usual mean scrub that they are barely recognized by the passer-by'. He recommended that, 'cleared around and surrounded by well-kept turf, they would prove ornaments to the whole district. But it may be urged that the squares are private property, and that their owners have a perfect right to keep them shut out from public view, if so disposed. Even so, it is quite possible to do this without making the margin inviting as a receptacle for miscellaneous rubbish, and without concealing the finest objects the squares contain' (fig. 176).[123]

Robinson proposed various simple measures to improve the beauty and utility of the city's squares both for the inhabitants and visitors to them. He took particular exception to the 'filthy and crowded marginal shrubbery' common to 'nearly all the enclosures': 'by allowing the grass to venture near the railing here and there, and dotting it with flowers, isolated shrubs, so as to permit pleasant peeps into the interior, quite a new aspect would be given to many of our now gloomy squares, and the change would by no means destroy privacy. No conceivable harm could come of making these little gardens attractive to the public, and in doing so, to those having "vested rights" also.'[124] Another contemporary writer, too, was dismayed by the boundary treatment of the squares, particularly their 'towering' hogged or clipped privet hedges, which were 'thick and impervious at top, scrubbed and straggling at bottom, concealing the view from the opposite causeway; and . . . revealing the less pleasing portions of the inclosure'.[125] 'Hedges', he proclaimed, 'ought to be uniform; but the screen close to the boundary must always conceal that growth of grass, flower, or shrub, which as viewed from either footways or houses, ought to present that which is pleasing at all seasons – the free growth of neat, well-turfed, and ornate lawn'.[126]

176 Adolphe-François
Pannemaker, *A Town Square
Opened Up*, engraving,
published in William
Robinson, *The Parks,
Promenades and Gardens of
Paris* (1869). Royal
Horticultural Society, Lindley
Library, London.

Robinson, like some of his contemporaries, also took issue with the disposition of the central portion, and particularly the fashion for raising arbours or covered seats within them – 'most of which have no pretension to ornament' or were 'decidedly ugly' (fig. 177).[127] Here, he argued, the ground is

usually so small that it is desirable to make the most of it. The best way to make it look mean and contracted is to build a structure varying in appearance from a wooden fowl-house to a bathing machine. Yet this is what is done in the

majority of the 'best' London squares. The eye is thus fixed on the contemptible objects in the centre, an agreeable spread of turf is made impossible, and the beauty of the trees or shrubs cannot be felt. It is unwise to desire uniformity in any art, but one principle deserves to be engraved on the mind of every person who has the care of squares, which is that the best way to obtain an excellent effect is by keeping the centre open and grassy, untortured by walks, hedges, or beds.[128]

The walks in London's squares were, Robinson affirmed, among their least attractive elements, as they were 'generally designed so as to cut through and destroy the prettiest spots in the square'. They were also disfigured by 'ugly, high and elaborate seats piled round the bases of the beautiful trees so as to cut short the effect of their stems as seen across the lawn'. He recommended that 'all the necessary seats, as well as tool-houses, and arbours, should be placed near or towards the sides, where they would be useful without being obtrusive. It is quite easy to so place such objectionable features that while convenient for shade and comfort, they shall not be objectionable from any point of view'.[129]

177 Adolphe-François
Pannemaker, *Structure in* [the]
Centre of a London Square,
engraving, published in
William Robinson, *The Parks,
Promenades and Gardens of Paris*
(1869). Royal Horticultural
Society, Lindley Library,
London.

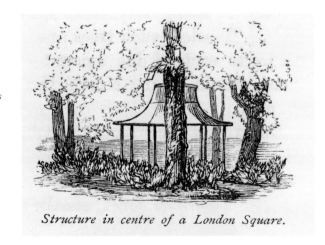

Structure in centre of a London Square.

178 A. Sargent, after
Adolphe-François Pannemaker,
*Streamlet in Paris Square with
Yuccas and Water-side Plants*,
engraving, published in
William Robinson, *The Parks
and Gardens of Paris* (1878).
Royal Horticultural Society,
Lindley Library, London.

Robinson, who was a great advocate of a natural style of gardening using hardy plants, was particularly critical of the planting of London squares, which he condemned as 'particularly lugubrious' and 'of a style quite apart': 'Hardy shrubs are not made a study of, and the bedding plants with which the country is ablaze in many parts are rarely seen [fig. 178]. Year after year the same tone of slimy melancholy is assiduously preserved. The trees crowd upon each other, and even those that tower above all, and assert their dignity in spite of their neglect, are not seen to advantage. Any flowers planted usually perish in the dismal shade.'[130]

Here Robinson's views were very similar to those put forward in articles published a few years earlier in *The Builder*. In November 1861, for example, one contributor had opined rather gently, that:

notwithstanding the beauty and general aspect of the London squares, the skilful arrangement and picturesque arrangement of the trees . . . it is clear that very great improvements may be made; particularly in spring, summer and autumn displays of flowers, and flowering plants; and in the winter, of a variety of evergreens. This could be attended with some expense; but we think that if the advantages and pleasures which would result

from this were taken properly into consideration, and a spirit of rivalry raised between the beauty of one square and another, there could be found no difficulty in this point.[131]

The author of 'Places, Squares and Trees of London' (1863) was sharper in his criticism of the 'wretched examples . . . of hortulan taste' that prevailed in some of the city's open spaces, and the squares in particular. He railed against the taste for vast gravelled areas in the central enclosures and the 'varicoloured walks or volutes to vie with the Persian shawls hung in the opposite shop windows', arguing that 'the repose of a well mixed plantation with a dozen plane trees, of ten years growth, would please the eye more, and might soon afford refreshing shade as well as ornament'. As to the overall improvement of squares and public gardens, 'there is much to be done, and great scope for the arborist and gardener: there is scarce one piece of intramural ground that can be called an ornamental garden; certainly nothing like the Hyde Park borders nor the flower walk of Kensington'. He concluded: 'what we want is the stately, shady, widespreading plane, the varied shrubbery, and the bed of transplanted flowers: these, with an emerald turf, and rich sanded walks, are all that can be desired to make [a square's] English garden a place of repose and of solace'.[132]

Comparison with London parks also drew the interest of yet another contributor to *The Builder*, writing in August 1864, who found a distressing contrast between the royal parks and the squares, observing that while the former were filled with 'glowing flower-borders and other "magical attractions", the latter were generally "most disgraceful": the same attention to planting out, cutting away redundant trees and arborage, thinning and pruning some of the bosquets, renewing others, and above all, well watering the whole, would render the railed-in spaces, dignified by the names of squares, crescents, oval and circuses, truly ornamental, as well as more cheering and healthful to our teeming and increasing population'. But, sad to say, he found the 'problem with squares' was that their inhabitants did not lavish sufficient expense in their 'horticultural embellishment'. To reflect upon the 'comparatively neglected state of nearly all the squares and open spaces' was, he said, unnecessary: one need only look to the parks for inspiration. It was, he recommended, in the interest of the inhabitants to make 'the misty depths of these urban wilds' as 'ornate as possible'. It was thus not the extent of the enclosure, but 'the care bestowed upon it that excites an interest, and there is ample scope for improvement in some of the widest and best we have'.[133]

For almost all contemporary critics, trees were generally regarded as the most redeeming feature of the London squares. Although described as being 'perhaps for eleven months of the year' rather etiolated and as 'smoke-blackened' as the surrounding houses, they were praised for making a splendid show in 'the bright May days . . . when every tree in every London Square forgets for the time being both London smoke and London fog, and clothes itself with a glorious foliage'.[134] Robinson's favourite Parisian critic, Robert Mitchell, had earlier noted that the inhabitants of the squares were 'above everything anxious about the health of the trees'.[135] Robinson, for his own part, remarked that 'in the West-Central districts are frequently seen Planes which would command admiration in their native forests. Huddled together, at first, with a number of miscellaneous trees, they, thanks to their constitutions and stature, now tower above the masses of overcrowded shrubs around them, and spread forth their boughs so freely that each tree seems as if it tried to fill up the square. When the multitudinous fires are active round them in winter, these trees give us in the dreary wastes of London a glimpse of the beauty of the wild woods'.[136]

Planes were not, however, the only trees that thrived perfectly 'even in the most smoky and crowded parts'; many others could be introduced which, if properly planted and attended to, 'would represent . . . the brake and forest beauty of every important cold region in America, Europe or Asia'. Robinson suggested that one way of encouraging 'desirable variety' would be the dedication of one square to the trees and shrubs of a particular country:

for example, one might have British trees and shrubs alone, another American trees, another Chinese and Japanese trees, and so on. It would be permanent too; and permanence in these matters simply means saving of constant trouble and expense. But there is no reason whatever why the squares should be devoted to hardy trees and shrubs alone. On the contrary, the best way would be to allow much latitude, so as to secure variety. When people begin to understand the management of city gardens, one of the first principles they will discover is that each square and small garden should differ as much as possible from its neighbours.[137]

While gardeners and aesthetes took pleasure in the manner in which the squares' trees thrived, those who viewed them purely in terms of the health of the metropolis disapproved of their success. A contributor to the *Sanitary Record* was of the opinion that the squares' 'ornamental trees' were 'overgrown so as to impede access of light to houses'.[138]

All of the aforementioned observations on planting were, it should be noted, made by 'outsiders', whose zeal to improve was quite at odds with the views of the square-dwellers. The latter, in fact, appear often to have been pleased that their gardens should convey an outward expression of unimproved rusticity. Not only was this evocation of 'country in town' an implicit aim of the inhabitants, it was intended to form a marked contrast to the surrounding houses and the cultivated gardens within the enclosures.

Although the guardians of the city's squares were accused of neglecting their enclosures, the minutes of many garden committees suggest otherwise – namely, that improvements were made on a regular basis, and that on some occasions the residents were capable of co-ordinating costly and ambitious refurbishments. The gardens were, however, generally improved piecemeal, and often evolved in an unplanned and idiosyncratic manner. Many committees were, in fact, starved of funds and relied heavily on the generosity of rich subscribers to improve their enclosures: garden ornament was supplied, plants were donated to fill gaps, and the gardeners or the contractors made do with what little was available. Critics disapproved of this ad hoc approach to gardening, where in the absence of a 'little supervision' the average enclosure became a 'receptacle for *rejectamenta* of every kind'.[139]

The squares were, in fact, generally perceived by the horticulturally minded as being inhabited and managed by deluded rustic dreamers. The ability of square-dwellers to see rusticity in what seemed to outsiders mere shabbiness is, in an extreme instance, literally defined as pathological. William Augustus Guy, in a case study in *The Factors of the Unsound Mind* (1881) describes the bizarre but perhaps telling condition of an 'amiable and gentle lady' whom he knew well, who had 'just fallen into an attack of mania'. She was, he reports, 'eager to make her escape from her bedroom which overlooked a London square; and more than once, as she looked out of [the] window, she spoke with delight of the handsome Deodara and a stream of water crossed by a bridge. She had transferred the principal ornaments of her countryside residence to the dingy London square, and saw them among the trees and railings.'[140] Were such phantasms the lot of the typical denizen of a London square? One hopes not!

Opening Squares to the Public

The thorny issue of the creation and retention of private square gardens within the metropolis gave rise to some soul-searching in the later nineteenth century: 'Sternly secluded by iron railings and locked gates, they have generally a dull look. You seldom see anyone in them. Apparently they are only used by a few nurserymaids with children. The public are shut out from their walks, or seats, or the cool shelter of the umbrageous trees. As the squares are private property, no one can justly complain that they are being so dealt with. We should trust, however, that means might be found to open up at least several of these moping melancholy squares.'[141] This debate must be seen in the context of the larger social upheavals that were taking place across the country in the mid-century, and particularly those that were fuelled by the growing public opposition to the enclosure of open space to the exclusion of the humbler classes. Up and down the land, from the late eighteenth century, people had begun to demonstrate their discontent by taking part in popular assemblies in public resorts, demanding greater access to, and preservation of, open green space.[142]

While the squares were not, in themselves, threatened with the mass invasions of people that from the mid-1850s regularly thronged Hyde Park, their inhabitants were doubtless perturbed by these popular tumults, and alarmed by the scenes of riotous demonstrators breaching the park's railings that were portrayed in the popular press (fig. 179). In the event, the assaults on the private enclosures were generally orderly and dignified affairs, and this measured approach gradually began to bear fruit, as the owners or guardians of some of the central squares were moved to open their gardens for limited periods to outsiders.

Such beneficence, however, was not the result of sudden civic-mindedness. From the late 1850s a variety of charitable institutions and religious and secular bodies began to petition the trustees of some London squares, whose enclosures were unkempt or under-utilised, for limited access to their central gardens. These appeals were motivated in part by the growth of the public parks movement, which from the 1840s had begun to foster a greater desire for universal access to open green space within close proximity of the town, but also by the surprising if unanticipated fact that some hitherto exclusive squares had begun to open their enclosures periodically to non-residents for the purpose of special events. The gardens of Lincoln's Inn Fields were, by way of a benign example, opened in November 1858 'to all respectable people' to view the gardeners' unusually fine 'Show of Chrysanthemums'.[143]

The success of such flower shows (fig. 180) doubtless galvanised the Secretary of the Playgrounds and General Recreation Society to approach the Trustees of Lincoln's Inn Fields to seek permission for children of the neighbourhood to play in the central garden for two or three hours 'of an Evening'. Although access was on this occasion denied, the trustees' refusal did not preclude others from trying their luck. Further petitions followed in the ensuing years, lodged by the St Giles District Board of Works and the West Central Day Industrial School, as well as a handful of local non-keyholding residents. These applications, too, were politely refused.[144] The vestrymen of St Giles were particularly vexed by the trustees' rebuff; they had hoped to persuade them to follow the example set by the Benchers of the Temple and Gray's Inn. The Inns of Court had recently begun to open their gardens, and had, in fact, even gone so far as to adapt their private pleasure grounds 'for the benefit of numerous infirm aged and sickly people of the Parish of St Clements Danes who resort to that open space for the sunshine & comparatively pure air'.[145] The Clerk of the Board of Works argued that, as the social character of the Fields had changed very considerably since the act that enabled 'the present and future Proprie-

tors and Inhabitants of the Houses in *Lincoln's Inn Fields* . . . to make a Rate on themselves for raising money sufficient to inclose, clean and adorn the said Fields' was passed in 1735: 'then, each Mansion in [the Fields] as well as those in the immediate neighbourhood was occupied by affluent and important families . . . now, out of 67 Houses a few only are

inhabited by families'. He hoped that he could rely upon the trustees' 'enlightened convictions of the necessity of moving in the Spirit of the Age, in complying with a want which is admitted by all parties, whether in our houses of Legislature or among that large and intelligent section of our Countrymen who are doing all they can to mitigate the evils incident to our overgrown Metropolis, in ameliorating the condition of our very great, poor, and pent-up populations, and which the use of such open Spaces cannot fail to effect'.[146]

Finally, in May 1874 the trustees relented, permitting Octavia Hill to escort a company of children from Drury Lane into the garden on a Saturday afternoon (fig. 181). In the event, the 'treat in the garden' at Lincoln's Inn Fields passed without incident, and this 'well-supervised' event was repeated over the following few years (the children were, however, forbidden from playing 'Cricket, Football, Rounders, Trap-bat & ball and any other game of Ball & Kite Flying').[147] The success of these days encouraged the trustees to 'experiment' further, and

also possibly persuaded them to improve the condition of the 'mangy jungles' of their enclosure:[148] in late spring 1877 they admitted a group of boys from the National Refuge for Homeless and Destitute Boys in Great Queen Street to use the gardens for exercise, although games and 'riotous behaviour' were banned. The Fields were, however, not wholly open to the public until 1895.

While most of Hill's energies were devoted to fighting campaigns for the renewal of disused urban burial-grounds as public open space, and for rights of access to common land, she also appreciated 'the value of land in any central position'. Hill identified the private squares as important open spaces for the recreation of the poor – places in which they could pursue 'happy outdoor amusements' without effort or expense, which lay within a short distance from their homes. Hill pronounced that the only harm that could be done to a square, were it 'lent' by the inhabitants for a 'Saturday afternoon at the end of the season to the poor of their own district for a flower-show' would be that the grass 'were trampled quite brown'.[149]

In such arrangements, Hill referred to the parochial flower shows organised for, and exhibiting plants belonging to, the working classes, which had begun to be staged in some of the Bloomsbury squares from the early 1860s (fig. 182).[150] The shows there were the brainchild of the Reverend Samuel Hadden Parkes, the senior curate at St George's Bloomsbury, and were run by the clergy, aided by better-off local residents and eventually by the aristocracy, who set the rules, managed the events, and provided and awarded the prizes. Although promoted by persons connected with religious communities, the events were 'done in a manner wholly untainted by sectarianism', and were described at the time as part of the 'cheerful window and clean room and comfortable fireside movement'.[151]

The aim of all such shows was quite simply to promote sensible attitudes towards the health-giving properties of fresh air and cleanliness. They were an instant success, and proved an 'inexpensive mode of giving a vast amount of pleasure to large numbers of persons'. They furthermore provided 'rational and innocent recreation' for people who would otherwise turn to the 'debasing influences of the music hall, the gin shop, or the beer house'.[152] The Bloomsbury Flower Show in Russell Square, held in July 1863, is of especial significance in terms of the history of the London square, as it was the first time that a large number of working-class people were invited into one of London's private squares. A report in the *City Press* reveals how startlingly novel this was: 'And where does the reader suppose this flower show is to be held? On the top of a house? In a stable? In the Museum Reading Room? Or in the sanded parlour of a public house? In none of these places, but in one less like[ly] than all, but most suitable for the purpose imaginable. The inhabitants of Russell-square have consented to allow the exhibition in their garden, which sounds as if the end of the world was near at hand.'[153]

Charles Dickens could hardly contain his excitement at discovering the 'glories' of the then aristocratic Russell Square when he attended the fourth annual 'Bloomsbury Bouquets' flower show in August 1864:

I should like to take any reader of this periodical, blindfold him, turn him round three times in the

garden of Russell-square, and ask him where he was. I will wager a mild amount of half-crowns that not one out of fifty shall answer correctly. You look round you far through the hanging branches of big trees, you see no signs of houses, you hear no sound of the ordinary traffic, and when Tom Cooper told me that there were frequently four or five games of croquet carried on at once on the expanse of lawn, I received the information without the least astonishment, and could, if called upon, have affirmed on oath that the place known as Holborn must be at least a hundred miles away.[154]

The garden was thronged with 'nicely dressed people', a band of volunteers played 'the inevitable Faust selections', and a big marquee was filled with a wide variety of flowers, including roses, fuchsias, geraniums, balsams, convolvulus, mignonette and dahlias. The format of the event was, in fact, loosely based on the traditional summer *fêtes champêtre*,

which were hosted by the householders of squares for their friends and neighbours.[155]

Outside the tent a police band, all the members in blue coats and oilskin-topped hats; numberless young ladies in the most delightful of summer costumes, with young gentlemen to match, behaving as the youth of both sexes do under such circumstances; numberless rich old people, bored and stupid; numberless poor old people, wondering and dazed 'which how they can wear them bonnets on the tops of their 'eads, and such rolls of 'air be'ind, good gracious!' numberless poor children; save those who were evidently exhibitors, there did not appear to be many poor people of middle age, they were mostly veterans or children, interspersed among the promenaders. And it was one of the curious sights of the day, to witness how thoroughly at home the children made themselves, and how, in blessed ignorance of childhood, they utterly ignored any deference to the powers that were. They sat in little knots under the trees, and played at being the owners of the ground; and they played at a game which culminated in the height of the fashionable promenade.[156]

The show was, according to Dickens, self-supporting, and attracted fifteen hundred subscribers, most of whom were 'well-to-do parishioners', and each of whom paid one shilling for admission. He was likewise impressed by the event, which clearly showed that 'the great arts of fighting against adverse circumstances, and of suffering and being strong, were practised among a certain portion of the poor with an exemplary patience worthy of emulation'.[157]

Open Squares and Open Spaces

The experiment of opening squares on a limited basis for public access received a significant boost when in 1872 Hugh Lupus Grosvenor, Marquess (later first Duke) of Westminster, contacted St George's Vestry with a view to converting Ebury Square into a public garden.[158] The enclosure, which had been laid out on the Grosvenor Estate in Pimlico in the 1820s, had, as reported in the local press, 'for some time shown a tendency to follow the downward path of Leicester-square, and had been allowed to fall into such a state of neglect as to become an eyesore to the neighbourhood'.[159] It was the peer's wish, as the landowner and a keen town planner, to 'give the public the benefit of the ground', and to try the experiment of an 'entirely open square in London' – without railings – in imitation of gardens on the continent.[160] The estate agreed to lay out and plant the garden on condition that the vestry provided for the proper 'control and management of the gardens for the use of the public'. The vestry, however, expressed concern that 'we had not quite arrived at the time to appreciate the continental management of such places and that in the present case it would be necessary for railings to be put up and a keeper appointed to look after the place'. In the event, the marquess's original 'liberal' proposal was carried out as intended for the benefit of the residents of Pimlico, and the railed garden was thrown open to its 'juvenile possessors' for annual summer parties in August 1872.[161] The Metropolitan

Board of Works subsequently took on the 'ornamental garden' and opened it to the public on a regular basis, but not until 1884.

Although 'opening the squares' was a sensible and humane suggestion, the residents of many squares objected to this so-called 'mania'.[162] A contributor to *The Graphic* remarked in 1870 that although, on 'general grounds', the public 'ought to have a right to be admitted to these places . . . the residents perhaps have some right to be considered', as opening the gardens to the public is 'apt to prove a nuisance by its social development so near your home'.[163] Another contributor in 1874 doubted whether 'the wholesale conversion of square gardens to public use is either politic or necessary. It may be imagined that the inhabitants of Grosvenor, Belgrave, and Berkeley Squares – to say nothing of those of Bedford, Russell, and Fitzroy – would scarcely view a project for their annexation to the public parks with any violent demonstrations of delight. Public gardens are excellent things, but private rights certainly merit a little consideration.'[164]

As the Duke of Westminster was a reforming landlord, he had a different point of view. He was aided in the transformation of Ebury Square by his friend Reginald, Lord Brabazon. Brabazon (later twelfth Earl of Meath),[165] who founded and became first chairman of the Metropolitan Public Garden, Boulevard and Playground Association (subsequently the MPGA, or Metropolitan Public Gardens Association), assisted the duke in arranging the leasing of Ebury Square to the association of Ebury Square in Pimlico at a peppercorn rent, on condition that the latter undertook to maintain 'this recreation ground [which] is highly prized by the inhabitants of this neighbourhood' (fig. 183).

Under the aegis of Brabazon, the MPGA was founded in 1882 with a view to protecting, preserving, safeguarding and acquiring for public use, disused burial-grounds, churchyards, open spaces, areas of land likely to be used for building purposes, strips of land adjoining footpaths and land situated within what was then known as the Metropolitan Police District Audits vicinity. The association's aims were supported by the provisions of the Open Spaces Act of 1881, which gave full power to the owners and trustees of squares to transfer such spaces either to the local vestry, the local Board of Works, or to the Metropolitan Board of Works, the grounds to be

maintained for the use and enjoyment of the public,
either as playgrounds or gardens. Well-kept gardens
and children's playgrounds would, the members
advocated, 'greatly enhance the value' of surrounding property.[166] In early 1884 the association appointed Joseph Forsyth Johnson and Fanny Wilkinson
as honorary landscape gardeners to assist them with
their projects.

The refurbishment of Ebury Square garden was
among the association's earliest achievements, and its
success led to a string of similar improvements at a
number of metropolitan enclosures. In 1884 it
obtained permission to lay out as a playground Mar-
lborough Square, Chelsea; it also requested the trustees of the then 'non-residential space' of Golden
Square to permit the children who lived in the
crowded vicinity to enter the garden during certain
hours of the day. In the East End it urged the
Mercers' Company to do likewise with the 'small

and at present useless piece of ground called York-
square, Stepney'. It also asked the Trustees of St
Bartholomew's Hospital to act in a similar manner
in regard to Bartholomew's Square. In urging these
changes, Brabazon described these 'small neglected
open spaces' as eyesores to their respective neighbourhoods, 'utterly useless to the landlords', and nuisances to the inhabitants of the neighbouring
houses.[167] An editorial in *The Times* was excoriating,
reporting that the squares' gardens had been 'given
over to neglect and disorder, a thick wall of grimy
bushes happily screening from sight refuse and
abominations of all kinds'. When such gardens were
improved, it was remarked that 'for broken pots and
pans and still less sightly objects have been substituted grass plots, gravel paths, seats and playing
places, plants and flowers'.[168]

Earlier, in 1882, the MPGA had collaborated with
the Duke of Westminster, this time on a scheme that

introduced the periodic opening of Lower Grosvenor Gardens to the poor of the parish.[169] It was arranged that the erstwhile private enclosure would open to the public on a regular annual basis from 15 August to 30 September, a period when most of the inhabitants of the surrounding houses were out of town. The association placed seats in the garden and appointed a caretaker. It was reported that 'no complaints were made of the behaviour of those who frequented it, and it is much hoped that it will form a precedent for the opening during the autumnal months of similar enclosures in other parts of London'.[170] The duke later expressed his satisfaction with this initiative, which he wished to see extended to other squares on his Belgravia and Mayfair estates.[171] It was not, however, in the duke's gift to open these spaces: he required the consent of the lessees and residents, who had legal rights over the gardens.

Again, the duke's benevolence aroused the anger of some inhabitants of the squares, and none was more incensed than the writer Mary Eliza Haweis: 'as a mother', she supported the residents of the 'fashionable old "squares"' who refused to throw open their central gardens; 'high-wrought children require an outlet from the prim nursery as much as the poor children from the fever-den . . . [but] the classes cannot mix while the habits of the poor remain uncleanly'.[172] Even those who, however mildly, favoured making the squares accessible to the public believed this could only take place if there were 'adequate police surveillance'.[173]

Some objectors also denounced the MPGA's initiatives to re-present the squares, splitting the enclosures into two to form separate recreation grounds and gardens, each appointed with a standard range of ornament and planting. Making the gardens 'afresh' in the new manner, they argued, threatened to destroy their historical character. Perhaps as a spokesman for others, a correspondent to *The Graphic* regretted this modernisation, remarking in 1874 that 'it is hoped that the energy of the new brooms will not sweep away all the ancient associations of the place'.[174]

Such views did not, however, deter a handful of improving landlords, who were galvanised by the MPGA to follow the Duke of Westminster's lead. The Marquess of Northampton was particularly generous, presenting Canonbury Square to the MPGA in 1884, and Northampton and Wilmington squares to the Vestry of Clerkenwell in the mid-1880s; Lady de Saumarez surrendered the freehold of Albion Square to Hackney Vestry in 1898; and Viscount Halifax followed suit, handing over Nelson Square in Southwark to the London County Council (LCC) in 1903. The marked success that attended these and earlier experiments greatly encouraged the MPGA to pursue further projects. As early as the spring of 1885 it had launched a public appeal 'for assistance to enable it to keep pace with the demands which are being made on its resources', and to safeguard, in particular, the future of the gardens at Carlton, Trafalgar, and Albert squares in the East End, Red Lion Square in Holborn, Soho Square in Westminster, Hoxton Square in Shoreditch, Walcot, St Mary's and Trinity squares in Lambeth, and Percy Circus in Clerkenwell.[175]

While some owners were disposed to hand over their gardens to the LCC, the vestries, the borough councils or the MPGA, most also demanded financial compensation. This was both an expensive and protracted enterprise. Ford and Sidney squares in Stepney were, for instance, acquired by the LCC under the provisions of the Open Spaces Act (1877) for £13,231, and Albert Square was compulsorily purchased in 1900 by the LCC under the LCC (General Powers) Act (1900) for £10,560 (fig. 184). It was considerably cheaper, but less desirable in the long term, for the LCC or the borough councils to rent or lease gardens from their respective owners and to lay them out and maintain them at their own expense. The MPGA, in fact, did not support the purchase of squares so much as 'merely making them *ineligible* for building on fair terms'.[176]

The truth of the matter was that simply improving the aforementioned 'useless and neglected squares' was in the end a cheaper business than buying them, given that the labour involved in the renovations was generally carried out by teams of unemployed, 'able-bodied men'. In advocating this employment, reformers affirmed that such efforts afforded 'health and recreation to many aged and ailing, the sick and the young, to whom the probably even modest distance to the nearest park or garden is a positive prohibition, and to many who have not perhaps once during their lives spent even one day in that country which it is the desire of this Association to bring to their doors'.[177]

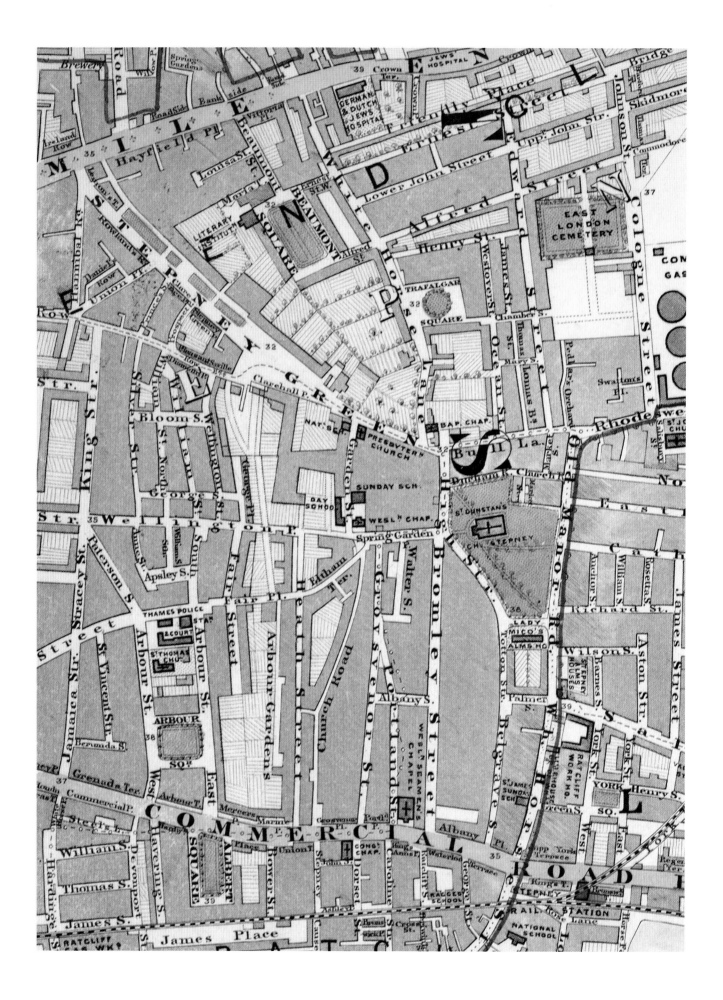

The success of one such self-starting initiative was reported in *The Times* on 30 June 1885:

Trafalgar-square, Stepney, an enclosure of only about an acre in extent situated in the midst of a dense population, was opened to the public on June 13, and was brilliantly illuminated after dark with coloured lights. The experiment succeeded perfectly. It was computed that between 1,000 and 2,000 persons entered the ground during the evening, the majority of whom had never seen anything of the sort before. Many were the expressions of delight and all appeared enchanted with the treat afforded them. Though belonging to the poorest classes, their behaviour compared most favourably with that of their wealthier brethren.[178]

The Builder was soon full of adulation for Brabazon and the MPGA for finding work for the unemployed in 'laying out afresh squares and other places which are now in a neglected state'. Such initiatives were, it reported, done with a view to creating 'permanent benefit to the community'. The same journal later trumpeted the MPGA's achievements, stating that this 'excellent society' had 'thrown open to outsiders' over 100 acres of greens, recreation grounds and the central gardens of a variety of squares from Islington to Mile End.[179]

The MPGA continued to play an important role in rescuing squares for public benefit – especially in the East End, where many were semi-derelict and threatened with redevelopment. In about 1887 they persuaded the London County Council and Shoreditch Vestry to purchase Goldsmith Square in Bethnal Green. The social investigator Charles Booth described the square shortly after its refurbishment in 1893 as 'now fairly respectable', and its enclosure as being divided into two – one half laid out as a 'new LCC playground' and the other as 'more of a garden with grass, flowerbeds & asphalt paths'.[180] The association was also instrumental in the acquisition and refurbishment of the central gardens at Albion and De Beauvoir squares, and collaborated with Octavia Hill and the Kyrle Society (whose aim was to promote the refining and cheering influences of natural and artistic beauty) on the restoration of the garden at Ion Square in Bethnal Green (fig. 185).[181] Most of these enclosures were 'rough fields,

uncared for, shut and entirely neglected' when they were acquired.[182] Albion Square was a particular disgrace, being described as 'very badly kept . . . no gates, no flowers, only mud heaps & trenches dug by the street boys who were playing in them; 40 or 50 year old trees, remnants of former care; & dilapidated iron railing round west the only things to shew it had once been cared for'.[183] Like others taken in hand and refurbished by the MPGA, the central gardens were later described as being well kept by the LCC (fig. 186).

The MPGA and the Kyrle Society were not the only bodies to project public improvements that had an impact on city squares: the Metropolitan Board of Works simultaneously pursued measures also aimed at making some of the hitherto gated precincts more accessible to the public. The board's overall objective was to remove physical barriers, wherever found, that impeded or obstructed pedestrian and vehicular traffic from freely entering squares (fig. 187). In pursuit of similar ends, amendments were made to the Metropolis Management and Buildings Act in 1882, which authorised the Board of Works to remove toll gates, bars, rails, posts and other 'obstructions' in certain parts of the metropolis, and Belgravia and Bloomsbury in particular. Although there was nothing to prevent even the Duke of Bedford – whose squares possessed a number of bars – from restricting vehicular access to his estate, it was now argued that such a practice had no place in London in the late nineteenth century: 'the restriction might have been right and proper originally, when the Bedford Estate was on the outskirts of London, but now that a large part of the metropolis lay north of the New-road the bars and gates caused great inconvenience, and their maintenance was an extreme assertion of the rights of property'.[184]

A natural and not wholly unexpected consequence of opening the squares to the public was that they became, like Trafalgar and Leicester squares and Clerkenwell Green, popular places for public assembly. No sooner had Ebury and Hoxton squares been re-landscaped and thrown open than they were used as rallying points for demonstrators on their way to an Irish Republican 'Monster Amnesty Meeting' in Central London. On 3 November 1872 hundreds of people assembled at these enclosures, as well as at Vincent and Finsbury squares, before processing en

185 (*right*) De Beauvoir
Square, Hackney, soon after it
was improved by the
Metropolitan Public Garden
Association (MPGA) in 1892,
photograph. Tower Hamlets
Local History Library.

186 (*below*) Albion Square in
Dalston, east London, was
secured and laid out by the
MPGA in 1899, photograph.
Private collection.

187 Barrier across Taviton Street at the north end of Gordon Square, Bloomsbury, *c.*1880, photograph. Bedford Estate Archive, CD2–15, Woburn Abbey.

masse to Hyde Park.[185] A contributor to the *Pall Mall Gazette* had predicted this outcome only days before the re-launch of Ebury Square, remarking 'it is hoped that the square will not be appropriated by agitators for political purposes. It will, indeed, be hard on the poorer classes if no open space is allowed to them for enjoyment without the accompaniment of the "mock-litany" ruffians and other followers of the Hyde Park agitators.'[186]

These gatherings had the effect of making residents who were already hesitant about opening their enclosures to the public even more reluctant to do so, and encouraged others to increase their gardens'

defences or to render their privacy 'more complete' through additional perimeter planting.[187] The MPGA also experienced a minor setback, as Brabazon was defeated in his attempt to open the gardens of Eccleston Square in Pimlico. The inhabitants 'did not feel convinced that the extra guardianship offered by the Metropolitan Public Gardens Association would certainly ensure the trees and shrubs from damage; and, moreover, they stated that several families living in the square were always in the town during the dead season'. A contributor to *The Graphic* recommended that 'in benevolent efforts of this sort it is well to bear in mind the proverb: "Be just before you are generous" . . . it must not be forgotten that in nearly every case these enclosures were made by private enterprise and for private objects'. The inhabitants, he continued, were not so much against opening the squares as eager to ensure that there was provision for their continued security and maintenance: 'plenty of old soldiers could be found to act as custodians, and, in their duty, the people living in the adjacent streets could still walk in the squares, while the right to play games should be reserved to them only'.[188] The rights of settled tradition thus seemed again to hold the day.

'Our Little Square Drags on its Humble Existence'

Sir: I live in a London Square, a nice quiet Square, with beautiful trees, mossy turf, and flowering shrubs, and delightful gates at each entrance to keep out everything that is noisy, and low, and vulgar. There is a rumour looming in the distance – if I may be allowed the metaphor – that a Society of Semi-lunatics are contemplating the removal of our gates of Eden; but this is, of course, too absurd even for these terribly levelling times. No, Sir – level down, if you will, our gracious, and noble, and right honourable Aristocracy, the pride of every true-born Briton, to the level of the mere professors of Law, Physics and Divinity, and level up, if you will, our mere working-classes to the level of our patrons of the Turf, or the Stock Exchange, but restrain the unhallowed hand that would level down our quiet-preserving gates.[189]

This satirical grievance, published in *Punch* in 1885, was one of many of the period in which a critic felt free to poke fun at the insularity and inherent conservatism of the inhabitants of the metropolis's 'miniature colonies'. The once fashionable squares of Mayfair, Belgravia, Marylebone, Tyburnia and Pimlico, and the northern suburbs of Bloomsbury and Islington were frequently portrayed as quaint, dingy, 'insufferably dull' and hopelessly desolate, much like their inhabitants; both squares and their denizens were now seen as curious relics of a bygone age besieged by a hostile modern world (fig. 188).[190]

The contemporary press mocked especially the inhabitants' persistent efforts to invoke and protect their *rus in urbe* and the tranquillity of their pre-

cincts.[191] Clearly it was difficult, if not downright foolish, for a square's occupants to imagine a degree of rurality amid the tumult and the clamour of the Victorian city. The American garden writer and designer Wilhelm Miller, writing in *The Times* in 1907, asserted that 'the desolate gardens of our London squares' were proof that efforts to recreate garden scenery in the midst of town 'must be failures, as they are attempts to do what is impossible'.[192] He continued:

The gardens of our squares are parodies of woodland and meadow. The foreigner who has heard of the English passion for gardening must suppose that passion to be extinct when he looks through the railings of a London square at the thickets of privet and the grass worn bare with the drip of the grimy, disconsolate trees. He cannot know that within these dreadful places the Englishman has attempted an impossible task and given it up in despair; that having an open space in the heart of a town he has tried to persuade himself that it is a still surviving piece of the country which he loves.[193]

Most of these squares' precincts, and those in the West End in particular, had lost what tenuous affiliation they once had with the open countryside and had become instead beleaguered islets of respectability within a new and constantly changing urban geography.

If *rus in urbe* was an elusive dream, the relative calmness of the squares was of a more practical importance to the residents. It was remarked in 1874 that 'Londoners choose squares to live in simply because they are quieter than streets. It is rather hard if a person who rents a house in a square for the sake of quiet suddenly finds the enclosure turned into a public garden, for after all there is nothing more annoying to the ears than the hum of multitudes and the crooning of children.'[194] Peacefulness seemed worth the price. Yet here too critics frequently assailed the idealised repose of the squares, declaring that they were so very silent and lifeless that any unexpected circumstance was deemed to be a 'serious threat' to their propriety: householders were alarmed by the rumbling of a passing carriage, deeply suspicious of the motives of an unknown passer-by, or distraught by the 'uncouth and indescribable bellowings' of peripatetic street criers (fig. 189).[195]

GETTING ONE'S MONEY'S WORTH.

She. "What's the good of spending all our Sunday Afternoons in walking round the Square, where there's never a Soul and hardly a Tree to speak of, and when there's the Park close by?"

He. "What's the good of having to pay a Guinea a Year for the use of the Square, if we don't use it as often as we can, I should like to know?"

One of the most amusing satirical accounts of the ostensible tediousness of living in a square was published in *Punch* in 1847 under the heading 'A Month's Residence in Middleton [*sic*] Square':

Diary, Sept. 3rd, 1847. Aroused at 8 o'clock by the tumult of an infuriated mob. On going down stairs, found the crowd to consist of three boys quarrelling about a top. – Mem. Seditious gatherings of the populace in masses in the overthronged streets, should be put to a stop by the legislature.

6th. Nothing particular since the 3rd.

9th. A cab drove through the Square, No. 131, K.K. There was a person inside. – N.B. The driver was rather below the middle stature . . .

13th. Another cab, but it was empty – couldn't get the number. This is a remarkable incident, for this makes the second cab which has been seen in the Square since that which brought my stepmother here last August.

19th. The postman called at the house opposite . . .

24th. Postman called again. How much the penny postage has increased correspondence.

26th. A policeman, T.999, passed *this very house*. He was followed by two boys, who wished to see where he could be going. What it is to live in crowded thoroughfares which are subject to the terrors of monthly visits of the executive and conservators of the peace!

27th. Important event. A private carriage drove rapidly into the Square at two minutes past twelve. The coachman remained nearly four seconds in earnest conversation with a man on the pavement.

30th. The result of the most minute inquiries about the carriage, has convinced me that the driver had lost his way.[196]

Nothing rankled with the silence-seeking residents more than the 'pest of street music'. It was

189 (*right*) Unknown artist, after George Cruikshank, *French Musicians, or, Les Savoyards*, June 1819, engraving. Author's collection.

190 (*below*) Charles Keene, *Characteristics*, engraving, from *Punch* 82 (1882): 191, showing a street-vendor and an organ-grinder in a London square. Private collection.

remarked in the *Literary World* in 1849 that 'if you want to know the character of a street or square, follow the organ-grinder'.[197] So pervasive was the street music generated by these 'Savoyard fiends' that there was hardly a square in the metropolis where the residents did not curse the 'organ-grinder's echo' (fig. 190).[198] The mischief was, in fact, so distracting that it was reported in 1862 that some people were 'driven to desperation', compelled to quit their squares and, in some instances, to leave London altogether to 'escape the distressing consequences of street music'.[199] Londoners who did not live in a square and were therefore not subjected to the curse of street music probably viewed the plight of the square-dwellers with a certain degree of Schadenfreude.

Even ghosts were sometimes credited with causing 'noisy and riotous proceedings', which greatly distracted the residents. In May 1867 the 'highly respectable inhabitants of Woburn-square', it was reported, were kept in a state of chronic annoyance by the 'nightly visits of large numbers of the ragged and noisy populations of St Giles in quest of a ghost said to be a denizen in their enclosed square garden'.[200] The crowds that assembled were so great that a considerable number of police were called in for 'special service of maintaining order, and making the populace move on'. The excitement centred on 'various absurd rumours of skeletons, women in white &c.', although it was 'by no means clear who was the first to detect the ghostly visitor, nor easy to find anyone who has seen any such appearance'. It was later affirmed that the ghost was nothing more than a patch of light 'thrown by a gas-lamp at the north end of the square'.[201]

Of course, the inhabitants themselves were not above creating their own forms of clamour; and this, too, invariably disturbed the more cantankerous residents of their own squares. In May 1872 Margaret Leicester Warren commented: 'What shall I write of on this long Sunday afternoon, sitting in the quiet and sadness of Onslow Square, the trees outside shivering in such a bitter wind and the architect's wife next door [Mrs Railton] playing over and over again "a few more years shall roll, a few more seasons pass", always wrong at the same chord!'[202] More disruptive were the lavish annual summer parties that were regularly held within garden enclosures, and to which all the rate-paying

householders were usually invited. These were sure to cause as much censure as pleasure, as did rowdy games or boisterous impromptu gatherings after the hours of darkness.

One may laugh at such reactions, when 'offensive sounds' are repeatedly cited as destroying the 'much-prized tranquillity' of the squares. Yet these superficial disturbances were, in fact, symptomatic of wider anxieties, which threatened to disrupt a square's social structure or besmirch its respectability.[203] In the last analysis, the communities' greatest concerns were for the often inevitable and gentle erosion of their social fabric, and the more general apprehension of the intrusion of unknown or undesirable elements, which posed potential threats to their comfort and privacy.

If inhabitants thus at times felt vulnerable to the encroachment of hostile outside forces or the reproaches of scoffing strangers, their sensitivity should have been (but often was not) aggravated by the fact that by the mid- to late nineteenth century there was little of the social solidarity that once bonded their communities. Many of the formerly fashionable West End squares – including Berkeley, Cavendish, Hanover, St James's and Grosvenor – had by the 1850s ceased to be exclusively residential, as some of their surrounding houses were given over to offices, clubs, lodging houses, learned societies, private academies or embassies. A contributor to *The Builder* in May 1877 described the phenomenon in reference to the changes that had taken place to the Bedford Estate in Bloomsbury during the preceding decades: 'by the mere force of the growth of London, the Bedford estate, as well as others of which we are not now speaking, was so hemmed in and built up that its original residential character was entirely changed, and . . . with this change in the habitable nature of the locality, came change in the class of inhabitants by whom it was populated'. This pattern was the same across London: the family 'as a rule' migrated to the suburbs or to 'those country places not as yet swallowed up in the great sea of suburb, to which railway accommodation has given a new and vigorous growth'. The squares' houses were then broken up into a 'collection of units' which were 'most convenient to those individuals who require only two or three rooms, but seek for them within easy access of the heart of the City traffic', and these were in turn 'offered indiscriminately to professional

men as offices; to bachelors, and even to married people as residences' (fig. 191).[204]

This demographic shift, nonetheless, introduced a range of new challenges. The influx of new occupants – many of whom, as non-resident and strictly day-time users of the amenity, were either unfamiliar with, or uninterested in, the established conventions of the place – took little if any interest in the management of the square and its enclosure. These circumstances had adverse consequences for the governance, presentation and viability of the squares, especially where they were neither cared for by the landlord, nor managed by a robust garden committee. The result was that many of the enclosures in the centre of town became increasingly neglected, and this led outsiders to conclude that they were unnecessary and unloved. An editorial in *The Graphic* in 1870 condemned the state of the 'noble garden' at Lincoln's Inn Fields: 'it is too much adapted indeed for a solitary walk, being mainly given up to the gardeners, for the majority of the occupiers of the square use their chambers only as offices, and do not go to them for rustic recreation. They have no families, moreover, to do their promenading there.' There were, he concluded, 'many gardens about London which are wasted for similar reasons'.[205]

If the squares themselves were often altered, they were, however, neither wasted nor uninhabited: they still retained sizable residential populations and their enclosures were, moreover, regularly used.[206] Outsiders who perceived them as wasted also, paradoxically, under the influence of the Open Space movement, regarded all forms of open space within the metropolis, as important. A contributor to *The Builder* in 1862 exclaimed 'every inch of open space in the Metropolis ought to be fought for, – given up only at the sword's point'; or as the landscape gardener Joseph Newton remarked in the following year: 'all squares, all trees, and every patch of verdure, have attained a value just in proportion to the denseness of the crowds compacted within the bills of mortality'.[207] There was, moreover, in many quarters of society a moral consensus that open ground 'in a waste state', regardless of its ownership, should be cultivated and, where possible, liberally and gratuitously thrown open for the enjoyment of all classes. The guardians of London's neglected gardens were therefore urged to shake off their indifference to the public advantage, and to make their gardens 'as ornate as possible'.[208]

Try as they might to insulate themselves from the hurly-burly of the streets, and the encroachments of modern London, the denizens of the squares, of whatever social stripe, could not escape the reality that their amenity was under threat. What was also becoming increasingly clear was that the greatest threat was not from without, but from within their own ranks: the indifference or complacency of many a square's residents, and their failure to safeguard and maintain their enclosures made these vulnerable to the advances of unscrupulous building speculators, who were eager to get their hands on the central gardens and to cover them with buildings. An anonymous contributor to the *Pall Mall Gazette* in 1893 summed up the sentiment. His essay entitled 'In a London Square' conveys wistful resignation in the face of threats to his square: 'there has always been to my eyes a strangely pathetic look about this little old-world corner of the great city. But a few yards off the full flood tide of traffic roars along with its ceaseless rumble of revolving wheels, yet rare are the carriages which turn into this sleepy London back-water, and I have no doubt that half the hurrying people who pass so near have never even heard the name of this peaceful sanctum.' He continued:

in 'true London fashion, though we live huddled up together year's end to year's end', few of us know aught about each other . . . Uncomfortable rumours will, on occasion, disturb the community – rumours that bruit abroad the certain intention of desecrating railways or handsome boulevards which are to break in burglariously upon us with scant warning, and wipe us off the face of the earth. Then it is that the air is full of giant scaffoldings and lofty cranes, ladders, and papered hoardings. But mercifully, these tales have never resolved into facts, and our little square drags on its humble existence, unimproved, unattacked. That it will last out my short lifetime I somehow feel contentedly secure, and this is all I patiently and hopefully desire.[209]

6

The Threatened Loss of 'Invaluable Lung Spaces'[1]

A contributor to *The Times* in April 1888 rejoiced at the passing of the Local Government Act, remarking that it was an 'important measure upon the interests of the inhabitants of the capital, because, practically, it would give the inhabitants of aggregate London the germ at any rate of direct control over their affairs'.[2] Londoners eagerly anticipated the creation of the London County Council (LCC) – almost the first democratic authority in the capital.[3] Not only did it signal the demise of the publicly unaccountable, and scandal-tainted Metropolitan Board of Works, but it gave Londoners reason to hope that their city would be significantly improved by 'the sort of energetic administration that had transformed Britain's provincial cities since the 1840s – a municipal gospel which included public health reform and slum clearance, the provision of gas, water, electricity and transport, and urban regeneration through street improvements, parks and other amenities'.[4]

London, in the late nineteenth century, 'lagged behind many provincial towns in its provision of what were increasingly regarded as the necessary social amenities of a "civilised" life'.[5] The new and reforming council, therefore, embarked with great gusto on a range of measures to improve the quality of living conditions in the metropolis through the use of statutory controls and sanctions for the benefit of the public. For instance, in 1894 it introduced the London Building Act which brought into public control the widening of streets, the lines of building

frontages, the extent of open space around buildings, and the height of buildings. It also launched a 'crusade to develop and implement its own cultural initiatives',[6] one of which was to be the provision and maintenance of public open spaces. This initiative promised to herald a 'new democratic age in which the municipality would now minister to the recreational tastes of its inhabitants'.[7]

Preserving London's 'Breathing Grounds'

Before the 1880s the state had not played a role in the cultural or recreational affairs of the city: its 'aims were limited and its legislation was little more than a response to immediate and pressing social concerns'. The state's encouragement for the provision of parks and open spaces, for instance, had been driven primarily by the practical concern for public health. From the late 1880s, however, the state began positively to intervene in the environment, and to 'encourage the growth of a social harmony by promoting a "national" culture, available to all its citizens'.[8]

In order to achieve these strategic aims, the LCC established the Parks and Open Spaces Committee under the chairmanship of Lord Meath.[9] Although the council was initially enthusiastic about the work of the Metropolitan Public Gardens Association (MPGA), it did not 'warm entirely to the idea that it might assume control of the small open spaces established by voluntary effort'. The council, in fact, only

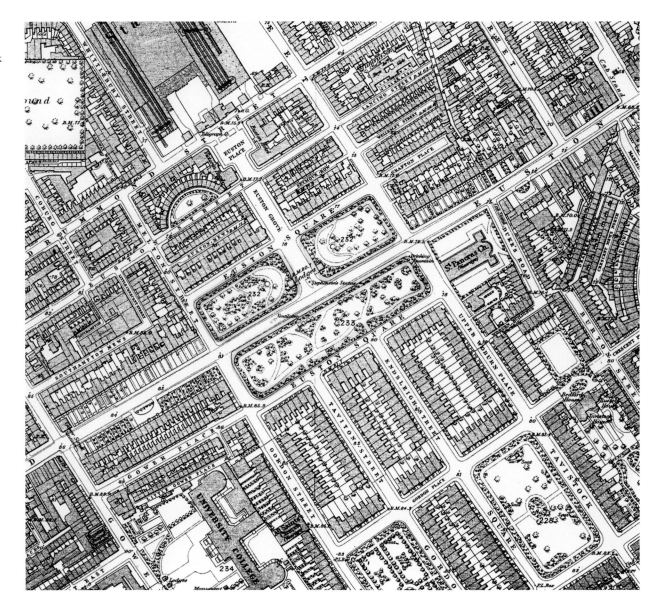

reluctantly accepted responsibility for a handful of MPGA-improved playgrounds – among them some of the converted East End squares – and in 1897 it even tried, unsuccessfully, to transfer the management of all open spaces under 10 acres in its control to the vestries. The objections were largely practical: new, small open spaces were costly undertakings to maintain – indeed, significantly more expensive than large parks.[10]

The LCC, however, regardless of the expense, continued to take an interest in providing small parks in crowded districts of the city. Indeed, it was compared favourably by George Haw in 1907 to a 'benevolent physician with healing in its train', adding as it did at the time some 3–4 acres a week to London's 'breathing grounds'.[11] The council, moreover, by vir-

tue of its remit to take a greater interest than the Metropolitan Board of Works in horticulture, gardening and town planning, also played an active role in efforts to protect open space throughout the Administrative County of London.[12] This approach reflected the increasingly popular view that saving the squares was not a mere parochial or local matter, but one that affected the welfare of the entire metropolis, and that the best way to protect the squares and enclosures was to enact legislation.[13]

No sooner had the Parks and Open Spaces Committee been established than it became embroiled in a dispute involving the preservation of Euston Square in St Pancras (fig. 192). Events began to unfold early in 1890 when the London and North Western Railway Company proposed to cover a

193 Edwardes Square,
Kensington, *c.*1912,
photograph. Kensington and
Chelsea Local Studies
collection.

'quarter of Euston-square with station premises, extending its borders to the edge of the high road'.[14] The company put forward its proposal as the free-holder of the square, having earlier bought the rights from all the occupants. When, however, the bill came before parliament, the LCC opposed it on the grounds that the company should not be permitted to destroy an 'unbuilt-on space'. The council's objection was upheld, and the company was prevented from build-ing on the land.[15]

The necessity of safeguarding square gardens again came to the fore in about 1896 when Albert Square, Stepney, was advertised for sale. Here the LCC had to obtain powers of compulsory purchase in order to preserve it as an open space. This cost a consider-able sum of money, but it was declared at the time that 'in that overcrowded part of London it was well worth the expenditure'.[16]

While the aforementioned cases were certainly victories in favour of the protection of squares in the face of proposed 'acts of vandalism', neither was as controversial or had so important a bearing on the future preservation of the squares as a whole than the proposed redevelopment of Edwardes Square, Kensington (fig. 193). The 'question' of the square arose in October 1903 when the gardens of

this 'socially select and largely self-governing enclave' were put up for sale by their freeholder the sixth Lord Kensington.[17] The gardens then comprised two discrete enclosures – the central 3-acre pleasance, and the communal front garden at Earl's Terrace – both of which had been subject to two acts of parliament (1819 and 1851). These acts contained clauses direct-ing that the enclosures be kept private for the exclu-sive use of persons occupying houses in the square. The inhabitants, however, were under the mistaken impression that their interest in the gardens would end in March 1910 on the expiry of the lease granted by the freeholder in 1820.

So great was the perturbation aroused by the impending sale that Kensington Borough Council was compelled to set up a special committee to consider whether to acquire the central garden as an open space, and the Parks and Open Spaces Com-mittee applied to parliament for power to prevent the square from being covered with buildings.[18] The case soon became a *cause célèbre* and was widely ventilated in the press with reference both to the particular case of Edwardes Square and to the ques-tion of the squares of London in general.

The sale of the square in November 1903 to a building company precipitated the proposal by the

LCC in 1904 of legislation for the preservation first of Edwardes Square, and afterwards of the London squares generally.[19] A bill was brought forward but was rejected by the House of Lords: 'the Lord Chairman suspected that the sacred rights of private property were involved and expressed disapproval'.[20] But parliament, having been satisfied on this point, the LCC obtained its London Squares and Enclosures (Preservation) Act (1906). This act, nevertheless, as we shall see, applied only to enclosures the owners of which expressed their agreement with its aims: in the event this meant that Edwardes Square remained unprotected.

Things took a turn for the worse in 1910 when the new owners applied for permission to build a cinema over the whole of the central garden and the carriageway in front of Earl's Terrace. Permission was refused by the LCC, a decision supported by the Royal Borough of Kensington; but there ensued a period of open hostility and intimidation waged by the freeholders against the residents, which included barricading the carriageway with 'timber and iron-work' and locking the residents out of their central garden.[21] Encouraged by a groundswell of public support in favour of preserving the square, the Kensington Garden Committee adopted the unprecedented course of taking the freeholder to law, where the court held that the powers granted in its nineteenth-century acts to 'the inhabitants of the houses of Edwardes Square and the other places around' were 'made for all time'. The 'perpetual' preservation of the enclosures was, however, only finally achieved when the House of Lords dismissed an appeal made by the freeholders in January 1912.[22]

The one-time Chairman of the LCC, Sir Willoughby Hyett Dickinson, later praised the Edwardes Square judgments, remarking that it was

> very difficult for a group of householders, interested in the preservation of a Square, to bring their legal rights to the test of a Court of Justice. If it had not been for the courage and resoluteness of two or three individuals residing in the Square the case would not have come before any Court and this important decision, which, in witness's [sic] opinion, affects many other Squares, would never have been obtained. The case would have gone by default. The interior of the Square would

to-day be covered with a lofty mass of brickwork; and other landlords would have realised what large profits might be made by selling to speculative builders the garden Squares of London.[23]

The London Squares and Enclosures (Preservation) Act

We have briefly noted how the agitation and litigation arising out of the sale of Edwardes Square galvanised the LCC to consider what steps might be taken by legislation to protect the squares from redevelopment. The means by which this protection evolved and was implemented deserves further explanation.

The LCC was in a unique position to promote a London-wide approach to 'the problem of the square'. In 1901 the council instructed the Parks and Open Spaces Committee to consider and report on the advisability of promoting legislation to prevent the squares and gardens in the County of London being built over.[24] This, in turn, led to a resolution in 1903 that resulted in the creation of an outline survey of the 'garden-squares, triangles, etc.' The template for this survey was Mrs Basil Holmes's exemplary audit of all burial-grounds existing in the County of London (1895); following her method, the committee employed 'returns' to form the basis for a schedule of the capital's squares and enclosures. The resultant document became known as the 'Particulars of the Garden Squares', and when completed in 1905 it became the first detailed survey of the squares in London (that is, the Administrative County of London) to record the name, locality, borough, approximate area, 'estate or reputed owner' of these open spaces, and the acts of parliament that affected their management (fig. 194).[25]

For the purposes of the survey, both 'garden squares' and 'enclosures' were included. Squares were defined as the 'generally recognised squares and a few "gardens", "crescents" etc. which are of practically the same character'. These gardens were originally provided as part of a built layout for the amenity of the houses overlooking them, from which they are generally separated by public roads. Squares that were considered mere 'street squares', such as Trafalgar and Sloane Squares, were not included. Enclosures, on the other hand, meant 'common gar-

194 Leinster Square, Bayswater, 1907, postcard. Author's collection. The photograph shows the square as it would have been at the time of the survey 'Particulars of the Garden Squares' in 1905.

dens in the front or rear of houses, shrubberies, road-side strips, and triangles at the junction[s] of roads'.[26]

Although these two broad categories of outdoor spaces were perceived as distinct, it was presumably advantageous to consider the effect of their combined acreage when quantifying their relative benefits to the metropolis. Not surprisingly, the survey threw up some interesting statistics: it named no fewer than 125 owners who possessed in aggregate 310 squares and 127 garden enclosures, making a total of 437 open spaces. The combined area of the squares was 287 acres, and of the enclosures 160 acres, making a grand total of 447 acres.

In 1905 the LCC, eager to see the introduction of legally binding measures to protect the squares, introduced a bill to parliament 'to prohibit or restrict the erection of Buildings and Structures on certain lands in the Administrative County of London'. The aim of the so-called London Squares and Enclosures (Preservation) Bill was to prevent building on these open properties forever, and to provide that the landlord could hand over the upkeep of the gardens to the council, if it were his wish. The House of

Lords Committee, however, rejected the bill on the grounds that it sought to impose restrictions without making sufficient provision for compensation for the landowners.[27]

The following year the LCC introduced another bill, which was finally passed as the London Squares and Enclosures (Preservation) Act.[28] This was, however, a feeble and much watered-down piece of legislation, which affected only sixty-four open spaces where the landowners had agreed to comply with the measures. The act, nonetheless, provided for the payment of compensation and for the substitution of lands, and generally foreshadowed later legislation.[29] It furthermore, put a temporary stop to the immediate threats to the squares.

One of the unforeseen benefits of the 1906 act was that it encouraged a handful of popular writers to take an interest in the history of the squares. Among them was the Hon. Mrs Evelyn Cecil, who included a 'faint sketch of the story of the squares' in her historical and horticultural survey, *London Parks and Gardens* (1907). And Edgcumbe Staley penned an amusing and light-hearted essay 'The Parks and Squares of London, and How to Make

CROMWELL GARDENS AND THURLOE SQUARE,
SOUTH KENSINGTON.

195 Cromwell Gardens, South Kensington, 1905, postcard. Author's collection. Beresford Chancellor remarks, in *The History of the Squares of London* (1907), that such Kensington squares differ greatly among themselves, 'in age, size, and importance': some 'have little or no history, and others are, from a variety of reasons, both interesting and historical'.

the Most of Them' (1907).[30] The most impressive of all, however, was E. Beresford Chancellor's *The History of the Squares of London* (1907).[31] The book was the first to deal in a comprehensive manner with the squares. The author's aim is to describe the formation of the squares, and 'to trace the occupancy of their houses to interesting, notable, and in some cases notorious, people, and, to here and there, enliven a mere dull enumeration of names and dates, by some story or anecdote' (fig. 195).[32]

Although the 'conscientious antiquary' succeeds in these objectives, Chancellor's *History* provides neither a clear historical overview nor a coherent chronological survey. The narrative, moreover, very curiously, does not touch on contemporary issues affecting the squares, including their physical decline, the numerous and real threats to their survival, and the concerted efforts that were being made at the time to preserve them.[33] His book was, in fact, in some ways possibly downright unhelpful in the attempt to save some squares that were threatened with imminent obliteration: Endsleigh Gardens was in his view 'rather an excrescence from the Euston Road than a proper square'; Mecklenburgh and Brunswick squares were 'uniformly monotonous';

and many more were too fragmentary, too uninteresting or too modern to warrant his approbation.[34] Only in 1918 did Chancellor finally begin actively to campaign for the preservation of squares. His outlook was, however, by this time rather gloomy: he lamented that they were now 'a thing of the past', that they were no longer economically viable to create, and that the 'existing squares were in many instances passing from their original character'.[35]

While these and other contemporary publications raised public awareness of the special qualities of the squares, they did not muster public support for their preservation. Here, however, the London Society was able to lend a helping hand. Founded in 1912, it was among the country's first environmental amenity societies. The society's explicit aim was to 'foster an intelligent interest in London both as the largest civic centre & as the Capital of the Empire & to induce a public spirit for the study and encouragement of its improvement';[36] and it proposed to achieve these ends by the '*united action of its* [London's] *citizens*'.[37] The society had considerable political clout as it functioned as an umbrella organisation, having close links with most of the leading bodies interested in the amenities of London, including the

196 The square-keeper at
work in St Peter's Square,
Hammersmith, *c.*1920,
photograph. Hammersmith
and Fulham Archives and
Local History Centre.

Architecture Club, the Commons and Footpaths Preservation Society, the Garden Cities and Town Planning Association, the Greater London Committee of the National Playing Fields Association, the London Survey Committee, the MPGA, the National Trust, the Royal Institute of British Architects, the Society for the Protection of Ancient Buildings, the Sunlight League and the Town Planning Institute.

The society took a particular interest in the London squares. Indeed, the preservation of St Peter's Square in Hammersmith in 1913 was among its earliest achievements (fig. 196).[38] The outbreak of the Great War in 1914, however, meant that the society was not called upon to campaign for the preservation of the squares again until 1922, as the fate of the squares took a back seat to other more pressing concerns.

London's Squares: A 'Most Kindly Nurse'[39]

There was, on the cusp of the twentieth century, as little consensus on the planting and laying out of squares as in the preceding two hundred years. A contributor to the *Gardeners' Chronicle* in 1895 affirmed that the gardens seldom showed 'much art'.

Trees and shrubs were 'usually of the most common species, disposed in the most tasteless manner'. Advocates of the modern school of gardening were inclined to the belief that 'the smaller the area to be dealt with the greater the call on the resources of the landscape gardener'. Onslow Square in South Kensington was considered to be among the most outstanding examples of his art, where beds of deciduous and evergreen shrubs, and trees 'of no great height or size of crown' gave diversity to the 'perfectly level area'. This plan was not, however, without its faults: the paths were considered too sinuous, there was insufficient open space in the middle of the ground left as a 'playing-place for children', and there were too few columnar-habited trees. The contributor supplied a plan prepared by Mr Hudson Gurney of Norwich showing an ideal garden plan (fig. 197).[40]

Earlier in the year Gurney had contributed a short essay to the *Chronicle*, in which he outlined how a square's garden 'might be arranged to give good effect from the street and from the inside, and yet remain private for the dwellers of the square'. The design of the garden should, he argued, be 'of a formal description, not being, as a rule, an irregular

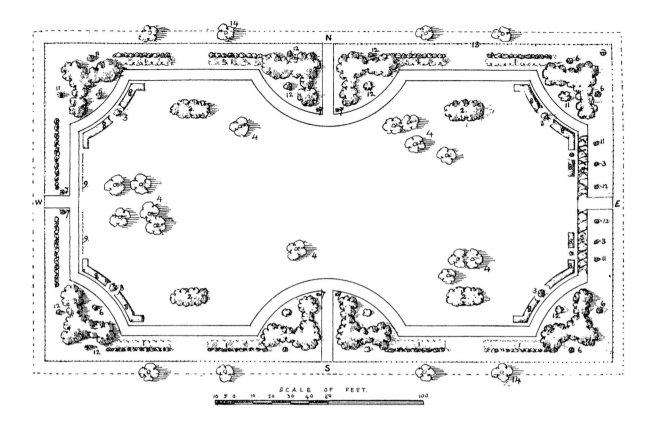

197 Unknown draughtsman, *Plan of Town Garden*, engraving, from *Gardeners' Chronicle*, 8 June 1895. Author's collection. The numbers on the plan relate to the proposed planting scheme and other features in the garden.

shape, and being surrounded by buildings'; 'it is a great mistake to make a pretence of being in the country, and laying out the naturally-flat ground into a sort of miniature hill-and-dale landscape'.[41] His contemporary the architect and writer Reginald Blomfield was of the same opinion: 'a London square is an entirely artificial affair. It is bounded by rectangular blocks of buildings and straight roads and fences. It would be reasonable to adhere to this simple motive.' Blomfield, however, despised the landscape gardener, whom he disparaged as making it his business to 'dispense with serious design', and who had a 'dislike of a simple straight line and a plain piece of grass almost to a mania'. Such an operative had, he contended, recently disfigured the interior layout of a Bloomsbury square.

In Bloomsbury, till within the last few years, there existed a good old-fashioned square garden, laid out in four grass plots, with a lime walk and a border of flowers running round the sides. It was restful and pleasant to look at. The grass plots were good for lawn tennis and the lime walks kindly to the citizen; but the landscape gardener appeared on the scene and speedily put all this to

rights. He cut up the grass plots and destroyed two sides of the lime walk, and heaped up some mounds, and made the most curiously unreasonable paths; and went his way, having destroyed one of the few square gardens in London with any pretence to design. Instead of trying to treat the square as a whole, or, better still, instead of leaving it alone, he deliberately turned his back on the adjacent architecture, and produced a result which has no distinction but that of immense vulgarity.[42]

Blomfield's savage polemic serves to remind us that the gardens of the squares were, in spite of their generally unprepossessing terrain and diminutive size, still worthy of the attentions of the landscape gardener, and that his efforts to recast the grounds of these very conservatively managed oases was a difficult business. What is certainly true is that most reforming outsiders failed to register just how little the inhabitants were concerned with what others thought of their enclosed pleasure grounds: it mattered little to them either that they gave 'good effect' from the street, or that ordinary passers-by were struck 'by what a melancholy-looking thing is the

198 Gardeners in St George's Square, Pimlico, *c.*1905, postcard. Author's collection.

garden in the London square' (fig. 198). Outsiders were deliberately denied the 'surprise . . . on entering one to find how charmingly they are arranged, and full of flowers'.[43]

The squares, like many other metropolitan gardens, suffered during the course of the Great War of 1914–18. The scarcity of labour meant that their lawns were 'less trimly mown', their 'shrubberies unweeded' and their drives and paths 'less smartly kept'.[44] The squares, nonetheless, generally fared better than the parks and public gardens, as many were not so reliant on public subsidy, nor were they compulsorily requisitioned for military purposes. Whereas the need for economy meant that the public parks and gardens were opened on a very limited basis and were kept to a lower standard than they had been before the war, the squares remained open regularly to their inhabitants, and their gardens were managed much as they had always been.[45]

Plans to bring square gardens under the plough for food production were mooted as early as 1916.[46] It was not, however, until the following year that central government began to exert pressure on the borough councils, under the provisions of the Cultivation of Lands Order (1917), to quantify and assess potential sites for cultivation.[47] The Board of Agriculture investigated, and expressed the view that the

square gardens, like the city's parks and open spaces, were 'of questionable utility' – their 'undrained London clay' soil was too heavy, and the 'atmospheric conditions' in the metropolis were too unfavourable to cultivation.[48]

These circumstances did not, however, dissuade patriotic citizens from offering up their central gardens with a view to producing food to contribute to the war effort. Indeed, in December 1917 the LCC received several requests from the public that it take for cultivation under the order the gardens in Tredegar Square, Bow, and Gibson Square, Islington. Both gardens were described at the time as 'of the ordinary type consisting in shrubberies, flower borders, and a lawn', and 'not used by the residents'. Although the pair of enclosures were eligible under the scheme, the Board of Agriculture declared them to be too small, at 5 rods each, to cultivate: the rent received from the cultivators would not cover the cost of reinstating the gardens after the war.[49]

It is a measure of the severity of the capital's wartime food-production crisis that in January 1918 Westminster City Council expressed support for a resolution passed at a meeting of the inhabitants of the borough 'in favour of the cultivation as allotments of all suitable open spaces whether in public parks and gardens, private squares or other enclo-

199 Mrs Kenyon Mitford (*left*) and Lady Selby Bigge (*right*), manning a flower stall at a produce sale in Berkeley Square on 29 June 1917, photograph; the produce was sold in aid of wounded soldiers.

sures'.[50] The Local Government Board approved of such initiatives, and expressed the view that while in 'ordinary circumstances' it was undesirable to curtail the open space available for recreation in London, 'so far as public health is concerned, there is no serious objection to such a proposal to cultivate a large and additional area of the parks and open spaces'.[51] The production of food was considered to be of paramount importance, and the land taken into cultivation could be restored to its former use on the conclusion of hostilities. In the event, however, none of the squares was cultivated, as the war ended before the authorities took any decisive action.

One of the more curious anomalies of the period was that the hardships imposed by the war on the public purse meant that for the first time in many years, the inhabitants of the squares found themselves in the enviable position of having their enclosures often better maintained than the public gardens.

This circumstance, not surprisingly, occasioned criticism from some outsiders, who disapproved of the fact that 'the flower-beds of squares' were being kept up during the war. These 'charming but wholly unnecessary' floral decorations were, it was reported, a waste of valuable labour: 'of all the forms of extravagance, this would seem, in the present circumstances the most criminal, seeing that the men thus withdrawn from useful labour are precisely those best qualified for food-producing work'.[52]

It is also particularly ironic, given earlier efforts to refurbish and throw open to the public some small square enclosures in the poorest districts of town, that these very gardens were among the first to suffer from cuts to the LCC's parks and gardens maintenance budgets. The 'fifth-class gardens' of Albert, Arbour, Beaumont, Munster, Nelson and Red Lion squares, and the 'sixth-class' enclosures of Carlton, Ford, Sidney and York squares were duly affected, and were ordered to be closed in the

200   Policewomen on parade in Eccleston Square, March 1918, photograph.

winter months with effect from October 1916 for the duration of the war.[53]

The West End's private squares, by contrast, did not suffer such a fate: they remained open to rate-paying residents, reasonably tidy, quiet and secluded. These circumstances meant that the squares were in the unusual position of performing a very useful role during the course of the war. Mrs Marion Repton, writing in *The Times* on 19 May 1916, suggested that 'our squares and other similar private spaces' could be devoted to a 'better cause': she recommended that they should be opened to wounded soldiers and sailors from neighbouring hospitals. There were, she observed, 'many such spaces in London, and a few long chairs and some of the many V.A.D.'s [Voluntary Aid Detachment nurses] to supervise the patients are all that are needed'. She was confident that 'the owners of such places would only be too glad to add to the comfort of our brave fellows during the coming summer' (fig. 199).[54]

Repton's 'excellent proposal' had, in fact, been anticipated in several West End squares: from September 1914, Vincent Square was occupied by troops, and it was later used on a regular basis for training,

as were a number of other squares (fig. 200); and by early 1916 the residents or guardians of Bedford, Mecklenburgh, Manchester, Berkeley and Queen squares had all given the freedom of their gardens to military patients at adjacent hospitals. The campaign launched and taken up in the columns of *The Times* was, nonetheless, a great catalyst to the throwing open of a number of private garden enclosures, and 'aroused no little interest in sympathy' from the public.[55] Indeed, what began as a mere 'suggestion' rapidly developed into what was referred to in the press as the 'movement for the admission of convalescent soldiers to the squares', and was 'received with warm and almost unanimous approval by residents, for whom the use of the gardens has hitherto been reserved'.[56] Within three weeks of the publication of Repton's letter, the residents or guardians of the most important West End squares, including Belgrave, Cambridge, Cavendish, Eaton (north side), Grosvenor, Hanover, Kensington, Oxford, Portman, Russell, St James's and Soho, had been encouraged to 'join the scheme',[57] and in some of these enclosures the residents had agreed to provide the wounded with seats, newspapers, books and tea, and

Queen Mary's Club, Eaton Square. W.

to 'do anything else they can for their comfort'.[58]
Squares that subscribed to the scheme sometimes
advertised their participation by flying flags or
posting notices bearing the words 'Sick and wounded
soldiers may rest here'.[59] The 'occasional right of
entry' to these gardens was not restricted solely to
British soldiers; Belgian soldiers on leave were also
granted permission to use the gardens of Manchester
Square through the offices of Les Vacances du Soldat
Belge.[60]

Advocates of this 'sensible use' of the squares,
pointed out that naval and military convalescents
were given a 'good deal of welcome latitude' to
enjoy the 'health-giving advantages of the grounds,
with their trees and shrubs and flowers and good
green turf'.[61] The squares, it was remarked, also
offered a 'special kind' of privacy, 'for no convalescent who sits in one of them need feel that he is
encroaching on the personal hospitality of the
owners. In fact, a square garden, being the property,
not of an individual, but of a community, is an ideal
compromise between a public park with its noise
and crowds and a private garden attached to a house,
and so meets the wants of the convalescent better
than either.'[62]

Invalid soldiers who were convalescing may have
regarded the squares close to their hospitals as 'oases
in desert London', but those who were 'well enough
to walk to the parks' preferred the latter 'as being
more lively'.[63] The parks were also preferable on
other accounts – not least because the soldiers could
exercise greater personal freedom within them. Hos-
pitalised servicemen were, like the rate-paying inhabitants, bound to observe the squares' byelaws, and
these were, in fact, in some instances made even
more stringent during the war to protect the amenity.
Some inhabitants, likewise, made special legal arrangements to ensure that 'no danger may ensue of
their privacy being lost when there ceases to be a
reason for the admittance of the wounded'.[64]

While the Squares for the Wounded campaign
was a great success, the 'Squares for London Children' initiative, launched in March 1917 by Mrs
Wilton Phipps, was less so.[65] An editorial in *The
Times* reported, nonetheless, that opening the squares
and other gardens provided much needed facilities,
and gave the 'greatest possible benefit to the health
and nerves of the children'.[66] Nursery children of
non-residents were admitted by special arrangement
to a limited number of squares' gardens on the con-

dition that they did so before regular opening hours;[67] and from 1916 the Education Committee of the LCC established a 'Classes in Parks and Open Spaces' programme for children from elementary schools, which was taken up by a few of the squares. Euston Square Gardens were, for instance, leased by the London and North Western Railway Company to St Pancras House of Fellowship, which made the enclosures available between 1917 and 1924 to the pupils of St Pancras Church of England School. Here, the children met under canvas awnings and were occasionally 'allowed [the] use of huts in bad weather'.[68]

In Euston Square open-air classes for gardening and dancing were launched, which occupied former military facilities thrown up in the enclosure in March 1915.[69] The largest of these was the YMCA's Military Centre Hut, which was the headquarters of the Rovers, Scouts and Cubs, and the Guides and Brownies.[70] The 'great hut' was one of a handful of temporary wartime buildings erected for the use of troops throughout the metropolis.[71] Most of the military buildings were large, undistinguished sheds, the erection of which often caused lasting damage to their garden settings (fig. 201).

This was not, however, true of the Washington Inn, which was built in St James's Square garden, and which ultimately led to the enclosure's tasteful refurbishment. Of the squares that placed their gardens at the disposal of the war effort, St James's was more dramatically transformed than any.[72] The householders and guardians of the square, who were keen 'to do the right thing', took the unprecedented step in October 1917 of handing over their garden for temporary use to the American YMCA.[73] The *New York Times* announced gleefully in June 1918:

Another cherished English tradition has been smashed by the advent of America into the war. For 200 years St James [sic] square has been regarded as sacred from all invasion. It lay green and pleasant amid some of the most stately mansions of London, but no one entered it from year's end to year's end save the gardeners, who rolled the turf or swept up the fallen leaves.

Today the American Y.M.C.A. has commandeered it [the enclosure] and turned it into a first-class country club for American officers, but has done it with gentle hands. The fine equestrian statue of William III is indeed surrounded by the buildings of the Washington Inn, but not one of the century-old planer [sic] trees has been disturbed, and the wings of the structure have been so disposed as to avoid their trunks. The result is that American officers, in the very heart of London, within five minutes' walk of Trafalgar Square, have a place of their own which might be miles in the country.

The Washington Inn (fig. 202) was built to provide hospitality to American soldiers, officers and men, who passed through London on their way to or from the trenches, and to those who were sent back wounded.[74] It was 'without question the most luxurious hostel of its kind', and must have offered a welcome respite from the devastation at the front. While it could not compare with the aristocratic splendour of the square's surrounding houses, it was 'substantially built in brick, ironwork, tiles, and wood', and boasted 110 bedrooms, hot and cold showers, a writing room, a well-stocked library and a dining room comfortably appointed with a grand piano, good furniture and 'engravings of famous pictures'; and these rooms, 'with their lofty beamed roofs and French windows, opening to the green turf and stately trees' were praised for giving 'the impression of being far away from the city and its dust and noise'.[75]

The garden was, however, neither very capacious nor particularly attractive: a correspondent to *The Times* had earlier described it as a 'thicket of grimy shrubs. You could not see across it. You had no idea of its spacious dignity.' And given the size of the Inn, its large windows were calculated less to offer a prospect of the verdure of the scene than to 'look out upon the town residences of Lords Derby, St Albans, Strafford, Kinnaird, and Falmouth; the Hon. Waldorf Astor and the Bishop of London'.[76] The YMCA officials compared their new West End establishment to a monastic community: 'in the centre is a green stretch of grass with William III on his pedestal in the middle, and all around is . . . their cloister, only no cloister ever designed by monk made so clever a use of vines to cover its inward face. From this cloister radiate, like spokes of a wheel, the wings, which are devoted to hotel purposes.'[77]

The Inn appears to have responded well to the layout of the square and its garden. The *New York*

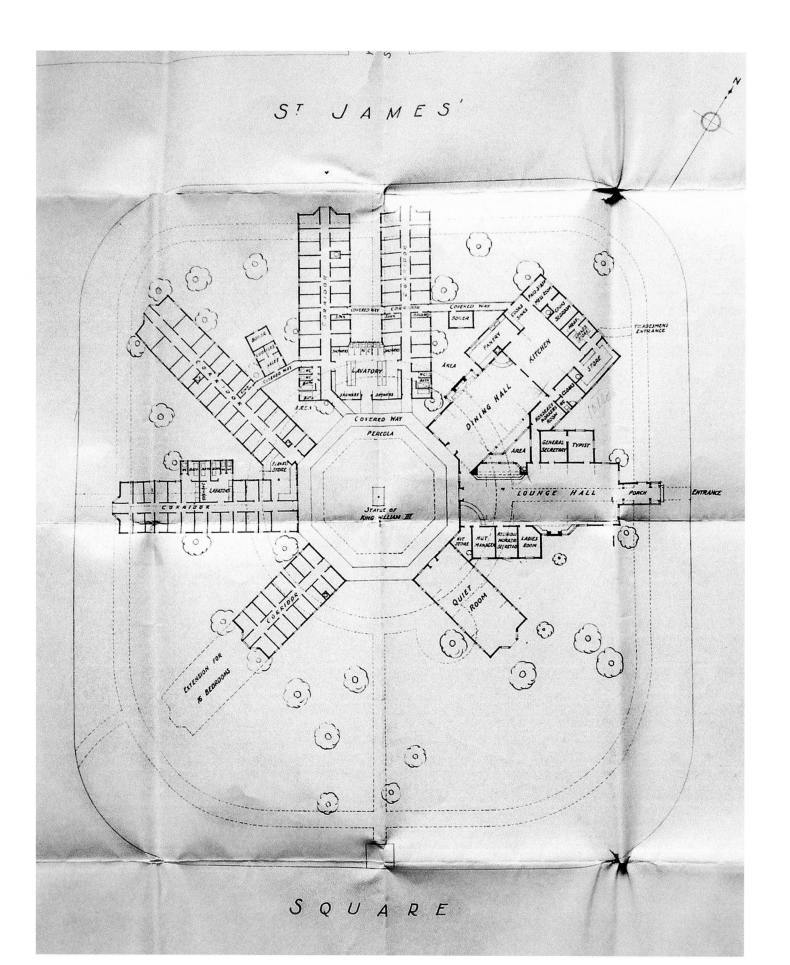

ST JAMES'

N

COVERED WAY
PERGOLA

STATUE OF
KING WILLIAM III

COVERED WAY

LAVATORY

CORRIDOR

CORRIDOR

SANITARY STORE

CLEANERS STORE

CORRIDOR

LAVATORY

CORRIDOR

EXTENSION FOR
16 BEDROOMS

DINING HALL

KITCHEN

PANTRY

STORE

TRADESMENS
ENTRANCE

AREA

GENERAL
SECRETARY

TYPIST

LOUNGE HALL

PORCH

ENTRANCE

HUT
MANAGER

RELIGIOUS
WORKER

SECRETARY

LADIES
ROOM

KIT
STORE

QUIET
ROOM

SQUARE

203 The central court of the Washington Inn in St James's Square, under construction, 1917–18, photograph. YMCA Archives, University of Minnesota.

202 (*facing page*) Unknown draughtsman, *Proposed American Y.M.C.A. Hostel for Officers, St James's Square*, 1917–18, pen and ink.

Times reported in August 1918 that 'the trees in the centre of the square were far too precious to be cut down' (fig. 203). 'The architect, being unable to dodge them, ingeniously included them in his plans, concealing the trunks with plaster but leaving a loophole for watering. It was not a new idea: the house of Ulysses in Ithaca formed a precedent.'[78] This comparison of the complex to the supposedly opulent palace of Odysseus would appear to be no more than a pretentious allusion. The Inn appears from contemporary photographs to have been little more than an encampment of primitive huts, set amid sooty trees. The *New York Times*'s journalist probably invoked Homer to conjure up the image of the return of the hero from the wars and his bid to re-establish himself in civil society.

In the event, the sprawling officers' complex in St James's Square had a short life. Although so substantially built that it 'might well last for a hundred years', the Inn was vacated by the YMCA in June 1920, and demolished by the spring of the following year.[79] The garden had been restored by the summer of 1921, and its 'spring-cleaning after the war' was praised in *The Times* in May 1923. The pleasure ground, described during its American occupation as 'all huts and typewriters and mess', was now restored to its 'ancient openness'. Many of the big trees

were cut down, the shrubberies uprooted, and the lawns made new. 'Magnolias and other flowering things ring the circuit. There is space, light, grateful shadow, gentle grandeur.'[80] The square was now, in fact, among the brightest and healthiest in the metropolis. Its former splendour had, however, changed forever, for after the war the social character of the square was further transformed by the decline in its already depleted residential occupation. More clubs and offices moved in, which prompted a reappraisal of the use of the garden, and which in turn led to its being thrown open to the public in 1933.

As a postscript to the physical changes that metamorphosed some of the squares during the course of the war, it is worth noting the imaginative transformation of the interior of Trafalgar Square from a windswept piazza into a 'shell-shattered French village' (fig. 204). In October 1918 a desolate landscape was created at the centre of the square, complete with a ruined farmhouse ('riddled with shot and shell holes, and the garden torn up and irretrievably damaged'), gun emplacements, sandbagged trenches, blasted trees, a shattered windmill and a wireless station. This remarkable *mise-en-scène*, which was presumably intended to evoke the bleak and melancholy 'Old British Front' at Ypres in Flanders, formed the backdrop to two large public appeals — the Feed

204 The Camouflage Fair in
Trafalgar Square, October
1918, postcard. Author's
collection.

the Guns campaign and the Camouflage Fair. The former was by all accounts a remarkable success, drawing in £29 million from Londoners towards the war effort.[81] The latter event, which was the last great 'flag day' staged by the Red Cross before the signing of the armistice on 11 November 1918, also proved to be very popular with the public: it appealed to all sections of society, and raised considerable sums for the charity.[82]

What are we to make of these curious campaigns of October 1918? It was not, in fact, unusual for official and semi-official events during the war to have had a theatrical quality about them. Paul Fussell remarks, in *The Great War and Modern Memory* (1975), that 'the devices of the theatre were frequently invoked at home to stimulate civilian morale and to publicise the War Loan'.[83] Trudi Tate concurs, suggesting in *Modernism, History and the First World War* (1998) that these elaborately staged events encouraged civilians to enact a 'fantasy of the war as circus, or fairground, replicated in bizarre simulacra in Trafalgar Square'.[84] While some people objected to what they called '"the circus business" in connection with national finance', implying that the state's money should be treated with 'greater dignity', there

were, nonetheless, others who were of the opinion that 'the end has justified the means', and that these events served to make the British recognise their 'individual responsibility' to pay for the war.[85] Regardless of their aims, there can be no doubt that both Feed the Guns and the Camouflage Fair were remarkable and costly productions, and their importance in the war effort to raise much needed money and boost public morale is underscored by the fact that they took place within Trafalgar Square – the rallying point of the nation and the cross-roads of the empire.

'Public Opinion Must be Marshalled to the Point of Taking Drastic Action'[86]

While the fashion for laying out squares and enclosures in new building developments ceased in the middle of the nineteenth century, there was from late in the century 'some reversion to this method of lay-out of housing estates developed by local authorities under the Housing Acts'.[87] The adoption of this method was credited at the time to the increased attention paid to town planning principles and the provision of amenities.[88] The LCC made

205 (above) Cottages on the north and west sides of New Square off Courtenay Street, photograph, from *Journal of the London Society*, no. 4 (July 1914). London Society Library. Contemporary critics praised the simple dignity of this quadrangle, with its 'well-kept lawn, in an oasis of peace and quiet amid the noise and unrest of the metropolis'.

206 (below) Holmewood Gardens, Streatham, *c.*1910, postcard. Author's collection.

'generous provision of open spaces of this kind' in many of its estates, including Tabard Gardens in Southwark (1919–25) and China Walk in Lambeth (1927–9), both of which were created through slum clearances.[89] These estates and many others that had large open green spaces were inspired by Parker & Unwin's planned settlement at Hampstead Garden Suburb in Golders Green (begun 1904), which had no fewer than three large 'squares'.[90] None of the aforementioned garden spaces was, however, a square in the traditional sense, although they were all based on a similar principle. Courtenay Square in Ken-

nington (fig. 205), on the other hand, laid out by Professor Stanley Adshead on the Duchy of Cornwall Estate, was hailed in 1914 as a 'proper' square.[91] Built between 1912 and 1919, the low-rise development was an admirable exercise in urban renewal. Rather unusually, the central garden was left unenclosed – 'something which no self-respecting Georgian developer would ever have allowed'.[92] A few private square-like enclosures were also formed in the outer suburbs, such as Holmewood Gardens, Streatham (1894), and Lissenden Garden, Camden (1899) (fig. 206).

While new developments recognised the advantages of the long-established practice of introducing green space into the urban environment, the LCC was also mindful of the danger to existing squares of rebuilding in the more central areas of the city. One of the chief objects of the council's Town Planning Scheme for Bloomsbury was the preservation of the garden squares in the neighbourhood in light of the potential redevelopment of the area. Under the scheme the ten squares within the area were scheduled as private open space and thus protected.[93]

Town planning may have promoted the creation of new square-like gardens, and spared Bloomsbury, but it did little to preserve individual squares. Indeed, it was criticised by some as hastening the demise of the genuine squares. The conservationist Stenton Covington, for example, writing in 1927, alleged that since the war, and despite town planning, 'Endsleigh-gardens and Mornington-crescent have ceased to exist'. These were, as we shall see, the first major square gardens to be given over to building land, and their loss provoked considerable public alarm. Squares were, in Covington's words, 'menaced':

> any day may see the announcement that another square is doomed [and that its] reprieve can only be obtained by payment of an impossible ransom . . . To most Londoners any serious destruction of its ancient gardens seems almost unthinkable. Painfully and at great cost, the present generation is trying to correct some of the evil legacies of the past in urban development, but little impression can be made on the dreary, drab, and uninviting stretches of London bricks and mortar. It would indeed be tragic if London lost, or permitted serious inroad upon, its garden squares, which for 200 years have added to the beauty, dignity, and health of the capital.[94]

Covington's cynicism was justified. Soon after the terrible calamity of war, many formerly prosperous areas such as Notting Hill – whose squares and terraces, in Osbert Lancaster's words, 'had once formed the very Acropolis of Edwardian Propriety' – began to decline 'slowly into slumdon': its vast stucco palaces were converted into self-contained flats where 'an ever increasing stream of refugees from every part of the once civilised world had found improvised

homes, like the dark age troglodytes who sheltered in the galleries and boxes of the Colosseum'.[95]

The government, moreover, passed legislation conferring additional powers and imposing additional duties upon local authorities in respect of housing, health, education, public assistance and public amenity.[96] The aims of these acts were to improve the health and welfare of the community, and to provide the best conditions 'for the production of that energy required for great enterprises, financial success and prosperity as well as for the social advancement and contentment of the inhabitants'.[97] Inevitably, however, they also had a downside: they promoted a surge in building activity in the outlying districts – often without 'any systematic and adequate provision of lung spaces' – and substantial redevelopment in the city centre, which injured or obliterated historic open spaces. Throughout London, back gardens and similar small open spaces were covered with buildings, and houses of one, two or maybe three storeys were pulled down and replaced by 'immense warehouses, stores, and offices, hotels or barrack-like flats'.[98]

Many of these rebuilding schemes had a devastating impact on the squares and their precincts, and prompted the Garden Cities Association and the London Society to co-organise a conference on the plight of the squares. The event, held in the autumn of 1922, was a great success, and was attended by representatives from the MPGA, the RIBA, the Town Planning Institute and the Commons and Footpaths Preservation Society. As a direct result of the event, memorials were sent to the LCC urging that body 'to take steps . . . to secure permanently these open spaces that are so valuable an asset not only to their owners, but to the health and amenities of London as a whole'.[99] The LCC was also encouraged to embark upon a 'comprehensive scheme' for preserving these 'valuable spaces' that were 'in danger of being used as building sites, so soon as the rights of the adjacent lessees to use them as private gardens comes to an end with the expiry of the leases'. It was, moreover, suggested that these areas, like churchyards and burial-grounds in use, should be 'sterilized and rendered ineligible as building sites, fair terms of compensation being, of course, paid to their owners for placing such a lien on their properties'.[100]

The question of the squares became increasingly urgent when in February 1923 concerns were raised

207 Pembroke Square, *c.*1912, photograph. Kensington and Chelsea Local Studies collection.

over the future of the neighbourhood of Kensington Square, and when in April of the same year it was announced that both Mornington Crescent and Endsleigh Gardens were 'in the market', and that building operations were poised to commence in Pembroke Square, Earl's Court (fig. 207).[101] The imminent destruction of these gardens prompted the LCC's Town Planning (Special) Committee to launch in February 1924 an inquiry to address the fate of the squares. They instructed their valuer, Mr Hunt, to prepare a detailed schedule of the squares. His brief was to determine which were in the hands of the authorities and therefore protected by the House of Lords judgment in the Edwardes Square case, and which were unprotected by the judgment and were thus 'in immediate danger through various causes', were in 'thickly populated districts', and were of high amenity value.[102] Harold Swann, Chairman of the Town Planning Committee, remarked that the inquiry would 'provide for the first time a basis of definite knowledge on which the whole problem can be judged in light of two essential qualifications – namely, what is reasonable, and what is financially possible'.[103]

These initiatives encouraged a handful of unscrupulous speculators to redouble their efforts to redevelop the squares in their possession. The 'ragged and beggarly' enclosure of Endsleigh Gardens[104] was particularly vulnerable, as its reputation had been tarnished by a celebrated murder in 1879, its few inhabitants had unwarily relinquished all rights over the enclosure, and the gardens had been desecrated by the erection of temporary buildings during the war.[105] Although attempts were made to save the gardens, their fate was sealed in July 1926, when a joint report of the Building Acts, Improvements and Parks committees recommended that no action be taken in the matter of their preservation 'either by acquisition or town planning'. It was argued that the sum demanded for the purchase of the land was too large, and that it was not necessary to preserve the garden as 'a score of similar squares existed within a half mile radius'.[106] Within weeks of this announcement, a hoarding was thrown up around the enclosure, and by the end of year the western portion of the gardens had been covered with the Society of Friends' London headquarters (figs 208 and 209). The Friends were thus the 'first to set the bad ex-

208 (*right*) St Pancras Church from Endsleigh Gardens, from the London Society's *London's Squares and How to Save Them* (n.d. [1927]), photograph. Gavin Stamp Collection.

209 (*far right*) The Society of Friends' London headquarters at the west end of Endsleigh Gardens, from the London Society's *London's Squares and How to Save Them* (n.d. [1927]), photograph. Gavin Stamp Collection.

210 (*below*) Bernard Partridge, *Wanted – An Open-Air Minister*, engraving, from *Punch* 171 (1926): 171.

211 (*facing page, top left*) Spencer Gore, *Mornington Crescent*, 1911, oil on canvas. Tate Collection.

212 (*facing page, top right*) Mornington Crescent Garden, from the London Society's *London's Squares and How to Save Them* (n.d. [1927]), photograph. Gavin Stamp Collection. 'A doomed site – Mornington Crescent, once an oasis of grass and trees which has already passed into the builder's hands, and is being prepared for factory developments, is a significant example of a fate which may await a number of London squares, particularly in Bloomsbury.'

ample of shutting out the light and air in one of the best planned areas of Central London'.[107] It was gloomily predicted at the time that the council's decision was bound to affect 'all the Bloomsbury Squares if and when they come up for sale' (fig. 210).[108]

Mornington Crescent fared no better than Endsleigh Gardens. Although appeals were made in 1924 for the retention of its 3-acre gardens, as they 'would be of great value to the children of the neighbour-

hood, which is now largely working class', they were purchased for £75,000 by the Carreras Cigarette Company and redeveloped as a garish Neo-Egyptian style factory (figs 211–13).[109]

Equally worrying was the announcement in November 1924 that the Foundling Hospital intended to quit its home and part with its 56-acre estate in Bloomsbury. The estate, which was then occupied by the hospital and its grounds, Mecklenburgh and Brunswick squares, and a large residential neighbourhood, retained 'a strong flavour of a bygone magnificence' (fig. 214).[110] The would-be purchasers were the Beecham Estates and Pills Company, which had recently acquired the Bedford Estate in Covent Garden, and which promoted a bill in Parliament to move Covent Garden Market to the site of the hospital, involving the 'absorption of the garden grounds of both Mecklenburgh and Brunswick Squares' (fig. 215).[111] This proposal aroused an 'intense opposition' not only from the residents of Bloomsbury, but also from the tenants of the market, as well as the principal authorities affected by the proposed removal, including the LCC, St Pancras and Holborn borough councils and many leading societies interested in the amenities, with the result that the bill was withdrawn.[112]

Although the threatened attack upon Brunswick and Mecklenburgh squares, through the Covent Garden Market Removal Bill, was averted, it was 'not too much to say that the chorus of criticism evoked by the measure both within and without the Houses of Parliament was due not so much to the removal of the market from its present position as to the condition that in the interests of wise Town

WANTED—AN OPEN-AIR MINISTER.

SPECULATIVE BUILDER (*to London*). "IT'S YOUR LUNGS I WANT!"

[Public protests are being made against the rumoured intention of converting the beautiful estate of the Foundling Hospital into a new Covent-Garden Market or otherwise building over this fine open space and its adjacent squares.]

213 Unknown artist, *Carreras Cigarette Factory*, Mornington Square, Camden, *c.*1928, poster. Camden Local Studies and Archives Centre.

Planning any radical alteration of a considerable area of Central London should not be left to the judgement of private corporations and individuals financially or otherwise interested in two important sites'.[113] The action of the promoters in withdrawing the bill was 'due to the tardy recognition of the widespread hostility to any undertaking calculated to imperil the amenities of the Metropolis'. It was remarked at the time, however, that the

withdrawal of the Bill (welcome as that event has been) must not be allowed to lull Londoners into

any false sense of security. With the examples of Mornington Crescent and Endsleigh Gardens so fresh in our memories we cannot allow the development of the Foundling Hospital to Site and the garden squares it contains to await haphazard determination at the hands of their ground landlords. It is of vital importance to London that the area should be treated with special sympathy and that Brunswick and Mecklenburgh Squares should be definitely protected and the amenities of the whole site as far as possible should be safeguarded.[114]

214 (*right*) Mecklenburgh
Square, Camden, 17 December
1926, photograph by H. F.
Davis.

215 (*below*) Unknown
draughtsman, proposal for the
redevelopment of the
Foundling Estate as a new
fruit and vegetable market,
from the London Society's
*London's Squares and How to
Save Them* (n.d. [1927]). Gavin
Stamp Collection.

'London's Squares and How to Save Them'

The great turning point in the campaign to save the squares took place at the Institution of Surveyors on the evening of 7 February 1927, when Mr Frank Hunt read his 'exhaustive paper' entitled 'The Garden Squares of London'.[115] In his address, Hunt put forward the case for the preservation of the squares very strongly from the town planning point of view, when he showed that the provision of these enclosures was an integral part of the original layout of the districts. There was, he believed, an urgent need to resolve the problem of the squares, especially in so far as the Minister of Health had intimated that

he hoped to 'enlarge the powers of local authorities to control built-up areas by extending thereto, in some form, the principles of town Planning'.[116] Such an extension would, Hunt remarked, 'present problems of the greatest magnitude'.[117]

The crux of the problem was, first, whether London squares needed regulations put in place to guarantee their preservation and, second, what those ought to be and how best to manage them. Hunt argued that local authorities who stipulated that certain grounds might not be built upon would be liable to pay compensation or find the owner another plot of land; for obvious reasons, this would reduce the incentive to preserve the squares. Another sug-

216 William Gaunt, *Prince's Square* (formerly Swedenborg Square), 1932, pen and ink with watercolour wash. Author's collection.

gestion mooted was that the local authorities might contribute maintenance for the upkeep of gardens as they stood; however, it was clear that the cost of maintaining a garden on behalf of the landowner would sooner or later exceed the sum needed to buy the freehold outright.

Sir Willoughby Hyett Dickinson wrote that there were potentially two paths that could be followed in this regard. The first was that local authorities be authorised to purchase the freehold of a garden, and that it then be either retained in its then state, or thrown open to the public. The second solution proposed an act of parliament that would secure the squares of London permanently as gardens, to be used for no other purpose.[118]

With regard to the first option – that the local authorities be allowed to take on the freehold of a garden – three issues were thought to arise: first, devoting the gardens to the public would arouse opposition from neighbouring householders; second, it would be difficult to justify the transfer of use from private to public; and third, if the local authorities were obliged to pay large sums to secure the land as open space, they would not do it, especially as few squares were large enough to serve as public recreation grounds (figs 216 and 217). Were the gardens, on the other hand, preserved by an act of parliament, it could be left to parliament to decide should there ever be a suggestion of opening them to the public.

217 Children at play on the merry-go-round in Bartholomew Square, March 1936, photograph by Reg Speller. The square, a 'small enclosure in the crowded district of Old Street' was laid out in the early nineteenth century on the site of the former burial ground of St Bartholomew's Hospital. It became a public recreation ground in 1895, and was among London's first floodlit playgrounds.

John Scurr, Labour MP for Mile End and alderman of the LCC, made good use of the contents of Hunt's speech when in February and March 1927 he introduced two bills in the Commons to preserve London squares, both of which ultimately promoted legislation with the passing of the London Squares Preservation Act of 1931. His bills provided that squares and enclosures should not be built upon without the consent of the Minister of Health, and if at any time the authorities consider that they should be acquired for the public then an enquiry was to be held and compensation paid if the acquisition were approved.[119] Although 'Scurr's Bills' proposed measures that would go some way to protecting squares, they were criticised by several of his supporters as 'too confiscatory'. Mr Basil Holmes, for instance, speaking on behalf of the MPGA, put forward a 'simpler' scheme – 'viz. to render the garden squares ineligible as building sites, fair terms of compensation being payable to the respective owners in each case, for the placing of this desirability upon their properties'. He did not suggest the purchase of

squares by any public body, but 'merely making them *ineligible* for building on fair terms'.[120]

The Commons and Footpaths Preservation Society came to the fore in July 1927, organising a conference that was attended by representatives of a variety of societies who were eager to devise a strategy for 'saving the Squares'. The proceedings were published by the London Society in *London's Squares and How to Save Them* (n.d. [1927]). In one of the pamphlet's essays, an anonymous author drew an analogy between the present plight of the square gardens and that of the commons some years earlier, recounting how the formation of the Commons and Footpaths Preservation Society in 1865 'revealed the ancient rights over these spaces that precluded owners from selling them at vast prices for use as delectable building sites'.[121] The public at large possessed no legal rights whatever over these lands, and 'although they had resorted to them for recreation from time immemorial, lords of the manor on every hand claimed the power to fence in the commons in order to develop them as building estates. Parliament, however, insisted that the retention of the commons was of the first importance to the whole community and that the 'legal rights and interests of the owners of the soil must give place to that consideration.' Accordingly, the Metropolitan Commons Act (1866) was passed, which forbade the enclosure of any of the commons in and around London, and 'provided machinery for the regulation of those lands as public open spaces'.[122] The public, it was argued, was now interested in the preservation of London squares as open spaces as well as from the point of view of amenity. Although they had no more right to use them than they had had to use the commons, the land could not lawfully be alienated and built upon 'any more than could a common while rights of common were in existence'.[123]

These trenchant views doubtless encouraged the government to set up a Royal Commission on London Squares in August 1927 to consider whether and on what terms squares and enclosures should be preserved as open spaces. The terms of reference of the commission defined the subject matter of enquiry as 'the squares or similar open spaces existing in the area of the Administrative County of London'. The commission was 'small, eminent, and largely titled', and was chaired by Charles Stewart Henry Vane-Tempest-Stewart, seventh Marquess of Londonderry.[124] The LCC contributed valuable material to it, which was supplemented by a questionnaire to affected parties. Its recommendations involved the permanent preservation of 'nearly all of London squares as open spaces, on very generous terms to the owners'.[125] These were in the main later embodied in the London Squares Preservation Act of 1931.

It was unusual to establish a royal commission for what some persons at the time considered a 'topic of relatively minor importance'.[126] However, the fact that the 'affairs of a capital city were involved, and more important those of the rich and propertied classes', brought it to the fore, or, as another investigator remarked at the time, it was felt that 'a commission would have more influence in obtaining evidence on this delicate subject'.[127]

The commission heard evidence from a wide range of witnesses, among them Sir Edgar Bonham Carter.[128] Bonham Carter was Chairman of the Finance Committee of the Commons and Footpaths Preservation Society and a member of the London Society and the MPGA, as well as a former member of the London

County Council Town Planning Committee, and the LCC Buildings Act Committee. Square gardens were, he argued, important from the point of view of town planning, public health, public amenity and traffic. He gave evidence on behalf of a number of 'well-known' amenity societies, which regarded the preservation of the square gardens and open spaces of a similar character as 'of the highest importance to London, and would consider the building over of any of them to be a public calamity'.[129]

Frank Hunt prepared most of the survey information for the commission, much of which was derived from earlier research, notably the LCC's 'Particulars of the Garden Squares'. To this, however, he added a supplementary series of tracings that illustrated the principal kinds of squares and enclosures in London (fig. 218).[130] Like his predecessors, Hunt quantified the squares to show their distribution and to impress upon the commission their impact on the metropolis. The results make fascinating reading. A very considerable part of the total number of squares was comprised in seven metropolitan boroughs: Kensington had 38 (48.78 acres); Westminster 25 (41.81 acres); St Pancras 24 (25.81 acres); Holborn 9 (30.38); Chelsea 12 (18.98 acres); St Marylebone 9 (17.5 acres); and Paddington 21 (12.7 acres). This meant that 138 squares (195.96 acres) of the total 231 squares (239.5 acres) in London were contained in these seven metropolitan boroughs – or nearly 60% of the number, and 82% of the total area of all the squares. Most of the squares lay north of the Thames (194 squares, at 224.01 acres); the boroughs south of the Thames contained only 37 squares (15.49 acres). Not only were there comparatively few garden squares in south London, these squares were on an average less than half the area of those in north London. As for enclosures, there were 200 across London comprising a total area of 160.64 acres: 147 of these lay north of the Thames (124.16 acres), and 53 south of the Thames (36.48 acres). The boroughs with the largest enclosures were Kensington, Paddington, Camberwell, Islington and Westminster.

When the royal commission published its report in September 1928 it concluded that squares were a 'very distinctive and attractive feature of the plans of the parts of London in which they are situate', that 'similar open spaces are not to be found except to a very limited extent in other towns in this or other countries', that 'beyond question' they added

LONDON COUNTY COUNCIL.
ROYAL COMMISSION ON LONDON SQUARES.
Appendix FH3 referred to in the Proof of Evidence of Mr Frank Hunt.
Sketches showing principal types of Garden Squares and Enclosures.

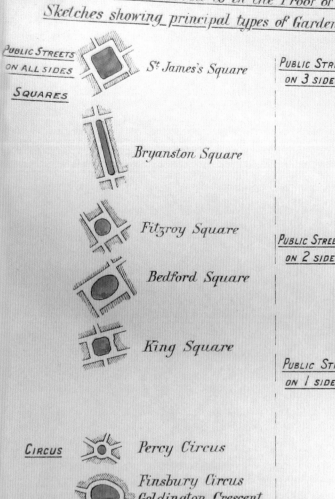

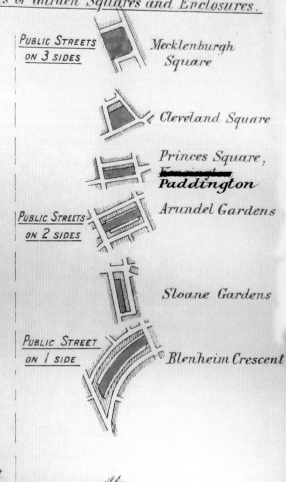

PUBLIC STREETS ON ALL SIDES

SQUARES

St James's Square

Bryanston Square

Fitzroy Square

Bedford Square

King Square

PUBLIC STREETS ON 3 SIDES

Mecklenburgh Square

Cleveland Square

Princes Square, ~~Kensington~~ **Paddington**

PUBLIC STREETS ON 2 SIDES

Arundel Gardens

Sloane Gardens

PUBLIC STREET ON 1 SIDE

Blenheim Crescent

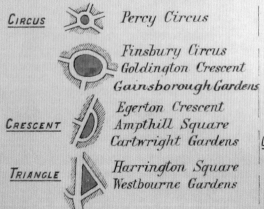

CIRCUS

Percy Circus

Finsbury Circus
Goldington Crescent
Gainsborough Gardens

CRESCENT

Egerton Crescent
Ampthill Square
Cartwright Gardens

TRIANGLE

Harrington Square
Westbourne Gardens

Goldsmith Square

INTERIOR GARDENS

Warrington Crescent
Randolph Crescent
Clifton Gardens

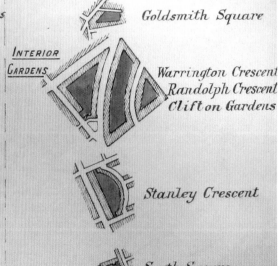

VARIOUS

Thornhill Square

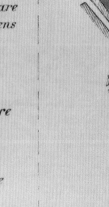

Oakley Square

Stanley Crescent

South Square, Gray's Inn

greatly to the amenities, not only of their immediate surroundings, but of London as a whole, and that the air spaces they afforded were of benefit to the well-being of the community (fig. 219).[131] Given these, and other compelling reasons, the commission recommended that squares should be preserved permanently as open spaces.[132] It also proposed conditions on which the squares should be preserved, and made suggestions for their improvement, including replacing perimeter hedges with grass borders, or, failing this, the contrivance of wide openings in the hedges; and the removal of the enclosures' 'thick, and frequently ugly' iron railings.[133]

It is a measure of the importance of the commission's findings that even the Prime Minister was involved in the aftermath: it was reported in October 1928 that Neville Chamberlain held out 'no hope of early legislation'.[134] He was, in this regard, right: only on 4 March 1931 did an act promoted by the LCC finally give effect to the commission's recommendations.

The London Squares Preservation Act (1931) was not only the 'rock upon which all preservation of squares is built',[135] but among the first acts of parliament to protect designed landscapes. The act, most importantly, gave protection to 461 squares and enclosures within the boundaries of the Administrative County of London, and constrained the potential for development within them. It was, however, far from perfect: it did not resolve the issue of the management of squares or the method of dealing with neglected squares; nor did it provide a mechanism for the review of the legislation. Sadly, it did not take long for these, and other shortcomings of the act, to cause further problems for these beleaguered urban havens.

'London Squares and a Traffic Tyranny'

The ever increasing tide of vehicular traffic in the metropolis (fig. 220) had a significant and detrimental impact on the squares: not only were they becoming open-air car parks, but the 'roar of the traffic' was rapidly eroding the tranquillity of these 'cool and shaded oases'.[136] A contributor to The Builder in May 1924 declared that given the 'intensification of street traffic', the inhabitants were justified in their desire to obscure views from the gardens to the road. Dense hedging and trees were an 'essential' foil: 'this

natural drapery and accompaniment reveals architecture to its further advantage'; furthermore, the greenery harboured the 'pleasures of bird life'.[137] An earlier contributor to the same magazine, was less convinced: lush vegetation was 'smothering' the city's open spaces, and obscuring views to the surrounding architecture. Grosvenor Square was singled out for particular criticism: what was once an airy open field was now an 'overgrown jungle'.[138] The painter, Sir William Orpen, writing in Country Life in 1924, was even more disdainful, alleging that most of London's squares would be 'far more imposing without their dank, dripping trees and railed off enclosures . . . Overcrowding trees', he remarks, contribute an air of 'dim sadness' to the squares, and impair the dignity of these formerly bright and airy places: 'Can one imagine filling up the Place Vendome with trees – dripping ones – wet clay and dank grass for the most part of the year?' Orpen alleged that it was impossible to enjoy London's cheerless enclosures: 'touch a leaf and your finger is black', and sit on the grass and 'your clothes are destroyed'.[139]

Road traffic and surface parking and their associated evils may have been annoying, but they were not so potentially destructive as underground car parking. While the 1931 act ensured that the majority of the square gardens would never fall into the hands of the 'overground builder', it neither protected their subsoil from underground development, nor controlled the buildings and the roadways around them.[140] These factors were to have profound consequences on the fabric of the West End squares.

In his essay 'London Squares and a Traffic Tyranny' (1934), the art critic Dugald Sutherland MacColl deplored the change in the social and economic fabric of the squares: 'old buildings, part stately, part homely' were being broken up. 'The flight to flats from spacious houses with basements and many stairs, a result of restricted families, unrestricted taxation, paucity and cost of service, combined with the western movement of business' was transforming the squares' 'old occupancy'; and building redevelopment meant that few still retained their 'old sober symmetry'. The 'brave days of the squares, as they were built to be', were, he lamented 'past or threatened'.[141]

Incensed by the prospect of the further degradation of the city's squares, MacColl railed against the 'frowsy perversion' of 'monster building' that threatened to dwarf the city's squares into 'well-like

218 (facing page) Unknown artist, 'Sketches Showing Principal Types of Garden Squares and Enclosures', 1927, Proof of Evidence of Mr Frank Hunt to the Royal Commission on London Squares. Parliamentary Archives, London, FCP/1/46, Appendix F.H.3.

courts',[142] and the swelling demand for 'wheeled transport' that was destined to transform these verdant refuges into busy thoroughfares or car parks.[143] He proposed that action be taken to 'preserve a tolerable proportion between the area of open space and the height of its surrounding architecture'. The 'growing fever of traffic', and poor traffic planning would inevitably reduce Portman and Bedford Squares to mere roundabouts; 'hugger-mugger' reigned at Cavendish Square; and St James's Square was disfigured by 'a many-storeyed slip of building . . . an overgrown, weedy hobble-dehoy'. MacColl declared that the trend of increasing levels of vehicular circulation had an 'insidious destructive' effect on the fabric of the city's squares: the 'grind, sizzle, and vibration' of lumbering tramcars and trolley vehicles would shake the very foundations of the buildings that surrounded the squares.[144]

When MacColl was writing there had only been talk of forming 'waiting places [car parks] under the gardens'; nothing had so far been done, and the 'mischief of a provisional arrangement' continued.[145] This began to change from October 1934, when an official at the Ministry of Transport announced that 'there is absolutely no room left in [central] London which is available for parking': provision must be made 'not only to palliate the ills of to-day, but also [to] anticipate the exigencies of to-morrow' (fig. 221). Subterranean development of the 'squares and similar open spaces' was identified as 'a real solution of the problem'. The preliminary works for such improvements should, it was reported, 'be put in hand forthwith'.[146]

That the subsoil of the squares remained unprotected by the 1931 act resulted from a proviso directing that the restrictions imposed by the bill 'should not prevent the owner of the enclosure from using the subsoil for the construction and maintenance of underground works and buildings'.[147] The owners or lessees of protected squares were 'specifically permitted to use the subsoil for the construction and maintenance of underground works, at the same time

222 Finsbury Square, 1939. Islington Local History Centre, Finsbury Library. The square is shown as it was being prepared for provision of air-raid protection.

taking over so much of the surface as may be necessary for the provision of entrances, exits, ventilation shafts, &c.'[148] While some saw the underground development of London's squares as an 'intelligent and far-sighted' solution to the problems of parking the ever increasing number of motorised vehicles in the congested West End, and in the squares in particular, many more disapproved of this measure as it was potentially destructive to the character of these erstwhile quiet residential precincts.

Serious plans to build car parks beneath the squares began to take shape from November 1938, when the Ministry of Transport considered options to create joint car parks and deep air raid shelters 'for providing as near as possible complete immunity from high explosive bombs as could be achieved'.[149] Initially an ambitious proposal was made for a 'grandiose car park scheme' to shelter 40,000 people under a Bloomsbury square.[150] There followed in February 1939 a scheme, developed by Messrs Tecton, architects, in collaboration with Dr O. N. Arup, for making similar 'structural shelters' in the Borough of Fins-

bury to provide refuge for over 39,600 persons; they were to be constructed under Charterhouse, King, Northampton and Finsbury squares and Percy Circus, and some were to be interconnected by tunnels. The projected construction in Finsbury Square was to be the largest of the shelters, being laid out over two floors, to garage 764 cars in 'normal circumstances', and to accommodate 12,000 persons in the event of war.[151] These plans and those at the other targeted squares were, however, later rejected: Finsbury Square garden was nonetheless requisitioned for use as a barrage balloon site, but only ten small underground shelters were excavated (fig. 222).[152]

Plans to create vast subterranean car parks under the squares were, like so many ambitious and expensive building projects, temporarily shelved with the advent of the Second World War. There was, however, from the early 1950s, as we shall see in Chapter 7, considerable eagerness on the part of the Ministry of Transport to resolve the traffic problem in central London, and the squares were, in the ministry's view, a soft target.

The writer Douglas Goldring, later Secretary of the Georgian Society, writing in 1936, despaired at the destruction of eighteenth-century London, remarking:

> it is no exaggeration to say that, since 1920, nearly every architectural feature . . . which was so characteristic of our national temperament and as expressive of our taste and culture as the Place Vendôme and the Place des Vosges are . . . expressive [of] the taste and culture of the French, has been either destroyed or partially ruined. Even the Squares of Mayfair and Bloomsbury – those masterpieces of by-gone town planning, that were so long a source of justifiable civic pride – have all, with the exception of Bedford Square, been hopelessly defaced . . . The new buildings which have been erected in the Squares have, in no case that I can recall, been designed to harmonize with their surroundings.[153]

Goldring was presumably referring in part to the University of London's proposed redevelopment of an 11.5-acre portion of the Bedford Estate north of the British Museum Extension, and in particular to the architect Charles Holden's 'great building, nearly a quarter of a mile long, with two towers'.[154] Holden's scheme proposed the obliteration of Torrington Square, and would have dominated the skylines of Bedford, Russell, Tavistock and Woburn squares (figs 223 and 224). It was argued by some at the time that the greater part of Torrington Square should be preserved 'as a pool of silence in the middle of London, Carlyle's "huge roaring Niagara of things", a beautiful garden, providing light, air, access and prospect for the University buildings, a place for recreation, garden parties, open-air plays, a hearth for our *lares et penates* including . . . the Officers' Training Corps Memorial'.[155] After a concerted campaign led by T. L. Humberstone, part of the square was saved in 1937, and became known unofficially as the 'University Garden'.[156]

If the future for the squares and their precincts looked grim in the mid-1930s, it began to look even gloomier with the looming prospect of war. It was widely predicted that, given the progress in the design and construction of military aircraft that led to great advances in the technique of bombardment,

aerial bombing of London was inevitable, and that such a grave menace would doubtless result in the indiscriminate destruction not only of single buildings but sometimes of whole districts of the metropolis.[157] The preparations for war would, therefore, necessitate the construction of a range of civil defences, including surface and subterranean air-raid shelters, emergency water tanks and trenches, many of which would be built in the squares, as they were among the largest open spaces in the most closely built-up quarters of the city. A great number of trench shelters were, for instance, constructed under the squares of Islington, including Arlington, Arundel, Barnsbury, Canonbury, Cloudsley, Gibson, Lonsdale, Milner and Union squares, and Annett's Crescent. Most of these were designed to accommodate several hundred civilians, and had electric lighting, seats, ladders, lavatories and a drinking-water supply (fig. 225).[158] In some places, such as Onslow Square in South Kensington, the trenches were also used during the war as accommodation for workmen involved in clean-up operations in the neighbourhood.[159] Similar preparations were made at many other metropolitan squares.

The government began its Air Raid Precautions (ARP) in 1935, but it was not until the Munich crisis of September 1938 that its policies began to affect the squares. During the crisis a great number of squares across the capital were 'hastily "trenched"' at the request of the Home Office to provide shelter for civilians during possible air raids in the event of war being declared (fig. 226).[160] Many of these trenches were 'placed more or less haphazard in every piece of open ground available' and were subsequently abandoned or filled in when war was thought to have been averted, only for some of the best sited of these 'relics' to be re-excavated and made 'permanent' the following spring, under powers conferred by the 1939 Civil Defence Act.[161]

Civilian building activity, and demolitions in particular, did not, of course, entirely cease during the early stages of the war. An anonymous contributor to *The Times* published a 'valediction' in June 1939, contending that 'the time has come when it may be said that Georgian Bloomsbury has ceased to exist as a distinct architectural unit on the map of London. This year and last the pick-axe has crushed heavily into that familiar area of brown-brick streets and squares': two sides of Russell Square were 'tumbling

223 (*right*) No. 30 Torrington Square, Bloomsbury, *c.*1910. The poet Christina Rossetti lived at this house in the square from 1876 until her death in 1894. Although she found the garden with its 'several graceful trees . . . attractive, almost picturesque', her friend and biographer Mackenzie Bell described the enclosure with its 'prim and somewhat sooty iron railings' as 'by no means inviting'.

224 (*below*) Adams, Holden & Pearson's preliminary designs for new buildings for the University of London, Bloomsbury, showing their relationship to Gordon and Russell squares, 1936, pencil. RIBA Library. The original intention was to build over Torrington Square, but part of the square was ultimately saved as a garden.

into ruins', the east side of Tavistock Square was a 'hoarded blank' and the south side 'merely a fragment', Euston Square was poised to be developed, part of Woburn and the whole of Torrington squares were 'receding before the Portland stone-bergs of London University', steelwork was rising on the north block of Brunswick Square, Mecklenburgh Square was 'threatened', and a 'tall new block' had destroyed the uniformity of Cartwright Gardens.[162] Other squares, too, were under threat: the residents of Fitzroy Square were, for example, struggling to preserve the fine Georgian 'street architecture' of the surrounding buildings.

When war was declared in September 1939 many of the private residents of the squares closed their houses, and office staff were evacuated. Trustees minutes suggest that it was, nonetheless, 'business as usual' at many squares' gardens: the gardeners (most of whom were too old to serve) did their best, 'under somewhat difficult conditions', to keep the gardens as trim and tidy as possible, in spite of the fact that many were encumbered by war-time buildings and

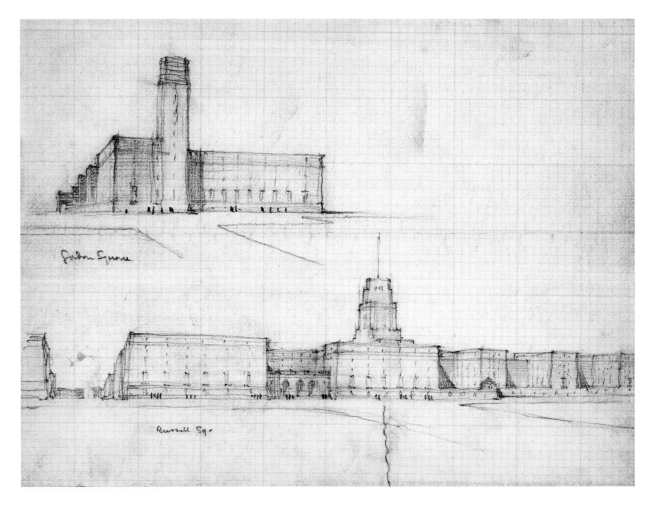

225 (*right*) Residents of Arundel Square in Barnsbury, north London, dig their own trenches and air-raid shelter on a local patch of waste ground, 23 September 1938, photograph.

226 (*below*) Air-raid shelter trenches being dug in the central garden at Lincoln's Inn Fields, *c.*1938, photograph.

227 (*right*) Unknown draughtsman, plan for the construction of an air-raid shelter under the east end of Ladbroke Square, 1941, pen and ink. Kensington and Chelsea Local Studies collection.

228 (*below*) Members of the Women's Auxiliary Air Force tethering a barrage balloon in Grosvenor Square, *c*.1943, photograph. Imperial War Museum (neg. no. 262341).

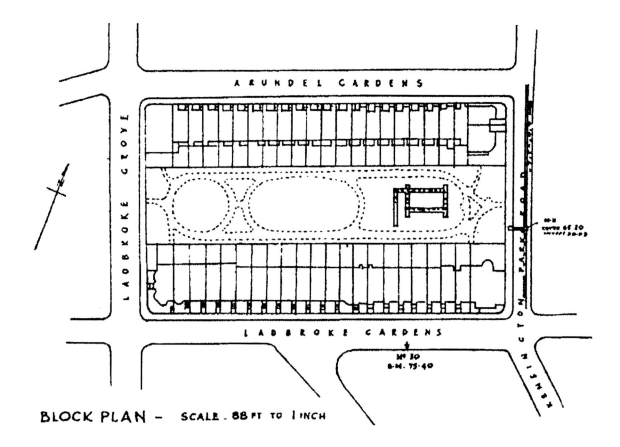

BLOCK PLAN – SCALE. 88 FT TO 1 INCH

civil-defence structures.[163] From spring 1940 air-raid shelters 'for public exhibition purposes' were dug in some of the squares, and latterly underground shelters, trenches and emergency water tanks were formed by order of the LCC's Town Planning and Building Regulation Committee (fig. 227). Every effort was supposed to be made to ensure that 'the amenity of the squares is impaired as little as possible, and that, if it became necessary to remove trees, other trees should, if possible, be planted to replace them'.[164] In practice, however, the workmanship was occasionally sloppy and the defences poorly sited and badly drained, causing considerable damage to mature trees.[165]

Squares served other useful purposes during the war, ranging from barrage balloon sites to 'war-time nurseries' or playgrounds for children (fig. 228). From mid-summer 1942 portions of Granville, Lloyd and King squares were, for example, opened for the use of children from day nurseries.[166] It was proposed that other squares be brought under the plough: from February 1939 the LCC gave consideration to the need for scheduling and zoning areas within the County of London 'for allotment purposes, sufficient for the potential demand'.[167] Later, in October, the Ministry of Agriculture launched its

229 Adrian Paul Allinson, *The A.F.S. 'Dig for Victory' in St James's Square*, 1942, oil on canvas. Westminster City Archives.

'Dig for Victory', and afterwards the 'Dig for Plenty' campaigns, exhorting able-bodied members of the public to grow their own fresh vegetables.[168] Surprisingly few squares, however, were given over to cultivation – sometimes on account of the ubiquity of ARP defences, the gardens' poor soil or the lack of a regular water supply, or because of strong local opposition.[169] The *Evening Standard*, nevertheless, reported in October 1939 that vegetables were being grown in Tavistock Square, and 'the land between the trench shelters' in Paultons Square, Chelsea, was also given over to allotments.[170] Later, in the spring of 1942, the inhabitants of St James's Square handed their central garden over to the Auxiliary Fire Service for vegetable production (fig. 229); and in December of the same year, a portion of Finsbury Square (above the air-raid shelter) was pegged out and cultivated.[171]

While only a scattering of squares were used for arable production, many more became settings for musical entertainments, and latterly 'Home Holidays'. Bartholomew, King, Northampton and Wilmington squares were, for example, frequently used during the war for band concerts, dances or children's entertainments.[172] The 'Holidays at Home

Programme' was instigated in 1943, and was described by the Ministry of Information as Britain's idea for providing annual relaxation for war workers without throwing too much strain on war transport. These festive events entailed the staging of concerts, games and flower shows, some of which took place in the squares. Among the best-documented is the 'War Fair, Holiday at Home Fete in Russell Square' (1943) (fig. 230). The private enclosed garden was metamorphosed temporarily into a public pleasure ground, decked with bunting, pennants and Union flags, and equipped with a skittle alley, a white elephant stall and other attractions, all of which were laid out in the lee of the giant plane trees and amid a mosaic of civil defences. The fair was a collaboration of the Holborn branch of the Red Cross and St John's Ambulance Brigade and Holborn Borough Council, and the money raised was put towards good causes and prisoners of war funds.

'The Battle of the Railings'

Of the many physical changes that took place to the squares during the course of the war, few were as controversial as the removal of their railings. While

230 A member of the Red Cross supervises a young boy attempting to drive a nail into Hitler's coffin at the War Fair in Russell Square, 1943, photograph. Imperial War Museum (neg. no. D 14682).

231 (*facing page*) The removal of the railings in Russell Square, 1942, photograph. Imperial War Museum (neg. no. HU 57738). The railings went for scrap for munitions.

there had been several earlier campaigns to dispense with the iron palisades, there had never been, until the advent of the Second World War, a moral imperative that sanctioned their official and almost total eradication (fig. 231).[173] The dependence of modern steel works on scrap iron ensured that the question of adequate scrap supplies would be one of the major points considered in the war. Not surprisingly, the often heavy and conspicuous railings round the squares became 'fair game for the zeal of reformers', most of whom, fuelled by patriotic enthusiasm, gave scant consideration to the aesthetic value they conferred on their surroundings.[174]

The movement to rid the squares of their railings began to gain momentum in April 1937 when Sir Thomas Inskip (then President of the Lord's Day Observance Society), presiding over the annual dinner of the Gardeners' Royal Benevolent Institution, proposed a toast in which he remarked that, as a garden lover, he would like to see the iron railings removed from the square gardens in the West End: it would be 'no bad thing for the residents in those

squares and for the people who dwelt in the neighbourhood if those gardens were available for wayfarers to rest in'.[175] These observations were subsequently published in *The Times*, and prompted Margot Asquith, to write in support, exclaiming that there was 'not a city in Europe where there are so few seats to sit upon or open spaces in crowded quarters where tired men and women can rest as there are in London. And except for the privilege of looking at the fine trees, of what benefit to the public are any of our dingy, uninhabited squares?'[176]

Inskip's plea also struck a chord with the London Society, and with Wyndham Deedes, Chairman of the London Council for Social Services, who campaigned to extend the benefits and amenities of these gardens to less fortunate members of the community.[177] Deedes had been trying since the early 1930s to persuade the residents of a clutch of London squares to open their gardens in the summer holiday months to some of the neighbours in adjacent poor areas, and especially 'the aged and invalids and mothers with small children, who never get away for a holiday at all'.[178]

The inhabitants of the squares did not generally share these sentiments: railings preserved their rights to property and ensured the very existence of these private spaces. They were therefore very attached to their railings and their much maligned perimeter hedges, stating that 'every year yards of this strong railing is smashed by cars whirling round the square at terrific speed and dashing into it. If railing and hedge do not prevent the intrusion of cars, what would be the fate of the children inside the square if such protection were removed?' Hedges also protected the tender planting in a 'draughty London square', minimised 'poisonous fumes from motor traffic', deadened the sound of traffic, and preserved the privacy so greatly valued by those who used the squares.[179]

The proposed campaign to remove the squares' railings was again aired in the press in April 1938. The architect Clough Williams-Ellis, writing in *The Times*, expressed his dislike of spiked railings, which he regarded more as a provocation than a deterrent. The English, he remarked, were as a nation 'great railers-off and railers-in', and 'the Englishman's home is his cage'.[180] He credited Winston Churchill with forming a plan during the First World War to melt down 'all the railings round our parks and square

gardens, and [convert] them into munitions'. This scheme was, however, abandoned when the armistice of 1918 supervened. He remarked that the 'expedient for the revealing of urban greenery having proved abortive, might we not yet deliberately uproot these disfiguring barriers while the going in the scrap metal market is so good – or do we in truth love them for their own sake and for all that they stand for and symbolize?'[181] Williams-Ellis proposed that the English, like most people on the Continent, could 'get along very well without elaborate defences'. In order to ascertain 'how destructive the public would be – especially on dark nights', he proposed that one half of the railings in Eaton Square 'be removed by way of a test case, and let us see the result and have an authoritative report on the desperate experiment. One can scarcely believe that the atrocities thus risked would be so very frightful.'[182]

All these views, and Williams-Ellis's in particular, marked the beginning of a spirited campaign that was to 'rage' throughout the Second World War, which was dubbed, at the time, 'The Battle of the Railings'. The campaign, according to the historian Celina Fox, was 'not simply a question of supplying scrap metal for munitions as the war ate into reserves', but a 'battle fought for democracy – for modern tastes and ideas'.[183] Railings, reported a correspondent to the *Evening News* in 1938, stood for privilege, 'as constant reminders of an outdated system of social hierarchy, for a lingering adherence to Victorian views of the sacredness of property'.[184] Fox contends that their removal was not, therefore, 'merely a pragmatic reaction to the circumstances of war, but bore a weightier aesthetic and political burden of meaning and was as symbolic, in its small way, of the yearning for a better world, for a more egalitarian society, as many more ambitious dreams of the epoch'.[185] The official battle lines for the campaign were drawn in May 1939, when the LCC's Town Planning and Building Regulation Committee addressed 'the question of the removal of railings around 54 garden squares'.[186] The explicit aim was to open the gardens to the public, although the scheme was also doubtless motivated by the desire to requisition railings for conversion into armaments.

The official campaign for 'goodwill' scrap metal began with the declaration of war in September 1939, though it had no immediate impact on the squares. There was, in fact, initially a marked reluctance on the part of square owners and inhabitants to contribute to the war effort, and, indeed, there appeared to be little reason to do so, as the Ministry of Supply made clear in the summer of 1940 that it did not propose to take away railings of historic interest and artistic value.[187] The ministry, however, very soon reneged on this promise: in February 1941 they compelled the LCC Parks and Gardens Committee to sacrifice 'on the patriotic altar' hundreds of tons of railings removed from Lincoln's Inn Fields and Leicester Square;[188] and soon thereafter this precedent was used to persuade the trustees and garden committees of Berkeley and St James's squares to accede voluntarily to the removal of their railings (fig. 232). James Melvin and Bryan and Norman Westwood writing in the *Architectural Review* in 1940, affirmed that the railings round parks and squares had always been 'fair game for the zeal of reformers', and that this impulse posed a 'danger' that 'patriotic enthusiasm may get the better of aesthetic sense and the buildings, and layouts of our cities may lose for ever an essential element of their design'.[189]

Culling the railings of the Bloomsbury squares on the Bedford Estate was a more difficult undertaking: the twelfth Duke of Bedford, as a pacifist, 'could not voluntarily offer them as a contribution to the war effort'.[190] The ministry, however, under the leadership of Lord Beaverbrook, waged a dirty campaign, and ultimately got its way: by November 1941 the railings around all of the Bloomsbury squares, excepting those at Bedford Square, had been requisitioned for scrap. The reprieve of the latter's 'beautiful railings of elliptical formation' was almost wholly due to the efforts of the Georgian Group.[191]

Under the voluntary scrap scheme, owners of the squares were generally, by their own admission, 'unwilling to take the patriotic course' to remove their railings, and to throw open their gardens.[192] Sacrificing the railings would, they argued, lead to a decline in value of their property, would endanger the users of the amenity, and would lead to their gardens' defacement. The inhabitants were also initially discouraged by the Ministry of Supply's ramshackle approach to the matter, and by conspicuous dumps of scrap that suggested that it was neglected or unwanted. In reality, most of the scrapped railings

232 Workmen removing the railings in Berkeley Square, 3 March 1941, photograph. Imperial War Museum (neg. no. HU 57684).

eventually found their way to Sheffield (and were not dumped in the sea, as is still commonly believed), where they were 'taken by the iron foundries, thus relieving the strain on the blast furnaces for pig-iron and allowing them to supply more to the steel works'.[193]

There were, predictably, mixed reactions to the removal of the railings. The *Architectural Review* expressed satisfaction with the throwing open of Berkeley Square, praising the result 'aesthetically and as a piece of urban planning'.[194] However, accounts abound of the rise in anti-social behaviour, vandalism and unintentional damage that ensued after the railings of many squares were removed. The borough councils reported that the gardens were being used by the general public as 'dumping grounds for

rubbish'; a letter in the *Daily Telegraph* reported that 'any lover of London's beauty would be heartbroken to see what unimpeded access had done to Berkeley Square, where the grass has been worn to mud;[195] and a Member of Parliament asserted in May 1942 that the removal of the railings at St James's Square was nothing short of a 'barbaric act of Socialism'.[196] The police, too, had strong views: they wanted to see erected a 'strong hoarding or fence' around Leicester Square, as 'if the garden were left open at night the responsibilities of Police would be unduly increased owing to prostitutes, vagrants and other undesirable elements resorting there'.[197]

The damage to the squares' gardens appears to have increased from March 1942, when compulsory powers to requisition scrap metal were introduced.

In the eyes of some inhabitants, this was the 'only just and reasonable solution', as all squares were treated equally, and the inhabitants were ostensibly eligible for compensation for the loss of their railings.[198] The reality, however, was that the promise of compensation was less important to the inhabitants than the protection of their amenity. This was especially true where they were still liable for garden rates even though their gardens were no longer exclusive. The inhabitants' infatuation with their railings is demonstrated by the fact that no sooner were they removed than they were replaced with makeshift solutions, including simple wires strung between existing shrubs, wooden stakes or concrete posts in order that 'a certain amount of privacy might be maintained'.[199] The residents of Cavendish Square, who saw their railings vanish in the autumn of 1942, swiftly re-enclosed their central garden with chestnut pales. This action, however, prompted an angry letter in The Times, in which the authors condemned the loss of a 'lunch-time open space'. War workers who spent their days in 'bomb-proof, bricked-up buildings' in the vicinity of Oxford Street reported that many of them had enjoyed a brief lunch hour in the quiet of Cavendish Square, and found themselves 'rested and refreshed by this short interlude in the sunshine and fresh air'.[200]

Other correspondents, too, appealed for help 'against the frantic desire to re-rail squares, &c., just when we are slowly coming to see the beauty and dignity of pavements and stretches of turf wide open to the eye'.[201] The residents of Hans Place Gardens, on the other hand, adopted a more relaxed approach to the loss of their railings. An inhabitant reported that they refrained from erecting temporary fencing after their railings had been removed, 'as has been done in many squares, for we thought that, if the garden was kept up as a garden, it would be appreciated by the public and treated with some respect'. They were, however, dismayed to find that within a short spell the garden's hedges were 'broken through, the flower-beds trampled upon, garden seats smashed, and the turf badly cut up'.[202]

Some outsiders were sympathetic to the plight of the inhabitants: Mr J. B. Abraham reported in *The Times* in September 1942 that while he was pleased to see the railings around the city's parks and gardens disappear, his rejoicing was 'short-lived, for the freedom resulting from the change has been sadly abused by all classes alike', and in particular by those who partook of 'the craze for taking short cuts across the grass instead of keeping to the paths'.[203] These 'destroyers' were known as 'short cut fiends';[204] and so numerous were the complaints of their depredations that the chief officer of the LCC Parks Department introduced plain-clothes patrols and additional keepers to prevent 'considerable damage' being done by 'gangs of youths and young girls bent on mischief and probably infected by the "destruction" complex of the moment'.[205]

Given the problems associated with the unregulated access to the squares, it is not surprising that by the summer of 1944 many private squares had reinstated their fencing. George Orwell grumbled in *The Tribune* on 4 August 1944 that 'the railings are returning – only wooden ones, it is true, but still railings – in one London square after another. So the lawful denizens of the squares can make use of their treasured keys again, and the children of the poor can be kept out.' Orwell saw the removal of railings as a 'democratic gesture' that had the potential to improve London 'out of recognition'. He hoped they would vanish permanently, and that this would lead to yet another 'improvement' – the replacement of their 'dreary shrubberies' with flower-beds. The author despised laurel and privet, in par-

ticular, which were not in his view 'suited to England and always dusty, at any rate in London'.[206] His remarks underscore the potential complexities of the horticultural class system: Orwell clearly perceived shrubberies as intensely symbolic of class, and therefore branded the squares as 'suburban'.

While Orwell condemned the squares' gardens as dreary and dusty, many Londoners who spent much of the war within the metropolis perceived them as alluring sanctuaries in an inhospitable world. Elizabeth Bowen's short story 'In the Square', written in a 'hot, raid-less patch of 1941 summer, just after Germany invaded Russia', encapsulates the mysterious charm and 'lucid abnormality' of the capital's bombed-out squares during the 'war climate': the 'violent destruction of solid things, the explosion of the illusion that prestige, power and permanence attach to bulk and weight, left us all, equally heady and disembodied'.[207] Such private, intramural spaces were detached from the experience of the everyday and the turmoil of the hostilities – they were, in Bowen's words, 'extinct scenes' which had 'the appearance of belonging to some ages ago'.[208] A handful of war-time melodies also attest to this popular sentiment, including 'In a Green London Square' (1941), and 'The Trees in Grosvenor Square' (1945) (fig. 233). None, however, is so powerfully expressive as 'A Nightingale Sang in Berkeley Square' (1940). The music publisher Reg Connolly, writing in *Variety* in January 1944, observed that the romantic ballad became a hit 'perhaps because it brought a touch of light, warmth and charm into black-out homes'.[209] First performed in June 1940, when German bombs were raining down on London, the song evokes the pre-Blitz charm and elegance of this 'famous London Square'.[210] It also, however, vaunts the special atmosphere of the square's garden, which became intensified during the calamity of war: the garden was a refuge, while the nightingale – no ordinary denizen of the metropolis – conjures up a degree of transcendence of the ordinary and the everyday, and its presence serves to transform the mere garden into an enchanted grove or an earthly paradise. The song, moreover, designates the square as a timeless oasis of peace and tranquillity without actually saying what is going on in historical time.[211]

7

Post-war Planning and the Square to the Present

In 1946 Geoffrey Dudley Hobson published an essay entitled 'The Future of London Square Gardens' in his sanguinary and controversial pamphlet *Some Thoughts on the Organization of Art after the War.*[1] Art, he remarked, is a 'social activity: it affects society and is affected by it; architecture is influenced by building regulations and town planning; horticulture by the policy adopted in public parks and gardens'. In the aftermath of the conflict it was, he believed, 'a good moment to consider the question – war has changed much in the world of Art, as in the other worlds of man; what are these changes and what should be our attitude towards them? What opportunities have they brought and how shall we use those opportunities?'[2]

'Are We to Try and Restore the Past?'

Hobson observed that the war had drastically changed the gardens of many squares of the west, south-west and west central districts of London. There, in Kensington, Bayswater, Marylebone, Bloomsbury, Westminster and Chelsea in particular, 'almost everywhere the railings are down and many of the enclosures have been devastated, by jeeps, by lorries, or Nissen huts, or allotments, or the multitudinous tread of Londoners – Berkeley, Grosvenor, Bryanston and Onslow Squares are among those that have suffered most, but very few have escaped all damage' (figs 234–6).[3] 'What', Hobson asked, 'is to be done about

it? These gardens cannot be left as they are; are we to try and restore the past, to put back the gardens as they were before the war, or are we deliberately to aim at something different? Here, clearly, is another problem, another opportunity, though it seems to have attracted very little attention.'[4]

He then lamented that, as a remnant of the past, the design of the average square

> could hardly be worse: starting from the outside, we are met first by an iron railing completely destitute of artistic merit; next comes a straggling hedge, usually of privet, broken at intervals by forest trees, the roots and shade of which effectually prevent the hedge from flourishing; on the inner side this tattered green line often expands into a dowdy jungle of evergreens, separated by a curving path from a central lawn. After seeing some 30 or 40 of these in an afternoon the mind is invaded by Freudian obsessions, the tall trees come to assume a phallic significance, and the paths to represent the soft contours of a woman's body.

It was, he opined, unlikely that such thoughts were on the minds of the original designers: the gardens owed their character and taste to a 'period which was so firmly convinced of the superiority of Nature to Art'.[5]

Thousands of similar gardens may be seen up and down the land round the smaller country and

Facing page: Montpelier Square, Brompton, May 1951, photograph. This square, which like many others lost its railings during the war, was enclosed by 'temporary' wire netting for many years. In 1946 the novelist H. J. Bruce rated the square 'high among the backwaters of unexpectedness that make the charm of London'.

234 (*right*) The central
pavilion or *reposoir* in Russell
Square, *c.*1940, photograph.
Camden Local Studies and
Archives Centre.

235 (*below*) The *reposoir* in
Russell Square after it was hit
by a flying bomb in 1944,
photograph. Camden Local
Studies and Archives Centre.

suburban houses. The hedges and railings reveal Victorian determination to keep the common herd at a distance; the enclosed space was useful for parking Victorian families; and two or three turns round the winding paths gave the overfed Victorian paterfamilias the illusion that he deserved his massive Sunday dinner. In a word, the great majority of Square gardens suggest a state of society and outlook on life which are as obsolete as the tall middle-class Victorian houses round some of them, with their narrow passage-halls, their dark corners, their steep mean stairs, their vile proportions, their vulgar ornaments, and their dank, beetle-haunted basements. Many of these have been replaced by civilized modern houses, as in Chelsea Square, or by blocks of flats as in Lowndes Square and elsewhere; are the gardens to be restored to what they were when the old houses represented the last refinement of domestic architecture in the greatest city in the world? Surely not.[6]

As an addendum to this critique, it may be said that Hobson was ambivalent about the necessity of rail-

ings. They were to his mind a 'secondary matter, which should be left to the decision of whatever body administers the gardens; so long as these are laid out to the best advantage, so long as the straggling hedges and the dowdy jungles are swept away . . . I think, we should be prepared to agree to the total or partial abolition of railings, or their universal reinstatement, provided that the new gardens are rather pleasanter to look at than the old'.[7]

Perhaps of greatest import in his informed analysis of London squares was Hobson's advocacy of a consolidated ownership, whereby 'all of the 461 enclosures, which by the terms of the London Squares Preservation Act of 1931 are to be kept permanently as open spaces, should be vested in a single body, either the L.C.C. or – perhaps better – specially appointed Trustees'. Money, he continued, would 'have to be found to make the necessary changes and provide for the upkeep of the gardens; a permanent staff would have to be engaged and a nursery garden taken somewhere near London where annuals could be grown for bedding out, and shrubs for ornamental vases kept in their off season' (Hobson

provided a detailed list of plants that would grow in London squares). He recommended that the trustees might begin to improve their squares by removing the unsightly shrubs and hedges, and importing new soil and manure – 'both badly needed' (fig. 237). The squares should, moreover, be redesigned, and the schemes for their refurbishment submitted to

public criticism at the Royal Academy or in other ways, though the Trustees would have the last word. The schemes would naturally be numerous – different Squares need different treatments. It is indeed essential that there should be plenty of variety – no stereotyped plan will do; the gardens should be so diverse and all so good that an American visitor would simply *have* to see them all – the first question he would be asked on returning to the cultured circle of his native town would be 'Did you see the London Squares?' and his name would be mud if he had to answer 'No!'.[8]

Hobson then concludes with a fanfare of visionary motifs:

Perhaps the Kew officials would undertake the management of one garden and demonstrate what plants and flowering trees will flourish in London, experimenting continually to increase the range of them; or work might be done by the Royal Horticultural Society, or by a firm of professional horticulturists. One of the smaller, formal gardens might be used annually for an exhibition of garden ornaments. It would be a gracious act to get a French designer to lay out the garden of Manchester Square in front of Hertford House . . . Other Squares might be, wholly, or in part, memorials; one of those in Bloomsbury, for instance, might have in the centre a large round lily pool to represent the Lake of Nemi; round it would rise grassy mounds or rock gardens like miniature hills; in one corner there should be a bust close to a mass of plants and trees – forsythia, broom, tree lupin, laburnum, evening primrose, etc. – whose golden boughs and blossoms would complete the memorial to the greatest scholar of his generation, who has had more influence on the mind of man than any Englishman since Charles Darwin – Sir James Frazer. But there is no end to the possibilities; it is indeed almost awe-inspiring to think of the beauty that might come to the great open spaces, such as Eaton Square and Cadogan Place; no city in the world has equal opportunities. London might become as attractive as Paris and in a completely different way.[9]

Hobson was, in fact, a post-war prophet, both as interpreter of the present and seer of the near future. Indeed, several of his recommendations were taken up shortly after the publication of his essay: officials from Kew, the Royal Parks, the Royal Horticultural Society and the Georgian Group began regularly to advise inhabitants on the rehabilitation and management of their central gardens. In addition, a few squares became, 'in part, memorials' – Grosvenor Square (known familiarly as 'Eisenhowerplatz' during the war) acquired its statue of Franklin Delano Roosevelt after the passing of the Roosevelt Memorial Act (1946), which also provided for opening the garden for the use and enjoyment of the public in perpetuity (figs 238 and 239);[10] and in 1955 Sir Edward Maufe's Merchant Navy memorial and its sunken lapidary garden were formed in Trinity Square.[11] Even Hobson's suggestion that a French designer should be employed to lay out a square was taken up: Jean-Charles Moreux, architect-in-chief of the National Museums and Palaces in France, embroidered the small triangular ground at Grosvenor Gardens in Victoria with an 'arabesque de broderie'. This 'Franco-British Experiment' was intended to honour Marshal Foch, whose effigy stands in the garden, and to evoke the spirit of France (fig. 240).[12]

These initiatives must have bemused Hobson, who, on the whole, was optimistic yet remained sceptical about the future of the square. There was, he remarked, 'no reason why the new gardens should be better than the old; projects which sound well on paper are, not infrequently, less admirable in practice. Of course there is not, there cannot be, any guarantee that all the new designs will be good – the

risk of failures must be taken. But, on the whole, there is a very fair chance of considerable improvement'.[13]

'These Good Things We Must Do our Best to Keep'

Hobson's importance notwithstanding, he was not the first to address the issue of London squares after 1945. The fate of squares was in fact a subject of detailed consideration even during the war, when plans were being drawn up for proposed reconstruction of the capital. The Minister of Works began the ball rolling as early as 1941, when he instructed the London County Council to prepare a plan that would bring a 'new order and dignity to the whole of the County of London'. Even in the face of unimaginable war, the LCC, for its part, welcomed this 'great opportunity to build a new London, a better, finer, more spacious city'.[14]

The resulting County of London Plan, prepared by Sir Patrick Abercrombie in collaboration with the architect J. H. Forshaw, was published in 1943. It was based on a sustained and even-handed analysis of the metropolis as they knew it, and drew attention to major defects in the city's structure, including traffic congestion, substandard housing, intermingling of housing and industry and a lack of open spaces. The plan was praised by Lord Latham, Leader of the LCC, who had commissioned it, as 'probably the greatest objective study of the infinite variety of planning problems connected with a great centre of population, one of the greatest centres of industry and commerce, and even of heavy industry in the country: the capital of a Commonwealth and an Empire and also the seat of national administration'. It was, he continued, 'more than a mere physical location and siting of roads, buildings and open spaces. It is a great sociological study of the [future] needs of the population, in their work and in their play' (fig. 241).[15]

The aim of this visionary plan was quite simple: to put in place a systematic framework for the redevelopment and improvement of the County of London after the destruction of the war; or, in Abercrombie's own words, to produce a 'balanced form of environment'.[16] Central to his plan was the creation of new open spaces and roads. Open space was to be, from Abercrombie's point of view, 'one of the

238 (*right*) Grosvenor Square in the aftermath of the war, 1946, photograph by H. Galwey. RIBA Library.

239 (*below*) Eleanor Roosevelt with the royal party at the unveiling of the memorial to President Franklin Delano Roosevelt, in Grosvenor Square, 12 April 1948, photograph: (*left to right*) Field Marshal Viscount Alexander, Major Hooker, Queen Mary, Queen Elizabeth, Mrs Roosevelt, King George VI and Viscount Greenwood.

most important of all the features of London': it was essential for both recreation and rest, and was 'a vital factor in maintaining and improving the health of the people'.[17] Although London possessed some of the 'most beautiful and extensive open spaces in the world', they were, in his view, 'very badly distributed'. Most of the existing open spaces were in the centre, with hardly any open spaces in the poor and congested quarters of the East End.[18] The plan he proposed, therefore, would introduce measures to establish a more balanced distribution of public open space across the county.

Although wartime bombing in Southwark and the East End facilitated – with a cruel irony – the creation of new public open space, existing squares had a somewhat different fate: they were to be identified as convenient and historic neighbourhood hubs from which to form new, larger open spaces. Since many of these had been rendered semi-derelict by the war, a prospect for absorbing them into larger landscape 'units' and thereby making possible

their ostensible rehabilitation was also seen as the means of saving them.

Although Abercrombie believed that London's 'domestic squares' were 'good things [that] we must do our best to keep', they should, nonetheless, in the future 'be open to full public use' (fig. 242).[19] For him, the loss of the squares' railings during wartime had brutally, 'brought them into the life of the community and destroyed their isolation'. He furthermore suggested that the honoured 'tradition of the domestic square should be developed in the areas of reconstruction', as the squares could provide 'communal gardens for adults with play centres for the children'. As for the squares that were to be found in the central business areas, these, he believed, should take the form of rest gardens for lunch-hour use.

Abercrombie's plan was finally given official status in 1947, and within the next few years its policies began to inform the local authorities' development plans. Its proposals, however, did not extend to the

241 Unknown artist, 'London: Social and Functional Anaysis', map published in the *County of London Plan* by Sir Patrick Abercrombie and J. H. Forshaw (1943). Private collection. The different areas of Greater London are represented in colour-coded form; this stylised representation gives a clear impression of the number of green spaces in the capital.

City of London. The City Corporation was to commission its own thirty-year plan for reconstruction, drawn up by Dr Charles Holden and Professor William Holford. Yet its aims, expressed in the *City of London Plan* (1947), were generally complementary to Abercrombie's, proposing the creation of a handful of new squares, circuses and places. In fact, however, these open spaces were all too often little more than 'islands enclosed by traffic roundabouts'. Although not intended as 'normal building sites', some of these new openings were inevitably seen as potential sites for car parking amid trees, grass and shrubs.[20]

The 'Business of the London Squares'

Once war finally ended, a number of squares were, rather hastily 'demobbed' from their wartime garb – lawns were ploughed up and resown, new benches were installed, and bulbs, flowering trees and shrubs, and spring and summer bedding were planted. Such efforts, however, were at best but superficial embellishments, calculated to relieve the 'drabness of recent

years' (fig. 243).[21] What was needed was a long-term and comprehensive strategy for the repair, future use and management of the gardens; and London citizens, who during the war had become accustomed, and were anyway generally well disposed, to state intervention, could only look to the government of the day for a solution.

Indeed, as early as December 1945, the Home Office had taken the initiative to organise centrally the 'removal of obstructions from London Squares'.[22] It stated that 'it was essential that the County of London Area should be viewed as a whole', that a register of contractors should be prepared, and that 'about 1,200 hands should be available'. The local authorities were asked to submit plans for the clearance of their areas and such plans would proceed by zones. It was anticipated that the work would begin in early 1946 and that it would take between eighteen months and two years to complete.[23]

The objective of the scheme was, first of all, to demolish and remove public and communal surface shelters and similar defence structures in the London

242 (*right*) Men cutting the grass with scythes in Russell Square, August 1948, photograph.

243 (*below*) Bloomsbury Square, winter 1946–7, photograph, published in 'There will be Blooms in Bloomsbury in 1947: A Plan to Brighten London Squares in the Coming Spring', *The Sphere*, 11 January 1947. Private collection.

Civil Defence Region, including trench shelters in city squares. Yet a Civil Defence circular, also dating from December 1945, stated that the priority was to remove obstructions that posed 'a definite menace' to the public, and that this must precede 'anything in the nature of amenity claims', as it was 'felt all round that it would be impossible to give any substantial consideration to London Squares while the more urgent problem of housing remained'.[24] The Ministry of Works' official line was the 'squares will have to wait'.[25]

Although the government reported that it was not in a position to take any 'active measures' towards restoring the amenities of the London squares, nonetheless the Home Office, the recently formed Ministry of Town and Country Planning and the Ministry of Works all conceded and favoured the idea that 'an increasing amount of attention is likely to be directed to the problem of restoring . . . dilapidated squares to something like their former splendour'. One historical factor, however, now began to loom. Clearly the questions of railings and enclosure troubled the government, and there was no easy solution that was going to satisfy those who, on the one hand, argued that the central areas should be converted into 'attractive public gardens', and those who, on the other, wished to see the gardens revert to their pre-war status. The Ministry of Works took the view that 'some form of fencing will undoubtedly be necessary . . . if any work of rehabilitation is not to be rendered useless'. It was, however, particularly keen that 'no reference at all' be made to the replacement of railings, insofar as the 'problem bristles with difficulties and the danger is not yet passed of violent criticism on the aftermath of the [war-time] railings campaign'.[26]

There then followed, on the recommendation of Herbert Stanley Morrison, MP, Secretary of State for Home Affairs and Minister for Home Security,[27] a series of studies to determine whether or not a type of fencing with or without the addition of a hedge would provide 'reasonably adequate protection' to the squares that had lost their railings.[28] Morrison's 'general inclination' was 'to abolish the closed gardens'; but knowing that there was an urgent need to address the problem of 'casual trespassing', even while recognising that labour and materials were in short supply, he promoted the inexpensive and expeditious solution of hedging. In this he was assisted by his colleague George Tomlinson, MP, and Minister of Works, who advocated experiments with potential forms of fencing – from steel mesh netting and cleft chestnut pales, to defensive grass banks – in the royal parks (fig. 244).[29]

Such practical suggestions side-stepped the more pressing issue of the extent to which the enclosure of some or all of the central gardens was either necessary or desirable. If only in practical terms, there was a reluctance on the part of government departments to take measures to encourage the general re-enclosure of squares as it had far-reaching legal and financial implications related to compensation. Nonetheless, Mr Ferriday at the Department of Works, attempted to compile a preliminary survey of squares in several metropolitan boroughs – includ-

ing Islington, Paddington, Westminster and Stepney – with a view to determining which central gardens could come under public control, and which should be reserved for key-holders. His overriding criterion for judgement was whether a square was residential or commercial in character (which took into account whether domestic premises had been adapted for commercial use, or whether new blocks of flats or offices had been built), and he also noted its proximity to public open space. As author of the survey, however, Ferriday was criticised internally for 'over-simplifying' the problem, insofar as his results showed 'a sharp cleavage between the poorer areas where he suggests that the squares should be open, and the wealthier areas, where he suggests enclosure'. It was recommended instead that the proper basis was simply that of need: if a square was needed for public recreation – particularly to prevent children from having to play in the streets – it should be open to the public. If it was not required by the public it could be closed.[30]

Throughout the late 1940s the 'business of the London Squares' thus remained contentious in both the Commons and the public press.[31] The government's line was conservative. While they did not want to see a return to the 'general use of massive iron railings', they wished to encourage some alternative form of protection, since 'the taking of the railings has resulted in untidiness' and a 'grave reduction in the amenity value they originally afforded'.[32] The government was anxious, however, that any assistance it might offer to compensate or restore the amenity of squares would also draw attention to the case of local authority parks and public open spaces, as well as the millions of private houses from which railings had been taken during the scrap campaign.

The outcome was perhaps predictable. The Commons declared in November 1945 that they did not propose to accept, in general, responsibility for replacing railings, even while allowing for the provisions of the Requisitioned Land and War Works Act (1945), which gave the Minister *carte blanche* powers to undertake works of rehabilitation where land had been damaged by government war work and use.[33] To that end, the government hoped that some owners of squares would be willing to incur the expense of refurbishing their own enclosures. But still there was the caveat: if the demand for grant aid became too great there would follow the question whether or

244 Temporary fencing in Piccadilly along the north side of Green Park, July 1949, photograph by H. Galwey. RIBA Library.

not expenditure of public money on restoring what were, in effect, private gardens for ratepayers in the square was expedient and in the public interest. The effect was clear. If restoration were to proceed on the grounds of amenity, it must be made practicable by the erection of only 'modified fencing', and that any cost beyond compensation must be a charge on public funds. This in turn would necessitate granting the general public rights of access.

The matter did not rest there, however. In January 1947 the Minister of Town and Country Planning, in consultation with the Minister of Works, issued an explanatory memorandum to the Lord President's Committee at the Home Office, outlining 'what action, if any, should be taken in connection with the restoration of London Squares'. It was his opinion that if indeed some squares needed protection to safeguard their amenities then they should be enclosed; the government, however, could not insist on the means of enclosure short of taking the somewhat contradictory position of encouraging the London local authorities to acquire them by lease or purchase and to maintain them as public open

spaces.[34] Clearly he saw this as a bad precedent. Indeed, it was in his view neither necessary nor even desirable that the majority of the squares should in fact be acquired as public open spaces – a judgement shared by the London County Council and the Planning Authority. Some gardens were, he remarked, 'the only gardens which the surrounding houses have to use and unrestricted public access makes it impossible to maintain grass and flowers. Provided that Squares are not too heavily enclosed the public interest will in many cases not suffer by leaving the Squares in private hands.'[35]

Reading between the lines, one can only conclude that at the war's end there were insufficient resources at all levels of government to allow it to consider taking clear control of the rehabilitation and maintenance of the city's hundreds of squares and their enclosures. It was also doubtless the case that government refused to make decisions in haste without adequate regard to long-term planning of the squares and their environs.

Yet resolution of such issues could not be postponed indefinitely. Much of the aforementioned

debate was finally resolved by the passage of the Town and Country Planning Act in 1947, which embodied most of the planning principles outlined in the Abercrombie plan. Under the act, the county was resolutely made the planning authority for the Administrative County of London (and also the City), and was required to carry out a survey and submit to the appropriate minister a plan and report for future development. This report, in the form of a development plan, set out proposals for the next twenty years, and was submitted in 1951 to the Minister of Housing and Local Government.

One of the most important aspects of the act was that it conferred powers upon borough councils to acquire the central gardens of squares after consultation with the LCC.[36] Where acquisition involved loss, a grant would be forthcoming; and in those instances where the cost of acquisition was less than the value of the land for public open space, a development charge would be payable. Other regulations, too,

would have a bearing on squares, including the Tree Preservation Order. This measure safeguarded the future of the gardens' trees, some of which were of major importance, such as the giant planes in Berkeley Square and Lincoln's Inn Fields (fig. 245); it also helped to protect trees that were threatened by the construction of underground car parks and transformer chambers for electrical substations.

Yet progress was slow. In 1948 the LCC's Town Planning, Parks and Finance Committees commissioned a joint report on the future use of land and buildings surrounding squares, and of the square gardens, so as to inform and advise on what was to become the Administrative County of London Development Plan (1951).[37] The recommendations the report put forward were based on a survey of seventy squares. The findings, however, were discouraging: the effects of the war had resulted in an increase in commercial uses around the squares in central London; less than a third of the squares were reported to have good garden maintenance arrangements – indeed, many had no arrangements whatsoever; and regardless of the standards of care, the condition of the gardens was 'poor'. The condemnation did not end there: less than half the squares, they found, still possessed 'some degree' of their former 'unity in the design of surrounding buildings', and a great number of premises overlooking the gardens were blighted by prominent advertisements that broke up what remained of the 'architectural unity'.[38]

The report concluded that insofar as 'the number of squares in the County is large, and both compensation and legal aspects are involved . . . first consideration should be given to squares in those areas where the need is greatest'. These areas were the so-called 'deficiency areas' where there were both a number of private squares, and where there was a deficiency in open space on the accepted standard of 2.5 acres per 1,000 population. In these areas preference was to be given to the acquisition of a borough's largest squares; the council had no interest in acquiring smaller squares as they believed that if they were opened to the public 'they might only become thoroughfares, which would lead to the destruction of amenities'. Of far greater importance was the acquisition of squares in the central areas zoned for business as 'precincts' (areas of proposed pedestrian priority). Here there was an 'acute need' for lunch-time open spaces. These could be 'quite small', such as Cavendish Square (in a 'business area'), or Bedford Square (in the 'Bloomsbury precinct'). The newly formed public garden at Grosvenor Square was furthermore cited as a good example of how this might be achieved.[39]

When the development plan was published in 1951 it called for 'neighbourhood conversion'. This policy involved the comprehensive redevelopment of large areas of historic fabric, as opposed to the earlier practice of piecemeal refurbishment of individual premises. It had been at the heart of the Abercrombie plan, and was praised in the architectural press for being both economical and socially desirable to the degree that it kept intact and encouraged the existing neighbourhood units, thereby promoting social cohesion.[40] While this policy, it should be noted, had the potential to be rather destructive to the historic character of some squares, elsewhere it led to the lateral conversion of the houses surrounding many squares – including Eaton and Eccleston squares and Clarence Gardens – where the central gardens remained more or less intact.

'A Square for Every Taste'

Post-war London thus saw a seemingly endless schedule of plans for the garden squares. Yet nowhere was there a truly comprehensive vision. One such view, however, did emerge in the pages of the *Architectural Review* in October 1947, when the gifted architect, draughtsman and writer Gordon Cullen demonstrated, with examples chosen from London, how Britain's squares 'could be made to serve life as it is lived in our towns today'. In 'A Square for Every Taste' he declared that 'town squares, once the preserve of privilege, have since the wartime salvage of railings become public spaces. It is unlikely and undesirable that they should all return to their former use, but so far no definite solutions have been put forward for bringing them into line with the needs of a changed society.' Squares, the piece continued, 'have a big future as well as an illustrious past. What is also clear is that they have a mediocre present. The authorities do not know what to do with them under the changing circumstances of a society which objects to being kept out of anything, objects to signs of privilege, yet by its impatience of restriction tends to destroy what it touches.'[41]

That this rhetoric should emanate from the pages of the *Architectural Review* is not so surprising. Hubert de Cronin Hastings, the owner and editor of the magazine, was the originator and principal proponent of what was then dubbed 'Townscape' – a movement described by its advocates as the 'conscious art of developing the character of a given place'. It was, in their view, 'the completion of the town planning process, since it gives to the accumulated labours of all the other branches of town design – sociology, traffic circulation, industry, housing, hygiene – the face and bearing of a living organism'.[42] Townscape was, above all, an organic and pictorial approach to design, and a celebration of the English genius in the production of harmony in variety.

Hastings, who had been profoundly affected by Christopher Hussey's *The Picturesque: Studies in a Point of View* (1927), was keen to promote what he saw as the role of the picturesque in Britain's cultural history, and to show the influence of the picturesque on mid-twentieth-century architecture and urban design. Two employees of the *Architectural Review* assisted him in this pursuit, the architectural historian Nikolaus Pevsner and Gordon Cullen. Pevsner was encouraged to research the contribution of 'planned squares' to English town planning, and Cullen to promote the practical reform of the city's squares (fig. 246).

In 'A Square for Every Taste', Cullen proposed new uses for old squares, set out principles for their redesign and devised a new nomenclature for the resulting spaces. As he saw it, 'Private Enclosed Squares' were those in which 'function and unity still march together [and] no change is advocated'; thus where a square was still residential it could remain a private or communal garden, enclosed by railings. 'Private Open Squares' were a variation on the first type, where the original perimeter railings were replaced by so-called 'hazards', or alternative boundary treatments, such as judicious planting and changes of level (fig. 247).[43] 'Collegiate Squares' were those where the traffic flow was to be reduced and reorganised to permit the formation of 'precincts', where pedestrians were to be given priority. These squares would be largely paved, and sprinkled with trees; there would be no attempt to 'preserve a few square feet of cat-ridden sooty turf in the smaller public squares' (fig. 248). 'Municipal Squares' were those places which, like Russell Square, were surrounded by large buildings and exposed to the 'continual roar and movement of fast traffic' – spaces where 'the monumentality should flow through with all its devices of the axis, fountains, seats and sculpture, and produce an unsubtle yet impressive effect of metropolitanism'. 'Exclusive Public Squares' were, like Grosvenor Square, openings in which the arrangement could be 'purely formal', with lawns, paving and ornamental trees. Lastly, 'Popular Public Squares' were, like Leicester Square, to be laid entirely to paving. In the case of Leicester Square itself there were, it was suggested, 'sufficient cafés round the square to rent space for tables, as is done in France, and gaily coloured velariums suspended between the trees would give protection from birds and rain'.[44]

In a subsequent article, Cullen put forward proposals to improve the character of the squares of Pimlico, 'the most stereotyped and anonymous of all the central London districts'. He developed his point that squares 'need not all have identical treatment simply because they come under the dictionary heading of SQUARE'. His aim was to 'show a few of the variations that are possible, variations that spring from the particular environment and which are intended to increase the usefulness of the square, to bring out its full value' (figs 249 and 250). Through a combination of compelling sketches and spirited text, Cullen explained the thinking behind his redesigns for Ebury, St George's and Warwick squares, and Pimlico and Grosvenor Gardens. He went into particular detail on the planting of Ebury Square garden, and was assisted to this end by the MPGA. The garden of this 'orthodox square' was to be a 'green bower' inside the 'structural enclosure' of the square's bleak and arid environment, and embellished with ornamental water, green grass and flowers, flowering shrubs, trees and seats.[45]

Squares and the London Development Plan

The London Development Plan (1951) was soon to prove a milestone in the process of post-war reconstruction: the document laid down proposed changes to land use, residential density, industrial relocation and community services. It also addressed the provision of public open space, and proposed measures to improve its distribution. To that end, its 'open space deficiency plan' identified thirteen boroughs found wanting in open space, including Shoreditch, Holborn, Deptford, Stepney, Finsbury, Islington and Southwark. The deficit estimate was in the region of 300 acres, for which the proposed remedy was the acquisition of private open space.[46]

Although the plan did not receive approval from the Minister of Housing and Local Government until 1955, its launch nonetheless swiftly generated a lively exchange between the boroughs and the LCC. While it is not necessary here to review the many, if sometimes dramatic, transformations of some of the county's squares that were brought about by the plan, it is important to examine the varied methods by which squares were used as vehicles to increase the provision of public amenity.

One of the more popular and innovative ways of creating new 'units' of public open space was through the 'extension' of existing squares. Such enlargements took place at Carlton and Ford squares in Stepney, Ion Square in Bethnal Green, King Square

246 *(facing page)* Nikolaus Pevsner, manuscript notes on the squares of the Bedford Estate, *c*.1942, pen and ink. Research Library, Getty Research Institute, Los Angeles.

Bedford Estate

Map drawn by Hy Holland, Hans Town Feb. 1793

No details on Bloomsbury or Bedford Sq. Bedford Ho to N. of Bloomsbury Sq has long straight back & || || avenues. But at far end, 3 streets N of ~~Tott~~ Bedford Sq N side on large lawn & clumped groups of trees or bushes

Printed Map of Estate by N.R. Hewitt c 1815

Bloomsbury Sq. 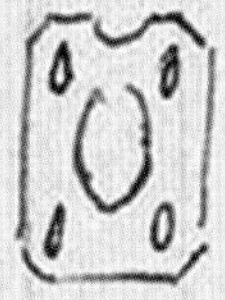 & no paths

Bedford Sq. 

Plots —

Russell Sq. 

In one Statue of Francis Duke of B
— — C.J. Fox

Houses up to Tavistock Sq, but no Square
N of Keppel St just begun

Large Map, drawn no date both houses pale pink, but Russell & Tavistock Sq. printed in in colour

Tavistock 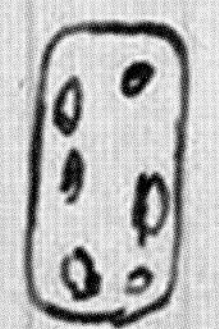 Houses only on E side

Between Tavistock & Russell Sq. only just starting

Russell Sq. similar to above but nippy in detail

247 (*right*) Gordon Cullen's proposals for alternative boundary treatments, or 'hazards', for St James's Square, from *Architectural Review* 103 (March 1948). RIBA Library.

248 (*below*) Gordon Cullen's sketch of a possible treatment for Manchester Square, from 'The Square as Quadrangle: The Collegiate Square', *Architectural Review* 106 (October 1949). RIBA Library.

in Finsbury, and Addington, Leyton and Lorrimore squares in Southwark, and Melbourne Square in Lambeth (figs 251 and 252).[47] Typically, a 'square extension' was the creation of a new public open space through the addition of neighbouring building land to an existing square – land formerly occupied by a square's surrounding premises, or contiguous sites that became available through slum clearances or demolitions. Such schemes frequently involved street closures to enable the creation of seamless open space, and further attempts were also made to forge 'links' between the new amenities. Interestingly, because many squares were protected under the London Squares Preservation Act, which forbade the building of new permanent structures on their central gardens, the original pleasure grounds frequently remained intact, embedded within successive treatments of the space.

249 (*right*) Gordon Cullen, *Ebury Square: The Ornamental Square*, proposed plan, from *Architectural Review* 112 (September 1952). RIBA Library.

250 (*below*) Gordon Cullen, *Ebury Square: The Ornamental Square*, proposed plan, perspective view, from *Architectural Review* 112 (September 1952). RIBA Library.

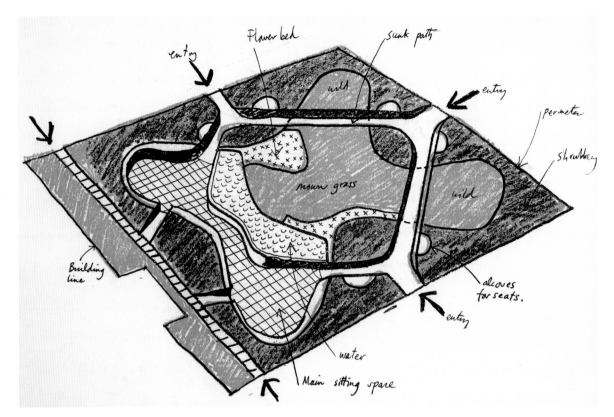

251 Nos 8–12 Melbourne
Square, Lambeth, c.1975,
photograph, showing some of
the original houses in the
square. Minet Library,
Lambeth.

252 (facing page) Unknown
draughtsman, plan for the
creation of Ion Square Open
Space through the extension
of Ion Square, February 1960.
London Metropolitan Archives.
Much of the area contained
within the heavy black line
was converted into public
open green space as an
extension of Ion Square (not
shown on the plan but
situated just above Warner
Place).

Many, indeed most, of these extension schemes
evolved through the close collaboration of the LCC
and the metropolitan boroughs: the former provided
grants towards the costs of acquisition and layout, to
a maximum of 50 per cent of the total sum, often
on condition that these new open spaces would
remain in their control and management.[48] Understandably, the LCC's valuer played a key role in this
process, as it was his responsibility to estimate the
cost of a proposed acquisition and expenses associated with clearances, partial redevelopment and subsequent maintenance (including stores, supplies,
equipment and staff). Other potential expenses for
consideration included rehousing liability, the re-
siting of industry, and development charges for loss
of development value under proposed legislation.
Some of these were recoverable from the War Dam-
ages Commission.

Each extension scheme ultimately had to fulfil the
planning requirements set out in the 1947 act, and
was referred to the Ministry of Housing and Local
Government for final approval. Once everything was
agreed and set in motion, it was left to the LCC's
Chief Officer of the Parks Department to determine
the layout of the newly enlarged garden. The design
treatment was typically inexpensive and formulaic,
based on guidelines established for 'amenity area'
landscaping, which at a minimum simply provided
for grass, trees, shrubs and herbaceous borders, a
rudimentary shelter, a 'paved sitting-out space' and
temporary accommodation for staff. Occasionally
play areas were laid out for young children with
seats, an area of grass and some screen planting (fig.
253).[49]

Yet the LCC was not interested solely in the acquisition of new open space; it also sought to improve

252

NELSON GARDENS
KITE PLACE
ST. PETER'S AV
WARNER PLACE
OLD BETHNAL GREEN
GOSSET STREET
Engineering Works
Div of PB & Ward Bdy
NORAH STREET
Queen Adelaide's Dispensary
POLLARD ROW
Club
ROBERTA STREET
IVIMEY ST
SQUIRRIES STREET
FLORIDA STREET
Cinema
The Hope (PH)
St James The Great Church
BETHNAL GREEN ROAD
BM 51·38
BM 49·34
BM 52·38
1
2
3
4
5
6

and maintain existing gardens. For instance, it offered to purchase the freehold interest in Beaumont Square in order to absolve Stepney Borough Council from its liability for the rent.[50] It did so on the proviso that the borough would undertake to put the central garden into 'reasonable order', and maintain it for the public benefit. The garden was described at the time as in 'an unkempt and derelict state which severely limits its public usefulness'.[51] The acquisition of the square and some of the properties around it was approved in June 1951, and the garden was embellished the following spring with the addition of a semi-circular seat recess and a birdbath. The borough council, however, was accused of 'vandalism' by the press and later the Chief Officer of the LCC's Parks Department on account of its 'unnecessary, unskilled, ruthless tree lopping' (fig. 254).[52]

Beaumont Square was not the only square to be 'despoiled' in the course of its refurbishment. The unfenced, scruffy and umbrageous garden of Golden Square received a lavish but unsympathetic makeover in the late 1950s, when it was taken over by Westminster City Council on lease from the trustees

of the square. Astragal reported in the *Architects' Journal* that the council's decision to remove all the plane trees from Golden Square may have been 'well-intentioned', but it was a 'visually disastrous, municipal garden policy', the outcome of which was to destroy the character of the square (fig. 255). He also condemned the council's unimaginative approach to the improvement of this and other of its public gardens: 'off we go again: Cotswoldey walling, rustic shack, boring windswept podium and patch of cobblestones'.[53] A contributor to the *Architect & Building News* was no less disapproving of Golden Square, likening it to a barren waste with 'simpering' flowerbeds and clumsy teak flower chests.[54]

Whereas most of the aforementioned initiatives, with the exception of Golden Square, were concerned primarily with creating public open space through 'partial redevelopment', others took place under the pretext of creating new housing through the redevelopment of squares, or the building of new ones. For instance, the present day Bevin Court in Finsbury, was contrived by the reconstruction of Holford Square (fig. 256). The redevelopment of the

256 Holford Square, 1939, photograph. Country Life Picture Library. Restored after war-time bomb damage, the square became a place of recreation for the inhabitants.

early nineteenth-century square, which had been severely damaged by war-time bombing, was initially intended to harmonise with the local street pattern, so that the enclosed layout of the square was if possible preserved, under the terms of the London Squares Preservation Act. However, as the scheme developed, and economic conditions worsened, as one commentator saw it, 'it became apparent that the atmosphere of crisis would radically influence, not only the detailed treatment and the technicalities of planning, but the whole conception of the ensemble'.[55] In the end, the retention of the enclosed central garden was rejected in favour of a 'peripheral solution', which saw a Y-shaped multi-storey modernist block (still in existence) raised on the north and west margins of the former garden (fig. 257).[56]

St Pancras Borough Council, in contrast, subscribed to what was called at the time the 'precinctual' principle – that is, the creation of compact, efficient and informal urban layouts for exclusive pedestrian use – when in the mid-1950s it redevel-

oped Clarence Gardens and Munster Square (figs 258 and 259).[57] These squares, which had been originally developed by John Nash on land east of Regent's Park, had been much damaged by the war. The fact that their central gardens were protected by the 1931 act, however, precluded their being built over, so the 'scope of the replanning was much restricted by the two existing large squares'. What finally emerged was an informal layout of new housing, 'so disposed as to form a series of varied and linked places and squares'. The whole area, moreover, had no formal road system, instead 'being treated as a pedestrian precinct'.[58] The *Architectural Review* published the schematic plans for this 'long-term redevelopment scheme' in 1956, remarking that 'while the squares and the paved ways and the spaces throughout the areas will be free for access by the general public, grass courts contained by, and adjacent to, the living-room sides of the blocks will be fenced and reserved for the private use of tenants as in some London squares'.[59]

Even more radical was St Mary's Square, the first permanent post-war housing scheme in Paddington (fig. 260). The square was created on the razed site of former terraced houses and mews, and comprises five blocks of flats built around a polygonal 'ring road', enclosing an internal court laid out with grass, shrubs and a single diagonal path.[60] The design of the small estate was presumably influenced by the writings of the architect and town planner Thomas Sharp. While Sharp had an informed appreciation of English townscape, and admired the urban tradition of the square, he did not advocate the imitation of eighteenth-century streets, squares and crescents. There was, he affirmed, 'no need for us to *imitate* anything. We must express our own purposes in our own modern way.'[61]

Such a 'modern way' even led to the curious proposal explored in the early 1950s to build new housing within the communal gardens of Lansdowne Gardens, Elgin Crescent, Arundel Gardens and Clarendon Road on the Ladbroke Estate. The scheme

entailed raising multi-storey blocks of flats at the tail ends of the gardens to 'illustrate a method by which these sites could be developed to provide a greater density' (fig. 261). It was promoted as allowing for 'additional building without necessitating any demolition', and of having the advantage of being easily repeated 'many times' in the neighbourhood's numerous communal gardens 'so that the building of additional blocks could be run on more advantageous lines due to the repetition of the actual buildings, and also the close proximity of the sites'.[62] Happily the scheme did not get beyond the drawing board.

Lastly, the London Development Plan also had a significant impact on the redevelopment of Parliament, Leicester and Trafalgar squares. The role and appearance of this trio of civic spaces were, given their central location, subject to protracted debate and numerous exercises in the then new discipline of spatial design. Many schemes proposed the reinstatement of the precinctual character of Parliament Square, or the forging of visual links between

260 (*right*) The internal court of St Mary's Square, Paddington, photograph, from *Architects' Journal* 108 (October 1948). RIBA Library.

261 (*below*) Collcutt & Hamp architects, proposals for housing to be built on part of the gardens at Lansdowne Gardens, Elgin Crescent, Arundel Gardens and Clarendon Road, *c.*1953, pen and pencil. RIBA Library.

view from the road.   view from the garden.

Trafalgar and Leicester squares.[63] Of these spaces, Parliament Square – 'the hub of Empire' – was perhaps the most important. The LCC had already begun to develop plans for its redesign as early as 1946 in collaboration with the Ministry of Works, who subsequently were 'under pressure to produce a non-controversial, inexpensive scheme to improve traffic flow around Parliament Square, while also producing a stately new civic space to impress visitors to the Festival of Britain'.[64] The ministry debated the possibility of introducing a form of square extension scheme, which would have created an isolated precinct for the Houses of Parliament and Westminster Abbey, protected from through traffic by diverting Victoria Street (in line with the objectives of the Abercrombie plan). These plans were, however, rejected in favour of a much simpler design by the architect Grey Wornum (fig. 262). The scheme, completed in 1951, is today still elegant and understated, reflecting the post-war move towards simplicity in civic spaces.[65]

Finally, to conclude our review of LCC-inspired redevelopments, it is interesting to note how the council appraised its own legacy. A joint report

issued in February 1956 by the architect, the valuer and the Chief Officer of the Parks Department recounts that the extension and acquisition of squares for the period 1951 to 1956 had in fact yielded only a very small quantity of new public open space.[66] Although the council was reasonably successful in collaborating with the City of Westminster in the opening of squares for lunch-time users, they were frustrated that a number of private owners declined to comply.[67] The council's greatest concern, however, was that a few squares still appeared 'neglected'. While most of the square gardens in public owner-ship were in 'reasonable order' and 'neatly main-tained by their respective authorities', there was 'some variation in the condition in which the private squares were maintained' – largely on account of the indifference of their owners, uncontrolled use by the public (especially children) and a lack of finance to 'maintain their appearance'. Finsbury, Brunswick and Arundel squares, and Percy Circus were singled out for particular criticism. Although there were mechanisms to reverse this decline, the authors of

the report did not, rather surprisingly, propose that these gardens should be taken into public ownership. In their opinion, the acquisition of a private square by a public authority 'does not necessarily result in an improvement of the amenity value of the open space. Because of the nature of their use (which may be limited), well maintained private squares have a delightful informal character which contributes a special quality to urban areas. On the other hand, a garden which is open to the public frequently requires quite a different layout treatment of a formal utilitarian kind which may, in some cases, differ materially from the previous standard of civic design'.[68]

Petrol Pumps in Squares: 'That is the Way the World is Going . . .'[69]

As car ownership and traffic increased in the capital after the war, car parking continued to be a problem in many central London squares. In the 1950s tem-porary expedients were adopted, including the use of bomb-sites, but as the LCC's Town Planning Committee admitted in January 1950 permanent solutions 'by way of accommodation at above, or below ground level must . . . be anticipated'.[70] Squares offered the 'most practical sites for such parks', and there were in the committee's estimation three choices: to create car parks on the surface, 'which would destroy all the amenity value of the square'; to build underground car parks, which would 'involve the removal of trees but would allow the retention of some amenity'; or to continue to let cars park on the streets, which was 'dangerous and obstructive, and would spoil the amenities of a large area'.[71]

The situation clearly troubled the Ministry of Transport, which in March 1953 announced a comprehensive plan for easing traffic congestion in central London. The plan, commissioned on the recommendation of the London and Home Counties Traffic Advisory Committee, proposed the phased construction of subterraneous car parking beneath nine squares – Grosvenor, Berkeley, Cavendish, St James's, Soho, Leicester, Finsbury and Portman squares and Lincoln's Inn Fields – and the building of a number of ancillary 'surface garages'.[72] It also proposed the felling of dozens of mature trees in the squares' gardens.

Tree-felling may have been acceptable at Grosvenor Square in the immediate aftermath of the war (where over sixty 'fine mature trees' were destroyed in the course of the garden refurbishment), as it was seen as a courageous step in post-war reconstruction, and was part and parcel of the creation of a major new public open space. But now the prospect of losing so many venerable trees across so many central squares, not surprisingly, provoked an angry public response.[73] Few opponents to the scheme, however, were as critical and as informed as Thomas Spencer, who even so early as 1929 had made a 'close study of the London traffic and car parking problems'. Now he contended that making car parks under squares was 'merely expensive "nibbling" and has already been objected to by many Londoners who value very highly the amenities of their squares'. Car parking, he declared, should be placed instead under parks, and on the outer perimeter of congested areas.[74]

The debate became even more contentious when in 1956 an outline application was submitted on behalf of Lex Garages to construct an underground car park for 323 cars with petrol pumps at ground level at Finsbury Square. The square's garden was at the time still scattered with the remains of air-raid shelters, as attempts to have them removed and the garden reinstated were frustrated by an ongoing dispute between the Home Office and Finsbury Borough Council, which was complicated by the square's then ownership by the Church Commissioners. The matter came to a head in 1957 when the 'stringent restrictions' that protected the square from redevelopment under the 1931 act were 'relaxed' temporarily to enable the passing of the Finsbury Square Act.[75]

In the event, the 1957 act was deemed unworkable, and a new bill was submitted. The dispute, therefore, continued; and Lord Grantchester, who in 1956 had conveyed the freehold of the square to the council on behalf of the Church Commissioners in the misguided belief that he was 'placing the Square in safe custody for the benefit of the public', began vigorously to campaign against the new bill.[76] The peer wrote to *The Times*, appeared on television, and organised a petition of protest that eventually contained more than 3,300 names. He alleged that 'the City workers who now find relaxation in the square will not wish to use what remains of it if petrol pumps come because of the noise and fumes'. He also voiced a wider objection that the use of the square for this purpose 'will create a precedent which might well be invoked in support of applications to develop other London squares in a similar manner'.[77]

Grantchester's efforts were futile. The second Finsbury Square Act was passed in June 1959,[78] and within the space of two and half years the square's much needed refurbishment was complete. The large oval-shaped garden was expanded to form a rectangle and laid out with a bowling green, a café and an informal garden. The square, however, was also fitted with steps, ramps, lifts, a filling station and a large underground car park.

Although it was hoped that this precedent would be ignored in future cases where there were objections to underground car parks, this was not to be so: by the early 1970s, Cavendish and Bloomsbury squares, and Cadogan Place Gardens had all suffered a similar fate (figs 263 and 264).[79] Regardless of the fact that most of the gardens' trees were saved, these examples served as awful warnings. As Kenneth

263 (right) Construction of
the car park beneath
Cavendish Square, *Paddington
Mercury*, 1 May 1970,
photograph. Private collection.

264 (below) The circular
diaphragm walling of the new
helical car park under
construction in Bloomsbury
Square, *c.*1964–5, photograph
by C. W. F. Holmes. RIBA
Library. The large tree in the
foreground survived the
dramatic excavations, and can
be seen in right foreground of
fig. 265.

Architect slams City Council over Cavendish Square trees

Browne remarked in the *Architectural Review* in February 1967, although such schemes may seem to have caused little disturbance to the appearance of the gardens, and gave the impression of being plausible and tempting, they were 'short term expedients which must be resisted for the sake of the environment'.[80] Such emerging consciousness of the important contribution squares made to the city's ecology was, in fact, increasingly shared and manifested by many other Londoners, as subsequent plans to excavate under Eccleston Square were met with robust opposition and were scrapped.[81]

'Save our Square'[82]

The future of Covent Garden once again became topical when in the early 1960s plans were put forward for the relocation of its fruit and vegetable market.[83] This time the threat was not that its removal would destroy another square or two, but

263 (right) Construction of the car park beneath Cavendish Square, *Paddington Mercury*, 1 May 1970, photograph. Private collection.

264 (below) The circular diaphragm walling of the new helical car park under construction in Bloomsbury Square, *c.*1964–5, photograph by C. W. F. Holmes. RIBA Library. The large tree in the foreground survived the dramatic excavations, and can be seen in right foreground of fig. 265.

as Kenneth Browne remarked, that 'Covent Garden itself, as a place, may be forgotten': that its 'special character could well be erased at one stroke by wholesale redevelopment'.[84]

The implacable Browne, then townscape editor of the *Architectural Review*, was eager to preserve the character of this 'urban cornucopia', and set out his proposals for doing so in 'A Latin Quarter for London: A Townscape Survey of Covent Garden and a Plan for its Future' (1964).[85] In it he voiced his despair that London was 'steadily being straightened out, having its eccentricities corrected, its character impoverished, not only by piecemeal replacement but also by the well-intentioned doctrine of the clean sweep (politely called comprehensive development). It is being made to conform to a desiccated conception of what it ought to be like with everything in compartments and no mixing by order.' There was, he believed, a 'dreary tendency for everywhere to become more and more the same'. That every problem rang up the 'same old standard solution' was a 'sad reflection on modern town planning'. Against such erosion of urban values in their

history, it was, in his view, 'essential that planners recognize and encourage the difference between places, emphasizing them, not destroying them'.[86]

The article was the first of many in which Browne was to promote a greater appreciation of the physical and social distinctness of the city's historic neighbourhoods: the leisured elegance and grace of Mayfair; the sleazy exoticism and insularity of Soho; the quiet respectability of Pimlico; and the dazzling vitality of 'Theatreland'.[87] Each of these areas had its complement of squares, each of which, for him, contributed to the essentially domestic quality of its surroundings.[88]

Browne's most poignant townscape survey was reserved for the squares of Bloomsbury – a neighbourhood with a great range of diverse squares, and one 'in grave danger of obliteration' (fig. 265).[89] The author had a special regard for this area, which he praised as 'London's finest example of a planned and civilized environment'.

Here are no axes or grand vistas, but instead each square forms a little world of its own, casually

COVENT GARDEN AS IT COULD BE

linked by undemonstrative terraces to other such worlds. The squares differ widely in size and shape, but always contain a central garden of large forest trees, left unpruned as though in a rural landscape. The regimented facades of the houses contrast happily with the informal and luxuriant foliage. Built to be quiet and calm, away from the traffic of the main streets, the enclosure afforded by the surrounding buildings of equal height gives much the same effect as a room. Non-directional, it suggests contemplation, not movement.[90]

The threat to the area was not, surprisingly, from the speculator, but from 'two of our leading cultural institutions, London University and the British Museum'.[91] The University of London, like 'some monstrous cuckoo . . . ever greedy for more space', proposed to 'smother' many of Bloomsbury's squares with 'bulky, dull buildings, overpowering in scale'; and the British Museum, for its own part, planned to redevelop a 7-acre site immediately south of the existing building to form a giant raised piazza, under which it proposed to place the British Library. The

creation of this 'draughty desert nobody wanted', which involved demolishing the western flank of Bloomsbury Square, was later shelved.[92]

Browne recommended that what was wanted for Bloomsbury was a townscape survey: 'here of all places it is the spaces and connections between them which count, and the preservation of a single building is not enough. The importance as urban landscape is such that a detailed townscape survey is needed now to determine what must be kept at all cost and what action is needed to pull back areas which have slipped.'[93] His concerns came in the wake of the reorganisation of the government of London. Under the London Government Act of 1963 the newly formed Greater London Council (GLC) was required to produce a development plan for the metropolis. The resulting document – the Greater London Development Plan (1976) – set out a series of strategic policies and proposals for the city's future development, covering population, housing, employment, roads, transportation, open space, areas for comprehensive development and other matters of strategic significance. The most controversial and least popular aspect of the plan was the comprehensive redevelopment of Covent Garden and the creation of a central London motorway loop (fig. 266). Indeed, the proposal was so unpopular that it provoked the neighbourhood's revolt and a clamorous protest movement that eventually forced the GLC to abandon it plans.

One should pause here to note how the Covent Garden protests reflected a change in the public and political mood, which from the early 1950s had begun slowly to turn against the insensitive redevelopment of London. This growing conservation movement was bolstered in the 1960s by the government's listing of 20,000 London buildings,[94] and was further strengthened by the 1968 Town and Country Planning Act, which increased penalties for neglecting or destroying protected buildings, and gave the council new compulsory purchase powers. Even more important, however, was the introduction of 'conservation areas' by the 1967 Civic Amenities Act, which opened up the planning system to greater public scrutiny, and which ultimately contributed to the protection and rehabilitation of hundreds of neighbourhood units across the capital, many of which possessed, or were built around squares.[95] The creation of conservation areas also galvanised the establishment of numerous garden square protection societies, which continue to play an important role in their gardens' management.[96]

The implementation of the Buchanan Report (1963) on traffic in towns, had also led to several significant improvements in some of the metropolitan districts, including the creation of a patchwork of 'environmental areas', or zones in which traffic controls were closely tied to a range of other environmental improvements, including housing, parking and open space. Barnsbury and Pimlico – both of which had a townscape of fine quality and an infrastructure of streets and squares – were the first areas of London to be designated as 'environmental areas', and both were gentrified as a result.[97]

The process of gentrification throughout the inner London boroughs had begun in the early 1960s, but was accelerated by the 1969 Housing Act, which increased improvement grants in designated 'improvement areas' (areas in which half of the existing housing lacked basic amenities), with a view to promoting the rehabilitation of old houses rather than their destruction for the building of new estates.

Not surprisingly, the fact that working-class families were displaced through the process, and their traditional and potentially attractive historic neighbourhoods were re-colonised by the middle-classes provoked a public outcry. Few instances were, in fact, as well ventilated as the gentrification of Gibson Square, which became the subject of a BBC Television social documentary entitled *Six Sides of a Square* (1966).[98]

Although gentrification was initially vilified, there is no question that it helped to save some parts of London from decay and demolition. For instance, the co-ordinated action of the 'gentrifiers' at Gibson Square spared their central garden (which had been open to the public since the war) the indignity of being bulldozed, having its trees uprooted, and its centre pierced by a 50-foot high ventilation shaft for the London underground (fig. 267).[99] Elsewhere, in De Beauvoir Town in Hackney, the newly settled inhabitants from professional classes worked alongside their working-class neighbours, the GLC, the Victorian Society, and the newly formed Hackney Society to prevent the council from flattening their planned Victorian suburb and its elegant square.[100]

Although these victories and others were significant, it was to be several decades before the conservation movement gained sufficient momentum to safeguard the vast majority of the capital's squares, and also before there were the resources to do so.

'The Square has a Future'

In August 1968 a leader in the *Illustrated London News* proclaimed triumphantly: 'The Square has a Future'. 'A new London Square is a rare event. Land in the centre of the capital is scarce and expensive. The regulations for town planning demand intensive development. The new Woodsford Square is in Kensington. Terraces of tall houses with gardens or patios are built round larger gardens shared solely by the residents. The result: a minimum of roads, the maximum of usable space.'[101]

When the builders Wates were planning this new residential area on the Ilchester Estate in Kensington, they called on the architects Fry, Drew & Partners to 're-create in modern terms the elegant way of life implicit in the inward-looking square' (fig. 268). Together with the surveyors of the Ilchester Estates, they were striving to create a 'self-contained, land-

scaped development . . . that will retain the peace and seclusion of a style of living increasingly rare in the centre of London'.[102]

The scheme, which has since been praised by the architectural historian Bridget Cherry as being a cut above the borough's more recent unremarkable housing,[103] was informed by historical research. It was, moreover, promoted by means of an elegant and informative brochure and an exhibition entitled 'The Rebirth of the London Square'.[104] The brochure provided a general history of the city's squares, and explained the basis for the scheme. Squares formed 'islands of activity or quiet', and were 'places to stop in for business or for pleasure'; their 'planning assumed wealth', their origins were aristocratic, and their exclusiveness was 'emphasized by enclosure'. Wates then commended the creation of Woodsford Square, as it 'offers the answer to many urban problems. It makes possible the control of traffic access, and forms an open space large enough to be a genuine park. Because it encloses a coherent area, a distinctive architectural treatment can have meaning, giving a sense of locality and identity. It offers, above

all, scope for the new excitement which people are finding in the relationship between their surroundings and the quality of life.'[105] The creation of the 'imaginatively laid out' Woodsford Square was not, however, as unusual as Wates would have us believe: it may have been the smartest, but modern variants on the square were, in fact, being formed across the capital in an array of private and public housing developments.[106]

The Barbican Estate in the City of London, raised between 1958 and 1975 on 35 acres of former building land, which had been levelled during the Blitz, was designed for middle- to higher-income residents; it was among the first new developments to adopt the premise of multi-level planning – that is, the segregation of pedestrians and vehicles – and the creation of pedestrian precincts.[107] The layout is loosely based on Le Corbusier's sketch and description of 1946 for the reconstruction of residential precincts within the heart of the town; as a commentator observed while the Barbican development was going up, 'wherever bombs have done their work verdure flourishes, and upon the wide green

268 'The Square has a Future', photograph, from *Illustrated London News*, 10 August 1968, announcing the opening of Woodsford Square off Addison Road in Kensington. London Society Library.

THE SQUARE HAS A FUTURE

spaces rise new buildings'.[108] Central to the planning of the Barbican was the provision of large areas of open space in the form of public, communal and domestic gardens, courtyards and squares. The premise of the square was, however, less frequently invoked in private developments than it was in major public housing schemes, and those developed and implemented from the 1950s by the LCC in particular, such as the Lansbury Estate in Poplar, the Brandon Estate in Southwark and the Ethelburga Estate in Battersea.[109]

The origins of the Lansbury Estate lie in Abercrombie and Forshaw's County of London Plan (1943).[110] The development, raised on bombed land in East London, also has close connections with the New Town Movement and the architects Frederick Gibberd, Geoffrey Jellicoe and Judith Ledeboer.[111] Begun in 1949, the estate on the north side of the East India Dock Road was intended to be an exemplar of post-war rebuilding for other local authorities. Here Jellicoe introduced a pair of open residential squares in the East Housing Site, the design of which was 'loosely based on the traditional London square'.[112]

The same design principles also informed the layout of the 56-acre Brandon Estate in Southwark, which was trumpeted in the *Architects' Journal* in November 1961 as the 'Welfare State's first major

addition to the new power symbols of the Metropolis'. Its six white nineteen-storey tower blocks and its mixed development of two- and three-storey housing, together with the South Bank, Elephant and Rotherhithe developments, marked a 'new stage in the LCC's slow but steady progress towards the regeneration of the decaying and formless mass of south London' (fig. 269).[113]

The primary objectives of this new estate were to achieve a high density of housing in the first part of a large redevelopment and slum-clearance scheme, and to make generous provision for playgrounds and open space. Another key point in the layout was the 'deliberate retention of links with the past, to avoid eradicating altogether the memory and sense of place of the older environment'.[114] One of the 'new ideas' developed at Brandon, which was singled out at the time for praise 'since it is so obviously good that the visitor is unlikely to realise that it is new', was the creation of a number of small and secluded courtyards, well planted and paved, and provided with seating; one of them was reported in 1957 to be 'to the scale and proportions of the characteristic older London squares'.[115] These courts, which were also laid out with a view to creating a network of safe pedestrian movement throughout the estate, were described in the contemporary architectural press as an 'essential amenity', and their invention

vaunted as a 'good example of the thoughtfulness and humanity of [the estate's] planning'.[116]

The mastermind behind the design of the Brandon Estate was the LCC's senior architect Edward 'Ted' Hollamby. Hollamby believed 'not just in high quality architecture but in the existence and nurturing of the public realm, of public architecture and civic design.'[117] As an early advocate of conservation, he was, moreover, keen to revive many old and established urban forms, including the square, street, courtyard, pedestrian precinct, patio and private garden, and adapt them to the requirements of contemporary programmes. In 'all these trends' there was, he remarked, 'a strong emphasis on enclosure because space enclosed means space comprehended, and space comprehended means scale – human scale'.[118]

Hollamby addressed the question of the visual relationships of urban planning and the quality it gives to towns in two articles published in *Architecture and Building* (1957).[119] In 'Space about Buildings', he explored, among other things, the collegiate tradition of interconnected and enclosed spaces as epitomised by the colleges and quadrangles of Oxford and Cambridge, as well as the London street and square, which he regarded as 'the most urban domestic form in the English planning tradition'.[120] In his second article, 'The Floor Around', Hollamby considered the visual appearance and function of 'the floor' in building groups developed at a high density.[121] Acknowledging his debt to Gordon Cullen, he examined ways in which contemporary designers could create a sense of 'delightful intimacy', shade and greenery in intensively used open space through the introduction of carefully planned seating, fencing, paths, pavements and forest trees.[122]

Doubtless Hollamby's informed approach to visual planning also guided the LCC architects in their development plan for the Ethelburga Estate. For here, from 1962, the open space created within the new estate was given over almost 'almost entirely' to '"landscaped" squares, some open and some closed'.[123]

The architects Peter and Alison Smithson, who from the mid-1950s were central figures in avant-garde architectural circles, and were hailed as the pioneers of 'New Brutalism', likewise admired some of London's 'domestic squares' – notably their layout and management, which is known to have influ-

enced some of their work. They esteemed in particular the 'vesica-shaped' Boltons in South Kensington, with its complement of paired villas each in a garden; and they also praised the fact that in the past, 'the Urban Estates had strict rules concerning the maintenance and use of individual properties and their collective open spaces, the squares and shared gardens'.[124] They did not, however, apply the premise of the square to a West End development, but to a Brutalist concrete housing estate on the Isle of Dogs in east London. Robin Hood Gardens was built between 1966 and 1972 and was formed of tower blocks encompassing a modern take on the traditional square, or what Peter Smithson later described, rather enigmatically, as 'the green space . . . in the central stress-free zone, in the form of a protected area shielded from urban traffic yet open to surveillance from the surrounding flats'.[125]

Redevelopment of Central London Squares

It is grimly paradoxical that as Woodsford Square was being launched in Kensington, and the Smithsons' role model for progressive social housing was been thrown up in a deprived quarter of east London, two of Bloomsbury's early nineteenth-century squares were teetering on the brink of demolition, and others lay in waste, or were threatened with imminent mutilation.[126]

Things had begun to look rather bleak for the whole area of Bloomsbury as early as 1959 with the unveiling of Sir Leslie Martin's planned mixed-use development scheme for the University of London, which proposed the destruction of 'much of the existing Georgian landscape' to create a 'larger secluded university precinct that could rival the spacious out-of-town sites'.[127] This proposal, as well as the Bedford Estate's own 'comprehensive redevelopment' schemes (1963–8), which would have seen the rebuilding of large stretches of the frontages at both Bloomsbury and Russell Squares, were rejected in 1969 (fig. 270).[128]

These were, however, only temporary setbacks. Martin's scheme was partially implemented from 1973, which brought about the destruction of most of Woburn and Torrington squares to make way for the School of Oriental and African Studies (SOAS), and the Institute of Education. The Trustees of Bedford Estate, too, were eventually able to carry

269 (*facing page*): Lorrimore Square, Brandon Estate, Southwark, 1959, photograph. RIBA Library. The church of St Paul's, formerly at the centre of the square, was destroyed by incendiary bombs in 1940. A new church was raised in its place in 1959/1960.

out some of their proposed redevelopment. They, however, proceeded more cautiously, deciding, in view of the 'obviously increasing importance then being attached to the preservation of the Georgian character of Bloomsbury', to appoint Professor Peter Shepheard as the estate's planning consultant. Shepheard was then President of the RIBA, and 'well known for his sensitivity to Georgian architecture and landscape'.[129] The estate's plans were negotiated with Camden Council, the Historic Buildings Section of the GLC and the Royal Fine Arts Commission, and were the subject of a planning inquiry in 1973.

Although the conservation lobby was reasonably effective in reducing the scope of the estate's redevelopment plans, one still must note that no less a figure than Nikolaus Pevsner presented evidence to the 1973 inquiry against the preservation of the historic frontages in Russell Square. The square, he declared, was a 'depressing experience': 'the east side has three big hotels: the Russell, the President and the Imperial; the western flank was 'disjointed . . . the University library tower . . . destroys the scale of the whole square', the 'north side is being ruinated right now', and the buildings on the south side were 'hopelessly dull'. Russell Square, he concluded, 'aesthetically – has to be given up'.[130]

Yet there was an upside to these dire events. Demolitions and threats to Georgian Bloomsbury, and to Tolmers Square in Euston (the 'locus classicus of London's intellectual squatting movement'),[131] succeeded anew in drawing public attention to the plight of the squares, and precipitated the initial stirrings of the movement for their preservation (fig. 271). While the Georgian Group, the Royal Fine Art Commission, the Society for the Protection of Ancient Buildings, the Victorian Society and the Garden History Society receive generous credit for their contribution to this movement, the achievements of one of the greatest and most tenacious champions of London squares has gone unrecognised. Philip Davies, now Planning and Development

272 Eccleston Square garden, photograph by Neville Capil, spring 2010.

Director (South) at English Heritage, became interested in the squares in 1973 as a conservation officer for the central area of Camden, covering Bloomsbury and Covent Garden. Appalled at the condition of the borough's squares, he set about to do what he could to improve them. Camden was then in the vanguard of local authorities interested in conservation area enhancement. This offered Davies an opportunity to improve several squares including Bedford Square (through the expansion of the footways, which was seen as an interim step towards a more comprehensive enhancement), and Fitzroy Square, where the carriageway was paved on three sides to designs by Sir Geoffrey Jellicoe.[132]

Subsequently, at Westminster City Council, Davies, in his own words, 'pressed repeatedly for a coherent programme of reinstatement, similar to that being pursued by Kensington & Chelsea but funding remained problematic'. Some improvements were, nonetheless, made to Princes and Norfolk squares in Bayswater, though most initiatives, including the re-railing of Onslow Square,[133] it should be noted, were privately driven by frontagers' groups or the great estates.

While many squares were thus improved by piecemeal refurbishment, Eccleston Square in Victoria was reformed by nothing less than what has been dubbed a 'coup d'état'.[134] The square's houses and central garden were desperately forlorn when in 1981 the residents association staged their dramatic overthrow of the long-standing and ineffectual garden committee. Within weeks of their victory, they mobilised a large volunteer workforce to cleanse the square of its accumulated rubbish; and, eager to put in place a strategy for the garden's restoration, they recruited from among their own ranks the photographer and botanist Roger Phillips to co-ordinate these improvements. This he did and, indeed, he continues to document life in the square to this day (fig. 272).[135]

Phillips, who established the Society for the Protection of London Squares, drew up a planting plan in collaboration with the Grosvenor Estate and the Royal Horticultural Society at Wisley, and superintended the garden's refurbishment. The results are exemplary. The square is regularly praised in the press, possesses an exceptional collection of ceanothus, camellias and roses, and has recently been

273   Damage to Soho Square after the 'Great Storm' of 15–16 October 1987, photograph by Jim Gray.

described as 'an extraordinary example of what can be achieved in a small square provided imagination, community involvement, hard work and an understanding of horticulture are applied'.[136]

Efforts in the 1980s to improve the capital's squares were also unexpectedly assisted by an act of God. The 'Great Storm' on 15 and 16 October 1987 shattered, toppled and uprooted hundreds of trees, mangled railings and ravaged the surroundings in many squares (fig. 273). The immediate effect of this freakish gale – the worst to hit England since 1703 – was catastrophic. But this 'arboricultural equivalent of the London Blitz' also brought promise: it galvanised inhabitants to carry out urgent repairs to their squares, and encouraged them to consider the opportunities presented by the devastation to replant and re-colonise their gardens. The great holes carved out of many a garden's dense canopy of majestic planes created new pools of sunlight, and within these appeared new flower-beds, garden benches and stretches of velvety turf. As Richard Girling remarked in 2007, on the twentieth anniversary of the storm: 'perhaps the greatest of the gale's achievements was to fire the public mood. As they came down around us, we suddenly remembered how much trees meant to us. They are central to the very idea of English landscape and art'.[137]

Epilogue

Giving 'New Life to the Enthusiasm for Squares'

The last decade of the twentieth century witnessed a remarkable surge of interest in London squares, in terms of not only their presentation, but also their stewardship, legal protection and long-term survival. This upsurge can be attributed to a number of factors, including a dawning recognition of the importance of green space in making cities attractive places to live, and a new emphasis in conservation on what is locally cherished rather than nationally listed or scheduled.

Campaigns and Initiatives for the London Squares

The newly established London Parks and Gardens Trust (LPGT) played a leading role in the movement to conserve London's squares.[1] Recognising that there was an urgent need to 'give new life to the enthusiasm for squares', and eager to promote a debate on their future, the trust initiated and organised a conference on the subject.[2] The London Squares Conference (1995) was well attended by design professionals, managers, owners, representatives from a variety of amenity societies, and MPs of both main parties, all of whom had an active or informed interest in squares, and many of whom were in a position to effect positive change.

The event was more than a mere forum for discussion of the capital's squares: it was, in the words of John Gummer, Secretary of State for the Environ-

ment, who delivered the keynote address to the conference, both a 'celebration' of the squares in all their forms, and a call to arms 'to fight for their retention, insist upon their enhancement, and, above all perhaps, demand that in the redevelopment of London, that remarkable concept – the square – takes its place again, not as pastiche, but as a form which can be given new life at the end of the millennium'.[3] These sentiments were echoed by Dudley Fishburn, MP, the conference chairman, in his introduction to the proceedings, in which he affirmed that squares were an 'integral part of London's life, its social life and its architectural order'. He continued: 'Taken individually, they are perhaps too small, too local to command the attention and finance needed. Taken together they present a compelling case for public attention and funds. If London is to be given a "lift" as the century turns, there can be no better place to start than on the restoration and conservation of its squares.'[4] The conference did, in fact, spark an array of new initiatives, which were to give a significant boost to the capital's squares; two of the most important were London Squares Day (now Open Garden Squares Weekend) and English Heritage's Campaign for London Squares.

The Open Garden Squares Weekend has unquestionably and single-handedly improved public awareness and the image of squares. In so doing, it has fulfilled the expectations of its founder, Caroline Aldiss, who organised the first open day in 1998

Facing page: Bedford Square, February 2009. The square was considerably improved in 2006 with the refurbishment of the lighting and paving, the removal of unnecessary clutter, and the creation of broad bound-gravel aprons around the oval garden. The project was funded by Camden Council, English Heritage, The Bedford Estates and The Crown Estate. Photograph by Phil Gyford.

with the support of the LPGT and English Heritage (fig. 274). The original one-day event was intended to draw attention to the contribution that the participating green spaces made to the capital, and the importance attached to their conservation. It also provided an opportunity for non-residents to explore private gardens that were not generally accessible to the public, and to enjoy them in a relaxed and convivial atmosphere of open-air concerts, historical exhibitions, craft displays and wine tastings. The annual weekend, now organised by the LPGT, has been a great success – indeed, it has become a regular fixture in the London garden calendar. Since the event began, tens of thousands of people have coursed through dozens of stoutly railed gardens that are normally closed to non-residents.[5] The visitors are grateful for the opportunity to gaze upon these 'secret gardens', and the squares' inhabitants seem content to open their squares to outsiders on this limited basis.

While the Open Garden Squares Weekend celebrates London's squares as they are, the English

Heritage Campaign for London Squares aims to reverse the decline in the capital's open spaces. Conceived by Philip Davies soon after he was appointed London Regional Director at English Heritage in 1997, the campaign 'set out clear priorities for action across London, based on a comprehensive assessment of squares' condition and significance, and using English Heritage grant funding as a catalyst for improvement'. The creation of the Heritage Lottery Fund in 1994 offered unprecedented levels of potential grant funding and thereby opened up real opportunities for cash-strapped local authorities.[6]

When the campaign was launched in 2000, some of the most prominent city squares were, indeed, in a poor state of repair. As Keith Hill, MP and Minister for London, remarked at the time: 'Many of London's squares fall short of the standards expected of a world class city. What is more their rundown condition can demoralise local communities and act as a barrier to regeneration . . . all too often they let us down because of poor presentation and manage-

275 Arnold Circus, Boundary Estate, east London, *c.*2009, photograph. Private collection.

ment. I have seen too many spoilt by decrepit fencing, broken surfacing and ugly intrusions. I have seen too many surrounded by a chaotic jumble of traffic islands, signs and rubbish. I have seen too many in the deep shade of unpruned trees.' The squares, he concluded, needed 'greater investment and enhancement'.[7]

The authors of English Heritage's campaign brochure stated that the primary objective of the initiative was 'to encourage all those responsible for the management and maintenance of these spaces to bring forward positive measures for their co-ordinated improvement, in particular the reinstatement of railings since they are such a vital component of the public realm'.[8] That is to say, railings are commended by English Heritage as 'essential management tools', as they provide an effective means of managing access, which ultimately safeguards the amenity.[9] Other English Heritage priorities include the reinstatement of layouts of footways and historic planting. English Heritage has never sought to restore squares to their original layouts (most of which are neither known nor documented in sufficient detail to warrant their re-creation), but aims to conserve

as well as possible their outstanding historic fabric, and to replace documented features that in the past contributed to the individuality of each square as a whole.

The campaign has been a resounding success: to date around £25m has been directed to the improvement of London's most important, neglected public and private squares.[10] Early successes included St George's Gardens, Russell, Brunswick and Bloomsbury squares, and Pond Square, Highgate. These have been followed by improvements to Gordon, Woburn, Bedford, Talbot, Tavistock and Fitzroy squares, and, Lincoln's Inn Fields, where a series of phased works was undertaken, culminating in the restoration of the gardens. In the spring of 2011 work began in Paddington on Sussex Gardens, in Marylebone on Park Crescent, and in Shoreditch on Arnold Circus (fig. 275).

In parallel with co-ordinated work on public squares by English Heritage in partnership with local authorities, the campaign has galvanised many private parties into taking action by demonstrating that the improvement of communal gardens can enhance the value of the surrounding properties. For

276   Russell Square, looking west towards Senate House, 2010, author's photograph. This view shows the refurbishment of the central garden carried out in the late 1990s.

instance, at Bedford Square the streetscape improvements completed in 2006 entailed repaving the public footpaths, realigning the carriageway, adding new street furniture, refurbishing the lighting, and reducing the square's visual clutter.[11] Here concessions were also made to modern use, including the formation of a broad bound-gravel apron for pedestrians around the garden oval within the square, and the provision of additional parking spaces.[12] English Heritage was also instrumental in encouraging the Crown Estate to restore Park Square, including the gates and railings, for the Queen Elizabeth's Golden Jubilee in 2002.

Lastly, English Heritage has supported a number of smaller projects by providing free professional and technical assistance in the preparation of landscape management plans, and repair and maintenance schemes. Among the recipients of this advice have been Central Square in Hampstead Garden Suburb, and Warwick Square in Pimlico. English Heritage ran the first and only London Squares Conservation Fair in 2003 in Bedford Square, with the support of

the Duke of Bedford and Camden Council; the organisation had its own stalls in the garden, offering visitors instruction in stone repair, railing design and repair, horticultural techniques, composting, tree care, biodiversity and insurance.

As well as by taking direct action, English Heritage has exercised a beneficial influence on other bodies seeking to maintain and improve London squares. In the late 1990s some of the great estates set up management plans in response to the 1993 Leasehold Reform, Housing and Urban Development Act, which threatened to destroy the unity of some of their squares and neighbourhoods. The schemes devised and implemented by the Grosvenor Estates in Mayfair and Belgravia are, for instance, exemplary, and have gone a great way to ensuring the continued conservation of their historic 300-acre early nineteenth-century layout of terraces, squares and crescents.[13]

Other initiatives, too, have taken shape in the aftermath of the conference. The LPGT's *Inventory of Public Parks, Gardens, Squares, Cemeteries, and Church-*

yards of Local Historic Interest in Greater London, which was begun in 1995 as a modest research project shortly after the trust was founded, has evolved into the *London Inventory of Historic Green Spaces*, a regular comprehensive survey of more than 2,500 squares, parks, gardens and open spaces in Greater London. As it provides detailed entries of all the squares listed in the 1931 act, and those created afterwards – most of which are not included in English Heritage's *Register of Parks and Gardens of Special Historic Interest* – it has become an important resource for a wide variety of individuals and organisations, including local authority planning and parks departments.[14]

Garden Square News is a forum for owners and residents of squares. Established in 1996, the twice-yearly magazine is the creation of the American journalist Holly Smith, and is, in her own words, a 'how-to manual', providing its readers with practical information to guide them in the management of their squares. Distributed to more than a hundred garden committees in Kensington and Chelsea, Westminster, and a variety of private estates across the metropolis, it also has many private subscribers in London and abroad. The magazine also promotes the improvement of squares through its annual London Squares competition.[15]

On an ecological note, since the turn of the century squares have become fully recognised for their significant contribution to sustaining biodiversity in the capital. In 2005 the London Parks and Greenspace Forum from the London Biodiversity Partnership commissioned a survey of more than 290 green spaces in central London, the results of which were published as *London's Small Parks and Squares: A Place for Nature? A . . . Habitat Action Plan for Parks and Squares*.[16] In important part, the study aimed to determine whether particular styles of gardening were associated with a richer bird life, and to develop best-practice guidelines for improving the biodiversity of public open spaces. The results have proven useful in informing private landscape restoration proposals as well as those undertaken through grants from English Heritage and the Heritage Lottery Fund. The survey proves, for example, that 'well-vegetated' garden squares provide excellent habitat for a wide range of bird species, including robins, dunnocks, wrens, long-tailed tits, great and blue tits, greenfinches and blackbirds – species commonly associated with woodland or woodland edge conditions. Gardens that contain a high percentage of trees, hedgerows and shrubbery, including some taller shrubs and pockets of denser growth, have the best range of breeding birds. Interestingly, the survey did not generally bring out a strong link between bird diversity and the presence of native trees and shrubs. The data also seem to suggest that a relaxed style of garden management can help make a garden more attractive to birds.

Unfortunately, the survey does not reveal much about the presence of mammals, amphibians and reptiles, as the methodology was 'not designed to pick up these species'. Nevertheless, it reports that foxes, grey squirrels, house mice and brown rats are 'street-wise enough' to travel between the small parks and squares on a regular basis. The survival of 'island populations' of wood mice in Eaton and Belgrave Squares are also noteworthy, as are the reports of hedgehogs in Ladbroke Square and St George's Gardens, Bloomsbury.[17]

Same Problem, Same Solution?

On Hampstead Heath's secluded walks
I'll hunt for thick, protruding stalks.
As dusk descends, I'll still be out,
To see what creepers are about:
With luck I'll take one home to bed,
Or pot one in the garden shed.
Now Russell Square's another nook
Where night-time growths deserve a look.
Some penis flytraps can be seen,
One glimpse of which would turn you green.[18]

Russell Square has been warmly praised as a good example of the comprehensive refurbishments brought about and partly funded through the Campaign for London Squares (fig. 276). The new layout, devised in the late 1990s by Land Use Consultants, in consultation with Camden Council, was based on a historical analysis of the square. The scheme was not, however, intended to be a reconstruction of the early garden, but rather an attempt to reform what had been censured as early as 1968 by a contributor to the *Architects' Journal* as an 'unfortunate muddle of different aesthetic ideas'.[19] The garden was restored to something like its nineteenth-century appearance: to this end, the railings and the perimeter hornbeam hedge were reinstated, and later 1950s additions such as the fountains and ad hoc planting were removed. Consideration was also given to the garden's present-day use and its maintenance. Thus the paths were laid in bound, rather than loose, gravel, and the path layouts were reconfigured to improve pedestrian circulation at the garden gates. The 1960s teahouse was rebuilt and extended, and a new *jet d'eau* was installed on the site of the former Reptonian *reposoir*. An evaluation by the Commission for Architecture and the Built Environment concluded that the garden, after these changes, was 'peaceful, green, uncluttered and relaxing'.[20]

What is perhaps less well known is that the refurbishment did not proceed without controversy: some of the changes (new high railings and the removal of much of the perimeter shrubbery, in particular)[21] were designed to deter gay men from using the garden as a night-time cruising area.[22] Some have suggested that this purge of London's 'queerest patch' had little to do with the public safety concerns of the neighbouring Bohemian community, and 'more than a little to do with the fact that the Russell Hotel, so beloved of US tourists, overlooks the square'.[23] Whatever the circumstances, John Beeson of *OutRage!* protested in 1999 that 'having created the problem, Camden is now considering closing the Square at night to stop gay men having sex there. This would end more than 50 years of gay cruising in Russell Square.'[24] Beeson made the following recommendation: 'If local people don't like gay sex in Russell Square, they should stay away. No one is forcing them to go there. They can use Bedford Square or Coram's Fields instead. In any case, what are these heterosexual whingers doing wandering around Russell Square at 2 a.m.? They should be at home looking after their children.' Beeson proposed that one third of the enclosure 'could be sectioned off with a high fence and thick shrubbery . . . [the] Entrance to the area would be marked with a warning sign. A similar system has worked well in the main parks in Copenhagen and Amsterdam for many years.'[25]

This is not, as we have seen, the first time that a square's central enclosure has been reordered and its management changed with a view to obviating what the authorities regarded as antisocial behaviour: as recently as 1993 Lincoln's Inn Fields was cleansed and re-railed by Camden Council to discourage the homeless from sleeping rough there.[26] Although many – and the Lincoln's Inn Fields Association in particular – were pleased to see the end of this 'city of the dispossessed', others objected to the new 'Colditz-like fence', and compared the 'unedifying spectacle' of rough sleepers being thrown off Lincoln's Inn Fields to 'some kind of 19th century clearance.'[27]

The alterations to both Russell Square and Lincoln's Inn Fields might lead us to believe that since the early eighteenth century there has been little change in the way in which we deal with antisocial behaviour in urban open spaces: the abuse of such places precipitates their enclosure. The successful stewardship of London's Georgian and Victorian squares, however, suggests otherwise. Secure enclosure and sustained maintenance are not in themselves enough to keep gardens in good order: their success is the more likely if underpinned by the familiar and heartening presence of the square keeper.[28] A uniformed figure reassures legitimate users, including mothers and children, and the elderly, and discourages the perpetrators of unacceptable behaviour; the presence of authority, moreover, fosters the development of peer-group pressure, which leads to changes in use and changes in perception that make the users of these invigilated spaces feel safe. The negotiation of what constitutes acceptable and unacceptable behaviour is, of course, subjective and constantly in flux, but in most squares it continues to be negotiated informally by the residents who pay a subscription for the use and benefit of a communal garden.

If there have been shortcomings in the management of gardens at Russell Square and Lincoln's Inn Fields it is because as 'public' gardens they are no different from urban parks now in local authority ownership, and as such suffer from the same problems: they are chronically under-funded by the public purse, and while they are given sporadic bursts of capital investment, there are no safeguards to financing their day-to-day and year-on-year maintenance. This was not, of course, always the case. Victorian parks were managed in much the same way as London squares. Indeed, the square keeper is very likely the role model for the Victorian park keeper, and the maintenance at many a London square set the standard for public parks and gardens across the metropolis.[29]

'Something's Missing Here': The Future of the London Square[30]

Developments around the turn of the century and since would appear to suggest that London's historic squares are probably now in better repair, more scrupulously maintained and more widely appreciated than they have been since the early nineteenth century (fig. 277). They are, moreover, broadly recognised as 'one of the defining features of London', and as England's most innovative and most universally admired urban landscape conceit.[31]

One can only hope that the momentum of this 'square renaissance' can be sustained, as there remains much to be done. The long history of the squares – the history that this study has begun to explore – suggests the need for continued concern. We can take nothing for granted about London's squares. By their nature as a unique urban phenomenon, they have been and are still today always vulnerable to any number of forces, both from without and within their immediate precincts. It remains to be seen, therefore, how they fare in light of future changes in demographics, land ownership, planning policy and even climate change.

To illustrate this uncertainty, it seems appropriate to end with a critical post-millennium issue. While London's historic squares are generally thriving, and have a reasonably rosy outlook, present building trends suggest that in future so-called squares may bear little resemblance to their precursors, and may function very differently from them. As Alina Congreve reported in *Garden Square News* in 2005, 'increased government pressure to develop housing at higher densities is making private residential developers look again at the garden square as a source of inspiration'. Congreve, a lecturer in the Department of Social Policy at the London School of Economics, refers specifically to Greenwich Millennium Village and to Wycombe Square and the Phillimores in west London, each of which is claimed by its respective developer to have been 'inspired by garden squares'.[32] Her criticism of these squares is based on two factors: the central communal garden at the Millennium Village, in her view, is poorly designed, and laid out without a view to its end users; and the layouts of all three squares are products of designers who have 'missed much of the point about why traditional squares work' (fig. 278). To explain, she observes that the average London square provides 'good quality open spaces in an urban environment', but those 'that really work well are well connected to the rest of the urban fabric of the city'. As examples she cites the highly regarded squares in Bloomsbury, which often have a main road on one side of the square and quieter roads on the other three sides, and many of those in Notting Hill, which, while enclosed on some sides, are 'well-connected into the urban fabric on other sides by a main road'.[33]

Such is not the case with the new squares in question. At Greenwich, Congreve affirms, the development has been located in the 'middle of a wilderness not connected to any of the rest of the city'. Less isolated, the Phillimores and Wycombe Square nonetheless 'make no effort to relate or connect with the pattern of streets in the surrounding area'. As a context for these squares' shortcomings, Congreve suggests that the 'fundamental mistake of providing open space, but in an isolated setting cut off from the rest of the city, has been the cause of blight on countless public housing projects in Britain since the 1950s. If garden squares are to provide a solution to our housing needs of the future, designers need to spend much more time looking at why current squares work before embarking on more schemes.'[34]

Congreve's argument is on the whole compelling: the squares she studied neither look nor function like traditional squares. She is right to warn, 'something's missing here'.[35] Nor is her criticism entirely new: in her dissertation of 1988, 'Type and Function in the Urban Square: A Case Study of London', Aspa Gospodini is critical of the functional and typological approaches to square design of the post-war period: 'Since most of the traditional squares are still popular spaces in our cities, it is difficult to avoid the inference that there is, indeed, something in the form of the old squares which has been misinterpreted by modern designs.'[36]

The Millennium Village is particularly revealing, as it was the first community to be built from scratch under the government's Millennium Communities initiative. The object was to provide eco-friendly housing within easy reach of schools, health centres, jobs, open space and public transport, and to embrace 'best practice on the use of energy and other natural resources . . . the latest innovations in building technology, and . . . challenging environ-

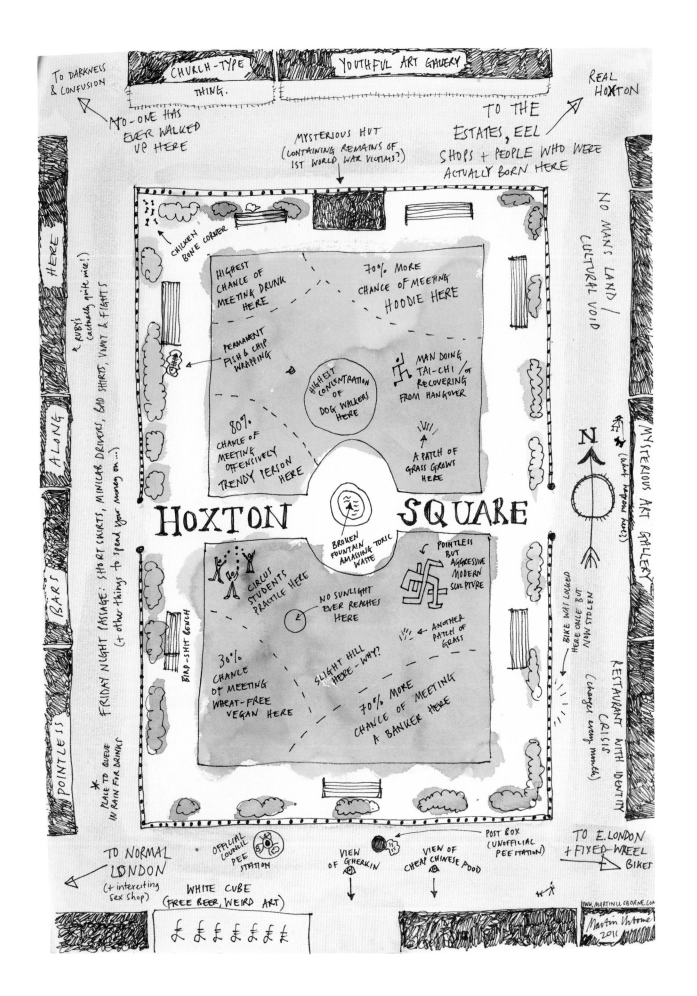

278 Becquerel Court, Millennium Village, Greenwich, 2011, author's photograph.

277 (facing page) Martin Usborne, *Hoxton Square*, 2011, ink with watercolour wash. Artist's collection. Usborne's spirited analysis, which recollects the plan of a London square in Horace Mayhew's 'Our Square' (1847; see fig. 149), conveys the complex social geography of a modern London square.

mental and ecological strategies'.[37] The village has received a number of plaudits, and is often cited as a good example of a mixed community, where people on different income levels can share the same part of the city. Yet, in fact, the village is not, as its name suggests, a picturesque hamlet laid out on an ancient green, but is instead, as one writer noted in the *Financial Times*, a jumble of 'bright cladding, vaulted roofs, private garden squares and a public ecology park', which straddles a 300-acre brownfield site on the Greenwich peninsula in south-east London. It was, in fact, raised on ground that was until recently occupied by the skeletal remains of Europe's largest gas works.[38] As Congreve remarks, 'the size of the site and the level of contamination deterred private developers from reclaiming the land until Government funding was forthcoming, including Government-funded improvements for transport links into the area'.[39]

According to English Partnerships, the government's regeneration agency, 'a new approach to the tradi-

tional London square' was deemed a desirable model for the new development, as it 'rekindles the traditional appeal of high-density housing'. Squares, it affirms, 'are common areas to be enjoyed and used by the residents and are designed to foster the neighbourly spirit which all thriving communities require'.[40]

To such ends, the village was, indeed, built around communal gardens. But, as Congreve contends, these central spaces neither look like squares, nor operate successfully as open spaces for communal use. Her reservations are confirmed by Heather Mulholland in her report *Perceptions of Privacy and Density in Housing* (2003), who is critical of the landscape design of the grounds for failing to deliver good-quality communal open space: she observes that the space is poorly laid out to accommodate a disparate mix of users, and there is a lack of provision for children. The report identifies four major shortcomings in the scheme: that the communal space is positioned at the back of the properties and enclosed by them; that this space is very much in the private zone at the back of the development, as opposed to the public, street-facing area at the front; that the communal space is too close to the houses and any lively activity there risks infringing the privacy of the residents; and that there is a lack of what is perceived as safe public open space close by for recreation. The third point has some especially grave consequences: it produces 'tensions between the households with, and those without, children over how the courtyards should be used. The former saw the courtyards as ideal places where their children could play safely and under supervision. The other residents perceived this as an invasion of their own privacy.'[41]

In response to such shortcomings, the report suggests that in higher density accommodation the provision of some outdoor space shared by the immediate neighbourhood is 'vitally important' as compensation for the necessary restrictions on private outdoor space, and that a combination of skilful design and good management are necessary to ensure that this space meets the needs of different households so that harmony prevails. Communal outdoor space must always 'be designed so that it offers an amenity for all those sharing it without disrupting the privacy of the residents in their homes. It should give scope for adults to enjoy quiet relaxation and for children to play games without causing annoyance to others.' The 'classic "garden square" as seen in Chelsea and South Kensington' is, in Mulholland's view, an 'excellent model for preserving privacy and amenity'. These squares were, she declared, successful for the following reasons: positioning the communal area in front of the properties put it more 'in the public realm' than if it had been in the private space at the rear; a quiet road, used primarily for access, intervenes to create more distance from the communal space; planting trees and hedges around the square gives some sense of privacy, but does not prevent the square from being overlooked by houses for safety; and putting in a clearly demarcated entrance that is gated, but not necessarily locked, keeps the communal space for the exclusive use of the neighbourhood.[42]

Finally, the report suggests as a matter of perhaps key importance that the communal gardens at the Millennium Village are unsuccessful because they are not governed by a code of behaviour. Squares, like public parks and gardens, have to accommodate a complex array of uses and users in a limited space,

and therefore require such a code in order to function. In squares, as we have seen, the code was traditionally negotiated among the residents, and was customarily displayed on signs or laid down in published rules.[43] The developer of the village had evidently given no forethought to how social interaction was supposed to take place within the new communal gardens. Restrictions, therefore, had gradually to be placed on the activities of children in some of the courtyards, but these were only introduced after 'major disputes arose over what were seen as breaches of privacy by some groups and as restrictions of freedom by others'.[44]

Far away in leafy Kensington, Wycombe Square and the Phillimores were laid out along more traditional, if somewhat starchy formal lines, and were intended for a very superior class of resident. Wycombe Square was completed in 2003 amid much fanfare, and promoted as 'the first new London garden square in 100 years' (fig. 279).[45] Reports in the press, however, suggested that the square's only distinction is that it boasts the highest average house prices in the Royal Borough, and possibly in the kingdom.[46] As a square, it must be said, it is neither fish nor fowl: the surrounding houses are separated from the central garden on three sides by a perimeter U-shaped road, and on the north side the square abuts the public pavement and carriageway. The square precinct gives the impression of being open to residents and outsiders: it is, therefore, neither entirely private nor wholly public. Although its pavements and central raised garden were conceived to be (at least under the planning conditions) part of the public realm, the reality is that the developers proposed from the outset to enclose the whole precinct with high railings with a view to excluding non-residents. However, as the planners denied them permission to do so, they resorted to hiring liveried security guards and installing CCTV to make casual visitors feel 'immediately conspicuous and unwelcome'.[47] Many local residents, with the exception, of course, of the square's inhabitants, have condemned the new square as a 'planning failure'.[48] This it may be, but for our purposes it is sufficient to say that the development is not a traditional London square: it was conceived and functions more or less as an American-style gated community – that is, a residential precinct surrounded entirely by a barrier, access to which is restricted to residents and their

284

guests, and where everything within the enclosure, including streets, pavements and gardens, are private and under the control of the community.

Although the neighbouring Phillimores was also advertised as a square, it too falls short of the most basic expectations of a traditional square. The development was formed through the conversion of Queen Elizabeth College, a handsome red-brick pile of 1912, built in the 'Wrenaissance' taste, surrounded by 4 acres of gardens and having a large central courtyard. The flats face the courtyard, and are separated from it by a pavement. Henry Tricks, writing in the *Financial Times* in 2003, reported that the 'key selling points for The Phillimores appear typically British – location, space, history, neighbourliness, and abundant greenery'. The fact that the agents marketing the development promoted it as a 'new square', doubtless bolstered its appeal; that this ploy of puffing it as a square succeeded is confirmed by Tricks, who reports that the agents were 'not shy of slipping in some old-fashioned British snobbery into their sales pitches if it helps the property stand out from its rivals'.[49]

Closer in its superficial appearance to a traditional square is the recently completed Phillimore Square (now Thornwood Gardens), described by its architects as a 'new London garden square which features eight substantial six bedroom houses to the west and east sides and a block of 32 apartments to the north' (fig. 280). Here the central garden is separated from the surrounding houses by a perimeter pavement and a road. But it, too, like the previous examples, is an 'insert', embedded in the well-established and eminently respectable neighbourhood overlooking Holland Park; and here, as in the Phillimores, the premises are large, comfortable, convenient for modern metropolitan living, and equipped with the most up-to-date security. This 'modern family living in a mix of houses and apartments', built around three sides of a central garden laid to lawn, and flanked on the long sides by low shrub beds is, however, like Wycombe Square, just another gated community.[50]

Although gated communities might conjure up images of socially cohesive groups of residents living in a geographical neighbourhood with well-defined boundaries to enhance secure feelings of community identity and belonging, this is not necessarily the case. Recent research by Sarah Blandy suggests that the 'physical structure of gated communities decreases urban and suburban permeability and, consequently, chance encounters in streets and everyday public spaces. These unplanned social interactions arguably enhance community cohesion and encourage a view of diversity as enjoyable, or certainly as tolerable, rather than frightening. Many gated-community residents, in contrast to this, become acculturated to their seclusion and increasingly dependent on it, which potentially leads, within the development, to 'destructive, negative cohesions . . . [based on] a nervous determination to exclude people seen as outsiders'.[51]

The blunt truth is that gated communities have little or nothing to do with London squares. If the modern squares we have examined are so called, it is only because their builders have appropriated the concept to capitalise on this ever popular, instantly recognisable and much admired 'upper middle class perquisite', as Anne Scott-James terms it.[52] That they have done so with little imagination, and with even less historical understanding of the concept, is reprehensible. Not only are the central communal gardens lacklustre in their layout, they are 'dead' spaces, as even the inhabitants are generally reluctant to use them: too obtrusive an attempt to ensure privacy and exclude outsiders inexorably deprives the gardens of any atmosphere of vitality and pleasure.

Traditional squares, as this book has shown, were more often than not designed to form conspicuous hubs of new neighbourhoods, and were lively, complex social organisms that shaped not only the life of their immediate surroundings, but that of the city around them. It is, therefore, particularly striking that although the new Kensington squares lie within a hundred metres of each other on the crest of

286

Campden Hill, there is no correspondence between them: each square is an independent and autonomous enclave, which turns its back on the adjacent streets and, indeed, the neighbourhood. The central space of the Phillimores is an invisible square or private courtyard, concealed on all sides by its surrounding buildings with no public access; that of Thornwood Gardens is semi-invisible, as the entrance to the precincts of this narrow cul-de-sac with a garden at its centre is separated from the public street by defensive railings and gates; and while Wycombe Square is wholly visible to outsiders, it is to all intents and purposes inaccessible. One can only regret that no effort has been made to integrate these new developments within their host communities, nor to create a degree of visual drama through 'the effects of surprise, intricacy, and seeming impro-

priety' – characteristics that Pevsner once admired in the squares of Regency London and Bath.[53]

As this book goes to print there are plans afoot to create a handful of squares at Chelsea Barracks in Lower Sloane Street. Here again the architects are confident that they will succeed in creating the first 'true' traditional London squares since the late nineteenth century. Whether they accomplish this, and what take on history these squares will have, has yet to be seen. Nor, I am sure, will these essays be the last. Squares will continue to be built anew and reinvented. We must hope that those who are in a position to create them will study to understand the wealth of opportunities that offer themselves through a careful analysis of the past, and all it can teach us about architecture, space and the environment at the service of communities.

Notes

Abbreviations

LMA London Metropolitan Archives
TNA National Archives
s.l. (*sine loco*) publisher unknown
SOL Survey of London

Prologue

1 Anne Scott-James and Osbert Lancaster, *The Pleasure Garden* (London: J. Murray, 1977; repr. Harmondsworth: Penguin, 1979), 88.
2 Scott-James and Lancaster, *Pleasure Garden*, 7.
3 Scott-James and Lancaster, *Pleasure Garden*, 88.
4 J. C. Loudon, 'Improvements in the North-Western Part of London', *Architectural Magazine* 5 (1838): 328.
5 John Timbs, *Curiosities of London, Exhibiting the Most Rare and Remarkable Objects of Interest in the Metropolis*, pt 2 (London: David Bogue, 1855), 679.
6 John Weale, *London Exhibited in 1851* (s.l.: n.p., 1851), 769.
7 London Society, *London Squares and How to Save Them* (s.l. [London]: London Society, n.d. [1927]), 7; Elain Harwood and Andrew Saint, *London* (London: HMSO, 1991), 95.
8 [James Ralph], *A Critical Review of the Public Buildings, Statues and Ornaments, in and about London and Westminster* (London: John Wallis, 1734), 30; John Clare, 'The Shepherd's Calendar', *The Shepherd's Calendar, with Village Stories and Other Poems* (London: James Duncan for John Taylor, 1827), 69.
9 *Once a Week*, 17 November 1866: 544.
10 *Sanitary Record: A Journal of Public Health* 9 (1878): 323.
11 Havelock Ellis, *Studies in the Psychology of Sex* (Philadelphia: F. A. Davis, 1906), 174.
12 Steen Eiler Rasmussen, *London: The Unique City* (London: J. Cape, 1937; repr., Harmondsworth: Penguin, 1961), 152-70.

13 William Holford in *Town Planning Review* 17, no. 1 (1938): 57.
14 Rasmussen, *London*, 167-8.
15 Rasmussen, *London*, 168.
16 See Elizabeth McKellar, *The Birth of Modern London* (Manchester: Manchester University Press, 1999), pp. xi-xii, and Michela Rosso, 'Georgian London Revisited', *London Journal* 26, no. 2 (2001): 45-6, for detailed analysis of the origins of Summerson's *Georgian London*, and a comparison of his objectives with those of Rasmussen.
17 Peter Borsay, *The English Urban Renaissance: Culture and Society in the Provincial Town, 1660-1770* (Oxford: Clarendon Press, 1989), 74.
18 McKellar in her work on London squares situates herself within the tradition of social display and identity formation, as in the work of Henri Lefebvre, *La production de l'espace* (1974), and Jürgen Habermas, *L'espace public* (1978).
19 Henry W. Lawrence, 'The Greening of the Squares of London: Transformation of Urban Landscapes and Ideals', *Annals of the Association of American Geographers* 83, no. 1 (1993): 90-118.
20 Lawrence, 'Greening of the Squares': 90-118.
21 Proof of Evidence of Mr Frank Hunt CVO Valuer to the London County Council, 15 November 1927, Royal Commission on London Squares, Appendix F.H.3, Parliamentary Archives, London, FCP/1/46. As Harwood and Saint have observed, the variations on the square are infinite, and 'few are anything like square' (Harwood and Saint, *London*, 96).
22 English Heritage quotes this number on its website *London Squares and Open Spaces* and in its *Campaign for London's Squares* (2000).
23 Todd Longstaffe-Gowan, 'Garden Squares', in *The London Town Garden, 1700-1840* (New Haven and London: Yale University Press, 2001), 183-233.

1 A New Attribute of 'the Seat Imperiall of this Kingdom'

1 J. F. Larkin and P. L. Hughes, *Stuart Royal Proclamations*, 2 vols (Oxford: Clarendon Press, 1973), 1:345–7.

2 The transformation of the fabric of London was, on the whole, a complex and far from uniform phenomenon. See Derek Keene, 'Growth, Modernisation and Control: The Transformation of London's Landscape, *c.*1500–*c.*1760', in *Two Capitals: London and Dublin, 1500–1840*, ed. Peter Clark and Raymond Gillespie (Oxford: Oxford University Press for the British Academy, 2001), 23–5; Elizabeth McKellar, 'Open Space in the City: From Fields to Squares and Gardens', in *The Birth of Modern London: The Development and Design of the City, 1660–1720* (Manchester: Manchester University Press, 1999), 188–223.

3 [William Weir], 'The Squares of London', in *London*, vol. 6, ed. Charles Knight (London: Charles Knight & Co., 1844), 193.

4 Jules Lubbock, *The Tyranny of Taste: The Politics of Architecture and Design in Britain, 1550–1960* (New Haven and London: Yale University Press for the Paul Mellon Centre for Studies in British Art, 1995), 4, 28. Lubbock affirms that the London square as a form of land use arose not from an alliance between the state and the nascent profession of architect–planners but from community action against development in favour of common rights to common fields.

5 McKellar, *Birth of Modern London*, 188–212.

6 Lubbock, *Tyranny of Taste*, 4–5.

7 Lubbock, *Tyranny of Taste*, 29.

8 See Norman George Brett-James, *The Growth of Stuart London* (London: London and Middlesex Archaeological Society, 1935), 453.

9 Richard Johnson, *The Pleasant Walkes of Moore-Fields* (1607), unpaginated. Local parishioners thwarted various informal attempts at enclosure, though they were less successful in preventing the erection of modest summer-houses on the edges of the common fields.

10 Johnson, *Pleasant Walkes*.

11 The development of Lincoln's Inn Fields is described in considerable detail in *Survey of London*, vol. 3: *St Giles-in-the-Fields, Part I: Lincoln's Inn Fields* [*SOL*, 3], ed. W. Edward Riley and Laurence Gomme (London: London County Council, 1912), 3–22.

12 Lincoln's Inn Fields are 10 acres in extent and were formed by the amalgamation of Purse Field, Cup Field and Fickett's Field.

13 *The Records of the Honorable Society of Lincoln's Inn: The Black Books*, 2 (1898), 439–40; *Register of Privy Council*, 3, fol. 45, quoted in *SOL*, 3:7.

14 *SOL*, 3:8.

15 *SOL*, 3:8.

16 *SOL*, 3:8, fn.

17 It is unclear whether Hollar depicts the fields as laid out to the designs of William Newton of *c.*1641 or Arthur Newman of *c.*1653. See R. Godfrey, *Wenceslaus Hollar: A Bohemian Artist in England* (New Haven and London: Yale University Press, 1995), no. 101.

18 'Petitions, Remonstrances, etc.', 1635–75, British Museum, 190 G 12 (51), quoted in *SOL*, 3:11.

19 This painting is at Wilton House, Wiltshire. It is reproduced in *SOL*, 3, pl. 6.

20 *SOL*, 3:18. In an agreement of 1657, Sir William Cowper and his colleagues had pledged to improve Cup Field in such a manner.

21 For a detailed account of the development of the fields, see *Survey of London*, vol. 34: *The Parish of St Anne Soho* [*SOL*, 34], ed. F. H. W. Sheppard (London: Athlone Press, 1966), 416–40.

22 *SOL*, 34:432.

23 TNA, PRO SP 16/181, no. 27.

24 Geoffrey Tyack, 'The Rebuilding of the Inns of Court, 1660–1700', in *The Intellectual and Cultural World of the Early Modern Inns of Court*, ed. Jayne Elisabeth Archer, Elizabeth Goldring and Sarah Knight (Manchester: Manchester University Press, 2011), 199.

25 Tia Sedley, 'Inner Temple Garden: "A New Faire Garden, Envoironed with Strong Brick Walls"', *London Gardener* 7 (2001–2): 46.

26 See David Jacques, '"The Chief Ornament" of Gray's Inn: The Walks from Bacon to Brown', *Garden History* 17, no. 1 (1989): 41–67; Deborah Spring, 'James Dalton and Francis Bacon: Two Garden Makers of the Inns of Court', *London Gardener* 14 (2008–9): 11–20; and Paula Henderson, 'The Evolution of the Early Gardens of the Inns of Court', in *Intellectual and Cultural World of the Early Modern Inns of Court*, ed. Archer, Goldring and Knight, 179–98.

27 Quoted in Hugh H. L. Bellot, *The Inner and Middle Temple: Legal, Literary, and Historic Associations* (London: Methuen, 1902), 248.

28 Henderson, 'Evolution of the Early Gardens': 184.

29 *Inner Temple Records*, 1:405, and *The Pension Book of Gray's Inn*, June 1631, 1:306, quoted in Henderson, 'Evolution of the Early Gardens': 182–3.

30 *House of Commons Journal*, 22:444, quoted in *SOL*, 3:19.

31 *Calendar of State Papers: Domestic Series, 1664*, vol. 91, no. 94.

32 Act for the Enclosure of Lincoln's Inn Fields, 1735. See also *The Old Bailey Online* (www.oldbaileyonline.org): Edward Swinney, Henry Harrison, Killing, murder, 27th August 1679; Roger Swiny, Killing, murder, 15th January 1680; and Charles Pynes, Robert Adderton, Killing, murder, 11th July 1694.

33 Johnson, *Pleasant Walkes*.

34 The word 'piazza' was used as late as 1768 to describe St James's Square. See *Public Advertiser*, 19 January 1768.

35 Francis Sheppard, *London: A History* (Oxford: Oxford University Press, 1998), 176; and Diane Duggan, 'The Architectural Patronage of Francis Russell, 4th Earl of Bedford, 1628–1638' (PhD diss., Courtauld Institute of Art, 2002), 86. There are compelling indications that Bedford – then still Lord Russell – began planning the development of the area as early as 1626, and that discussions with Inigo Jones could conceivably have begun at the same time.

36 Duggan, 'Architectural Patronage', 122, 125. King James certainly associated the uniform appearance of such new brick houses with the international standing of his capital,

and asserted that they were greatly admired 'by Ambassadors of foreign nations and others'. Howard Colvin, ed., *History of the King's Works*, vol. 3: *1485–1660* (London: HMSO, 1975), 153–4.

37 Giles Worsley, 'Inigo Jones and the Origins of the London Mews', *Architectural History* 44 (2001): 88–95.

38 The erection of the chapel of ease may have been a concession made to obtain the licence to build, and was probably, from Bedford's point of view, an essential attraction for the success of the new development.

39 The house was demolished and the gardens given over to building land in the eighteenth century.

40 I am grateful to John Harris for acquainting me with this view, and for dating it to *c*.1649.

41 Gordon Higgott, 'Inigo Jones in Provence', *Architectural History* 26 (1983): 24–34.

42 Juan de la Corte, *Horse Tournament in the Plaza Mayor, Held to Honour the Arrival of Charles Stuart, Prince of Wales, in Madrid in 1623*, painted *c*.1630.

43 Jesús Escobar, *The Plaza Mayor and the Shaping of Baroque Madrid* (Cambridge: Cambridge University Press, 2004), 212–13. Escobar makes the same observation. Memo from Jo: Granville to Francis Bedford, 27 December 1632, Alnwick Castle Archives, 2, B3 E2.

44 Malcolm Smuts, 'The Court and its Neighborhood: Royal Policy and Urban Growth in the Early Stuart West End', *Journal of British Studies* 30 (1991): 140–1.

45 Duggan, 'Architectural Patronage', 133–5, 138, 140–3. Owing to a lack of forward planning the streets and the piazza were paved before the sewer was completely installed.

46 *Survey of London*, vol. 36: *The Parish of St Paul Covent Garden* [*SOL*, 36], ed. F. H. W. Sheppard (London: Athlone Press, 1970), 130.

47 *SOL*, 36:129–31; St Paul's Covent Garden, Churchwardens' Accounts, 1656–1960, TNA, accession 426.

48 Duggan, 'Architectural Patronage', 162–4. The earl's grand plans to erect an equestrian 'statua . . . in Brasse' of the king in the middle of the piazza did not materialise.

49 The tree was planted in 1657. The erection of the column in the piazza appears to have created a fashion for isolated columns in London in the late seventeenth century. See Stephen Priestley, 'The Fountain and Gardens in New Square, Lincoln's Inn: A Brief History', *London Gardener* 3 (1997–8): 27.

50 Duggan, 'Architectural Patronage', 161, 164; TNA, PRO SP 16/402, no. 75. This aim was included in the articles of Bedford's 'first proposicion' for his new development.

51 For an analysis of the prevalence of sculpture in French public squares, see Robert W. Berger, *A Royal Passion: Louis XIV as a Patron of Architecture* (Cambridge: Cambridge University Press, 1994), 154–62; Jean-Louis Harouel, *L'embellissement des villes: l'urbanisme français au XVIIIe siècle* (Paris: Picard, 1993); Hilary Ballon, *The Paris of Henri IV: Architecture and Urbanism* (Cambridge, Mass.: MIT Press, 1991). I am grateful to Andrew Saint for these references.

52 Duggan, 'Architectural Patronage', 164.

53 Churches were occasionally built within the central gardens, but seldom on the main square until after the 1820s; and for much of the eighteenth century they 'found no place at all' in new residential development. Sheppard, *London*, 177.

54 *The Diary of John Evelyn*, ed. William Bray, 2 vols (New York and London: M. Walter Dunne, 1901), vol. 2: 9 February 1665.

55 L. Stone, 'The Residential Development of the West of London in the Seventeenth Century', in *After the Reformation*, ed. B. C. Malament (Manchester: Manchester University Press, 1980), 167–212; Smuts, 'Court and its Neighborhood', 117–49.

56 St Albans was in France in 1633–6, 1641–4 (living at the Louvre and St Germain-en-Laye), and 1644–8 (with Queen Henrietta's household at the Palais Royal and Château de Colombe). Anthony R. J. S. Adolph, 'Jermyn, Henry, Earl of St Albans', *Oxford Dictionary of National Biography*.

57 St Albans commissioned Sir Christopher Wren – whose career he had furthered by introducing him to the best builders in Paris in 1665 – to design St James's Church. As steward of Greenwich, 1660–76, he supported the restoration and extension of the Queen's House and the redevelopment of Greenwich Palace, and, in 1662, brought André Le Nôtre over from France to design the park at Greenwich. *Survey of London*, vol. 29: *St James Westminster, Part I* [*SOL*, 29], ed. F. H. W. Sheppard (London: Athlone Press, 1960), 56–76.

58 TNA, PRO SP 29/75, no.27.

59 TNA, PRO SP 44/13, p. 340.

60 TNA, PRO C104/148 (deed). The houses referred to as 'Pyatza Houses' are now nos. 1 and 2 St James's Square.

61 Balthasar de Monconys, *Journal des voyages de Monsieur de Monconys, publié par le Sieur de Liergues son fils* (Paris: Louis Billaine, 1677), pt 2: 11; Samuel Sorbière, *Relation d'un voyage en Angleterre* (Paris: Thomas Jolly, 1664), 38.

62 Roland Fréart, *A Parallel of the Antient Architecture with the Modern*, trans. John Evelyn (London: John Place, 1664), Evelyn's dedication to Charles II.

63 John Summerson, *Georgian London* (London: Pleiades Books, 1945; repr. Harmondsworth: Penguin, 1978), 42.

64 McKellar, *Birth of Modern London*, 203–4.

65 See Keene, 'Growth, Modernisation and Control', 23.

66 References to the early planning of Marine Square are found in Marine Square Papers, Ellesmere MS EL 10389–10433, Huntington Library, San Marino, California.

67 For instance Jeffreys, Queen and Fish Street squares were little more than street widenings, and Bear Garden Square was described in 1720 as 'convenient for Butchers and such like, who are taken with such rustick Sports as the baiting of *Bears* and *Bulls*'. John Stow, *Survey of the Cities of London and Westminster*, rev. John Strype, 2 vols (London: Churchill et al., 1720), 2:28.

68 There were elms in the fields in 1614. A baptismal register of St Andrew's Holborn records 'Thomas, a child born under Red Lyon Elmes in the Fields in High Holborn, baptised iii August 1614.'

69 Narcissus Luttrell, *A Brief Historical Relation of State Affairs*, 6 vols (Oxford: Oxford University Press, 1857), 4:309.

70 *The Records of the Honorable Society of Lincoln's Inn: The Black Books*, 2:347, quoted in *SOL*, 3:9.

71 National Register of Archives, c9/92/3.

72 For a detailed account of the area, see *Survey of London*, vol. 46: *South and East Clerkenwell*, ed. Philip Temple (London: Yale University Press, 2008), 243–79.

73 In 1611 the priory was converted for charitable purposes to Sutton's Hospital in Charterhouse, in which use it continues to this day.

74 The plan is no longer attributed to Ralph Agas, but is still known by his name.

75 James Howell, *Londinopolis* (London: J. Streater, for H. Twiford, 1657), 343.

76 Free-standing statues were common enough in early eighteenth-century London for Edward Hatton to dedicate a section of *A New View of London, or, An Ample Account of that City* (London: R. Chiswell, 1708) to 'An Alphabetical Account of the Publick Statues in and about the City'. His book lists over ninety works of sculpture, which adorned churches, livery company halls, city gates, courts, noblemen's houses and gardens. Only a small proportion of these were, however, set up in gardens and, of these, all except the fountain and statue dedicated to Charles II in Soho Square were based on antique originals. See Todd Longstaffe-Gowan, 'Brazen Proclamations: The Deployment of Statuary in Some Early London Garden Squares', *Sculpture Journal* 18 (2009): 52–66.

77 National Register of Archives, C66/3181, no. 24.

78 *Survey of London*, vol. 33: *St Anne Soho* [*SOL*, 33], ed. F. H. W. Sheppard (London: Athlone Press, 1966), 33, 42.

79 Gregorio Leti, *Del teatro brittanico, o vero, Historia dello stato, antico e presente, corte, gouerno spirituale, e temporale, leggi, massime, religioni, & euuenimenti della Grande Brettagna*, 2 vols (London: Roberto Scott, 1683 [1682]), 1:74.

80 Leti, *Del teatro*, 1:74.

81 Leti, *Del teatro*, 1:74. At the time he was writing he remarked that yet another 'superbissima piazza' was being planned for Lord Arlington's estate in Piccadilly, which, like Soho Square, was to be surrounded by palaces. He refers here to the ill-fated Arlington Square, which was, in fact, never realised.

82 The outline of the 'fountaine' appears on John Ogilby and William Morgan's *Large and Accurate Map of the City of London* (1676).

83 King's Square, like the Piazza Navona in Rome, was surrounded by houses; and while Bernini's fountain was fed with waters from the Acqua Vergine, the fountain at King's Square was fed by a windmill several hundred yards to the north.

84 Leti, *Del teatro*, 1:74.

85 The square is recorded in leases of 1683 as 'King Square' (*SOL*, 33:42). By this time the statue of Charles II had been erected in the centre of the square, which was presumably named in honour of the reigning monarch.

86 [Hatton], *New View of London*, 789. Hatton goes on to describe in detail the figures and inscriptions of the base and plinth.

87 Stow, *Survey*, 87.

88 Provision for the maintenance of the 'Fountaine and Garden in the middle of the said Square' was made in the house leases of 1680–1. National Register of Archives, c6/291/12.

89 The Soho Square model became more widely imitated after 1726. For a detailed account of the building history of Golden Square, see 'Golden Square Area', *Survey of London*, vol. 31: *St James Westminster, Part II: North of Piccadilly* [*SOL*, 31], ed. F. H. W. Sheppard (London: Athlone Press, 1963), 138–75.

90 McKellar, *Birth of Modern London*, 129; Westminster Cathedral, deed of 21 April 1684 for 22 Golden Square, quoted in *SOL*, 31:145.

91 Royal National Ear, Nose and Throat Hospital deeds, 28 October 1685, quoted in *SOL*, 31:145. The garden may have been completed by 1688, when one Mathew Capell, at No. 25, paid £1 'towards Gravelling the Square'. National Register of Archives, c8/350/89.

92 Stone, 'Residential Development', 180. These amenities were provided at St James's Square from *c.*1665, Leicester Fields from *c.*1670, and Golden Square from *c.*1690.

93 For a detailed history of the square, see *SOL*, 29:56–75.

94 TNA, PRO SP 29/361, no. 204.

95 Greater London Record Office, Harden deeds, X142, X145; Greater London Record Office, (M) acc. 401/182–3.

96 'Models' for rebuilding were put forward in September 1666 by Christopher Wren, John Evelyn, Robert Hooke, Sir William Petty, Richard Newcourt and Valentine Knight.

97 See John Evelyn, *Fumifugium, or, The Inconveniencie of the Aer and Smoak of London Dissipated* (London: Gabriel Bedel and Thomas Collins, 1661).

98 Augustin-Charles d'Aviler, *Cours d'architecture qui comprend les ordres de Vignole* (Paris: N. Langlois, 1696), 308–9.

2 Adorning Squares in the 'Rural Manner'

1 Daniel Defoe, *A Tour thro' the Whole Island of Great Britain* (1725; repr., Everyman ed., London: Dent, 1962), 1:314.

2 *Applebee's Original Weekly Journal*, 14 September 1725.

3 *Weekly Medley*, 13 September 1718.

4 John Fielding, *The New London Spy* (London: J. Cooke, 1771), 60.

5 Guy Miège, *The Present State of Great Britain* (London: J. Nicholson, 1707), 135.

6 Guy Miège, *The New State of England Under Their Majesties K[ing] William and Q[ueen] Mary* (London: R. Clavel, H. Mortlock and J. Robinson, 1694), 231; Miège, *Present State of Great Britain*, 135.

7 [Joseph Pote], *The Foreigner's Guide*, 2nd ed. (London: J. Pote, 1740), 118.

8 The reservoir was excavated some time in the thirteenth century to supply water for the Greyfriars of Newgate Street in the City.

9 The statue was not erected until 1780, after the New Road had compromised the views north.

10 [William Weir], 'The Squares of London', in *London*, vol. 6, ed. Charles Knight (London: Charles Knight & Co., 1844), 203; 'Mr Repton, Letter to the Trustees of Blooms-

bury Square, March 3rd 1807', Bedford Estate Archive, Woburn Abbey.

11 [Pote], *Foreigner's Guide*, 122 (and 1729 ed.). The square is described in the *Weekly Medley*, 13 September 1718, as 'the New-square which is building near Tyburn road'.

12 Arthur Murphy, 'An Essay on the Life and Genius of Henry Fielding', in *The Works of Henry Fielding, Esq., with the Life of the Author*, 3rd ed., vol. 1 (London: A. Millar, 1766), 128.

13 John Ingamells, *A Dictionary of British and Irish Travellers in Italy, 1701–1800* (New Haven and London: Yale University Press, 1997), 617.

14 [James Ralph] in *London Magazine, or, Gentleman's Monthly Intelligencer* 3 (March 1734): 104.

15 *Post Boy*, 23 June 1719.

16 *Weekly Medley*, 13 September 1718. It is also possible that the landscape gardener Charles Bridgeman, who was resident on the estate, and an old friend of the Earl of Oxford, had a hand in this matter.

17 [Ralph], *London Magazine*: 105.

18 The reservoir was filled in between 1764 and 1765, and replaced with buildings.

19 Béat Louis de Muralt, *Letters Describing the Character and Customs of the English and French Nations: With a Curious Essay on Travelling*, 2nd ed. (London: T. Edlin, 1726), 78–9.

20 Thomas Fairchild, *The City Gardener* (London: T. Woodward and J. Peele, 1722), 11–12.

21 Fairchild, *City Gardener*, 12.

22 Fairchild, *City Gardener*, 13–14.

23 Fairchild, *City Gardener*, 14. The author remarked that he was 'sensible that it [his plan] may be very much improved'.

24 Fairchild's recommendations were not new. In 1712 John James (*The Theory and Practice of Gardening* (s.l.: n.p., 1712), 18) had 'earnestly' recommended the planting of 'small Groves of Evergreens' in 'some Squares' as they would 'look very well when seen from the Building' and they would 'make a diversity from other Wood; which having lost its Leaves, appears quite naked all the Winter'.

25 Fairchild, *City Gardener*, 16–21.

26 Fairchild, *City Gardener*, 21–6

27 Fairchild, *City Gardener*, 27, 38.

28 Fairchild, *City Gardener*, 27–34.

29 Fairchild, *City Gardener*, 40–2. Fairchild does not prescribe a height for his hedge. It was presumably approximately 8 feet, as were Alston's at Grosvenor Square Wilderness, planted by *c.*1729–30.

30 Jan Woudstra, 'The Wilderness in Seventeenth and Eighteenth Century Gardens' (MA thesis, University of York, 1986).

31 For a similar wilderness plan, see Nino Strachey, 'The Helmingham Plan: An Eighteenth-Century Survey of the Gardens at Ham House', *London Gardener* 2 (1997–8): 36–41.

32 Fairchild, *City Gardener*, title page.

33 Fairchild, *City Gardener*, 14, 41–3.

34 Fairchild, *City Gardener*, 42–3.

35 Preamble, 12 Geo. I, c. 25, public (St James's Square Act).

36 *Survey of London*, vol. 36: *The Parish of St Paul Covent Garden*, ed. F. H. W. Sheppard (London: Athlone Press, 1970), 131.

37 [Pote], *Foreigner's Guide*, 124. The first new squares to be built along the lines of Grosvenor Square appeared not in London but in Bath. For a detailed account of the building of the square, see 'Grosvenor Square', *Survey of London*, vol. 40: *The Grosvenor Estate in Mayfair, Part II: The Buildings*, ed. F. H. W. Sheppard (London: Athlone Press, 1980), 112–70.

38 [Pote], *Foreigner's Guide*, 124.

39 Mark Girouard, *The English Town* (New Haven and London: Yale University Press, 1990), 161.

40 Elain Harwood and Andrew Saint, *London* (London: HMSO, 1991), 96.

41 See Julie Schlarman, 'The Social Geography of Grosvenor Square: Mapping Gender and Politics, 1720–1760', *London Journal* 28, no. 1 (2003): 5–28.

42 Draft agreement between John Alston and Sir Richard Grosvenor, 1729, Grosvenor Papers, Westminster City Archives 1409/10/4, misc. 6. The unusual shape of the garden is attributed to the estate's surveyor John Mackay.

43 'Articles of Agreement for the Building of the Garden of Grosvenor Square', 1729, Grosvenor Papers, Westminster City Archives, 1409/10/4, misc. 6.

44 [Ralph], *London Magazine*: 142; Girouard, *English Town*, 160.

45 Ingamells, *Dictionary of British and Irish Travellers*, 435.

46 *British Journal*, 18 March 1727; 'Agreement for the Laying-Out of Grosvenor Square', 24 June 1725, item 8, Messrs Glyn, Mills Archives, quoted in Gunnis Papers, Henry Moore Institute Archives, Leeds.

47 James Peller Malcolm, *London Redivivum*, 4 vols (London: J. Nichols, 1802–7), 4:131–2.

48 *British Journal*, 18 March 1727.

49 L. Stone, 'Residential Development in the West End of London in the Seventeenth Century', in *After the Reformation: Essays in Honor of J. H. Hexter*, ed. Barbara C. Malament (Philadelphia: University of Pennsylvania Press; Manchester: Manchester University Press, 1980), 196.

50 Specifications included in 'Articles of Agreement for the Building of the Garden of Grosvenor Square'.

51 [Pote], *Foreigner's Guide*, 124–6.

52 [Ralph], *London Magazine*: 142, quoted in 'Conclusion of the Review of the Public Buildings, &c.', *Weekly Register*, 30 March 1734. For an interesting insight into Ralph, see Eileen Harris and Nicholas Savage, *British Architectural Books and Writers, 1556–1785* (Cambridge: Cambridge University Press, 1990), 381–4.

53 Published comments on the square from 1734 onwards treated the irregularity of the buildings as an excusable defect of the grand plan.

54 *Post Boy*, 11–14 December 1697.

55 Narcissus Luttrell, *A Brief Historical Relation of State Affairs*, 6 vols (Oxford: Oxford University Press, 1857), 4:316; *Post Boy*, 11–14 December 1697; *Survey of London*, vol. 29: *The Parish of St James Westminster, Part I* [SOL, 29], ed. F. H. W. Sheppard (London: Athlone Press, 1960), 67. There are no surviving drawings of the work, but it may possibly be

associated with a bronze equestrian statuette of William III – in the triumphant posture of Marcus Aurelius – crowning a plinth decorated with inscriptions and reliefs now in the Royal Collection. I am grateful to Jonathan Marsden, Deputy Surveyor of the Queen's Works of Art, for acquainting me with this sculpture.

56 The gilded bronze monument was destroyed on 10 August 1792. François Souchal, ed., *French Sculptors of the 17th and 18th Centuries: The Reign of Louis XIV*, 4 vols (Oxford: Cassirer, 1977–93), 1:253–7; Anthony Blunt, *Art and Architecture in France, 1500 to 1700* (London: Penguin, 1953), 213.

57 12 Geo. I, c. 25, extract. So considerable was the accumulation of debris that 3,792 cubic yards of soil was removed from the surface of the square when it was replanned in 1727. St James's Square Trust, Minutes of the Trustees, 1726–1835, Westminster City Archives, 395, 15 March 1727. For a detailed description of activities that have taken place in the square from the late seventeenth century onwards see Denys Forrest, *St James's Square: People, Houses, Happenings* (London: Quiller Press, 1986).

58 The act was a 'private act' – that is, local and personal in its effect, giving special powers to the residents and/or making exceptions to the law in its particular geographic area.

59 Although this and ensuing acts for the enclosure, embellishment and protection of squares are not referred to by historians or geographers as Parliamentary Enclosure Acts, the motives for these enclosures was clearly the same. For the rich and powerful the parliamentary process lay to hand to enable them to 'snatch' such common waste land; see J. R. Wordie, 'The Chronology of English Enclosure, 1500–1914', *Economic History Review* 36 (1983): 488.

60 *SOL*, 29:66.

61 Until about 1730 the trustees met frequently, sometimes at only a few days' interval, but thereafter they normally convened only very formally once a year.

62 See *SOL*, 29:56–76.

63 *Weekly Journal, or, British Gazetteer*, 18 March 1727.

64 St James's Square Trust, Minutes of the Trustees, 7 February 1727. The basin was lined with clay and finished with a bed of flints.

65 St James's Square Trust, Minutes of the Trustees, 6 February 1727, 15 March 1727.

66 Susan Jenkins, *Portrait of a Patron: The Patronage and Collecting of James Brydges, 1st Duke of Chandos (1674–1744)* (Aldershot: Ashgate, 2007), 84. Chandos lived in St James's Square between 1720 and 1735, and commissioned John Theophilus Desaguliers and John Lowthrop to assist him in his hydrological pursuits. In about 1722 he had built a 'Great Octagonal Bason' at Canons at Stanmore, north London. He was also involved in the York Buildings (Water) Company.

67 St James's Square Trust, Minutes of the Trustees, 27 February 1727. The decision to build a reservoir may have been galvanised by a 'violent fire' that destroyed the Duke of Kent's house and damaged the adjoining houses. *Evening Post*, 14 December 1725.

68 Extract from the will made in 1724 by Samuel Travers of

St James's, Westminster, MP, Auditor-General to the Prince of Wales, and (probably) Surveyor-General of Crown Lands. *SOL*, 29:67.

69 Three subsequent attempts to raise statues in the square also failed: the first by Lord Ranelagh, who tried in 1710–11 to raise a statue of William III; the second in 1721, when the French sculptor Claude David endeavoured to raise an equestrian statue of George I; and the third in 1724, when Samuel Travers made provision in his will for an equestrian statue in brass.

70 See [James Ralph], *A Critical Review of the Publick Buildings, Statues and Ornaments, in and about London and Westminster* (London: John Wallis, 1734), 32.

71 Timothy Clayton, *The English Print, 1688–1802* (New Haven and London: Yale University Press, 1997), 75; Sheila O'Connell, *London 1753* (London: British Museum Press, 2003), 243–5.

72 12 Geo. I, c. 25, extract. The precedent had been established in 1707 when a bill had been brought in 'for beautifying and preserving the Square called Lincoln's Inn Great Fields'. Nothing, however, came of it.

73 'Commissioning Papers Relating to the Queen's Statue', document 6, Lambeth Place Library. For a detailed account of this commission, see Terry Friedman, 'Foggini's Statue of Queen Anne', in *Kunst des Barock in der Toskana* (Munich: Bruckmann, 1976), 39–56.

74 Talman's choice for the queen's statue was doubtless made in the spirit of improvement that guided so many guardians of the city's squares; he was, in this respect, also in good company, as three eminent architects had proposed to build imposing churches on the same site between 1688 and 1712: Sir Christopher Wren in *c*.1688, Thomas Archer in 1711–12, and Colen Campbell in 1712.

75 'Commissioning Papers', document 13.

76 Lincoln's Inn Fields, Minutes of the Trustees, 1735–1879, British Library, Add. MSS 35077–35081, 2 June 1735.

77 Lincoln's Inn Fields, Minutes of the Trustees, 2 June 1735, 4 August 1735

78 Lincoln's Inn Fields, Minutes of the Trustees, 2 August 1736, 23 July 1741

79 Lincoln's Inn Fields, Minutes of the Trustees, 19 May 1736.

80 Lincoln's Inn Fields, Minutes of the Trustees, 3 December 1735.

81 Lincoln's Inn Fields, Minutes of the Trustees, 6 June 1753, 29 November 1774.

82 Lincoln's Inn Fields, Minutes of the Trustees, 6 May 1754, 18 February 1805, 14 May 1810.

83 Lincoln's Inn Fields, Minutes of the Trustees, 6 June 1753, 6 August 1753, 15 April 1760, 14 May 1774, 31 May 1774, 30 November 1776.

84 Lincoln's Inn Fields, Minutes of the Trustees, 24 February 1798, 17 June 1805.

85 Horace Mayhew, 'Our Square', *Lady's Newspaper*, 31 July 1847.

86 Lincoln's Inn Fields, Minutes of the Trustees, 2 August 1736.

87 Lincoln's Inn Fields, Minutes of the Trustees, 9 May 1771, 1 Nov 1742, 2 May 1743.

88 Lincoln's Inn Fields, Minutes of the Trustees, 14 November 1739, 22 December 1756, 22 January 1760.

89 Lincoln's Inn Fields, Minutes of the Trustees, 6 June 1753, 13 December 1752, 26 February 1752, 11 July 1740, 14 May 1774.

90 Lincoln's Inn Fields, Minutes of the Trustees, 25 February 1760.

91 Lincoln's Inn Fields, Minutes of the Trustees, 18 November 1805.

92 Accusations included permitting beggars to enter the fields and lay 'filth and nastinese [sic] there' (6 June 1753), suffering children to be disorderly (6 May 1754), and sleeping on duty (14 February 1759).

93 *Country Journal*, 16 April 1737; [Ralph], *Critical Review*, 30. The improvements were to be paid for by voluntary subscriptions from the inhabitants.

94 'Golden Square Area', *Survey of London*, vol. 31: *The Parish of St James Westminster, Part II: North of Piccadilly*, ed. F. H. W. Sheppard (London: Athlone Press, 1963), 138–75.

95 *The London and Westminster Guide, Through the Cities and Suburbs* (London: W. Nicoll, 1768). The stone statue of the reigning monarch, attributed to John Nost II (carved *c.*1727), was erected in 1753.

96 [Ralph], *Critical Review*, 101–2.

97 'An Act to enable the present and future Proprietors and Inhabitants of the Houses in *Red Lion Square*, in the County of *Middlesex*, to make a Rate on themselves, for raising Money sufficient to enclose, pave, watch, clean, and adorn, the said Square', 10 Geo. II, c. 15.

98 Lincoln's Inn Fields, Minutes of the Trustees, 6 June 1753.

99 An account of the conviction of a 'disorderly person' discovered in the square was proposed by the trustees to be published in the *Daily Advertiser*. Lincoln's Inn Fields, Minutes of the Trustees, 9 June 1736.

100 Malcolm Smuts, 'The Court and its Neighborhood: Royal Policy and Urban Growth in the Early Stuart West End', *Journal of British Studies* 30 (1991): 131.

101 In legal terms this meant simply that land formerly held in severalty fell under the power of one owner or group, who could do with it what he pleased; this land did not necessarily have to be enclosed but it had to be improved or more intensively cultivated, and it was also free of all common rights, except possibly for a right of way. See Wordie, 'Chronology of English Enclosure'; and Michael Williams, 'The Enclosure and Reclamation of Waste Land in England and Wales in the Eighteenth and Nineteenth Centuries', *Transactions of the Institute of British Geographers* 51 (November 1970): 55–69.

102 This trend began from the second quarter of the seventeenth-century. See Stone, 'Residential Development', 193–5; Smuts, 'Court and its Neighborhood', 126–7.

103 [Pote], *Foreigner's Guide*, 128. The same message was projected in other contemporary guidebooks aimed at foreign visitors, including J. B. Küchelbecker, *Der nach Engelland reisende curieuse Passagier, oder Kurze Beschreibung der Stadt London und derer umliegenden Oerter* (Hanover: Nicolaus Förster und Sohn, 1726), and *De leydsman der vreemdelingen* (Amsterdam: Dirk onder de Linden, 1759).

104 [Ralph], *Critical Review*, 5.

105 P.Q., *St James's Park: A Comedy* (London: John Cooper, 1733), 57–8. See also Laura Williams, '"To recreate and refresh their dulled spirites in the sweet and wholesome ayre": Green Space and the Growth of the City', in *Imagining Early Modern London* (Cambridge: Cambridge University Press, 2001), 202.

3 *'Squares that Court the Breeze'*

1 Thomas Hosmer Shepherd and James Elmes, *Metropolitan Improvements, or, London in the Nineteenth Century* (London: Jones & Co., 1827), 2.

2 *Rambler*, no. 61, 16 October 1750.

3 James Thomson, *Liberty: A Poem* (London: A. Millar, 1735–6), pt iv, lines 701–2.

4 Originally published in weekly numbers beginning on 29 December 1753, the whole work was finished by 1756.

5 'A Londres, le peu de hauteur des maisons, la largeur des rues, la plupart longues et droits, fait qu'on s'oriente aisement: à chaque distance de rues il y a des places spacieuses, les unes ont au milieu une statue, dans un boulingrin, ou un pièce d'eau, ou des bosquets, le tout bien entretenu et qui sert de promenade aux gens de la place; ces places sont immenses et de toute beauté: il y en a à chaques distance; elles sont innombrables. L'on ne bâtit aucun nouveau quartier que par places, qui forme quatre ailes de maisons.' Louis-Sébastien Mercier, *Parallèle de Paris et de Londres*, 1781, ed. Claude Bruneteau and Bernard Cottret (Paris: Didier Érudition, 1982), 60.

6 'Les nouveaux quartiers de Londres sont coupés & se communiquent par des places quarrées, dont plusieurs sont d'une fort grande étendue: les Anglois les appellent *squarres* [sic]. Fermées la plupart, come la Place Royale l'est à Paris, elles ont au milieu ou des boulingrins, ou des pièces d'eau. Celle de *Grosvenor* a un jardin distribué en allées. Quelques-unes ont des statues équestres des derniers rois . . . Les maisons qui bordent ces places, ne sont point assujetties à une exacte uniformité: parmi des façades toutes nues, on en voit de plus ou moins ornées, suivant le caprice ou le goût du propriétaire.' [P.-J. Grosley], *Londres*, 3 vols (1765; Lausanne: n.p., 1770), 1:71–2.

7 'Un étranger se doit faire un plaisir de parcourir toutes les places de Londres dans le quartier de Westminster, qui est plus grand que Paris. Il y a plus de vingt places très spacieuses, toutes quarrées, entourées de très-belles maisons, car il n'y a point d'hôtels à grandes portes cochères. Ces superbes places, comme celle de *Gro[s]venor*, sont embellies ou par des statues équestres ou pédestres, ou obélisques, ou par des bassins ou bosquets fermés par des grilles de fer, dont les habitans de la place ont la clef, & s'y promènent lorsqu'il fait beau temps, ce qui n'arrive jamais passé le mois d'Octobre les brouillards envéloppent alors & sans cesse cette Babilone.' François La Combe, *Tableau de Londres et de ses environs, avec un précis de la constitution de l'Angleterre, et de sa Decadence* (1777; London: Société Typographique, 1784), 14. Many of the eighteenth-century so-called 'foreigner's guides' – whether in English,

French, German or Dutch – reported the ever changing numbers of squares in the metropolis.

8 James Boswell, *The Life of Samuel Johnson* (London: Baynes and Sons, 1826), 1:370.

9 Morris R. Brownell, *Samuel Johnson's Attitude to the Arts* (Oxford: Clarendon, 1989), 5.

10 See Nicholas Hudson, 'Samuel Johnson, Urban Culture, and the Geography of Post-Fire London', *Studies in English Literature, 1500–1900* 42 (2002), 577–600.

11 Boswell, *Life of Johnson*, 3:244.

12 Brownell, *Samuel Johnson's Attitude*, 130.

13 John Gwynn, *London and Westminster Improved, Illustrated by Plans. To which is Prefixed, A Discourse on Publick Magnificence* (London: Dodsley, 1766), p. v.

14 Boswell, *Life of Samuel Johnson*, 2:415.

15 Gwynn, *London and Westminster Improved*, 77.

16 Gwynn, *London and Westminster Improved*, 80.

17 Gwynn, *London and Westminster Improved*, 80.

18 Gwynn, *London and Westminster Improved*, 1.

19 John Wood's extemporised projections in Bath were also influential, and entailed linking Queen Square with the Circus (from 1754) by Gay Street (begun 1750) to form a sequence of planned open spaces.

20 Dance had more than six years' architectural training in Italy between 1758 and 1764. For nearly fifty years he 'exercised an enlightened supervision over the growth and redevelopment of the City'. Howard Colvin, *A Biographical Dictionary of British Architects 1600–1840* (London: J. Murray, 1978), 249.

21 John Trusler, *The London Adviser and Guide, Containing Every Instruction and Information Useful and Necessary to Persons Living in London and Coming to Reside There* (London: the author, 1790), 1.

22 John Britton, Edward Wedlake Brayley et al., *The Beauties of England and Wales, or, Delineations, Topographical, Historical, and Descriptive of Each County*, 18 vols (London: Vernon & Hood, and others, 1801–15), 3:657.

23 John Summerson established the pattern of estate development in London in *Georgian London* (London: Pleiades Books, 1945).

24 Donald Olsen, *Town Planning in London: The Eighteenth and Nineteenth Centuries* (New Haven and London: Yale University Press, 1964), 3–38.

25 Leases varied from thirty-one years in the 1630s on the Bedford Estate, to sixty-one years on the Bloomsbury Estate in the eighteenth century. From the latter part of the eighteenth century to the middle of the nineteenth century, the ninety-nine-year lease became standard.

26 Summerson, *Georgian London* (repr. Harmondsworth: Penguin, 1978), 163.

27 Olsen, *Town Planning in London*, 19–20.

28 Gwynn was doubtless referring to Portman Square when he recommended that new squares should be formed along the lines of Grosvenor Square. He projected such a new square adjacent to Portman Square, as a pendant to Grosvenor Square north of Oxford Street. See Gwynn's plan of Westminster 'shewing several improvements propos'd' in *London and Westminster Improved*. (Portman Square was still being formed at the time.)

29 Todd Longstaffe-Gowan, 'Portman Square Garden: "The Montpelier of England"', *London Gardener* 12 (2006–7): 78–93.

30 Sir John Soane's Royal Academy Lecture XI, presented in March 1815. See David Watkin, ed., *Sir John Soane: Enlightenment Thought and the Royal Academy Lectures* (Cambridge: Cambridge University Press, 1996), 649.

31 Journey to England by an Irish Clergyman in 1761 and 1772, 'Itinerarium Bristoliense', entry of 9 September 1773, British Library, Add. MS 27951.

32 The square was referred to as Bentink Square on 'A Plan of Part of an Estate in the Parish of St Marylebone . . . belonging to Henry William Portman Esqr, Surveyed by James Buck of Paddington Road Middlesex in the Year 1777', Portman Estate Archives.

33 Note by G. Scott-Thomson in Eliza Jeffries Davis, 'The University Site, Bloomsbury', *London Topographical Record* 17 (1936): 76.

34 Elain Harwood and Andrew Saint, *London* (London: HMSO, 1991), 96.

35 S. P. Cockerell, 'Report to the Governors of the Foundling Estate Hospital', 1790, London Metropolitan Archives, Foundling Hospital Records, A/FH. The squares were originally proposed to have 'basons of water in each'.

36 Hermione Hobhouse, *Thomas Cubitt, Master Builder* (London: Macmillan, 1971), 59; [William Weir], 'The Squares of London', in *London*, vol. 6, ed. Charles Knight, 2nd ed. (London: Henry G. Bohn, 1851), 199.

37 Bodleian Library, MS Douce, e.35, fol. 29.

38 Burton would later, from 1817, spearhead the development of Burton Crescent – now Cartwright Gardens – on the Skinner's Estate.

39 Olsen, *Town Planning in London*, 52 fn. For Russell Square, Burton's plan was estimated to cost £2,570 and that of Gubbins (Lord Bedford's surveyor) £3,000; the alternative prices for Tavistock Square were £1,650 and £1,850.

40 Charles Sloane (1728–1807) was Surveyor of the King's Gardens from 1764 to 1769.

41 Humphry Repton, *Observations on the Theory and Practice of Landscape Gardening* (London: J. Taylor, 1803), 205.

42 George Carter, Patrick Goode and Kedrun Laurie, *Humphry Repton, Landscape Gardener, 1752–1818* (Norwich: Sainsbury Centre for the Visual Arts, 1982), 156.

43 The 'walk & belt of shrubs' of Repton's plan were recommended by the trustees as features to be adopted. Letter dated 8 August 1807, Bedford Estate Archive, Woburn Abbey. For a detailed description of the development of Russell and Bloomsbury squares see Stephen Daniels, *Humphry Repton: Landscape Gardening and the Geography of Georgian England* (New Haven: Yale University Press, 1999), 181–2.

44 *Public Advertiser*, 14 July 1755.

45 *Gazette and New Daily Advertiser*, 14 March 1767.

46 J. M. Beattie, *Policing and Punishment in London, 1660–1750* (Oxford: Oxford University Press, 2001), 224–5.

47 *Gazette and New Daily Advertiser*, 14 March 1767.

48 For an excellent account of the social significance of keys and the control of them, see Amanda Vickery, *Behind*

Closed Doors: At Home in Georgian England (New Haven and London: Yale University Press, 2009), 25–48.

49 The keys and locks at Lincoln's Inn Fields were changed five times between 1736 and 1824 (Lincoln's Inn Fields, Minutes of the Trustees, 1735–1879, British Library, Add. MSS 35077–35081). See Vickery, *Behind Closed Doors*, which describes how the business of delineating space, marking boundaries and shutting one area off from another lay at the heart of the experience of eighteenth-century English domestic life.

50 Lincoln's Inn Fields, Minutes of the Trustees, 20 August 1821.

51 Lincoln's Inn Fields, Minutes of the Trustees, 14 December 1816.

52 Lincoln's Inn Fields, Minutes of the Trustees, 13 July 1822.

53 Minutes of the Trustees of Portman Square, Portman Estate Archives, 26 July 1797.

54 For an analysis of the behaviour and spatial distribution of crowds in England's four largest provincial towns for the period 1790–1835 – an analysis of direct relevance to the eighteenth-century understanding of the topography of the metropolis – see Mark Harrison, 'Symbolism, "Ritualism" and the Location of Crowds in Early Nineteenth-Century English Towns,' in *The Iconography of Landscape*, ed. Denis Cosgrove and Stephen Daniels (Cambridge: Cambridge University Press, 1988), 194–213.

55 *Daily Journal*, 4 May 1724.

56 Todd Longstaffe-Gowan, 'Portman Square Garden': 90.

57 Lincoln's Inn Fields, Minutes of the Trustees, 1 February 1808.

58 See Beattie, *Policing and Punishment*, 114–225.

59 *Morning Chronicle*, 8 March 1815.

60 See *The Old Bailey Online*, ref. nos t17800628–81, t17800628–69, and o17800628–1 (www.oldbaileyonline.org). Both men were indicted for 'breaking the peace': 'together with an hundred other persons and more, [they] did, unlawfully, riotously, and tumultuously assemble, on the 6th [and 7th] of June, to the disturbance of the publick peace, and did begin to demolish and pull down the dwelling-house of the Right Honourable William Earl of Mansfield, against the form of the statute, &c.'

61 *Notes and Queries*, 2nd ser., 9 (14 April 1860).

62 [John Stewart], *Critical Observations on the Buildings and Improvements of London* (London: J. Dodsley, 1771), 14.

63 Samuel Richardson, *The History of Sir Charles Grandison*, 1753, ed. Jocelyn Harris, vol. 1 (Oxford: Oxford University Press, 1972), 125.

64 [James Ralph], *A Critical Review of the Publick Buildings, Statues and Ornaments, in and about London and Westminster* (London: John Wallis, 1734), 108–9.

65 Whately's work was not published until five years after it was written: Thomas Whately, *Observations on Modern Gardening* (London: T. Payne, 1770), 3.

66 The attribution of *Critical Observations* to John Stewart was made by Eileen Harris and Nicholas Savage in *British Architectural Books and Writers, 1556–1785* (Cambridge: Cambridge University Press, 1990), 168–71.

67 [Stewart], *Critical Observations*, 2.

68 [Stewart], *Critical Observations*, 6–7.

69 [Stewart], *Critical Observations*, 7–8.

70 [Stewart], *Critical Observations*, 8.

71 [Stewart], *Critical Observations*, 8–9.

72 The gap on the north side of Cavendish Square was filled in 1771, thereby terminating the open 'visa' from Hanover Square. The last building carcases were erected in Grosvenor Square by 1731, and the open views to the north gained from Queen Square were obstructed by the erection of houses in Upper Guilford Street by c.1795. See Rudolf Ackermann's aquatint view of Queen Square, 1812, London, Guildhall, catalogue no. p5444500.

73 The sheep in Cavendish Square were evicted in 1771, soon after the erection of the statue. For more information, see John Archer, '*Rus in urbe*: Classical Ideals of Country and City in British Town Planning', *Eighteenth-Century Culture* 12 (1983): 162.

74 This was not, of course, unique to squares; other urban garden and landscape settings produced a similar sense of anomaly, and a distressing confusion of symbolic categories. For instance, one foreign observer was in 1710 surprised to find that St James's Park contained neither woodland nor birds, but 'merely avenues' of trees, and a considerable number of grazing cattle and deer. Zacharias Conrad von Uffenbach, *London in 1710, from the Travels of Zacharias Conrad von Uffenbach*, trans. and ed. W. H. Quarrell and Margaret Mare (London: Faber & Faber, 1934), 12.

75 [Stewart], *Critical Observations*, 9–10.

76 'Passimque armenta videbant / Romanoque foro et lautis mugire Carinis', Virgil, *Aeneid*, viii:359. From the early nineteenth century the Forum was sometimes referred to by English travellers as the 'Papal Smithfield'.

77 [Stewart], *Critical Observations*, 10–11.

78 [Stewart], *Critical Observations*, 10–11.

79 [Stewart], *Critical Observations*, 11–12.

80 [Stewart], *Critical Observations*, 12–13.

81 [Stewart], *Critical Observations*, 13–14. Stewart is, however, 'almost disposed to excuse' the iron-railed enclosure of Lincoln's Inn: 'the vast extent of field, still further extended by the proximity of the gardens, the lofty trees in prospect, the noble piece of water in the middle, conspire to create an illusion, and we feel ourselves as it were fairly beguiled into the country, in the very centre of business and care'.

82 Stewart compares the squares of London to those of Bath, praising the latter for their 'uniformity, beauty and convenience'. [Stewart], *Critical Observations*, 20.

83 [Stewart], *Critical Observations*, 2.

84 [Stewart], *Critical Observations*, 21.

85 [Stewart], *Critical Observations*, 14.

86 [Stewart], *Critical Observations*, 14–15

87 Charles Jenner, *Town Eclogues* (London: T. Cadell, 1772), Eclogue iv, 'The Poet', p. 26.

88 William Mason, *An Heroic Epistle to Sir William Chambers* (London: J. Almon, 1773), p. 4. The poem is a satire on Chambers's *A Dissertation on Oriental Gardening* (London: W. Griffin, 1772).

89 Rarely, until the late eighteenth century, was it felt that

these elements were balanced, and that there prevailed a 'regularity' throughout in the structures and 'neatness' of the gardens. St James's Square was among the first garden squares to be praised for its handsome regularity.

90 A letter from Paris reported that 'all the People at the solemnity of erecting the King's Statue were bareheaded when they came into the Square of Lewis le Grand, and . . . Soldiers uncovered themselves before his Statue with as much Devotion as they do before their consecrated Host'. *Flying Post, or, Post Master*, 10 August 1699.

91 This pamphlet was a compendium of Ralph's articles, which appeared in the journal *Critical Review* from April 1733.

92 [Ralph], *Critical Review*, 101; Harris and Savage, *British Architectural Books and Writers*, 382.

93 [Ralph], *Critical Review*, 101.

94 The equestrian statue of George I by C. Buchard (fl. 1716) was the first to be raised in a London square after the defacement of the effigy of the same monarch in Grosvenor Square in 1727.

95 By 1539–40 Michelangelo had made the statue the focal point of the new piazza.

96 *Survey of London*, vol. 34: *The Parish of St Anne Soho*, ed. F. H. W. Sheppard (London: Athlone Press, 1966), 433; *Gentleman's Magazine* 18 (1748): 521; *General Evening Post*, 2 August 1748.

97 *Old England's Journal*, 17 March 1753.

98 The French sculptor Beaupré (fl. 1764–83) is credited with the statue; Ingrid Roscoe, ed., *Biographical Dictionary of British Sculptors, 1660–1851* (New Haven and London: Yale University Press, 2009), 88.

99 *Gazette and New Daily Advertiser*, 17 July 1766.

100 David Hughson, *London: Being an Accurate History and Description of the British Metropolis and its Neighbourhood, to 30 Miles Extent, from an Actual Perambulation*, vol. 4 (s.l.: n.p., 1807), 395.

101 James Peller Malcolm, *Londinium Redivivum*, 4 vols (London: J. Nichols, 1802–7), 4:131–2; [Stewart], *Critical Observations*, 90–1.

102 [Grosley], *Londres*, 1:71–2; La Combe, *Tableau de Londres*, p. 14.

103 Timothy Clayton, *The English Print, 1688–1802* (New Haven and London: Yale University Press, 1997), 75.

104 Anna Maude, '"Pleasurable Mementoes": Sutton Nicholls's Views of the London Square in the First Half of the Eighteenth Century', *London Gardener* 16 (2010–11).

105 John Wood the elder, *An Essay towards a Description of the City of Bath*, 2 vols (s.l. [Bath]: W. Frederick, 1742), 2:14.

106 Simon Varey, *Space and the Eighteenth-Century English Novel* (Cambridge: Cambridge University Press, 1990), 27.

107 14 Geo. III, c. 52, extract.

108 The plan would appear to have been commissioned by Assheton Curzon, later first Baron and first Viscount Curzon. Curzon lived at No. 66 Brook Street – just off Grosvenor Square – between 1759 and 1820, and was presumably a trustee of the square. Richardson was working for Curzon at Kedleston Hall, Derbyshire, in the early 1770s.

109 The cartographer Richard Horwood's representation of the garden on his *Plan of the Cities of London and Westminster the Borough of Southwark, and Parts Adjoining Shewing Every House* (London: R. Horwood, 1792–9) corroborates the layout of the garden to the Kedleston plan.

110 Richard Alan Ryerson, ed., *Adams Family Correspondence*, vol. 6: *December 1784–December 1785* (Cambridge: Belknap Press of Harvard University Press, 1993), 242. The Adams family took up residence in Grosvenor Square in June 1785.

111 C. P. Moritz, *Travels, Chiefly on Foot, through Several Parts of England, in 1782 . . . Translated from the German, by a Lady* (London: G. G. and J. Robinson, 1795), letter of 17 June 1782.

112 The central garden of Leicester Square as it is portrayed in Hodges' painting of *c.*1790 suggests that the new planting scheme approximated that of the Elysian Garden (begun in the early 1780s) at Audley End. William Tompkins depicted the latter in a minutely detailed painting of 1788. See Mark Laird, *The Flowering of the English Landscape Garden: English Pleasure Grounds, 1720–1800* (Philadelphia: University of Pennsylvania Press, 1999), 341–50.

113 Samuel Rawle's engraved view was published in 1801. See also an aquatint view of Leicester Square published by Rudolph Ackermann in *c.*1815 (London, Guildhall, catalogue no. p5404647).

114 *Survey of London*, vol. 33: *The Parish of St. Anne Soho*, ed. F. H. W. Sheppard (London: Athlone Press, 1966): 52. See also 'A List of Trees & Plants Planted in Soho Sq.', British Library, Add. MS 39167 g(2), fol. 144. Garden maintenance was in 1796 carried out by 'James Alexander, of No. 35 Wardour Street, Gardener', Add. MS 39167 g(2), fol. 146.

115 *The Letters of Sir Charles Bell* (London: John Murray, 1870), 101; see also 187–8 n., 227, 232, 327; Britton, Brayley et al., *The Beauties of England and Wales*, 3:657.

116 Lincoln's Inn Fields, Minutes of the Trustees, 4 January 1827.

117 Lincoln's Inn Fields, Minutes of the Trustees, 12 December 1795

118 Malcolm, *Londinium Redivivum*, 4:331.

119 Hughson, *London*, 4:384. Euston Square was the 'Bedford Nursery'. For a detailed history of Russell Square see Land Use Consultants, 'The Historical Development of Russell Square', unpublished report for London Borough of Camden, May 1997.

120 B. Lambert, *The History and Survey of London and its Environs from the Earliest Period to the Present Time*, 4 vols (London: T. Hughes and M. Jones, 1806), 3:532.

121 J. A. Andersen [A. A. Feldborg], *A Dane's Excursions in Britain*, 2 vols (London: Mathews & Leigh, 1809), 1:11. 'Sundry portions' of brick walls were substituted by 'open Iron Railings' around the edges of Hyde Park and Green Park in 1826. *Fifth Report of the Commissioners of His Majesty's Woods, Forests and Land Revenues* (London: n.p., 1826), 14.

122 [Weir], 'Squares of London,' 193.

123 Hughson, *London*, 4:384.

124 H. L. H. von Pückler-Muskau, *Letters from Albion to a Friend on the Continent* (London: Gale, Curtis & Fenner, 1814), 132–3.

125 Philippar remarks: 'En Angleterre toutes les places publiques sont ornées, au centre, d'un jardin entouré de grilles', and described the placing of gardens in squares as 'Cette méthode, qui offre l'advantage d'attenuer la sévérité qu'offre cette regularité de construction'. François Philippar, *Voyage agronomique en Angleterre, fait en 1829* (Paris: Rousselon, 1830), pl. iii.

126 J. P. Malcolm, *Anecdotes of the Manners and Customs of London during the Eighteenth Century* (London: Longman, Hurst, Rees and Orme, 1808), 472.

127 Sarah Lloyd, 'Amour in the Shrubbery: Reading the Detail of English Adultery Trial Publications of the 1780s,' *Eighteenth-Century Studies* 39 (2006): 421.

128 See Samuel Fullmer, *The Young Gardener's Best Companion, for the Thorough Practical Management of the Pleasure Ground and Flower Garden; Shrubbery, Nursery, Tree Plantation and Hedge* (London: n.p., 1781), 78.

129 Lincoln's Inn Fields, Minutes of the Trustees, 21 November 1803, 8 July 1828, 29 May 1845.

130 John B. Papworth, *Select Views of London* (London: R. Ackermann, 1816), 36. Papworth may be referring to Martial's epigram 9:68, where he inveighs against a schoolmaster, whose noisy school on the Quirinal Hill disturbs his sleep in the early morning hours.

131 John Claudius Loudon, *An Encyclopaedia of Gardening* (London: Longman, Hurst, Rees, Orme, and Brown, 1822), item 2041, p. 1188.

132 Hobhouse, *Thomas Cubitt*, 71.

133 John Claudius Loudon, Letter to the editor, 22 December 1803, *Literary Journal* 2 (1803): cols 739–42.

134 Loudon, *Encyclopaedia of Gardening*, item 2041.

135 Humphry Repton, 'Mr Repton, Letter to the Trustees of Bloomsbury Square, March 3rd 1807', Bedford Estate Archive, Woburn Abbey.

136 Humphry Repton, *An Enquiry into the Changes of Taste in Landscape Gardening* (London: n.p., 1806), 33. This essay was republished by John Claudius Loudon in *The Landscape Gardening and Landscape Architecture of the Late Humphrey [sic] Repton* (London: Longman & Co.and A. & C. Black, Edinburgh, 1840).

137 Repton, *Enquiry*, 63.

138 Repton, *Enquiry*, 60, 63.

139 Repton, *Enquiry*, 63.

140 Loudon, *Encyclopaedia of Gardening*, item 2041.

141 'Mr Repton, Letter to the Trustees of Bloomsbury Square, March 3rd 1807'.

142 Neil Bingham, 'Humphry and John Adey Repton's Unexecuted Design for Burlington Place, Piccadilly', *London Gardener* 12 (2006–7): 11–19.

143 Repton coined the term 'landscape gardening' in 1803. John Loudon, *The Landscape Gardening and Landscape Architecture of the late Humphry Repton, Esq.* (London: Longman & Co.and A. & C. Black, Edinburgh, 1840) 30.

144 A criticism repeated in Loudon, *Encyclopaedia of Gardening*, item 1189.

145 Repton, *Enquiry*, 64.

4 'Genuine Squares', 'New Squares' and 'Places'

1 The West End was, as we have seen, a cluster of suburban estates.

2 Alexander Cavalié Mercer, *Journal of the Waterloo Campaign, Kept throughout the Campaign of 1815* (s.l. [London]: Peter Davies, 1927), 331. I am grateful to Roger Bowdler for bringing this quotation to my attention.

3 The author of 'On the Ridiculous Consequence Assumed from Superiority of Places of Residence', *Monthly Mirror* 15 (1803): 239, refers to London's new West End estates as 'the new colonies'.

4 [John Stewart], *Critical Observations on the Buildings and Improvements of London* (London: J. Dodsley, 1771), 21.

5 Letter from James Peller Malcolm, published in the *Gentleman's Magazine* 83 (November 1813): 427–9; 'A Plan of Ground to be Lett on Building Leases for 95 Years at Sommers Place', fly-sheet advertising the new properties for sale (c.1790–1800), author's collection.

6 'John Newton to William Cowper, Letter iv, 29 April 1780', in *The Works of John Newton*, 3rd ed. (London: n.p., 1824), 330.

7 'Walpole to Horace Mann, 17 July 1776', in *Letters of Horace Walpole, Earl of Orford, to Sir Horace Mann*, 4 vols (London: Richard Bentley, 1843–4), 2:384.

8 Robert Fishman, *Bourgeois Utopias: The Rise and Fall of Suburbia* (New York: Basic Books, 1987); W. G. Hoskins, 'Suburban Growth and Infilling', in *Local History in England*, 2nd ed. (London: Longman, 1972).

9 John Summerson, *Georgian London* (London: Pleiades Books, 1945; repr. Harmondsworth: Penguin, 1978), 280. Other patterns of suburban growth included village development, country villa building and roadside development.

10 Summerson, *Georgian London*, 280–1.

11 Henry Holland senior, the builder, was the father of the architect Henry Holland (1745–1806).

12 Jacob Leroux's first polygon was devised in 1768 as a speculation in Southampton. This scheme was abandoned by 1776. S. Robertson, 'The Polygon, Southampton: Recent Fieldwork', *Hampshire Studies* 56 (2001).

13 Neither the square nor the circus was realised.

14 Henry Leroux, the son of Jacob Leroux, was a speculating surveyor working on the Northampton Estate in Canonbury.

15 In the event, only one of the four proposed squares was built. *Victoria History of the Counties of England*, vol. 10: *A History of the County of Middlesex: Hackney Parish*, ed. T. F. T. Baker (Oxford: Oxford University Press for the Institute of Historical Research, 1995), 33–5.

16 *Survey of London*, vol. 47: *Northern Clerkenwell and Pentonville* [*SOL*, 47], ed. Andrew Saint and Philip Temple (New Haven and London: Yale University Press, 2008), 268–95.

17 *SOL*, 47:269.

18 For instance, St Mark's Myddelton Square; St Mary's The Boltons; St Luke's Redcliffe Square. The churches of St Michael Chester Square and St George Warwick Square were built on the edges of the enclosures.

19 *Survey of London*, vol. 45: *Knightsbridge*, ed. John Greena-combe (London: Athlone Press, 2000), 97–8.

20 Addington Square was finished only in the 1840s. Bridget Cherry and Nikolaus Pevsner, *London*, vol. 2: *South*, The Buildings of England (Harmondsworth: Penguin, 1983), 55.

21 *Survey of London*, vol. 22: *Bankside*, ed. Howard Roberts and Walter H. Godfrey (London: London County Council, 1950), 129.

22 *Survey of London*, vol. 46: *South and East Clerkenwell*, ed. Andrew Saint and Philip Temple (New Haven and London: Yale University Press, 2008), 10, 298–300.

23 Frank A. J. L. James and Anthony C. Peers. 'Conservation Plan for the Royal Institution of Great Britain', unpublished proposal, submitted by Rodney Melville and Partners to the Royal Institution, June 2003, 22–3.

24 John Noorthouck, *A New History of London, Including Westminster and Southwark* (London: R. Baldwin, 1773), 732; Thomas Hosmer Shepherd and James Elmes, *Metropolitan Improvements, or, London in the Nineteenth Century* (London: Jones & Co., 1827), 16.

25 Grosvenor Estate Minute Books, Westminster City Archives, Acc. 1049/5/1, entries of 13 March 1789 and 18 May 1792.

26 Jill Lever, *Catalogue of the Drawings of George Dance the Younger (1741–1825) and of George Dance the Elder (1695–1768), from the Collection of Sir John Soane's Museum* (Oxford: Azimuth Editions, 2003), 132–3, 374–5.

27 Mireille Galinou suggests that the original plan of 1794 for a circus 'upwards of 57 Acres' and its successor, exhibited in 1803, are probably the work of John Shaw, who became the official architect and surveyor to the Eyre Estate in 1805; see her *Cottages and Villas: The Birth of the Garden Suburb* (New Haven and London: Yale University Press, 2010), 71–7.

28 Galinou also discusses other contemporary developments based on 'circular geometries', including Michael Novosielski's crescent in Brompton of 1786 (originally Novosielski Street; demolished in 1843). Galinou, *Cottages and Villas*, 77.

29 Fishman, *Bourgeois Utopias*, 64.

30 J. Mordaunt Crook, 'Metropolitan Improvements: John Nash and the Picturesque', *London: World City, 1800–1840*, ed. Celina Fox (New Haven and London: Yale University Press, 1992), 77–96.

31 Geoffrey Tyack, 'Nash, John', *ODNB*.

32 Crook, 'Metropolitan Improvements', 77, paraphrasing R. B. Pugh, *The Crown Estate: An Historical Essay* (London: HMSO, 1960).

33 Crook, 'Metropolitan Improvements', 77–96.

34 John White senior was Surveyor of the Portland Estate.

35 Commissions of Woods, Forests, and Land Revenues, Report no.1, 1812, TNA, CRES (Records of the Crown Estate and its predecessors) 60/2.

36 Mordaunt Crook, 'Metropolitan Improvements', 80.

37 Lord Brougham's comments on the Regent's Canal Bill, 7 May 1812, *The Parliamentary Debates from the Year 1803 to the Present Time* (London: T. C. Hansard, 1812), 23:72.

38 'Report of Mr John Nash, Architect in the Department of Woods: With Plans for the Improvement of Mary-le-bone Park', in *Some Account of the Proposed Improvements of the Western Part of London, by the Formation of the Regent's Park, the New Street, the New Sewer, &c.* (London: W. & P. Reynolds, 1814), appendix 3, pp. xxii–xxiii.

39 Shepherd and Elmes, *Metropolitan Improvements*, 11.

40 House of Lords, *Report of Mr John Nash, Architect in the Department of Woods: With Plans for the Improvement of Mary-le-Bone Park*, appendix 12(B) (1812), 98; and 'Approved Report of Mr John Nash Relative to improvements in Mary-le-bone Park, and to the Grand New Street from thence to Charing Cross', *Monthly Magazine* no. 44 (1813): 26.

41 House of Lords, *Report of Mr John Nash*, appendix 12(G), 132.

42 House of Lords, *Report of Mr John Nash*, appendix 12(B), 98.

43 House of Lords, *Report of Mr John Nash*, 99. Nash's initial design and the principles behind it, were to earn him the reputation as a 'master pragmatist and virtuoso of scenographic art'.

44 *Survey of London*, vol. 21: *Tottenham Court Road and Neighbourhood*, ed. J. R. Howard Roberts and Walter H. Godfrey (London: London County Council, 1949), 142–3.

45 James Anderson, 'Marylebone Park and the New Street: A Study of the Development of Regent's Park and the Building of Regent Street, London, in the First Quarter of the Nineteenth Century' (PhD diss., Courtauld Institute of Art, University of London, 1998), 239–47.

46 Shepherd and Elmes, *Metropolitan Improvements*, 88.

47 Shepherd and Elmes, *Metropolitan Improvements*, 88–9.

48 Shepherd and Elmes, *Metropolitan Improvements*, 89.

49 John Claudius Loudon, *An Encyclopaedia of Gardening* (London: Longman, Rees, Orme, Brown, Green, and Longman, 1835), 1213. In the 1822 edition of the same work, Loudon remarked that 'This mode he would adopt on account of its originality.'

50 Like his contemporaries, Soane appropriated and applied the principles of the picturesque, as they offered a means of incorporating within the same landscape contrasting categories, such as the sublime and the beautiful, the wild and the cultivated, and the general and the particular. John Soane, Lecture X: 'Gardens and City Plans', 1815, in *Lectures on Architecture, as Delivered to the Students of the Royal Academy from 1809 to 1836*, ed. Arthur T. Bolton (London: Soane Museum, 1929), 152. Soane argued in this Royal Academy lecture that the new generation of planners and architects had much to learn from ornamental gardening: what was needed to inject life into London's streets were such garden attributes as irregularity, contrast and surprise.

51 The term 'Metropolitan Picturesque' is attributed to Malcolm Andrews, who employed the term in his essay 'The Metropolitan Picturesque', in *The Politics of the Picturesque: Literature, Landscape and Aesthetics since 1770*, ed. Stephen Copley and Peter Garside (Cambridge: Cambridge University Press, 1994). See also Andrea Fredericksen, 'The Metropolitan Picturesque' (PhD diss., University of California at Los Angeles, 1997), who argues that the

'Picturesque City' was a 'distinct urban model that, while not traditionally avant-garde, represents an important configuration of landscape theory and city construction which profoundly shaped modern architecture and planning'.

52 John Nash, letter to Alexander Milne, 2 January 1823, TNA, CRES uncatalogued.

53 Uvedale Price, *An Essay on the Picturesque as Compared with the Sublime and the Beautiful*, 2nd ed., 2 vols (London: n.p., 1796–8), 2:207.

54 John Nash, letter to Alexander Milne, 17 April 1822, TNA, CRES 2/771.

55 John Nash, letter to Alexander Milne, 18 January 1822, TNA, CRES 2/771.

56 John Nash, letter to Alexander Milne, 24 January 1822, TNA, CRES 2/771.

57 St James's Square Trust, Minutes of the Trustees, 1726–1835, Westminster City Archives, 395, 4 May 1759, 14 May 1799, 28 June 1816, 7 June 1817.

58 St James's Square Trust, Minutes of the Trustees, 2 and 4 September 1817.

59 The Duchess of St Albans, the Countess of Surrey, Viscountess Falmouth, Lady Grantham, Mrs Byng and Mrs Boehm. St James's Square Trust, Minutes of the Trustees, 8 June 1818.

60 Gamma, 'London Changes', *Once a Week*, 28 July 1860: 128.

61 [Washington Irving], 'Rural Life in England', *Edinburgh Magazine and Literary Miscellany* 84 (July 1819): 211.

62 John Britton and Augustus Pugin, *Illustrations of the Public Buildings of London*, 2 vols (London: J. Taylor, 1828), vol. 2.

63 Summerson, *Georgian London*, 196.

64 Hermione Hobhouse, *Thomas Cubitt, Master Builder* (London: Macmillan, 1971), 71. The duke experimented at Woburn with grasses, heaths, willows, pines and other ornamental plants and shrubs, of which he caused several catalogues to be published. E. A. Smith, 'Francis Russell, fifth Duke of Bedford', *Oxford Dictionary of National Biography*; F.M.L. Thompson, 'John Russell, sixth Duke of Bedford', *Oxford Dictionary of National Biography*.

65 Hobhouse, *Thomas Cubitt*, 71. In 1850 George Scharf, who lived at No. 1 Torrington Square, recorded on a sketch that the square was planted with 'Plain Liburnum Lillac and Elm Plane Lilac [and] Sycamore'.

66 'The Species of Plants which Thrive in the Smoky Atmosphere of London and its Immediate Neighbourhood', *Gardener's Magazine* 8 (1832): 243–4; G. Berry in *Garden* 20 (1881): 372.

67 Annual Report, 1851, fol. 11, Bedford Estate Archive, Woburn Abbey.

68 Gamma, 'London Changes': 128; T. Cubitt, letter to Christopher Heady, 26 December 1823, Bedford Estate Archive, Woburn Abbey.

69 T. Cubitt, letter to Messrs Lawson, 7 November 1851, Bedford Estate Archive, Woburn Abbey.

70 John Timbs, 'Belgravia', *Curiosities of London*, new ed. (s.l. [London]: Longmans, 1868), 43; Hobhouse, *Thomas Cubitt*, 88–9.

71 Walter Thornbury and Edward Walford, *Old and New London: A Narrative of its History, its People, and its Places*, 6 vols (London: Cassell, Petter and Galpin, 1897), 5:2.

72 Britton and Pugin, *Illustrations*, 2:292–3.

73 The square was raised upon the site of a 10-acre nursery. Timbs, 'Belgravia', 43.

74 Britton and Pugin, *Illustrations*, 2:vi.

75 Britton and Pugin, *Illustrations*, 2:294.

76 [William Weir], 'The Squares of London', in *London*, vol. 6, ed. Charles Knight (London: Charles Knight & Co., 1844; 2nd ed., London: Henry G. Bohn, 1851), 205.

77 Either William Porden or Thomas Cundy I was responsible for the revision of Wyatt's and the Robertsons' schemes. See Hobhouse, *Thomas Cubitt*, 89.

78 [Weir], 'Squares', 205.

79 Hobhouse, *Thomas Cubitt*, 90. The nurseryman John Allen planted the southern gardens of the square; Cubitt planted out the northern gardens after 1842. Hobhouse, *Thomas Cubitt*, 132, 144.

80 [Weir], 'Squares', 205.

81 Victoria Square was developed on the plan of the architect Matthew Cotes Wyatt.

82 'On the Ridiculous Consequence': 240; Hobhouse, *Thomas Cubitt*, 105.

83 'On the Ridiculous Consequence': 240.

84 Hobhouse, *Thomas Cubitt*, 148.

85 Britton and Pugin, *Illustrations*, 2:292–3.

86 Hobhouse, *Thomas Cubitt*, 218–19; *Builder*, 27 January 1844: 48.

87 Gordon Toplis, 'Urban Classicism in Decline: The History of Tyburnia', *Country Life*, 15 November 1973: 1526–8; G. Toplis, 'Back-to-Front Splendour in Bayswater: The History of Tyburnia, II', *Country Life*, 22 November 1973: 1708–10

88 Toplis argues that the Cockerell plan probably evolved as early as *c*.1804. See 'Urban Classicism in Decline': 1526.

89 This scheme predates Nash's proposals for Regent Street. Cockerell's plan, moreover, proposed to link his new development to an existing landscape garden, whereas Nash proposed to create a new park at the end of his processional route.

90 This was the first building boom after the Napoleonic Wars.

91 J. C. Loudon, 'Improvements in the North-Western Part of London', *Architectural Magazine* 5 (1838): 330.

92 [Weir], 'Squares', 206

93 Peter Cunningham, *Modern London, or, London as It Is* (s.l.: n.p., 1851), p. x. The monotony of the new district was criticised by Louis Énault in *Angleterre, Écosse, Irlande: voyage pittoresque* (Paris: n.p., 1859), 7.

94 John Weale, 'Squares', in *London Exhibited in 1851, Elucidating its Natural and Physical Characteristics, its Antiquity and Architecture* (London: J. Weale, 1851), 770.

95 The term 'mushroom aristocrats' was used by George Augustus Sala to describe 'your yesterday nobility . . . millionaires, ex-Lord Mayors, and low people of that sort' who inhabited Tyburnia and Belgravia. See G. A. Sala, *Gaslight and Daylight*, 2nd ed. (s.l.: n.p., 1861), 101.

96 Gamma, 'London Changes': 125–6. The first inhabitant of

a new square was commonly referred to as 'bait', a 'call bird' or a 'decoy'.

97 Wilkie Collins, *Basil: A Story of Modern Life* (London: Sampson Low, Son & Co., 1862 (another ed.)), 1–2. Collins lived all his adult life in neighbouring Marylebone.

98 [Weir], 'Squares', 204.

99 The site of Thomas Lord's original cricket ground: the first great match was played here on 31 May and 1 June 1787, and the Marylebone Cricket Club was founded here.

100 Thomas Whipham, *Montagu Square: An Account of its History and Development* (Olympic Press: n.p., 1990), unpaginated. Messrs Jonathan Harrison and Thomas Butler played a part in the building of Montagu Square. Harrison was the principal builder of Bryanston Square. Designs for Blandford Square – a companion for Dorset Square – were drawn up but were abandoned.

101 *Gardener's Magazine* 2 (1827): 97.

102 Loudon, *Encyclopaedia of Gardening*, 1213.

103 [Weir], 'Squares', 207.

104 [Weir], 'Squares', 206.

105 *Survey of London*, vol. 37: *Northern Kensington* [*SOL*, 37], ed. F. H. W. Sheppard (London: Athlone Press, 1973), 89–90, 260.

106 *SOL*, 47:275–97.

107 Elain Harwood and Andrew Saint, *London* (London: HMSO, 1991), 102.

108 *SOL*, 47:245.

109 *SOL*, 47:193–9.

110 *SOL*, 47:227.

111 *SOL*, 37:212, quoted from *Builder*, 29 January 1845.

112 Allason worked for the Earl of Shrewsbury at Alton Towers, where 'He was engaged in laying out the gardens and for this period he was much employed as a landscape gardener.' *Gentleman's Magazine* 221 (May 1852): 526.

113 Michael Girouard, *The English Town* (New Haven and London: Yale University Press, 1990), 170.

114 The successive stages in the complex evolution of the district are documented by a series of plans dating from 1842 to 1849. That these large gardens survived the vicissitudes of taste and the tumultuous financial events that plagued and protracted the development of north Kensington to become a basic element in the executed plan of the district is a credit to Allason's sustained involvement and the inherent attractiveness of his original concept.

115 Annie Thomas, *False Colours*, 3 vols (London: n.p., 1869), 1:7.

116 *SOL*, 37:229.

117 *Westminster Review* 43 (June 1845): 132.

118 *SOL*, 37:211. Royal Borough of Kensington and Chelsea, Kensington Central Library, 1844/6/87.

119 *SOL*, 37:212.

120 James Pennethorne, 'Plan no. 1 to Accompany Report of Octr. 3d 1846', London Metropolitan Archives, NBW/OW/VP/8.

121 *Survey of London*, vol. 42: *Southern Kensington: Kensington Square to Earl's Court*, ed. Hermione Hobhouse (London: Athlone Press, 1986), 184–95; Harwood and Saint, *London*, 14–15.

122 Henry Worsley, 'Juvenile Depravity', *Eclectic Review* (1850): 200–21; Mrs S. C. Hall [Anna Maria Hall], 'The Daily Governess', *Tales of Woman's Trials* (London: Chapman & Hall, 1847), 373.

123 'The Pioneers of London', *Tait's Edinburgh Magazine*, new ser., 20 (1853): 403. The plight of the urban poor, and the lack of accessible green space in town had earlier been the subject of Sir Edwin Chadwick's *Report on the Sanitary Condition of the Labouring Population of Great Britain*, House of Lords Paper (1842), part of which was commonly referred to in the nineteenth century as the 'Effect of Public Walks and Gardens on the Health and Morals of the Lower Classes of the Population'. The social reformer – then a resident of Tyburnia – advocated the preservation of disused burial-grounds as public open spaces, and their subsequent conversion into public gardens.

124 'Pioneers of London': 402.

125 'Pioneers of London': 403.

126 *Morning Chronicle*, 7 September 1837.

127 Bedford, Belgrave, Berkeley, Bloomsbury and Cavendish squares, Covent Garden, Eaton, Euston, Finsbury, Fitzroy, Golden, Grosvenor, Hanover, St James's and Leicester squares, Lincoln's Inn Fields, and Manchester, Portman, Princes, Queen, Russell, Soho, Tavistock, Trinity and Wellclose squares. Samuel Leigh, *Leigh's New Picture of London*, rev. ed. (London: n.p., 1834), 210.

128 Leigh, *Leigh's New Picture of London*, 216.

129 W. S. [Turner], 'Suggestions for a Society for Promoting the Improvement of the Public Taste in Architectural and Rural Scenery', letter to the editor, 6 April 1835, *Gardener's Magazine* 11 (1835): 280.

130 Jonas Dennis, *The Landscape Gardener: Comprising the History and Principles of Tasteful Horticulture* (London: J. Ridgway and Sons, 1835), 74–5.

131 Dennis, *Landscape Gardener*, 40.

132 J. C. Loudon, *Gardener's Magazine* 11 (1835): 282.

133 Loudon, *Encyclopaedia of Gardening*, 336–7.

134 J. C. Loudon, *The Suburban Gardener, and Villa Companion* (s.l. [London]: privately printed, 1838), 30.

135 In 1839 Alexis de Chateauneuf proposed to transform the space into a commemorative grove. Stephan Tschudi-Madsen, *The Works of Alexis de Chateauneuf in London and Oslo* (Oslo: Foreningen til Norske Fortidsminnesmerkers Bevaring, 1965), 28–37; Reuben Percy, 'Amusements of the People', *Mirror of Literature, Amusement and Instruction* 21 (1833): 341.

136 Robert B. Shoemaker, *The London Mob: Violence and Disorder in Eighteenth-Century England* (London: Hambledon and London, 2004).

137 John Gywnn had realised the important pivotal function of such a new square in 1766. John Gwynn, *London and Westminster Improved, Illustrated by Plans* (London: Dodsley, 1766), 85.

138 The square was originally to be called King's Square.

139 *Morning Chronicle*, 18 August 1837.

140 *Morning Chronicle*, 18 August 1837.

141 *Morning Chronicle*, 7 September 1837, 6 September 1837, 20 September 1837.

142 *Morning Chronicle*, 20 September 1837.

143 'Trafalgar Square', *The Times*, 8 May 1844. See also 'The Opening of Trafalgar Square', *Punch* 6 (1844): 200.

144 *The Times*, 8 May 1844.

145 See Rodney Mace, *Trafalgar Square: Emblem of Empire* (London: Lawrence and Wishart, 1976).

146 Brougham, *Parliamentary Debates*, 23:72.

147 James Malton, *Letters Addressed to Parliament and to the Public in General* (Dublin: the author, 1787), 253; *Morning Chronicle*, 7 September 1837. Leicester Square had been described as a 'dirty place' from the late eighteenth century.

148 'Metropolitan Improvements', *Punch* 5 (1843): 18.

149 *Punch* 16 (1849): 257.

150 Charles Dickens, 'Leicester Square', *Household Words* 7 (1858): 67.

151 Charles Dickens, *The Life and Adventures of Nicholas Nickleby* (London: Chapman and Hall, 1839), 16.

152 'This Key can be obtained: price Sixpence at *Lady's Newspaper*. Our Square will be published every week till the entire map is completed.' *Morning Chronicle*, 29 July 1842.

153 Horace Mayhew, 'Our Square', *Lady's Newspaper*, 31 July 1847

154 Mayhew, 'Our Square', *Lady's Newspaper*, 7 August 1847.

155 In 1823 the estate of Prince Heinrich Reuss-Lobenstein-Ebersdorff was reported by his countrymen to be 'as large as St James's-square, or Moorfields'. *Bell's Life in London and Sporting Chronicle*, 8 June 1823.

156 Mayhew's essays doubtless subsequently inspired Edward Rose's farcical comedy called *Our Square* ('Our Square', *Era*, 16 February 1884), performed at the Winter Gardens, Southport. Rose's play in turn galvanised J. Pen to produce a series of sketches entitled 'Stories of Our Square' (1894), published in the *Newcastle Courant*, which documented the day-to-day life in a dingy but 'picturesque and cheery' old square.

157 *Punch* was co-founded by Mayhew with Douglas William Jerrold and William Makepeace Thackeray.

158 *Punch* 5 (1843): 104.

159 'London Out of Town', *Punch* 11 (1846), 62.

160 Theodore Edward Hook, *Peregrine Bunce, or, Settled at Last* (London: n.p., 1857), 332–3.

161 *Punch* 6 (1844): 243.

162 'Savage Assault on a Square-Keeper', *Punch* 5 (1843): 154; 'The Historian in Leicester Square', *Punch* 17 (1849): 165; *Lloyd's Weekly Newspaper*, 22 July 1855.

163 'A Month's Residence in Middleton Square', *Punch* 13 (1847): 168–9; Charles Dickens, 'A City Square', *Penny Satirist*, 2 March 1839 (later repr. in *Nicholas Nickleby*).

164 Rev. Derwent Coleridge, 'Love at a Rout', *Poems of Withrop Mackworth Praed*, rev. and enlarged ed., 2 vols (New York: W. J. Widdleton, 1865), 1:338–43; Thomas Hughes, 'Tom Brown at Oxford', *Macmillan's Magazine* 2 (May–October 1860): 138.

165 'Old Humphrey on Autumnal Scenes', *Visitor, or, Monthly Instructor* (1847): 461.

166 Henry J. Slack, 'Spring-Time in Bloomsbury Square', *Ainsworth's Magazine: A Monthly Miscellany of Romance, General Literature and Art* 16 (1849): 123–4.

167 John Fisher Murray, *The World of London*, 2 vols (Edinburgh: Blackwood, 1843), 2:61.

168 'The Historian in Leicester Square': 165.

169 T. B. Macaulay, *The History of England from the Accession of James II*, vol. 1 (London: Longman, Brown, Green, and Longmans, 1849), 355–8.

170 Dickens, *Nicholas Nickleby*, 353.

171 [Weir], 'Squares', 193–208. The bookseller and social reformer Charles Knight (1791–1873) remarks in the *Penny Magazine* (1835) that 'the tendency of the improvements which have since [1765] taken place has been to extend an air of comfort and luxury through our streets and squares rather than to erect structures individually great' (26 September 1835, 375–6).

172 [Weir], 'Squares', 193.

173 [Weir], 'Squares', 194–5.

174 [Weir], 'Squares', 199.

175 [Weir], 'Squares', 201.

176 [Weir], 'Squares', 196.

177 Edmund Hodgson Yates, 'Broken to Harness: A Story of English Domestic Life', *Temple Bar* 11 (1864): 372.

178 *Building News* 3 (1857): 1, quoted in Arthur M. Edwards, *The Design of Suburbia* (London: Pembridge Press, 1981), 26.

179 Hieronymo Wyrardisbury, 'Squares and Villas', *Building News* 4 (1859): 606, quoted in Donald Olsen, *The Growth of Victorian London* (London: Batsford, 1976), 217.

180 Twenty squares were formed between 1855 and 1900 in the boroughs of Chelsea, Fulham, Islington, Kensington, Paddington, St Pancras and Wandsworth.

181 Girouard, *English Town*, 71; Harwood and Saint, *London*, 95, 144.

182 Helen C. Black, *Notable Women Authors of the Day* (London: Maclaren, 1906), 45–6; Andrew Saint, correspondence with the author, March 2011.

5 Squares 'Going Down in the World'

1 'Five Speeches on Ecclesiastical Affairs, Delivered by Edward Horsman, Esqr., M.P., in the House of Commons, in the Sessions of 1847 and 1848', *Eclectic Review* new ser., 2 (1851): 489.

2 'Social Rivalry, or the Dangers of Modern Luxury', *Friends' Intelligencer: A Religious and Family Journal* 14 (1858): 366; see also Fanny Fern, 'The Advantages of a House in a Fashionable Square: A House in St John's Square', in *Fern Leaves from Fanny's Port-Folio*, 2nd ser. (London: Sampson Low, Son & Co., 1854); Charles Dickens, 'A Rogue's Life', *Household Words* 13 (1856): 158; Georgiana May Step, 'Reine Marguerite', *Christian Parlor Magazine* 9–10 (1852): 257.

3 *Penny Cyclopaedia* 14 (1839): 112; T. Roger Smith and W. H. White, 'Model Dwellings for the Rich', *Society of Arts Journal* (November 1875): 460–1.

4 Henry Mayhew, *The Great World of London* (London: David Bogue, n.d. [1856]), pt 9, p. 60.

5 Thomas Moore, 'The Summer Fête', *The Poetical Works of Thomas Moore* (London: Longman, Brown, Green, Longmans and Roberts, 1856), 119; 'A Sketch of the Peculiari-

ties of London', *London University College Magazine* 1 (1849): 224.

6   *Blackwood's Edinburgh Magazine* 46 (1839): 220.

7   'Squares of the West', *Builder*, 13 August 1864.

8   Henry Mayhew and John Binny, *The Criminal Prisons of London and Scenes of Prison Life* (London: Griffin, Bohn, 1862), 57.

9   Mayhew and Binny, *Criminal Prisons of London*, 59.

10 Mayhew and Binny, *Criminal Prisons of London*, 58.

11 Mayhew and Binny, *Criminal Prisons of London*, 59.

12 Mayhew and Binny, *Criminal Prisons of London*, 59–60.

13 Mayhew and Binny, *Criminal Prisons of London*, 60.

14 Mayhew and Binny, *Criminal Prisons of London*, 60.

15 Mayhew and Binny, *Criminal Prisons of London*, 60.

16 'The earliest air he breathed was in a smoky London Square; / Where in a dingy brick and mortar pile his high-born parents lived in handsome style, / Kept their state coach, and many a liveried knave, / And large sad parties once a fortnight gave.' H. T. Lyte, 'Tale Fourth: Edward Field', *Tales in Verse* (London: William Marsh, 1825), 103.

17 *Galaxy* 5 (1868): 397; *Punch* 91 (1886): 215.

18 Heman Humphrey, 'Publick Squares', *Family Magazine* 3 (February 1836): 430. This 'sprightly outline' of one of the 'brighter features in the overgrown British metropolis' is an extract from one of a series of letters published in the *New York Observer* written by Dr Humphrey. *Friend* 9 (1836): 185.

19 Many knew the London square as filled with 'troops of children of all ages and sizes, from the baby in arms to the boy or girl of fifteen, to say nothing of the occasional presence of the "quite grown up" young men and maidens who play lawn-tennis'. A. E. Q.[uekett?], 'In and Out of a London Square (a Chat of a Childhood Passed in Lincoln's Inn Fields)', *Temple Bar* 116, (1899): 382. The author is presumed to be the son of Professor John Thomas Quekett, who was a Trustee of Lincoln's Inn Fields from 1856 until his death in 1862.

20 Theodore Edward Hook, *Peregrine Bunce, or, Settled at Last* (London: n.p., 1857), 332–3.

21 C. M., 'Education', *New Monthly Magazine* 5 (1823): 564.

22 Elizabeth Hamilton, *Letters on the Elementary Principles of Education*, vol. 1 (Philadelphia: Isaac Pierce, 1813), 249–50.

23 Lady Margaret King was the daughter of the Irish peer Robert King, second Earl of Kingston, and married Stephen Moore, second Earl Mountcashell. She was a disciple of Mary Wollstonecraft.

24 Margaret King Moore, 'General Observations Respecting Children of All Ages', *Advice to Young Mothers on the Physical Education of Children* (Florence: Jos. Molini, 1835), 305.

25 C. R. Aikin, 'Remarks on the Protective Power of Vaccination', *London Medical Gazette* 18 (1836): 11. See also Hook, *Peregrine Bunce*, 332–3.

26 Humphrey, 'Publick Squares': 430.

27 Catherine Grace Frances Gore, 'Temptation and Atonement', *Tait's Edinburgh Magazine* 13 (1846): 749.

28 The Hon. Mrs Henry Clifford, 'Cousin Geoffrey's Chamber', *London Society* 14 (1868): 52.

29 Augustus Mayhew and Henry Mayhew, *The Greatest Plague of Life* (London: David Bogue, 1847), 94.

30 A. E. Q., 'In and Out of a London Square', 382.

31 A. E. Q., 'In and Out of a London Square', 383.

32 A. E. Q., 'In and Out of a London Square', 384.

33 Hook, *Peregrine Bunce*, 332–3.

34 Lincoln's Inn Fields, Minutes of the Trustees, 1735–1879, British Library, Add. MSS 35077–35081, 1 August 1859.

35 Lincoln's Inn Fields, Minutes of the Trustees, 11 October 1837.

36 Minutes of the Trustees of Portman Square, Portman Estate Archives, 24 April 1795; Lincoln's Inn Fields, Minutes of the Trustees, 6 May 1754.

37 See the complaint concerning 'destruction of garden seats and other injuries in the garden by Mrs Peacock's son & others', Lincoln's Inn Fields, Minutes of the Trustees, 7 June 1831; see also 29 June 1835, 1 May 1843.

38 Lincoln's Inn Fields, Minutes of the Trustees, 18 June 1868.

39 'Physical Exercises and Recreation for Girls', *Museum and Journal of Education* 3–4 (1867): 202; *Living Age* 83 (1864): 174.

40 Edmond Warre, *Athletics, or, Physical Exercise and Recreation* (London: n.p., 1884), 88.

41 Minutes of the Trustees of Portman Square, 7 May 1879, 29 June 1899, 3 June 1890, 1 May 1894.

42 'Hygienic Excess', *Punch* 77 (1879): 174.

43 'London Squares', *Graphic*, 1 August 1885.

44 *Entomologist's Monthly Magazine* 14 (1878); and John T. Carrington, *Entomologist: An Illustrated Journal of British Entomology* 11 (1878), 93.

45 *Literary World*, 14 February 1879, 107; *Congregationalist* 8 (1879): 614; and *Evangelical Magazine and Missionary Chronicle* 9 (1879): 257.

46 John Timbs, *Knowledge for the People* (London: n.p., 1831), 144.

47 Cornelius Nicholson, 'The Cockney House Sparrow and the Early Breakfast-Shop', *Zoologist: A Popular Miscellany of Natural History* 9 (1851): 3138.

48 'Sketch of the Peculiarities of London': 226–31; *Cassell's Popular Natural History*, vol. 3 (London: Cassell, Petter and Galpin, 1871), 151; Charles Dickens, 'Town and Country Sparrows', *All the Year Round*, 20 June 1868: 44.

49 J. B. of Fulham, 'Evils Produced by the Birdcatchers in the Vicinity of London', *Magazine of Natural History* 1 (1829): 288.

50 'Parks of London', *Friend* 29 (1856): 109; *Builder*, 14 January 1882: 38; Andrew Wynter, 'Metropolitan Improvements: Artistic and Structural', *Once a Week*, 17 November 1866: 544

51 John Weale, *London Exhibited in 1851* (London: J. Weale, 1851), 769.

52 'On the Etiology of Cholera', *Medico-Chirurgical Review and Journal of Practical Medicine* 18 (1833): 197.

53 'Health in London', *London Medical Gazette* 30 (1842): 612. See also Humphrey, 'Publick Squares'; Theodore Dwight, 'Sketches of London', *American Penny Magazine* 1 (1845): 660.

54 'Health in London': 612.

55 'Public Health and Mortality', *Quarterly Review* 66 (1840): 124.

56 Lincoln's Inn Fields, Minutes of the Trustees, 21 July 1849.

57 'The Dirt of London', *Chambers's Edinburgh Journal* no. 495 (24 July 1841): 209.

58 'Beauties of Ignorance', *Common School Journal* 2 (1839): 312.

59 William Guy, 'Lectures on Public Health', *Medical Times* new ser., 3 (1851): 397.

60 Michelle Allen, *Cleansing the City: Sanitary Geographies in Victorian London* (Athens, Ohio: Ohio University Press, 2008), 44.

61 The Metropolitan Sewers Act, 1848, made citizens legally bound to use the public sewers to dispose of their private waste. See Allen, *Cleansing the City*.

62 Allen, *Cleansing the City*, 43.

63 Henry Mayhew, *London Labour and the London Poor* (London: Charles Griffin and Company, n.d. [1864]), 2:395.

64 Caption for an illustration of Leicester Square, *Punch* 16 (1849): 257.

65 In the eighteenth century, in its heyday, Leicester Square had been home to some distinguished residents, including William Hogarth, Sir Joshua Reynolds and Sir Isaac Newton.

66 'Laughable Position of the Leicester-Square Statue', *Illustrated Police News*, 27 November 1869.

67 Annie S. Wolf, *Pictures and Portraits of Foreign Travel* (Philadelphia: E. Claxton & Company, 1881), 82. The Metropolitan Board of Works was created by the passing of the Metropolis Management Act, 1855. It was not a directly elected body, but consisted of members nominated by the vestries, who were the principal local authorities.

68 TNA, C 12/979/14. 'Leicester Square Area: Leicester Estate', *Survey of London*, vol. 34: *The Parish of St Anne Soho* [*SOL*, 34], ed. F. H. W. Sheppard (London: Athlone Press, 1966), 416–40.

69 *SOL* 34:434.

70 Leicester Square Scrapbook, vol. 1, p. 34, Westminster Public Library.

71 Charles Dickens, 'Leicester Square', *Household Words* 7 (1858): 67.

72 'Panoptics and Polytechnics', *Chambers's Journal of Popular Literature, Science and Arts* 5 (1854): 361.

73 *Notes and Queries* 5th ser., 2 (1874): 46. Eliakim Little, Robert S. Littell, *Littell's Living Age* 160 (1884): 366.

74 Walter Thornbury, 'London Squares', II: 'Russell-Square, Leicester-Square, and Grosvenor-Square', *Belgravia: A London Magazine* 1 (1867): 471.

75 Walter Thornbury and Edward Walford, *Old and New London: A Narrative of its History, its People, and its Places*, 6 vols (London: Cassell, Petter and Galpin, 1897), 3:171.

76 Also known as the Town Gardens Protection Act. Alexander McKenzie, *The Parks, Open Spaces and Thoroughfares of London* (London: Waterlow & Sons, 1869), 12.

77 Act for the Protection of Certain Garden or Ornamental Grounds in Cities and Boroughs, 1863, 26 Vict., c. 13. *Builder*, 7 November 1863: 799.

78 *Solicitors' Journal & Reporter* 12 (1868): 74

79 'Laughable Position'; John Hollingshead, *The Story of Leicester Square* (London: Simpkin and Marshall, 1892), 65. See *Chambers's Journal of Popular Literature, Science and Arts* 55 (1878): 728. Dickens supplies an amusing account of the dismal state of other statues in the city's 'enclosures' in 'Our Eye-Witness among the Statues', *All the Year Round*, 26 May 1860: 164–6.

80 Diane Chappelle, *Land Law*, 7th ed. (Harlow: Pearson Longman, 2006), 447–50. *Tulk* v. *Moxhay* (1848), 41 ER 1143 (Chancery).

81 *English Illustrated Magazine* 3 (1878): 718; William Robinson, *The Parks, Promenades and Gardens of Paris* (London: John Murray, 1869; 2nd ed. as *The Parks and Gardens of Paris Considered in Relation to the Wants of Other Cities and of Public and Private Gardens*, London: Macmillan, 1878), 126–7; *Time: A Monthly Miscellany of Interesting and Amusing Literature* 2 (1880): 427.

82 Articles on the squares of Marylebone, Holborn, Bloomsbury, Soho and Belgravia appeared in *Builder*, 10 May 1873: 364; 1 November 1873: 857–8; and 15 November 1873: 897–8; and in *Academy* 6 (1874): 53, 293, 317, 380.

83 Edwin Chadwick, 'On the Structural Arrangement Most Favourable to the Health of Towns', *Report to Her Majesty's Principal Secretary of State for the Home Department from the Poor Law Commissioners on an Inquiry into the Sanitary Condition of the Labouring Population of Great Britain* (London: HMSO, 1842), 386. The inhabitants of Lincoln's Inn Fields condemned the proposal to build the new Court of Law and Equity over their square, asserting in a petition to parliament in June 1841 that the Fields 'situated in the midst of a neighbourhood very densely peopled, and, combined with the Gardens of Lincoln's Inn, forms the largest and finest open area in the Metropolis with the exception of the Parks . . . nothing short of irresistible necessity would justify covering with buildings an open space so essential to the health and comfort of the Inhabitants of fields and their vicinity'. Lincoln's Inn Fields, Minutes of the Trustees, 14 June 1841.

84 *Macmillan's Magazine* 32 (1875): 329, quoted in Octavia Hill, *Homes of the London Poor*, new ed. (London: Macmillan, 1883), 91.

85 *Chambers's Journal of Popular Literature, Science and Arts* 51 (1874): 528.

86 *Macmillan's Magazine* 32 (1875): 329.

87 John Forrest Dillon, *The Law of Municipal Corporations*, 2nd, rev. and enlarged, ed., 2 vols (New York: J. Cockcroft, 1873), 2:611; Robinson, *Parks and Gardens*, 124–5.

88 Robinson, *Parks and Gardens*, 125.

89 *Galaxy* 5 (1868): 397.

90 Henry B. Wheatley, Review of Tom Taylor, *Leicester Square: Its Associations and its Worthies* (1874), in *Academy* 6 (1874): 228.

91 Adolphe Trébuchet, 'Boards of Health: Report on the Labours of the "Conseil de Salubrité" of Paris, from 1829 to 1839', cited in Thomas Milner, *The Elevation of the People, Moral, Instructional and Social* (London: n.p., 1846), 449.

92 'Public Walks: Report', *The Times*, 7 September 1833.

93   Milner, *Elevation of the People*, 366–8.

94   Isaac Taylor, 'Seeing is Believing', *People's Magazine: An Illustrated Miscellany for Family Reading*, 6 April 1867.

95   Charles Dickens in *All the Year Round*, 7 June 1862: 303.

96   The area was probably the model for the dust heap described in Dickens's *Our Mutual Friend* (published in serial form, 1864–5).

97   Dickens to Angela Burdett-Coutts, 16 March 1852, *Letters of Charles Dickens*, vol. 6: *1850–1852*, ed. Madeline House, Graham Storey, Kathleen Tillotson and Nina Burgis (Oxford: Clarendon Press, 2002), 626.

98   Dickens, *All the Year Round*: 303.

99   '"May difference of opinion," etc.', *Punch* 41 (1861): 174 (an anonymous contributor to *Punch* quoting an excerpt from the *Opinion Nationale*).

100 '"May difference of opinion," etc.': 174.

101 Thomas Hood remarked as early as 1838: 'all fashions transplanted from Paris flourish vigorously on our soil'. Thomas Hood, 'The Comic Annual', *Mirror of Literature* 30 (1838): 10. See also 'The Poor of Paris', *All the Year Round*, 22 October 1864: 248–53.

102 McKenzie, *Parks, Open Spaces and Thoroughfares of London*, 3.

103 McKenzie, *Parks, Open Spaces and Thoroughfares of London*, 11. Similar sympathies can also be found in contemporary prose. For instance, the author of 'The White Cat: A Peep at Fairyland' (1870) described a square where 'nobody is allowed a key – because there are no railings to keep anyone out. Everybody who can find sitting or standing room (which is not easy on bright summer evenings) may enter and gaze at the brilliant flowers.' 'The White Cat', *London Society* 17 (1870): 154.

104 Robinson, *Parks and Gardens*, 116.

105 Robinson, *Parks, Promenades and Gardens*, 85–6.

106 Robinson, *Parks, Promenades and Gardens*, 86.

107 Robinson, *Parks and Gardens*, 116–17.

108 Robinson, *Parks and Gardens*, 110.

109 Robinson, *Parks, Promenades and Gardens*, 120, 91, xxiii. Robinson makes no mention of Edward Cresy's Square d'Orléans, laid out in La Nouvelle Athènes (today in the Quartier St Georges, 9th arrondissement) in 1829–30; see Diana Burfield, *Edward Cresy, 1792–1858: Architect and Civil Engineer* (Donington: Shaun Tyas, 2003), 65–8.

110 See Howard Saalman, *Haussmann: Paris Transformed* (New York: Braziller, 1971).

111 Robinson was acquainted with Alphand.

112 Robinson, *Parks, Promenades and Gardens*, 111.

113 Robinson, *Parks, Promenades and Gardens*, 83.

114 Robinson, *Parks and Gardens*, 26.

115 Robinson, *Parks and Gardens*, 115.

116 Robinson, *Parks and Gardens*, 118.

117 Robinson, *Parks and Gardens*, 121.

118 Robinson, *Parks and Gardens*, 119.

119 Robinson, *Parks and Gardens*, 120–1.

120 The aim of the London Recreational and Playground Society was to provide playgrounds for poor children in populous places. See the *Philanthropist, and Prison and Reformatory Gazette*, 1 November 1858: 263; see also 'Going out to play', *Chambers's Journal of Popular Literature, Science and Arts* 9 (1858): 148.

121 *Gardeners' Chronicle*, 10 March 1877: 308.

122 Robinson, *Parks and Gardens*, 121.

123 Robinson, *Parks and Gardens*, 122.

124 Robinson, *Parks and Gardens*, 122.

125 'Squares of the West', *Builder*, 13 August 1864: 600–2.

126 'Squares of the West'. See also William Laxton in *Civil Engineer and Architect's Journal* 25 (1862): 221.

127 'Some Notes on London Flowers and Greenery', *Builder*, 30 November 1861: 821. In this article it is reported that Mr Broome suggested building glasshouses or conservatories instead of arbours, as they would be 'both useful and graceful features in the London squares'. See also William Robinson, 'London Gardens', *Garden* 2 (1872): 95.

128 Robinson, *Parks and Gardens*, 123.

129 Robinson, *Parks and Gardens*, 123.

130 Robinson, *Parks and Gardens*, 123.

131 'Some Notes on London Flowers and Greenery': 821.

132 'Places, Squares and Trees of London', *Builder*, 2 May 1863: 317.

133 'Squares of the West': 602. The value of houses in Park Lane was said to have doubled after the old garden walls were replaced with 'Elysian borders'.

134 *Transactions of the Microscopical Society of London* 1 (1853): 280; *British Chess Magazine* 4 (1884): 239.

135 Robinson, *Parks and Gardens*, 118.

136 Robinson, *Parks and Gardens*, 124.

137 Robinson, *Parks and Gardens*, 124.

138 'Ornamental Grounds', *Sanitary Record* new ser., 2 (1881): 271.

139 *Gardeners' Chronicle*: 308.

140 William Augustus Guy, *The Factors of the Unsound Mind, with Special Reference to the Plea of Insanity in Criminal Cases* (London: De la Rue, 1881), 41.

141 *Chambers's Journal of Popular Literature, Science and Arts* 51 (1874): 528.

142 The most notable achievement was the passing of the Metropolitan Commons Act, 1866, which provided for the improvement, protection and management of commons near the metropolis.

143 The garden and the beadle were instructed to admit 'all respectable people to view them' for a fortnight between 1 p.m. and 4 p.m. The display was advertised in *The Times* and other daily newspapers. Lincoln's Inn Fields, Minutes of the Trustees, 1 November 1858.

144 Lincoln's Inn Fields, Minutes of the Trustees, 1 November 1858, 1 August 1859.

145 Lincoln's Inn Fields, Minutes of the Trustees, 1 August 1859; 'The Children in the Temple Gardens', *Pall Mall Gazette*, 16 September 1870.

146 Transcription of a letter from the Clerk of the Board of Works of St Giles District to the Trustees of Lincoln's Inn Fields, 28 June 1859, Lincoln's Inn Fields, Minutes of the Trustees, 1 August 1859. Non-residents of the Fields were granted keys from 1861.

147 Lincoln's Inn Fields, Minutes of the Trustees, 10 June 1875, 8 June 1876, 7 May 1877. See also Octavia Hill, *Our Common Land: (And Other Short Essays)* (London: Macmillan, 1877), 133.

148 'Children in the Temple Gardens'.

149 Octavia Hill, *Homes of the London Poor* (London: Macmillan, 1875), 209.

150 Joyce Bellamy, '"A New Gleam of Social Sunshine": Window Garden Flower Shows for the Working-Classes, 1860–1875', *London Gardener* 9 (2003–4): 60–70; 'A City Flower Show', *Sanitary Record* 7 (1877): 44.

151 *Gardener's Magazine*, 21 July 1866: 323.

152 S. Hadden Parkes, *Window Gardens for the People, and Clean and Tidy Rooms: Being an Experiment to Improve the Homes of the London Poor* (London: S. W. Parkes: 1864), 53.

153 *City Press*, quoted in *Gardener's Magazine*, 30 May 1863: 175

154 Charles Dickens, 'Bloomsbury Bouquets', *All the Year Round*, 20 August 1864: 33–4.

155 George Augustus Sala parodied these annual 'Watteaulike' garden parties which were staged in Sarcophagus Square in his 'Episode in the Career of Professor MacPelvis', *Gentleman's Magazine* 65 (1878): 257.

156 Charles Dickens, 'Bloomsbury Bouquets', *All the Year Round*, 20 August 1864: 34

157 Dickens, 'Bloomsbury Bouquets': 34.

158 Grosvenor was created duke in 1874.

159 *Lloyd's Weekly Newspaper*, 28 July 1872.

160 'Proposed Public Garden in Ebury Square', *Builder*, 27 July 1872: 582–3.

161 *Lloyd's Weekly Newspaper*, 25 August 1872.

162 'Public Gardens and Private Rights', *Graphic*, 5 September 1874: 222.

163 'London Gardens', *Graphic*, 9 April 1870.

164 'Public Gardens and Private Rights'.

165 Brabazon succeeded to the earldom in 1887.

166 Reginald Brabazon, 'Public Playgrounds for the Children of the London Poor', *The Times*, 22 January 1884. The MPGA endeavoured, as far as possible, to keep the two types of spaces entirely distinct, as it was a 'mistake to allow children to disturb the quiet and rest which public gardens should afford to adults'. *The Times*, 30 May 1885.

167 *The Times*, 22 January 1884.

168 *The Times*, 19 November 1904.

169 *Quiver* 20 (1885): 337.

170 Private correspondence with Joyce Bellamy, Secretary of the MPGA, August 2009.

171 Hugh Lupus Grosvenor, 'Work for the Unemployed', editorial, *The Times*, 27 March 1885.

172 M. E. Haweis, 'Rus in urbe, or Gardening in London', *Contemporary Review* 48 (July–December 1885): 97.

173 W. Beatty-Kingston, *A Journalist's Jottings* (London: n.p. [Chapman and Hall], 1890), 116.

174 'Public Gardens and Private Rights'.

175 Reginald Brabazon, 'Work for the Unemployed', editorial, *The Times*, 13 March 1885; 'London Gardens and Playgrounds', *Builder*, 8 August 1885: 177.

176 Notes for Lieutenant-Colonel K. Vaughan Morgan, CBE, MP, Parliamentary Archives, FCP/1/48.

177 Brabazon, 'Work for the Unemployed'.

178 Reginald Brabazon, 'Open Spaces', letter to the editor, *The Times*, 30 June 1885.

179 'London Gardens and Playgrounds'.

180 Charles Booth, 'Survey of Life and Labour in London', 1886–1903, no. 352, p. 25, Archives Division of the British Library of Political and Economic Science (http://booth.lse.ac.uk/).

181 Here the MPGA secured the enclosure and undertook the refurbishment of the landscape. The costs of the improvements were, however, met by the Kyrle Society.

182 Description of Ford Square (formerly Bedford Square), east London. Booth, 'Survey of Life and Labour in London', no. 350, p. 101.

183 Booth, 'Survey of Life and Labour in London', no. 347, p. 49.

184 *Builder*, 25 March 1882: 364; 17 June 1882: 752.

185 M. Berlin, 'Common People, Common Land: A History of London's Open Spaces as Places of Protest', unpublished conference paper, read at the London and Middlesex Archaeological Society, 44th annual local history conference, 21 November 2009.

186 *Pall Mall Gazette*, 22 July 1872.

187 Charles Hare, Report of the Treasurer, 25 May 1891, 27 April 1892, Manchester Square Garden, Minutes of the Trustees, Manchester Square Garden Trust.

188 'London Squares', *Graphic*, 1 August 1885: 115.

189 *Punch* 88 (1885): 143.

190 Mary L. Dodds, *Rose Dunbar's Mistake, or, Whom Have I in Heaven?* (London and Edinburgh: n.p., 1879), 21.

191 'Sport in a London Square', *Punch* 77 (1879): 165.

192 [Wilhelm Miller], 'English Ideals of Gardening', *The Times*, 16 November 1907.

193 [Miller], 'English Ideals of Gardening'.

194 'Public Gardens and Private Rights': 222.

195 'On Some Nuisances and Absurdities in London', *Builder*, 26 September 1874.

196 *Punch* 13 (1847): 168–9.

197 'The Colonel's Club, Meeting CLIII', *Literary World* 4 (1849): 277.

198 'Mrs Argentine Stepney', *Ainsworth's Magazine* 22 (1852): 211; Victor Baune, letter to Michael Bass, MP, 4 May 1864, Michael Thomas Bass, *Street Music in the Metropolis: Correspondence and Observations on the Existing Law and Proposed Amendments* (London: J. Murray, 1864), 7–8; *Punch* 46 (1864): 27. The 'Street-Organ Nuisance' had long been a cause of concern: it had been discussed in the House of Commons many years earlier, during the debates that led to the passage in 1839 of the Metropolitan Police Act (2 & 3 Vict., c. 47, s. 57).

199 Bass, *Street Music in the Metropolis*, 7.

200 'A Ghost in a London Square', *Lancet* 1 (1867): 688; *Pall Mall Gazette*, 31 May 1867: 265.

201 See 'Story of a Phantom', *Tait's Edinburgh Magazine* 25 (1858): 16.

202 Margaret Leicester Warren, *Diaries*, 2 vols (Taunton: privately printed, 1924), 2:185. I am grateful to Andrew Saint for this reference.

203 *Punch* 88 (1885): 143.

204 'The Removal of Obstacles to the Architectural Improvement to London', *Builder*, 26 May 1877: 520.

205 'London Gardens', *Graphic*, 9 April 1870.

206 'London Squares', *Graphic*, 1 August 1885.

207 'Save Leicester Square', *Builder*, 6 December 1862: 870; J. Newton, FRHS, 'Open Spaces and Squares', *Builder*, 7 November 1863.

208 'Squares of the West'.

209 *Pall Mall Gazette*, 30 June 1893.

6 The Threatened Loss of 'Invaluable Lung Spaces'

1 London Society, *London's Squares and How to Save Them* (s.l. [London]: London Society, n.d. [1927]), 10.

2 'The Local Government Bill', *The Times*, 20 April 1888. The London County Council (LCC) replaced the Metropolitan Board of Works in 1889.

3 The London School Board predated the London County Council by nearly twenty years.

4 John Davis, 'The Progressive Council, 1889–1907', in *Politics and the People of London: The London County Council, 1895–1965*, ed. Andrew Saint (London: Hambledon Press, 1989), 27.

5 Chris Waters, 'Progressives, Puritans and the Cultural Politics of the Council, 1889–1914', in *Politics and the People of London: The London County Council, 1895–1965*, ed. Andrew Saint (London: Hambledon Press, 1989), 49.

6 Waters, 'Progressives, Puritans', 50.

7 Waters, 'Progressives, Puritans', 52.

8 Waters, 'Progressives, Puritans', 50.

9 In February 1914 it was renamed the Parks and Open Spaces and Allotments Committee, but reverted to its former title of Parks and Open Spaces Committee when the third Smallholdings and Allotments Committee was formed in 1921. The title was later shortened to Parks Committee.

10 London County Council, *London Statistics* 16 (1905–6): 150–3, quoted in Waters, 'Progressives, Puritans', 55.

11 George Haw, 'Lantern Lecture, London County Council Election', *Daily News*, 2 March 1907: 6, quoted in Waters, 'Progressives, Puritans', 52.

12 The Administrative County of London comprised what is known as inner London, and excluded the City.

13 'The Disputed Rights in Kensington', *The Times*, 27 May 1910.

14 'Open Spaces in Parliament', *The Times*, 22 February 1890

15 Precis of Evidence to be submitted by Sir Willoughby Dickinson to the Royal Commission on London Squares, 1926–7, Parliamentary Archives, FCP/1/46.

16 Precis of Evidence to be submitted by Sir Willoughby Dickinson.

17 'The Edwardes Estate: North of West Cromwell Road', *Survey of London*, vol. 42: *Southern Kensington: Kensington Square to Earl's Court*, ed. Hermione Hobhouse (London: Athlone Press, 1986), 249–60.

18 'Gardens in Squares', *The Times*, 7 November 1903; London County Council [LCC] Minutes, 3 November 1903, London Metropolitan Archives [LMA], LCC/MIN/1722.

19 London Society, *London's Squares and How to Save Them*, 44.

20 Stenton Covington, 'London's Garden Squares', *Star*, 28 February 1927.

21 'The Disputed Rights in Kensington', *The Times*, 26 May 1910.

22 'The Edwardes Square Dispute', *The Times*, 24 December 1913: 9, *The Times*, 21 January 1914: 8; *The Times*, 23 January 1912: 3.

23 Precis of Evidence to be submitted by Sir Willoughby Dickinson.

24 LCC Minutes, Parks and Open Spaces Committee, 20 July 1900 to 10 October 1902, LMA, 303, 15 November 1902.

25 'Particulars of the Garden Squares', May 1904, Parliamentary Archives, FCP/1/48.

26 Proof of Evidence of Mr Frank Hunt, CVO, Valuer to the London County Council, 15 November 1927, Royal Commission on London Squares, Parliamentary Archives, FCP/1/46.

27 London Squares and Enclosures (Preservation) Bill, 1905, Minutes and Correspondence, LMA, LCC/LP/01/117. While the bill would have prohibited the erection of buildings and structures on specified lands in the Administrative County of London, it did not propose to acquire the estates, expropriate the lands or disturb the legal ownership. It was remarked in *London's Squares and How to Save Them* (9–10), that 'though it did not give the landlord monetary compensation it gave him the right to put the burden of maintaining the ground on the local authority and still permitted him to collect the full benefit of the amenity of the gardens from the houses round. It preserved right of heredity and gave permission for the landlord to exchange the open space for another equally desirable, if he could procure one. If the Bill had been passed it would have secured to London in perpetuity many green gardens which it now possesses and the landlords could not have argued that they had been very great losers by this measure.'

28 London Squares and Enclosures (Preservation) Bill, 1906, Minutes and Correspondence, LMA, LCC/LP/01/142.

29 London Society, *London's Squares and How to Save Them*, 14; Richard Catt, 'Small Urban Spaces, Part 8: Protecting London Squares', *Structural Survey* 15, no.1 (1997): 33–8.

30 *Fortnightly* 81 (1907): 311.

31 See the obituary of the author in *The Times*, 5 February 1937.

32 E. Beresford Chancellor, *The History of the Squares of London: Topographical and Historical* (London: Kegan Paul, Trench, Trübner, 1907), p. x.

33 L. W. Chubb, letter to B. W. Horne, 24 June 1925, Evidence before the Royal Commission on London Squares, Parliamentary Archives, FCP/1/46.

34 Chancellor, *History of the Squares of London*, 245, 255.

35 'Value of London Squares: History of Health', *The Times*, 6 December 1918; E. Beresford Chancellor, 'The Squares of London', *British Architect* 88 (February 1919): 14.

36 Minutes of the London Society, 17 January 1912, London Society Archives.

37 See *Journal of the Town Planning Institute* 14 (1927): 59, 67, 200.

38 It was achieved through the collaboration of the MPGA and other local interest groups. 'The Saving of St Peter's Square', *Journal of the London Society* no. 2 (January 1914): 7–8.

39 It was remarked in *The Times* on 3 June 1916: 'With its multitude of squares, if they are all put to this sensible use [i.e. made available for the use of wounded soldiers during the war], London, we are sure, will prove to be, in an unexpected sense, a "most kindly nurse".'

40 'A Plan for Laying-Out a London Square', *Gardeners' Chronicle*, 8 June 1895: 718.

41 'Gardens in London Squares', *Gardeners' Chronicle*, 13 April 1895: 456.

42 Reginald Blomfield, *The Formal Garden in England*, 3rd ed. (London: Macmillan, 1901), 224.

43 'Gardens in London Squares': 456.

44 'Untidiness in London Parks', *The Times*, 15 May 1916.

45 'Gardens for the Wounded: Questions in the County Council', *The Times*, 31 May 1916.

46 The food production campaign, launched in 1915, gave compulsory powers to extend cultivated land into the metropolis. It was not, however, invoked until the end of 1917, when the situation became critical.

47 Cultivation of Lands Order, 1917, LMA, LCC/MIN/8713, and LCC/MIN/8923.

48 'Vacant Land in London: The LCC and the Parks', *The Times*, 22 January 1917; F. W. Parker and George Berry (inspectors at the Board of Agriculture), 'Land at Bedford Estate at the Rear of the British Museum: Report as to the Suitability for Cultivation', 26 January 1917, LMA, LCC/MIN/8922.

49 Frank Hunt, Cultivation of Land Orders, 1917: Tredegar Square, Stepney, 7 December 1917, LMA, LCC/MIN/8923; Frank Hunt, Cultivation of Land Orders, 1917: Gibson Square, Islington, 7 December 1917, LMA, LCC/MIN/8923.

50 Minutes of the Parks and Small Holdings and Allotments Committee, 1 February 1918, LMA, LCC/MIN/8713. Bethnal Green Metropolitan Borough quickly followed suit. In the event, however, the squares were not cultivated.

51 Agenda of the Parks and Small Holdings and Allotments Committee, 1 March 1918, LMA, LCC/MIN/8713.

52 'Too Many Flowers', letter to the editor, *The Times*, 27 May 1916.

53 MPGA, 'Closing of Small Gardens', letter to the LCC, 25 September 1916, Agendas of the Parks and Small Holdings and Allotments Committee, LMA, LCC/MIN/8713, item 49.

54 'London Squares and the Wounded', *The Times*, 19 May 1916.

55 *The Times*, 26 March 1918.

56 By 29 May 1916 *The Times* had received 218 messages in support of Repton's scheme.

57 Bedford Square also joined the scheme.

58 'Rest Gardens for the Wounded', *The Times*, 24 May 1916; see also London Squares: A Debt to the Wounded', *The Times*, 20 May 1916; 'Rest Places for the Wounded: The Use of London Squares', *The Times*, 22 May 1916; 'Wounded in the Squares: Safeguards to Privacy', *The Times*, 26 May 1916; 'Gardens for the Wounded: Spread of the Scheme', *The Times*, 27 May 1916; 'Tea in London Squares: Another Offer to the Wounded', *The Times*, 29 May 1916.

59 'Gardens for Wounded Soldiers: Spread of the Scheme'.

60 Letter to the editor, *The Times*, 24 May 1916. Les Vacances du Soldat Belge was an organisation based in London whose aim was to minister to wounded Belgian soldiers.

61 *The Times*, 23 May 1916.

62 'Convalescents in the Squares', *The Times*, 3 June 1916.

63 'Gardens for the Wounded', *The Times*, 31 May 1916.

64 'Wounded in the Squares: Safeguards to Privacy'.

65 Her views were first aired in *The Times* on 26 March 1916.

66 'Children Deprived of Playgrounds: Loan of Gardens Wanted', *The Times*, 7 June 1918. The open-air school movement had begun in 1904, and was promoted to prevent the development of tuberculosis in children.

67 Letters of 13 October 1916, 20 October 1916 and 21 December 1916, Agendas of the Parks and Small Holdings and Allotments Committee, LMA, LCC/MIN/8713.

68 'Classes in Parks and Open Spaces, 1917', 28 February 1917, memo from the Education Committee to the Parks and Small Holdings and Allotments Committee, LMA, LCC/MIN/8922; Euston Square, St Pancras, 'Returns of Squares', LMA, LCC/PK/Gen/01/19.

69 Euston Square, St Pancras, 'Returns of Squares'.

70 'Princess Beatrice to Visit Euston Square', *St Pancras Gazette*, 10 June 1927.

71 Trinity Square garden, Tower Hill, was put at the disposal of the Admiralty and a temporary hospital was built there, which was in use from October 1914. Minutes of the Parks and Small Holdings and Allotments Committee, 21 October 1914, LMA, LCC/MIN/8713.

72 Todd Longstaffe-Gowan, 'The Washington Inn: The "House of Ulysses" in St James's Square', *London Gardener* 13 (2007–8): 89–95.

73 'Rest Places for the Wounded: The Use of the Squares', *The Times*, 30 May 1916; St James's Square Trust, Minutes of the Trustees, 1836 to the present, 9 October 1917.

74 The American YMCA assisted in the maintenance and promotion of the morale and welfare of the Allied military forces during the war. Their efforts were co-ordinated by the National War Work Council on behalf of the International Committee of North American YMCAs.

75 *The Times*, 14 June 1918; *New York Times*, 16 June 1918.

76 *The Times*, 3 May 1923; *New York Times*, 25 June 1918.

77 *New York Times*, 16 June 1918.

78 *New York Times*, 25 June 1918.

79 *The Times*, 14 June 1918, 3 January 1921.

80 *The Times*, 3 May 1923.

81 Ian F. W. Beckett, *The Great War, 1914–1918*, 2nd ed. (Harlow: Pearson/Longman, 2007), 359.

82 Flag days, or 'flower days' as they were sometimes known, originated in 1912, and entailed organising respectable young women to sell flower emblems on the streets in aid of reputable charities.

83 Paul Fussell, *The Great War and Modern Memory* (London: Oxford University Press, 1975), 194. Jim Aulich and John Hewitt, *Seduction or Instruction? First World War Posters in Britain and Europe* (Manchester: Manchester University Press, 2007), 102.

84 Trudi Tate, *Modernism, History and the First World War* (Manchester: Manchester University Press, 1998), 132.

85 'The Outlook', *Land and Water*, 14 March 1918: 4.

86 London Society, *London's Squares and How to Save Them*, 8.

87 Royal Commission on London Squares, Proof of Evidence of Mr Frank Hunt, CVO. The first Housing Act was passed in 1890.

88 For an example on the Ladbroke Estate see 'An Early Garden Town-Planning Scheme in London', *Architectural Review* 38 (1915): 85.

89 I am grateful to Elain Harwood at English Heritage for this information.

90 Royal Commission on London Squares, Proof of Evidence of Mr Frank Hunt, CVO.

91 'The Duchy of Cornwall Estate at Kennington', *Journal of the London Society* no. 4 (July 1914): 13–18.

92 Elain Harwood and Andrew Saint, *London* (London: HMSO, 1991), 105.

93 Royal Commission on London Squares, Proof of Evidence of Mr Frank Hunt, CVO, paras 114–17. The scheduled open spaces were Argyle, Brunswick, Gordon, Mecklenburgh, Queen, Regent, Russell, Tavistock, Torrington and Woburn squares.

94 Covington, 'London's Garden Squares'.

95 Osbert Lancaster, *All Done from Memory* (Cambridge, Mass.: Houghton Mifflin Co., 1953), 8.

96 In addition to legislation already in force (the Open Spaces Act, 1906, and the Public Health Acts Amendment Act, 1907) a number of acts passed into law in the postwar period: the Land Settlement (Facilities) Act, 1919; Housing Act, 1925; Town Planning Act, 1925; Public Health Act, 1925; and the Parks Regulation (Amendment) Act, 1926.

97 William Simpson, 'Open Spaces for Public Health: Some Observations on the Destruction of Open Spaces in London and its Suburbs', *New Health* 2 (1927): 1.

98 Simpson, 'Open Spaces': 2.

99 'London Squares and Garden Enclosures', *Architects' Journal* 57 (1923): 793.

100 Basil Holmes, Secretary of the MPGA, 'Euston Square', letter to the editor, *The Times*, 2 August 1923.

101 'London Open Spaces', *The Times*, 9 April 1923; 16 May 1923.

102 'Erection of Buildings on Gardens and Recreation Grounds', Town Planning (Special) Committee, Report by the Valuer, 16 May 1924, Parliamentary Archives, FCP/1/48; 'London Squares: Preservation for Public Use', *The Times*, 30 June 1925.

103 'London Squares: Preservation for Public Use'.

104 The southern half of Euston Square had been renamed Endsleigh Gardens in 1879.

105 'Spring in London', *Glasgow Herald*, 6 May 1893.

106 *The Times*, 4 July 1923.

107 London Society, *London's Squares and How to Save Them*, 14.

108 E. Bonham Carter, letter to L. W. Chubb, 3 July 1923, Royal Commission on London Squares, Parliamentary Archives, FCP/1/46.

109 'Open Space in London: Need for Preservation Policy', *The Times*, 8 March 1924. The surveyors acting on behalf of the Hall Estate in St Pancras had intimated as early as 1909 that they intended to dispose of the whole of their estate, including the enclosed garden of Mornington Crescent. The capacious crescent, which had been laid out in the 1820s, was by the turn of the twentieth century down at heel: the surrounding houses were in multiple occupancy, and the garden was leafy but somewhat shabby. The atmosphere is evocatively captured in Spencer Gore's many portraits of the square painted between 1909 and 1911. The spectre of its sale did not, however, rear its head again until the spring of 1915, when the property was marketed for sale for building purposes. The Parks Committee considered the matter, but decided in the end to take no action.

110 London Society, *London's Squares and How to Save Them*, 4.

111 'The Future of the Foundling', *The Times*, 28 November 1924; London Society, *London's Squares and How to Save Them*, 4.

112 London Society, *London's Squares and How to Save Them*, 4.

113 London Society, *London's Squares and How to Save Them*, 36.

114 London Society, *London's Squares and How to Save Them*, 37.

115 A detailed account of the lecture was published in 'London's Lungs', *Architect & Building News*, 11 February 1927.

116 'Garden Squares of London: Value to the Public. Mr F. Hunt on Future Control', *The Times*, 8 February 1927.

117 'London's Lungs'.

118 Precis of Evidence to be submitted by Sir Willoughby Dickinson.

119 London Squares and Enclosures (Preservation) Bill, 23 February 1927, and London Squares and Enclosures (Preservation) Bill No. 2, 10 March 1927. Scurr had looked for guidance to earlier legislation relating to Brighton. The 'Brighton Precedent' was established in 1884 when Brighton Corporation passed an Improvement Act, which dealt with the preservation of ten squares and crescents. The act gave the corporation power to purchase the soil of the squares subject to the rights of use of the adjoining owners, for whom the corporation was to act as trustee.

120 'Mr Basil Holmes' [unofficial] Views re Mr Scurr's Bill on London Squares', n.d. [1927], Parliamentary Archives, FCP/1/48.

121 The Commons and Footpaths Preservation Society is Britain's oldest national conservation body.

122 London Society, *London's Squares and How to Save Them*, 42. It was noted that this measure was taken without compensating the owners for the 'abolition of their rights to enclose and build over the commons if they could overcome the opposition by the commoners as legal users of the commons'.

123 London Society, *London's Squares and How to Save Them*, 43.

124 R. V. Vernon and N. Mansergh, eds, *Advisory Bodies: A Study of their Uses in Relation to Central Government, 1919–1939* (London: George Allen & Unwin, 1940), 272.

125 *Royal Commission on London Squares: Report and Appendices*, Cmd. 3196 (London: HMSO, 1928).

126 Dudley Fishburn, MP, 'Opening Speech and Welcome to Delegates', in *London Squares: The Proceedings of the London Squares Conference, a Forum on the Past, Present and Future of London's Squares, 1995*, ed. Chris Sumner (London: London Historic Parks and Gardens Trust, 1997), 7.

127 H. F. Gosnell, 'British Royal Commissions of Inquiry', *Political Science Quarterly* 49 (1934): 91.

128 Other witnesses included Frank Hunt, Alderman Charles Pascall, Cecil A. Levy, Herbert Morrison, the Rt Hon. Sir Willoughby Hyett Dickinson, Harry C. Bickmore, Edmund Rushmore Abbott, Sir Edgar Harper, Maurice Webb, Francis Campbell Ross Douglas, Arthur C. H. Borrer, H. Arthur Steward, Ernest Humbert, Lionel Walford, Gerald Eve, Arthur Stretton Gaye, Edward F. M. Elms, C. S Sanders, Joseph Stower, P. F. Story, Edward Willis and William Loftus Hare. Royal Commission on London Squares, Minutes of Evidence, 15 November 1927 to 28 February 1928, London Society Archives.

129 Sir Edgar Bonham Carter, Proof of Evidence to be given before the Royal Commission on London Squares, 1927, Parliamentary Archives, FCP/1/44. The organisations for which Sir Edgar spoke included the Commons and Footpaths Preservation Society, the Garden Cities and Town Planning Association, the London Society, the London and Greater London Committee of the National Playing Fields Association, and the MPGA.

130 Royal Commission on London Squares, Proof of Evidence of Mr Frank Hunt, CVO Appendix F.H.3.

131 *Royal Commission on London Squares: Report and Appendices*, 27.

132 *Royal Commission on London Squares: Report and Appendices*. With the exception of five enclosures (Imperial Square, West Kensington Gardens, and Torrington, Alexander and Blandford squares), all enclosures falling within the scope of the inquiry were recommended for permanent preservation as open spaces.

133 'Oases in London', *The Times*, 29 April 1937.

134 London Council for Social Services, London Squares Sub-Committee, Minutes, 29 October 1928, Parliamentary Archives, FCP/1/44. Chamberlain wrote to the London Society in June 1927, inviting it 'to recommend the names of two or three gentlemen (from which he could select one) to serve on the Royal Commission which it was proposed to set up to consider the question of the preservation of the existing squares', Minutes of the Executive Committee of the London Society, 29 June 1927, London Society Archives.

135 David Marcus, 'Legal Aspects of London Squares', in *London Squares: The Proceedings of the London Squares Conference*, ed. Sumner, 24

136 'Our London Squares', *Builder*, 30 May 1924: 861; Royal Commission on London Squares, Minutes of Evidence of Edmund Rushworth Abbott, Town Planning Institute, 10 January 1928, Parliamentary Archives, FCP/1/48, para. 12. See also debate on the London Squares Preservation Bill, 4 March 1931, *Parliamentary Debates, House of Lords*, 5th ser. (1931), vol. 80, cc. 235–47, and in particular the remarks of Earl Howe and Lord Ponsonby of Shulbrede.

137 'Our London Squares', 861. See also *Journal of the London Society* no. 75 (May 1924): 4.

138 'Open-Air Life in London', *Builder*, 17 March 1922: 413.

139 Sir William Orpen, 'Are the Squares of London Used to Advantage', *Country Life*, 19 April 1924: 560.

140 'Underground Car Parks: Growing Burden on the Streets', *The Times*, 14 July 1936.

141 Dugald Sutherland MacColl, 'London Squares and a Traffic Tyranny', *Nineteenth Century and After* 115 (1934): 336.

142 MacColl, 'London Squares': 336. See John Betjeman 'we see the squares of London being transformed into wells for blocks of flats – witness Berkeley Square', 'Antiquarian Prejudice' (lecture delivered in 1937), *First and Last Loves* (London: John Murray, 1952), 49. 'Berkeley Square, St James's Square and Leicester Square are all changing and becoming little green wells among blocks of flats and cinemas', John Betjeman, *Tennis Whites and Teacakes*, ed. Stephen Games (London: John Murray, 2007), 146.

143 As early as 1927 the London and Home Counties Traffic Advisory Committee had promoted car parking in various squares, including Bedford, Charterhouse, Finsbury, Lowndes, Soho and Trinity squares, Royal Crescent, West Smithfield, and Finsbury Circus. 'Motor-Parking in London', *The Times*, 3 December 1927; 'London Motor Traffic', *The Times*, 5 December 1927.

144 MacColl, 'London Squares', 336.

145 MacColl, 'London Squares', 337. The Automobile Association had prepared a model of an underground car park for Leicester Square as early as 1924. Stenson Cooke, 'Underground Car Parks', *The Times*, 25 November 1935.

146 'Underground Car Parks: Growing Burden on the Streets', *The Times*, 14 July 1936.

147 'London Squares: Preservation Bill in Committee', *The Times*, 6 March 1931.

148 'Underground Car Parks: Growing Burden on the Streets'.

149 J. E. Arnold James, *Air Raid Precautions: Report to the Finsbury Borough Council by Messrs. Tecton, Architects, on the Structural Protection for the People of the Borough against Aerial Bombardment* (London: Borough of Finsbury, 1939), 2.

150 'Shelter Policy', *The Times*, 21 April 1939.

151 'Car Park and A.R.P. Shelter: Finsbury Square Scheme', *The Times*, 26 July 1939. See Civil Defence Act (1939), Clause 7, Powers of Local Authorities to construct underground shelters and other premises required for civil defence; and Clause 8, Powers of Local Authorities to construct underground car parks suitable for use as air raid shelters.

152 The war-time history of the square is reported in 'Underground Park for 350 Cars', *The Times*, 18 July 1961.

153 Douglas Goldring, *Pot Luck in England* (London: Chapman & Hall, 1936; 1938 ed.), 258–9.

154 Thomas Lloyd Humberstone, *Torrington Square Saved!* (London: William Rice, 1938), 2.

155 Humberstone, *Torrington Square Saved!*, 9.

156 Humberstone, *Torrington Square Saved!*, 21–2; *Evening News*, 16 December 1937.

157 There had been aerial attacks on London during the First World War. Ann Saunders, ed., *The London County Council*

Bomb Damage Maps, 1939–1945 (London: London Topographical Society and London Metropolitan Archives, 2005), 4.

158 'Air Raid Shelters: Trenches', Islington Borough Council Minutes, 1939–40, Islington History Centre, 15 December 1939, p. 258.

159 'Public and Communal Shelters', Kensington Borough Council Minutes, 1944–5, Kensington and Chelsea Local Studies, 12 December 1944, p. 40, item 2.

160 'Trenches and Trees', *The Times*, 10 June 1939.

161 Civil Defence Act (1939), Clause 7(2): provision to construct 'any such underground shelter or premises . . . in any protected square or in any allotment, common or open space'; James, *Air Raid Precautions*, 3; W. F. Deedes, *A.R.P.: A Complete Guide to Civil Defence Measures* (London: Daily Telegraph, n.d. [1939]), 25.

162 'The Building of Bloomsbury: Beauty in Brick and Stucco, A Valediction', *The Times*, 20 June 1939.

163 Report of the Treasurer, Manchester Square Garden, 24 June 1941, Manchester Square Garden Trust.

164 LCC, Parks Department, 'Air Raid Precautions, Squares and Small Open Spaces: Underground Tanks for Emergency Water Supply, Lincoln's Inn Fields', 28 August 1939, LMA, LCC/MIN/9012, 19 January 1940.

165 'Trenches and Trees'.

166 'Open Spaces', Finsbury Borough Council Minutes, 1942–3, Islington History Centre, 13 July 1942, p. 167, item 11; 'War-time Nurseries', 14 July 1942, p. 251, item 101.

167 Agendas of the Parks Committee, 1939–50, LMA, LCC/MIN/8717, p. 6.

168 'The Man with the Spade: New Allotments in London', *The Times*, 5 February 1940.

169 'War-time Food Production in Allotments and Private Gardens', Chelsea Borough Council Minutes, 1939–40, Kensington and Chelsea Local Studies, 13 December 1939, p. 174, item 10.

170 *Evening Standard*, October 1939 [undated clipping in a scrapbook in the London Society Archives]; 'Allotments', Chelsea Borough Council Minutes, 1939–40, Kensington and Chelsea Local Studies, 28 August 1940, pp. 91–2, item 10.

171 Emergency Committee, 'Finsbury Square: Cultivation', Finsbury Borough Council Minutes, 1942–3, Islington History Centre, 6 May 1942, p. 57, item 15.

172 'Musical Entertainments in Open Spaces: 1939 Season', Finsbury Borough Council Minutes, 1939–40, Islington History Centre, 17 April 1939, p. 49; 1942–3, 'Open Spaces – Musical Entertainments', 11 May 1942, p. 69, item 24; 'Open Space Entertainments: Season 1942', 13 July 1942, p. 168; 1944–5, '"Holidays-at-Home" Programme', 8 May 1944, pp. 60–6.

173 Celina Fox, 'The Battle of the Railings', *AA Files* no. 29 (1995): 50–60, supplies a very detailed account of the phenomenon.

174 James Melvin, Bryan Westwood and Norman Westwood, 'Railings for Scrap: A Pictorial Survey', *Architectural Review* 87 (1940): 171–4.

175 'Sir Thomas Inskip's Pleas for the Removal of Railings', *The Times*, 14 April 1937.

176 'London Square Gardens: Removal of Railings', *The Times*, 17 April 1937.

177 'Railings Round Squares', Minutes of the Executive Committee of the London Society, London Society Archives, 28 April 1937. The London Council for Social Services had been an active participant in the movement for the preservation of London squares.

178 Wyndham Deedes, letter to *The Times*, 24 April 1937.

179 Lilias Bathurst, letter to the editor, *The Times*, 4 May 1937.

180 Clough Williams-Ellis, letter to *The Times*, 9 April 1938.

181 Field-Marshal Goering announced in 1938 a plan to deliver up the iron railings throughout Germany to help make good the shortage of scrap metal, declaring that most of the railings were 'out of date, and not in conformity with modern tastes and ideas'. Quoted in Clough Williams-Ellis, letter to *The Times*.

182 Clough Williams-Ellis, letter to *The Times*.

183 Fox, 'Battle of the Railings', 50.

184 *Evening News*, 9 April 1938.

185 Fox, 'Battle of the Railings', 51.

186 Agenda of the Parks Committee, 19 May 1939, LMA, LCC/MIN/8717.

187 By August 1941 none of the private squares in Chelsea had contributed its railings to the war effort. *The Times*, 1 August 1941.

188 Fox, 'Battle of the Railings', 54.

189 Melvin, Westwood and Westwood, 'Railings for Scrap'.

190 Duke of Bedford, letter to Mr Matthew, 27 October 1941, Bedford Estate Archive, Woburn Abbey.

191 Alan Oliver, letter to *The Times*, 24 October 1940.

192 Hilda Reid, letter to *The Times*, 15 August 1941.

193 Fox, 'Battle of the Railings', 52–3.

194 *Architectural Review* 89 (1941): 128.

195 'Maintenance of Garden Squares', Finsbury Borough Council Minutes, 1942–3, Islington History Centre, 7 August 1942, p. 238, item 24(d); Geoffrey L. Butler, letter to *Daily Telegraph*, 28 December 1941. See also City of Westminster Minutes, Westminster City Archives, 6 September 1945, p. 175.

196 St James's Square Trust, Minutes of the Trustees, 1836 to the present, 12 May 1942.

197 C. Carter (Assistant Commissioner, New Scotland Yard), letter to the Chief Officer, Parks Department, LCC, 6 June 1940. LMA, LCC/MIN/9012, 5 July 1940.

198 Hilda Reid, letter to *The Times*, 15 August 1941.

199 Report from the Treasurer, Manchester Square Garden, 7 July 1942, Manchester Square Garden Trust.

200 Miss Barbara Donnington, Mr N. A. Gruner and Mr B. M. Phillips, letter to *The Times*, 5 September 1942.

201 Mrs Basil Williams, letter to *The Times*, 5 September 1942; see also C. Every Brown, letter to *The Times*, 3 September 1942. *The Times* reported on 5 September that they had received many letters on this topic.

202 Mr John R. Villiers (Chairman of the Hans Place Garden Committee), letter to *The Times*, 5 September 1942.

203 J. B. Abraham, letter to the editor, *The Times*, 10 September 1942.

204 This term was coined by the *Evening News*, 21 October 1941.

205 Report dated 21 January 1941, LMA, LCC/CI/PK/1/45. The patrols were apparently materially effective in limiting the nuisance.

206 George Orwell, *Tribune*, 4 and 18 August 1944.

207 Elizabeth Bowen, *Ivy Gripped the Steps* (New York: Alfred A. Knopf, 1945), Preface. The stories in the collection were written in war-time London between the spring of 1941 and the late autumn of 1944. I am very grateful to Chloe Chard for introducing me to this compelling quotation.

208 Elizabeth Bowen, 'In the Square', *The Demon Lover and Other Stories* (London: Jonathan Cape, 1945), 7.

209 *Variety*, 5 January 1944: 189.

210 It was rapidly parodied as 'A screaming bomb fell in Berkeley Square', owing to several 'incidents' that occurred in the square at the time. Quentin Reynolds, *The Wounded Don't Cry*, 4th ed. (s.l. [London]: Cassell, 1941), 175. 'Famous London Square Hit: Four Big Bombs but No Casualties', *The Times*, 2 October 1940.

211 I am grateful to Chloe Chard for her insights into these war-time melodies.

7 Post-war Planning and the Square to the Present

1 G. D. Hobson, *Some Thoughts on the Organization of Art after the War* (London: Batsford, n.d. [1946]).

2 Hobson, *Some Thoughts on the Organization of Art*, 3.

3 Hobson, *Some Thoughts on the Organization of Art*, 7. Pelham, Hereford, Philbeach, Nevern and Leyton squares, Gloucester Circus, Greenwich, and the Paragon, Blackheath, too, were badly scarred by V1 flying bombs; and the central garden at Ebury Square was partly destroyed in June 1944 by a direct hit.

4 Hobson, *Some Thoughts on the Organization of Art*, 7.

5 Hobson, *Some Thoughts on the Organization of Art*, 9.

6 Hobson, *Some Thoughts on the Organization of Art*, 10.

7 Hobson, *Some Thoughts on the Organization of Art*, 12.

8 Hobson, *Some Thoughts on the Organization of Art*, 10–11.

9 Hobson, *Some Thoughts on the Organization of Art*, 11–12.

10 Roosevelt Memorial Act, 9 & 10 Geo. VI, c. 83.

11 The garden was tacked on to the north side of Sir Edwin Lutyens's 1914–18 memorial. It was derided in the *Architects' Journal* ('No Home for the Sailors', 122 (1955): 615) for cutting up and destroying a third of the square; it was, moreover, attacked for being unrelated to the neighbouring buildings, and 'entirely unrelated to the garden', the remainder of which was in 'a sorry condition'. It was lamented that the whole garden had not been restored and laid out to form the memorial.

12 'How to Keep the Public off the Grass', *Architects' Journal* 116 (1952): 128–9.

13 Hobson, *Some Thoughts on the Organization of Art*, 14.

14 Sir Patrick Abercrombie, commentary to the film *Proud City* (1945).

15 Patrick Abercrombie, 'Some Aspects of the County of London Plan: Discussion', *Geographical Journal* 102 (1943): 238.

16 Abercrombie, 'Some Aspects of the County of London Plan': 228.

17 Abercrombie, 'Some Aspects of the County of London Plan': 236; J. H. Forshaw and Patrick Abercrombie, *County of London Plan, Prepared for the London County Council* (London: Macmillan, 1943), 36.

18 Abercrombie, 'Some Aspects of the County of London Plan': 231.

19 Abercrombie, commentary to *Proud City* (1945).

20 'Reconstruction in the City of London', *Architects' Journal* 105 (1947): 425–31.

21 'A Place in the Sun', *Evening News*, 25 February 1949.

22 Minutes of a meeting held between Sir Alexander Rouse, A. Croad (London Regional Works Adviser), A. J. Edmunds, and S. L. G. Beaufoy, HMA, at the Home Office, 3 December 1945, TNA, HLG 71/365. Although it was the responsibility of the local authorities to restore the squares, the Home Office had to foot the repair bill. Therefore the sanction of the Home Office had to be obtained before any work of restoration was undertaken.

23 Minutes of a meeting held at the Home Office, 3 December 1945.

24 Civil Defence circular, 'Organisation of Demolition of Public and Communal Surface Shelters and Similar Civil Defence Structures in the London Civil Defence Region', drafted by the Home Office, 14 December 1945, TNA, HLG 71/365.

25 Ministry of Works, letter to S. L. G. Beaufoy at the Ministry of Town and Country Planning, 10 January 1946, TNA, HLG 71/365.

26 Ministry of Works, letter to S. L. G. Beaufoy.

27 Herbert Stanley Morrison was also Lord President of the (Privy) Council and Chairman of the Lord President's Committee.

28 Ministry of Works, letter to S. L. G. Beaufoy, 29 January 1946, TNA, HLG 71/365. It should be noted that the problem of protection existed not only for squares, whether in London or in the provinces, but also for many churches, as well as public parks, recreation grounds and playing fields, where railings had been removed.

29 Tomlinson concluded that clipped hawthorn with a 'backbone' of two or three strands of wire woven through panels of wire mesh would form a 'most impenetrable barrier', and would 'prevent people from crawling through the hedge' and gaining access at night. It would not, however, work if the boundaries were overhung with trees, which agile trespassers could climb in order to gain entry to the gardens. George Tomlinson, letter to Herbert Morrison, 3 July 1946, TNA, HLG 71/365.

30 E. G. Elliot, memorandum to Mr Littler, 22 November 1946, TNA, HLG 71/365.

31 At question time in the House of Commons on 26 February 1946 Captain Bullock, who feared that squares were inadequately protected from building development, asked the Minister of Town and Country Planning whether any decision had been taken as to the plan for making use of the gardens in London squares; and Sir Wavell Wakefield asked the same minister if he had considered 'utilising the space underneath these gardens for public garages, so that revenue obtained would help maintain the gardens above'.

32 'London Squares: Replacement of Railings by Hedges', memorandum prepared by the Minister of Works, November 1946, TNA, HLG 71/365.

33 Requisitioned Land and War Works Act, 1945, 8 & 9 Geo. VI, c. 43, s. 52.

34 Only the London County Council had power of compulsory acquisition, though the metropolitan borough councils could acquire by agreement.

35 Minister of Town and Country Planning, 'London Squares', memorandum to the Lord President's Committee, 17 January 1947, TNA, HLG 71/365.

36 Section 114(5) of the Town and Country Planning Act, 1947.

37 London County Council [LCC], London Squares, Joint Report, 8 November 1948, LMA, LCC/MIN/9022.

38 LCC, London Squares, LMA, LCC/MIN/9022.

39 LCC, London Squares, LMA, LCC/MIN/9022.

40 'Conversions', Architects' Journal 120 (1954): 728–36; '7–10 Clarence Gardens, NW1', Architects' Journal 120 (1954): 811.

41 Gordon Cullen, 'A Square for Every Taste', Architectural Review 102 (1947): 131; the article was reprinted in Cullen's The Concise Townscape (London: Elsevier, 1961), 97–102.

42 Townscape Manifesto (London: Architectural Press Archive, 1953/4), 1. A copy of the manifesto is in the Getty Research Institute, Los Angeles, Nikolaus Pevsner Papers, 840209.

43 The theme of 'hazards, or the art of introducing obstacles into the landscape without inhibiting the eye' was developed further in the Architectural Review 103 (1948): 99–105.

44 Cullen, 'A Square for Every Taste': 131–4.

45 Gordon Cullen, 'Pimlico Square', Architectural Review 112 (1952): 164–71.

46 'Private open space' was defined in the London Development Plan as land being used as private grounds for sport, play, rest or recreation, or as ornamental gardens or pleasure grounds, or for agricultural purposes. It also referred to certain houses with large grounds on which there was thought that no other development would be appropriate. It should be noted that, whereas the London Squares Preservation Act (1931) had a tally of 414 squares, the plan added another forty-seven open spaces that were not within the jurisdiction of the act, including Clifton and Gloucester Gardens, Egerton Terrace, the rear garden at Castellain Mansions, and Torrington Square. All of these gardens were zoned for open space purposes in the development plan. Furthermore, 'privately-owned squares' and 'small squares' were zoned as non-programmed sites under the heading 'Industry, Commerce, Offices, Special Areas', while 'small public squares' were zoned as non-programmed sites under the heading 'Public Buildings, Hospitals, Shopping, Roads'. A few of the smallest of these gardens such as Harrington Gardens, Kensington, and Cheyne Gardens, Chelsea, were not so zoned because of the limitation of scale of the town map.

47 Ion Square is now known as Ion Gardens, Addington Square as Addington Square Gardens, Leyton Square as Leyton Square Gardens, Lorrimore Square as the Brandon Estate, and Melbourne Square as Mostyn Gardens.

48 In practice, however, many of these gardens ultimately reverted to the borough councils on condition that they undertook to maintain them.

49 Layout, Melbourne Square, Lambeth, LMA, LCC/MIN/8719, 6 July 1956.

50 The acquisition of Beaumont Square provided the LCC with 'necessary amenity open space' for the contiguous Ocean Street housing scheme.

51 Beaumont Square, Stepney, LMA, LCC/MIN/8718, 1 June 1951.

52 'Vandalism in Stepney', Architects' Journal 115 (1952): 653; LMA, LCC/MIN/8793, 14 October 1955.

53 Astragal, 'London's Squares', Architects' Journal 117 (1953): 385, 383.

54 Architect & Building News, 22 January 1953: 104.

55 'Flats in Holford Square Finsbury', Architectural Review 111 (1952): 404.

56 The resulting scheme was designed by the architects Skinner, Bailey & Lubetkin. 'Flats in Holford Square Finsbury': 406.

57 The 'precinctual' principle of urban design was originated by Sir Alker Tripp in 1935. See 'Precinctual Planning', Journal of the Town Planning Institute 45 (1959): 267.

58 'Housing, etc.: Regent's Park', Architectural Review 119 (1956): 32–5.

59 'Housing, etc.': 34.

60 'Flats at Paddington', Architects' Journal 108 (1948): 331–4.

61 Thomas Sharp, Town Planning (Harmondsworth: Penguin Books, 1940), 104.

62 Collcutt & Hamp Architects, Proposals for Lansdowne Gardens, Elgin Crescent, Arundel Gardens and Clarendon Road, RIBA Drawings Collection, PA 1220/14.

63 'Proposals for Trafalgar & Leicester Squares', Architectural Review 110 (1951): 248–52.

64 Barbara Simms, 'Parliament Square: The Significance of the Grey Wornum Landscape', London Gardener 13 (2007–8): 73–89.

65 Simms, 'Parliament Square': 85.

66 Administrative County of London Development Plan, Parks Committee and Town Planning Committee, 'Joint Report . . . by Architect to the Council and Chief Officer of the Parks Department', LMA, LCC/MIN/9036, 24 February 1956.

67 Soho, Berkeley, Golden, Hanover and Ebury squares were opened, but St George's, Eccleston, Warwick, Byranston, Dorset, Manchester, Montagu and Portman squares remained closed. Administrative County of London Development Plan, LMA, LCC/MIN/9036, 24 February 1956.

68 Administrative County of London Development Plan, LMA, LCC/MIN/9036, 24 February 1956. When a review of the 1951 plan was carried out in 1960, the LCC gave statistical details of the new open spaces that had been created during the decade. The total area of open space had increased by 6.3 per cent.

69 Quoted from a debate on the Finsbury Square Bill, 25 June 1959, Parliamentary Debates, House of Lords, 5th ser. (1959), vol. 217, cc. 255–96. When Lord Grantchester asked

Mr Rosset Chinn, managing director of Lex Car Parks, in June 1959 whether he would like to see more petrol pumps installed in London's squares, the latter replied: 'that is the way the world is going . . . and that is that . . . too bad if some people don't like it'.

70 Cavendish Square, St Marylebone, Proposed Underground Car Park, LMA, LCC/MIN/9023, 27 January 1950.

71 Cavendish Square, LMA, LCC/MIN/9023, 27 January 1950.

72 'Central London Parking Plan: Garages beneath Squares', *The Times*, 13 March 1953.

73 'Safeguarding Trees in City Squares', *The Times*, 26 July 1954; 'Underground Car Park', *Architects' Journal* 120 (1954): 157.

74 Thomas Spencer, 'Underground Car Parks', *The Times*, 29 July 1954.

75 Finsbury Square Bill, Minutes of the Parks and Town Planning Committee, 22 March 1957, LCC/MIN/9037. The borough council was able to override the statutes of the 1931 act and disregard a covenant into which they had entered because charitable property was involved, and the Attorney-General had intimated that he would raise no objection to the bill.

76 Debate on the Finsbury Square Bill, *Parliamentary Debates, House of Lords*.

77 'Petrol Pumps in London Squares', *The Times*, 30 May 1959.

78 The bill had been four times through a select committee, twice through the House of Commons and twice through the House of Lords.

79 Petrol pumps were not, however, installed at these squares.

80 Kenneth Browne, 'Townscape: West End 5, Mayfair', *Architectural Review* 141 (1967): 133.

81 John Goulden, correspondence with the author, August 2010.

82 Slogan of the Gibson Square Protection Society, 1963.

83 The market was finally relocated to Nine Elms in 1974.

84 Kenneth Browne, 'A Latin Quarter for London: A Townscape Survey of Covent Garden and a Plan for its Future', *Architectural Review* 135 (1964): 193.

85 Browne's article was a response to the *Study for the Relocation of Covent Garden Market, London, for the Covent Garden Market Authority, Part 1–2* (London: Fantus Company, 1963).

86 Kenneth Browne, 'Townscape: West End 2, Soho', *Architectural Review* 140 (1966): 29.

87 Browne, 'Latin Quarter for London': 193.

88 Browne, 'Townscape: West End 5, Mayfair': 133.

89 The critic Ian Nairn shared this view. In the mid-1960s he remarked: 'as anything more than an area on a map, Bloomsbury is dead. Town planners and London University have killed it between them – a notable victory. The splendid plane trees are still there to soothe . . . but instead of their gay yet discreet stock-brick buildings, there are doughty intrusions like the droppings of an elephant.' Ian Nairn, *Nairn's London: Revisited by Peter Gasson*, rev. ed. (Harmondsworth: Penguin, 1988), 96.

90 Kenneth Browne, 'Townscape: West End 8, Bloomsbury', *Architectural Review* 142 (1967): 453.

91 Browne, 'Townscape: West End 8, Bloomsbury': 453.

92 Browne, 'Townscape: West End 8, Bloomsbury': 455–6. John Nash had proposed to build a square on the south side of the museum in 1820s. John Summerson, *John Nash: Architect to King George IV*, 2nd ed. (London: Allen & Unwin, 1949), 179.

93 Browne, 'Townscape: West End 8, Bloomsbury': 453.

94 Listing began in Britain on 1 January 1950: 'listed building' status gives a building statutory protection. Buildings may be listed because of age, rarity, architectural merit or method of construction, or any combination of these attributes.

95 A conservation area is an area of special architectural or historic interest, the character or appearance of which it is desirable to preserve or enhance.

96 For instance, the Gibson Square Protection Society (1963), the Norland Conservation Society (1969), the Ladbroke Association (1969) and the Pembridge Association (1972).

97 Donald Appleyard, M. Sue Gerson and Mark Lintell, 'The First Environmental Areas: Barnsbury and Pimlico', in *Livable Streets* (Berkeley and Los Angeles: University of California Press, 1981), 157–83.

98 Astragal, 'Two Sides', *Architects' Journal* 143 (1966): 729–30; Mary Cosh, 'Six Sides of a Square', letter to Astragal, *Architects' Journal* 143 (1966): 917.

99 Astragal, 'Canon to Right of Them', *Architects' Journal* 138 (1963): 1164. John Betjeman was President of the Gibson Square Protection Society. The residents received the support of the Georgian Group, the Victorian Society, the Islington Society, the Royal Fine Arts Commission, the LCC and Islington Borough Council.

100 Stephen Inwood, *A History of London* (London: Macmillan, 1998), 882.

101 'The Square has a Future', *Illustrated London News*, 10 August 1968: 15.

102 *The Rebirth of the London Square: A Wates Exhibition*, promotional brochure, 1968, London Society Archives.

103 Bridget Cherry and Nikolaus Pevsner, *London*, vol. 3: *North West, The Buildings of England* series (New Haven and London: Yale University Press, 2002), 452.

104 The historians who prepared the exhibition made use of Kensington Central Library, the Guildhall Library, the National Monuments Record and the Royal Institute of British Architects.

105 *The Rebirth of the London Square*.

106 Cherry and Pevsner, *London*, vol. 3: *North West*, 452.

107 For a description of 'multi-level planning' see Edward Hollamby, 'Space about Buildings', *Architecture and Building* 32 (1957): 294–301.

108 Sherban Cantacuzino, 'The Barbican Development, City of London', *Architectural Review* 154 (1973): 71.

109 I am very grateful to Andrew Saint for drawing my attention to material relating to the development of these estates.

110 *Survey of London*, vol. 43: *Poplar, Blackwall, and the Isle of Dogs*, ed. Hermione Hobhouse (London: Athlone Press, 1994), 212–23.

111 Gibberd was the master planner for Harlow New Town,

Geoffrey Jellicoe prepared the preliminary plan for Hemel Hempstead New Town, and Ledeboer planned one of the neighbourhoods at Hemel Hempstead.

112 Geoffrey Jellicoe, correspondence with the author, April 1990.

113 'Housing at Brandon Estate, Southwark', *Architects' Journal Building Studies*, 2nd series: Flats: General, 1 November 1961, 826.

114 'Housing at Brandon Estate, Southwark': 826. Some original mid-nineteenth century houses were retained on the estate, including some in Lorrimore Square. The Pepys Estate, built by the GLC from 1963 on the site of the Deptford Victualling Yard, also incorporated old buildings within the new development. It possesses one 'generous grassy square', Bridget Cherry and Nikolaus Pevsner, *London*, vol. 2: *South, The Buildings of England* series (Harmondsworth: Penguin, 1983), 410.

115 See 'Housing at Brandon Estate, Southwark': 830.

116 Hollamby, 'Space about Buildings': 298; 'Housing at Brandon Estate, Southwark': 830.

117 Jonathan Glancey, Obituary of Edward Ernest Hollamby, *Guardian*, 24 January 2000. Hollamby was senior architect with the LCC between 1949 and 1962, and, having moved to the London borough of Lambeth, rose to become director of architecture, planning and development in Lambeth, a position he held from 1969 to 1981.

118 Hollamby, 'Space about Buildings': 296–7.

119 I am grateful to Andrew Saint for these references.

120 Hollamby, 'Space about Buildings': 298. Hollamby's design assistant David Gregory-Jones had explored the subject in 'Squares and Backs', *Keystone* (winter 1956–7): 295–300.

121 Edward Hollamby, 'The Floor Around', *Architecture and Building* 32 (1957): 352–7.

122 Hollamby, 'The Floor Around': 356. Courtenay Square is singled out for special praise.

123 Andrew Saint, email correspondence with the author, 22 March 2011.

124 The Smithsons continued: 'These rules were set to maintain the consistency of place in keeping with the original urban intention: the rules reinforced the function implied by the urban form. In return, the lessees were given a sense of stability and protection in knowing what the rules were and that they were common to all; the rules established how these spaces were to be "possessed", how they were to be collectively owned and used.' Alison Smithson and Peter Smithson, *The Charged Void* (New York: Monacelli Press, 2005), 189–90.

125 Smithson and Smithson, *The Charged Void*, 177. The estate was, in fact, a miserable failure, and has since been compared to a prison. I am grateful to Niall Hobhouse for this reference. Hobhouse suggests that the Smithsons, writing fifteen years after Robin Hood Gardens had 'failed', may have felt that it would have sounded the wrong note politically to make an explicit formal echo to the London square. Niall Hobhouse, email correspondence with the author, 15 March 2011.

126 Cherry and Pevsner, *London*, vol. 3: *North West*, 452.

127 Richard Clarke, Elizabeth McKellar and Michael Symes, *Russell Square: A Lifelong Resource for Teaching and Learning*, FCE Occasional Paper no. 5 (London: Birkbeck, University of London, Faculty of Continuing Education, 2004), 60.

128 'Draft Proof of Evidence for Planning Inquiry by J. M. Sword, General Manager, Bedford Estates', 1973, Getty Research Institute, Los Angeles.

129 'Draft Proof of Evidence', Getty Research Institute.

130 Nikolaus Pevsner, 'Draft: 44–49 and 52–60 Russell Square', c.1973, Getty Research Institute, Los Angeles, Nikolaus Pevsner Papers.

131 In the early 1970s the residents of Tolmers Square fought for the preservation of their community, and for rehabilitation rather than redevelopment. See *Battle for Tolmers* (London: Tolmers Village Association, 1974); Nick Wates, *The Battle for Tolmers Square* (London: Routledge & Kegan Paul, 1976).

132 Philip Davies, correspondence with the author, September 2010.

133 Davies, correspondence with the author. 'The Railings Go Back in a London Square: Onslow Square, Kensington', *Concrete Quarterly*, no. 105 (1975): 18–19. The railings were reinstated at Euston Square in the early 1970s.

134 John Goulden, *Eccleston Square, 1830–2010: Renaissance of a London Garden Square* (London: privately published, 2010), unpaginated.

135 Roger Phillips was awarded an MBE for 'Services to London Garden Squares' in 2010. *Garden Square News* 15, no. 1 (2010): 16.

136 London Wildlife Trust, *London Wildweb* (http://www.london.gov.uk/wildweb/).

137 Richard Girling, 'Order after the Storm', *Sunday Times*, 9 September 2007.

Epilogue   Giving 'New Life to the Enthusiasm for Squares'

1 The London Parks and Gardens Trust (formerly the London Historic Parks and Gardens Trust) is an independent charitable trust established in 1994. Its aims are to increase knowledge and appreciation of historic parks and gardens in London, and it seeks to conserve London's green spaces for the education and enjoyment of the public.

2 John Gummer, MP, 'Keynote Conference Speech', in *London Squares: The Proceedings of the London Squares Conference, a Forum on the Past, Present and Future of London's Squares*, 1995, ed. Chris Sumner (London: London Historic Parks and Gardens Trust, 1997), 5.

3 John Gummer, 'Keynote Conference Speech', 4–5.

4 Dudley Fishburn, MP, 'Introduction', in *London Squares: The Proceedings of the London Squares Conference, a Forum on the Past, Present and Future of London's Squares*, 1995, ed. Chris Sumner (London: London Historic Parks and Gardens Trust, 1997), 3.

5 One third of the 207 participating gardens in 2011 were squares; the remainder were private gardens that are not ordinarily open to the public.

6 Philip Davies, correspondence with the author, September 2010.

7 Keith Hill, Foreword, in English Heritage, *A Campaign for London's Squares* (London: English Heritage, 2000), 1.

8   English Heritage, *Campaign for London's Squares*, 2.

9   Drew Bennellick, correspondence with the author, 15, 17, 18 September 2010. Bennellick worked closely with Philip Davies on the English Heritage campaign.

10 Davies, correspondence with the author.

11 The refurbishment was carried out by Camden Council. The project cost £740,000 and was funded by the council, English Heritage, the Bedford Estate and the Crown Estate.

12 The apron was insisted upon by the traffic engineers at Camden Council. Although it is frequently cited as being an original feature of the square layout, it has no historical basis.

13 Grosvenor Estate, *A Guide to the Belgravia Estate Management Scheme* (London: Grosvenor Estate, 1998), 4. (For more information, see www.grosvenor-gardens.co.uk.)

14 The inventory is available at *London Gardens Online* (http://www.londongardensonline.org.uk). In 2010 the Department for Communities and Local Government issued a policy statement (*Planning for the Historic Environment*, Planning Policy Statement 5 (London: The Stationery Office, 2010)), which requires local planning authorities to take into account the significance of heritage assets, whether designated or not, in reaching development management decisions, and to refer to the Historic Environment Record, a series of linked computer databases that hold information on known archaeological sites, finds, landscapes, buildings and other aspects of the historic environment.

15 The first competition took place in 1997. The London Gardens Society also hosts a London Garden Squares Competition.

16 Of the more than 290 green spaces examined in the survey, 116 were squares.

17 Peter Sibley, Jan Hewlett, Denis Vickers, Chris Gannaway, Kevin Morgan and Nigel Reeve, *London's Small Parks and Squares: A Place for Nature?, A Report from the London Biodiversity Partnership's Habitat Action Plan for Parks and Squares on a Survey of more than 290 Green Spaces in Central London* (London: London Biodiversity Partnership, n.d. [2005]), 46.

18 Anon., 'The Botanist', *OutRage!* (May 1999).

19 'Guide to London's Landscapes', *Architects' Journal* 148 (1968): 601.

20 Commission for Architecture and the Built Environment (CABE), Russell Square case study (www.cabe.org.uk/case-studies/russell-square/evaluation).

21 The new perimeter railings, like the modern replacement railings at Lincoln's Inn Fields, are considerably higher than the originals.

22 Mark Turner, 'Welcome to the Cruising Capital of the World', *Observer*, 30 July 2006.

23 Julie Burchill, 'The Age of Reason: Swallow the Bait', *Guardian*, 26 June 1999.

24 Beeson refers to the fact that from the late 1940s when the management of the garden was handed over by the Bedford Estate to the Local Authority it had been open almost twenty-four hours a day to all and sundry. This regime changed in the early 1990s when the square was locked at night to prevent what the London Borough of Camden has described as the use of the garden by 'undesirables' for casual sex.

25 '"Zone of Toleration" for Gay Sex in Russell Square?', *OutRage! Queer Intelligence Service*, London, 28 May 1999 (see http://rosecottage.me.uk/OutRage-archives/russell.htm).

26 Between 150 and 200 people were sleeping rough in the fields in 1993. Mary Carter and Heather Petch, 'Society: Hollow Victory in the Fields. London's biggest site for rough sleepers has been cleared, to the DoE's [Department of the Environment's] delight. But is this type of operation really so desirable?', *Guardian*, 31 March 1993.

27 'Second Front: Pass Notes, no. 90: Sir Matthew Farrer', *Guardian*, 16 February 1993; Laurence Pollock, 'Housing: A Policy that's Built on Sand', *Guardian*, 12 February 1993.

28 The Perambulator, 'To the Barricades', *London Gardener* 14 (2008–9): 23–6.

29 David Lambert, *The Park Keeper* (London: English Heritage, 2005), commissioned by English Heritage from the Parks Agency.

30 Alina Congreve, 'Three New Squares Critiqued: Something's Missing Here', *Garden Square News* 10, no.1 (2005): 20–2.

31 *Open Garden Squares Weekend, 12–13 June 2010* (London: n.p. [Transport for London?], 2010), 5.

32 Congreve, 'Three New Squares Critiqued', 20.

33 Congreve, 'Three New Squares Critiqued', 22.

34 Congreve, 'Three New Squares Critiqued', 22.

35 Congreve, 'Three New Squares Critiqued', 20.

36 Aspa Gospodini, 'Type and Function in the Urban Square: A Case Study of London' (PhD diss., University College London, 1988). In the abstract, Gospodini remarks: 'Since most of the traditional squares are still popular spaces in our cities, it is difficult to avoid the inference that there is, indeed, something in the form of the old squares which has been misinterpreted by modern designs.'

37 Gareth Huw Davies, 'Why Buy? 21st-Century Living', *Sunday Times*, 27 May 2001.

38 Steven Cook, 'The Greenwich Guinea Pigs: Millennium Communities', *Financial Times*, 12 February 2003.

39 Congreve, 'Three New Squares Critiqued', 20.

40 Congreve, 'Three New Squares Critiqued', 20. Squares, it should be noted, were not the only open spaces created within the village: 50 acres were also set aside for general recreation.

41 Heather Mulholland (Mulholland Research & Consulting), *Perceptions of Privacy and Density in Housing: Report on Research Findings Prepared for the Popular Housing Group* (London: Design for Homes Popular Housing Research 2003), 147. One courtyard was dubbed the 'Chardonnay Garden' 'because it was intended for quiet adult pursuits such as relaxing outside with a glass of wine or reading'.

42 Mulholland, *Perceptions of Privacy*, 24.

43 The Perambulator, 'Don't Eat the Ducks: Transgression in Public Parks', *London Gardener* 11 (2006–7): 39–42.

44 Mulholland, *Perceptions of Privacy*, 15.

45 'A Square is Born', *Garden Square News* 8, no. 1 (2003): 5.

46 Karen Robinson, 'Sampling the Lifestyle on Millionaires' Row', *Sunday Times*, 4 April 2004; 'Diamond Banks Property Sale', *Financial Times*, 27 March 2009; 'Despite the Downturn, Streets of London are Still Golden', *The Times*, 29 December 2009.

47 Congreve, 'Three New Squares Critiqued', 22. Even the Head of Planning for the Royal Borough of Kensington and Chelsea, and three councillors for Campden Hill Ward were 'interrogated by intimidating security guards' when they tried to enter the square. Cllr Tim Ahern, who later became Mayor of the Royal Borough, described the guards that accosted him as 'a couple of little Hitlers, trying to make it [the square] a no-go area'. He wrote several letters of complaint to the developers, which had no effect. Pippa Brill, '"Public Square" Seems to Be a Planning Failure', *Garden Square News* 12, no. 2 (2007): 6.

48 Brill, '"Public Square"': 6.

49 Henry Tricks, 'A Very British Form of Luxury Home', *Financial Times*, 31 May 2003.

50 Both the Phillimores and Thornwood Gardens (Phillimore Square) are the work of Nilsson Architects.

51 Sarah Blandy, email correspondence with the author, September 2010; Sarah Blandy, 'Secession or Cohesion? Exploring the Impact of Gated Communities in England', in *Community Cohesion in Crisis: New Dimensions of Diversity and Difference*, ed. John Flint and David Robinson (Bristol: Policy Press, 2008), 253. Blandy is Senior Lecturer in the School of Law in the Faculty of Education, Social Sciences and Law at the University of Leeds.

52 Anne Scott-James and Osbert Lancaster, *The Pleasure Garden: An Illustrated History of British Gardening* (London: J. Murray, 1977; repr. Harmondsworth: Penguin, 1979), 87.

53 Nikolaus Pevsner, *Visual Planning and the Picturesque*, ed. Mathew Aitchison (Los Angeles: Getty Research Institute, 2010), 93, 98.

Select Bibliography

Allen, Michelle, *Cleansing the City: Sanitary Geographies in Victorian London* (Athens, Ohio: Ohio University Press, 2008)

Andersen, J. A. [A. A. Feldborg], *A Dane's Excursions in Britain*, 2 vols (London: Mathews & Leigh, 1809)

Appleyard, Donald, M. Sue Gerson and Mark Lintell, 'The First Environmental Areas: Barnsbury and Pimlico', in *Livable Streets* (Berkeley and Los Angeles: University of California Press, 1981)

Archer, Jayne Elisabeth, Elizabeth Goldring and Sarah Knight, eds, *The Intellectual and Cultural World of the Early Modern Inns of Court* (Manchester: Manchester University Press, 2011)

Archer, John, 'Country and City in the American Romantic Suburb', *Journal of the Society of Architectural Historians* 42 (1983): 139–56

——, '*Rus in urbe*: Classical Ideals of Country and City in British Town Planning', *Eighteenth-Century Culture* 12 (1983): 159–86

Beattie, J. M., *Policing and Punishment in London, 1660–1750* (Oxford: Oxford University Press, 2001)

Beresford, Camilla, *The Development of Garden Squares* (London: English Heritage, 2003)

Bingham, Neil, 'Humphry and John Adey Repton's Unexecuted Design for Burlington Place, Piccadilly', *London Gardener* 12 (2006–7): 11–19

Blandy, Sarah, 'Secession or Cohesion? Exploring the Impact of Gated Communities in England', in *Community Cohesion in Crisis: New Dimensions of Diversity and Difference*, ed. John Flint and David Robinson (Bristol: Policy Press, 2008), 239–58

Blomfield, Reginald, *The Formal Garden in England*, 3rd ed. (London: Macmillan, 1901)

Borsay, Peter, *The English Urban Renaissance: Culture and Society in the Provincial Town, 1660–1770* (Oxford: Clarendon Press, 1989; first published as 'The English Urban Renaissance: The Development of Provincial Urban Culture, c. 1680–c. 1760', *Social History* 2 (1977): 581–603)

Boswell, James, *The Life of Samuel Johnson*, 4 vols (London: Baynes and Sons, 1826)

Bradley, H. Gilbert, *Dorset Square: A Short History* (London: Dorset Square Trust, 1984)

Britton, John, Edward Wedlake Brayley et al., *The Beauties of England and Wales, or, Delineations, Topographical, Historical, and Descriptive of Each County*, 18 vols (London: Vernon & Hood, and others, 1801–15)

Brownell, Morris R., *Samuel Johnson's Attitude to the Arts* (Oxford: Clarendon Press, 1989)

Byrom, Connie, *The Edinburgh New Town Gardens: 'Blessings as well as Beauties'* (Edinburgh: Birlinn, 2005)

Cecil, Mrs Evelyn (Alicia Amherst), 'Squares', in *London Parks and Gardens* (London: A. Constable, 1907), 217–41

Chalklin, C. W., and M. A. Havinden, eds, *Rural Change and Urban Growth, 1500–1800: Essays in English Regional History in Honour of W. G. Hoskins* (London: Longman, 1974)

Chancellor, E. Beresford, *The History of the Squares of London: Topographical and Historical* (London: Kegan Paul, Trench, Trübner, 1907)

Chastel-Rousseau, Charlotte, '*Rus in urbe*: les squares en Grande-Bretagne à l'époque Georgienne, 1714–1820', in *La nature citadine au siècle des lumières: promenades urbaines et villégiature*, ed. Daniel Rabreau et Sandra Pascalis, Annales du Centre Ledoux, vol. 5 (Paris: Arts & Arts, 2005)

——, 'The King in the Garden: Royal Statues and the Naturalization of the Hanoverian Dynasty in Early

Georgian Britain, 1714–1760', in *Sculpture and the Garden*, ed. Patrick Eyres and Fiona Russell (Aldershot: Ashgate, 2006), 61–70

Clarke, Richard, Elizabeth McKellar and Michael Symes, *Russell Square: A Lifelong Resource for Teaching and Learning*, FCE Occasional Paper no. 5 (London: Birkbeck, University of London, Faculty of Continuing Education, 2004)

Cohen-Portheim, Paul, *The Spirit of London*, 3rd rev. ed., ed. Raymond Mortimer (London: Batsford, 1950)

Collins, Wilkie, *Basil: A Story of Modern Life* (London: Richard Bentley, 1852; another ed., London: Sampson Low, Son & Co., 1862)

Colvin, Howard, *A Biographical Dictionary of British Architects 1600–1840*, 2nd ed. (London: J. Murray, 1978)

Congreve, Alina, 'Three New Squares Critiqued: Something's Missing Here', *Garden Square News* 10, no. 1 (2005): 20–2

Cosgrove, Denis, and Stephen Daniels, eds, *The Iconography of Landscape: Essays on the Symbolic Representation, Design and Use of Past Environments* (Cambridge: Cambridge University Press, 1988)

Cosh, Mary, *The Squares of Islington*, vol. 1: *Finsbury and Clerkenwell* (London: Islington Archaeology & History Society, 1990)

——, *The Squares of Islington*, vol. 2: *Islington Parish* (s.l. [London]: Islington Archaeology & History Society, 1993)

Cowan, Carrie, 'The Early Garden Committee Meetings of Some Westminster Squares', *London Gardener* 15 (2009–10): 89–100

Cruickshank, Dan, and Neil Burton, *Life in the Georgian City* (London: Viking, 1990)

Daniels, Stephen, *Humphry Repton: Landscape Gardening and the Geography of Georgian England* (New Haven: Yale University Press: 1999)

D'Aviler, Augustin-Charles, *Cours d'architecture qui comprend les ordres de Vignole* (Paris: N. Langlois, 1696)

Dasent, Arthur I., *The History of St James's Square and the Foundation of the West End of London* (London: Macmillan, 1895)

Defoe, Daniel, *A Tour thro' the Whole Island of Great Britain* (1725; repr., Everyman ed., London: Dent, 1962)

Dibdin, Emily, *A London Square and its Inhabitants* (London: Religious Tract Society, 1878)

Duggan, Diane, 'The Architectural Patronage of Francis Russell, 4th Earl of Bedford, 1628–1638' (PhD diss., Courtauld Institute of Art, 2002)

English Heritage, *A Campaign for London's Squares* (London: English Heritage, 2000)

Escobar, Jesús, *The Plaza Mayor and the Shaping of Baroque Madrid* (Cambridge: Cambridge University Press, 2004)

Fairchild, Thomas, *The City Gardener* (London: T. Woodward and J. Peele, 1722)

Fielding, John, *The New London Spy* (London: J. Cooke, 1771)

Fishman, Robert, *Bourgeois Utopias: The Rise and Fall of Suburbia* (New York: Basic Books, 1987)

Fitzroy Square Trustees, Minutes of the meetings, 1806–43, Trustees of the Fitzroy Square Frontagers

Forrest, Denys, *St James's Square: People, Houses, Happenings* (London: Quiller Press, 1986)

Forshaw, J. H., and Patrick Abercrombie, *County of London Plan, Prepared for the London County Council* (London: Macmillan, 1943)

Fox, Celina, 'The Battle of the Railings', *AA Files* 29 (1995): 49–60

Friedman, Terry, 'Foggini's Statue of Queen Anne', in *Kunst des Barock in der Toskana* (Munich: Bruckmann, 1976), 39–56

Fullmer, Samuel, *The Young Gardener's Best Companion, for the Thorough Practical Management of the Pleasure Ground and Flower Garden; Shrubbery, Nursery, Tree Plantation and Hedge* (London: n.p., 1781)

Fusch, Richard, 'The Piazza in Italian Urban Morphology', *Geographical Review* 84 (1994): 424–38

George, M. Dorothy, *London Life in the Eighteenth Century* (London: Kegan Paul, Trench, Trübner, 1925)

Giedion, Sigfried, 'The Dominance of Greenery: The London Square', in *Space, Time and Architecture: The Growth of a New Tradition*, 5th rev. ed. (Cambridge, Mass.: Harvard University Press, 1967), 716–33

Girouard, Mark, *The English Town* (New Haven and London: Yale University Press, 1990)

Glanville, Philippa, 'The Century of Squares', in *London in Maps* (London: Connoisseur, 1972)

Golby, John, and A. W. Purdue, *The Civilisation of the Crowd: Popular Culture in England, 1750–1900* (London: Batsford, 1984)

[Grosley, P.-J.], *Londres*, 3 vols (1765; Lausanne: n.p., 1770)

Grosvenor Estate, *A Guide to the Belgravia Estate Management Scheme* (London: Grosvenor Estate, 1998)

Gwynn, John, *London and Westminster Improved, Illustrated by Plans. To which is Prefixed, A Discourse on Publick Magnificence* (London: Dodsley, 1766)

Hamilton, Geoffrey Heathcote, *Queen Square, its Neighbourhood and its Institutions* (London: Leonard Parsons, 1926)

Harding, Vanessa, 'Gardens and Open Space in Early Modern London', in *London's Pride: The Glorious History of the Capital's Gardens*, ed. Mireille Gallinou (London: Anaya, 1990), 44–55

——, 'City, Capital, and Metropolis: The Changing Shape of Seventeenth-Century London', in *Imagining Early Modern London: Perceptions and Portrayals of the City from Stow to Strype, 1598–1720*, ed. J. F. Merritt (Cambridge: Cambridge University Press, 2001), 117–43

Harris, Eileen, and Nicholas Savage, *British Architectural Books and Writers, 1556–1785* (Cambridge: Cambridge University Press, 1990)

Harwood, Elain, and Andrew Saint, *London* (London: HMSO, 1991)

Hobhouse, Hermione, *Thomas Cubitt, Master Builder* (London: Macmillan, 1971)

Hobson, G. D., 'The Future of London Square Gardens', in *Some Thoughts on the Organization of Art after the War* (London: Batsford, n.d. [1946])

Hudson, Nicholas, 'Samuel Johnson, Urban Culture, and the Geography of Post-Fire London', *Studies in English Literature, 1500–1900* 42 (2002): 577–600

Hughson, David, *London: Being an Accurate History and Description of the British Metropolis and its Neighbourhood, to 30 Miles Extent, from an Actual Perambulation*, 6 vols (s.l.: n.p., 1805–9)

James, Frank A. J. L., and Anthony C. Peers, 'Conservation Plan for the Royal Institution of Great Britain', unpublished proposal, submitted by Rodney Melville and Partners to the Royal Institution, June 2003

James, John, *The Theory and Practice of Gardening . . . Done from the French Original [of Antoine Joseph Dézallier d'Argentville]* (s.l.: n.p., 1712)

Jenkins, Susan, *Portrait of a Patron: The Patronage and Collecting of James Brydges, 1st Duke of Chandos (1674–1744)* (Aldershot: Ashgate, 2007)

Jenner, Charles, *Town Eclogues* (London: T. Cadell, 1772)

Johnson, B. H., *Berkeley Square to Bond Street: The Early History of the Neighbourhood* (London: John Murray, 1952)

Kalm, Pehr, *Kalm's Account of his Visit to England on his Way to America in 1748* (London: Macmillan, 1892)

Keene, Derek, 'Growth, Modernisation and Control: The Transformation of London's Landscape, *c.*1500–*c.*1760', in *Two Capitals: London and Dublin, 1500–1840*, ed. Peter Clark and Raymond Gillespie (Oxford: Oxford University Press for the British Academy, 2001), 7–38

Küchelbecker, J. B., *Der nach Engelland reisende curieuse Passagier, oder Kurze Beschreibung der Stadt London und derer umliegenden Oerter* (Hanover: Nicolaus Förster und Sohn, 1726)

La Combe, François, *Tableau de Londres et de ses environs, avec un précis de la constitution de l'Angleterre, et de sa Decadence* (1777; London: Société Typographique, 1784)

Laird, Mark, *The Flowering of the English Landscape Garden: English Pleasure Grounds, 1720–1800* (Philadelphia: University of Pennsylvania Press, 1999)

Land Use Consultants, 'The Historical Development of Russell Square', unpublished report for London Borough of Camden, May 1997

——, 'Bloomsbury Square: Initial Historical Research', unpublished report for London Borough of Camden, 1998

——, 'Conservation Management Plan for Woburn Square', unpublished report for University of London, 2004

——, 'Conservation Management Plan for Tavistock Square', unpublished report for London Borough of Camden, 2007

Lawrence, Henry W., 'The Greening of the Squares of London: Transformation of Urban Landscapes and Ideals', *Annals of the Association of American Geographers* 83, no. 1 (1993): 90–118

Leinster Square Garden Committee, Minutes and accounts, 1920–52, Westminster City Archives 0792/2

The Letters of Sir Charles Bell (London: John Murray, 1870)

Lincoln's Inn Fields, Minutes of the Trustees, 1735–1879, British Library Manuscripts Department, Add. mss 35077–35081

Lloyd, Sarah, 'Amour in the Shrubbery: Reading the Detail of English Adultery Trial Publications of the 1780s', *Eighteenth-Century Studies* 39 (2006): 421–42

'London Gardens', *Garden* (3 August 1872)

London Parks and Gardens Trust, *London Inventory of Historic Green Spaces* (formerly *Inventory of Public Parks, Gardens, Squares, Cemeteries, and Churchyards of Local Historic Interest in Greater London*), available online at http://www.londongardenstrust.org

London Society, *London's Squares and How to Save Them* (s.l. [London]: London Society, n.d. [1927])

London Squares and Enclosures Preservation Bill, 1905, *Parliamentary Debates, House of Lords*, 5th ser. (1905), vol. 141, cc. 429–30

London Squares and Enclosures (Preservation) (No. 2) Bill, 1927, *Parliamentary Debates, House of Commons*, 5th ser. (1927), vol. 203, c. 1375

The London Squares Preservation Act, 1931, *Parliamentary Debates, House of Lords*, 5th ser. (1931), vol. 80, cc. 235–47

Longstaffe-Gowan, Todd, 'A Palmyrene Eye-Catcher in Hanover Square Gardens?' *London Gardener* 6 (2000–1): 50–9

——, 'Garden Squares', in *The London Town Garden, 1700–1840* (New Haven and London: Yale University Press for the Paul Mellon Centre for Studies in British Art, 2001)

——, 'Portman Square Garden: "The Montpelier of England"', *London Gardener* 12 (2006–7): 78–93

——, 'Brazen Proclamations: The Deployment of Statuary in Some Early London Garden Squares', *Sculpture Journal* 18 (2009): 52–66

Loudon, John Claudius, Letter to the editor, 22 December 1803, *Literary Journal* 2 (1803): cols 739–42

——, *An Encyclopaedia of Gardening* (London: Longman, Hurst, Rees, Orme, Brown and Green, 1822, and later eds)

——, *The Suburban Gardener, and Villa Companion* (s.l. [London]: privately printed, 1838)

Lubbock, Jules, *The Tyranny of Taste: The Politics of Architecture and Design in Britain, 1550–1960* (New Haven and London: Yale University Press for the Paul Mellon Centre for Studies in British Art, 1995)

Luttrell, Narcissus, *A Brief Historical Relation of State Affairs: From September 1678 to April 1714*, 6 vols (Oxford: Oxford University Press, 1857)

McCaig, Verena, 'Square Routes: An Investigation into the Conservation Issues Facing the Urban Landscape of the

Suburban London Square' (MSc diss., University of Bath, 2009)

MacColl, Dugald Sutherland, 'London Squares and a Traffic Tyranny', *Nineteenth Century and After* 115 (1934): 335–7

McKellar, Elizabeth, *The Birth of Modern London: The Development and Design of the City, 1660–1720* (Manchester: Manchester University Press: 1999)

McKenzie, Alexander, *The Parks, Open Spaces and Thoroughfares of London* (London: Waterlow & Sons, 1869)

Malcolm, James Peller, *Londinium Redivivum*, 4 vols (London: J. Nichols, 1802–7)

Malton, James, *Letters Addressed to Parliament and to the Public in General, on Various Improvements of the Metropolis* (Dublin: the author, 1787)

Manchester Square Garden, Minutes of the Trustees, March 1891–, Manchester Square Garden Trust

Martin, Valerie, 'Mecklenburgh Square and its Garden', unpublished report 2003

Mason, William, *An Heroic Epistle to Sir William Chambers* (London: J. Almon, 1773)

Mayhew, Henry and John Binny, *The Criminal Prisons of London and Scenes of Prison Life* (London: Griffin, Bohn, 1862)

Mercier, Louis-Sébastien, *Parallèle de Paris et de Londres* (1781), ed. Claude Bruneteau and Bernard Cottret (Paris: Didier Érudition, 1982)

Monconys, Balthasar de, *Journal des voyages de Monsieur de Monconys, publié par Sieur de Liergues, son fils* (Paris: Louis Billaine, 1677)

Montagu Square Garden, Minutes of the Trustees, 1814–1998, Westminster City Archives MSGT

Muralt, Béat Louis de, *Letters Describing the Character and Customs of the English and French Nations: With a Curious Essay on Travelling*, 2nd ed. (London: T. Edlin, 1726)

Murphy, Arthur, 'An Essay on the Life and Genius of Henry Fielding', in *The Works of Henry Fielding, Esq., with the Life of the Author*, 3rd ed., vol. 1 (London: A. Millar, 1766)

A New Critical Review of the Publick Buildings, Statues and Ornaments, in and about London and Westminster, 2nd ed. (London: printed by C. Ackers for J. Wilford and J. Clarke, 1736)

Ogborn, Miles, 'Designs on the City: John Gwynn's Plans for Georgian London', *Journal of British Studies* 43, no. 1 (2004): 15–39

Oldfield, Trenton James Hamilton, 'The Process of Enclosing Open Space in Contemporary London' (PhD diss., London School of Economics, 2008)

Olsen, Donald, *The Growth of Victorian London* (London: Batsford, 1976)

——, *Town Planning in London: The Eighteenth and Nineteenth Centuries* (New Haven and London: Yale University Press, 1964; 2nd ed. 1982)

'On the Ridiculous Consequence Assumed from Superiority of Places of Residence', *Monthly Mirror* 15 (1803): 238–41

Orpen, William, 'Are the Squares of London Used to Advantage?' *Country Life* (19 April 1924): 599–600

Palin, William, '"This Unfortunate and Ignored Locality": The Forgotten Squares of Stepney', *London Gardener* 12 (2006–7): 94–112

Palmer, Susan, 'From Fields to Gardens: The Management of Lincoln's Inn Fields in the Eighteenth and Nineteenth Centuries', *London Gardener* 10 (2004–5): 11–28

——, 'Lincoln's Inn Fields, Part II: The Management of the Gardens in the Twentieth Century', *London Gardener* 12 (2006–7): 54–67

Papworth, John B., *Select Views of London* (London: R. Ackermann, 1816)

Paul, Anthony, *A History of Manchester Square, London* (London: Manchester Square Trustees, 1971)

Pevsner, Nikolaus, *Visual Planning and the Picturesque*, ed. Mathew Aitchison (Los Angeles: Getty Research Institute, 2010)

Philippar, François, *Voyage agronomique en Angleterre, fait en 1829, ou, Essai sur les cultures de ce pays comparées à celles de la France* (Paris: Rousselon, 1830)

[Pote, Joseph], *The Foreigner's Guide, or, A Necessary and Instructive Companion both for the Foreigner and Native, in their Tour through the Cities of London and Wesminster [sic]*, 2nd ed. (London: J. Pote, 1740)

P. Q., *St. James's Park: A Comedy* (London: John Cooper, 1733)

Priestley, Stephen, 'The Fountain and Gardens in New Square, Lincoln's Inn: A Brief History', *London Gardener* 3 (1997–8): 24–9

Princes Square Garden Committee, Minutes of the Committee, 1861–1940, Westminster City Archives 0792/1

Pückler-Muskau, H. L. H. von, *Letters from Albion to a Friend on the Continent* (London: Gale, Curtis & Fenner, 1814)

——, *Tour in Germany, Holland and England in the Years 1826, 1827, 1828*, vol. 4 (London: n.p., 1832)

Queen's Gardens Association, Bayswater, Minutes of the Association, 1859–1969, Westminster City Archives, 1659

[Ralph, James], *A Critical Review of the Publick Buildings, Statues and Ornaments, in and about London and Westminster* (London: John Wallis, 1734)

Rasmussen, Steen Eiler, *London: The Unique City* (London: J. Cape, 1937; repr. Harmondsworth: Penguin, 1961)

Report of the Select Committee on Public Walks (London: n.p., 1833)

Repton, Humphry, *Observations on the Theory and Practice of Landscape Gardening* (London: J. Taylor, 1803)

Robinson, William, *The Parks, Promenades and Gardens of Paris* (London: John Murray, 1869; 2nd ed. as *The Parks and Gardens of Paris Considered in Relation to the Wants of Other Cities and of Public and Private Gardens*, London: Macmillan, 1878)

Rosso, Michela, 'Georgian London Revisited', *London Journal* 26, no. 2 (2001): 35–50

Royal Borough of Kensington, Report of Housing and Town Planning (Garden Squares) Sub-Committee, 1949, Royal Borough of Kensington and Chelsea, Local Studies and Archives

Royal Commission on London Squares: Report and Appendices, Cmd. 3196 (London: HMSO, 1928)

Ryerson, Richard Alan, ed., *Adams Family Correspondence*, vol. 6: *December 1784–December 1785* (Cambridge: Belknap Press of Harvard University Press, 1993)

Saint, Andrew, ed., *Politics and the People of London: The London County Council, 1895–1965* (London: Hambledon Press, 1989)

St James's Square Trust, Minutes of the Trustees, 1726–1835, Westminster City Archives, 395

Schlarman, Julie, 'The Social Geography of Grosvenor Square: Mapping Gender and Politics, 1720–1760', *London Journal* 28, no. 1 (2003): 5–28

Scott-James, Anne, and Osbert Lancaster, 'The London Square', in *The Pleasure Garden: An Illustrated History of British Gardening* (London: J. Murray, 1977; repr. Harmondsworth: Penguin, 1979)

Shepherd, Thomas Hosmer, and James Elmes, *Metropolitan Improvements, or, London in the Nineteenth Century* (London: Jones & Co., 1827)

Smithson, Alison, and Peter Smithson, *The Charged Void* (New York: Monacelli Press, 2005)

Smuts, Malcolm, 'The Court and its Neighborhood: Royal Policy and Urban Growth in the Early Stuart West End', *Journal of British Studies* 30 (1991): 117–49

Soane, John, *Lectures on Architecture, as Delivered to the Students of the Royal Academy from 1809 to 1836*, ed. Arthur T. Bolton (London: Soane Museum, 1929)

Souchal, François, ed., *French Sculptors of the 17th and 18th Centuries: The Reign of Louis XIV*, 4 vols (Oxford: Cassirer, 1977–93)

[Stewart, John], *Critical Observations on the Buildings and Improvements of London* (London: J. Dodsley, 1771)

Stone, Lawrence, 'The Residential Development in the West End of London in the Seventeenth Century', in *After the Reformation: Essays in Honor of J. H. Hexter*, ed. Barbara C. Malament (Philadelphia: University of Pennsylvania Press; Manchester: Manchester University Press, 1980), 167–212

Summerson, John, *Georgian London* (London: Pleiades Books, 1945; repr. Harmondsworth: Penguin, 1978)

Sumner, Chris, ed., *London Squares: The Proceedings of the London Squares Conference, a Forum on the Past, Present and Future of London's Squares*, 1995 (London: London Historic Parks and Gardens Trust, 1997)

Survey of London, 47 vols (London: [various publishers], 1900–2008)

Thompson, F. M. L., ed., *The Rise of Suburbia* (Leicester: Leicester University Press: 1982)

Thornbury, Walter, and Edward Walford, *Old and New London: A Narrative of its History, its People, and its Places*, 6 vols (London: Cassell, Petter and Galpin, 1897)

Thurloe Square Garden Square Committee, Minute book, 23 January 1919–9 September 1967, and other related papers to 1973, Royal Borough of Kensington and Chelsea, Local Studies and Archives

Timbs, John, *Curiosities of London, Exhibiting the Most Rare and Remarkable Objects of Interest in the Metropolis* (London: David Bogue, 1855; new ed., s.l. [London]: Longmans, 1868)

Trusler, John, *The London Adviser and Guide, Containing Every Instruction and Information Useful and Necessary to Persons Living in London and Coming to Reside There* (London: the author, 1790)

Uffenbach, Zacharias Conrad von, *London in 1710, from the Travels of Zacharias Conrad von Uffenbach*, trans. and ed. W. H. Quarrell and Margaret Mare (London: Faber & Faber, 1934)

Varey, Simon, *Space and the Eighteenth-Century English Novel* (Cambridge: Cambridge University Press, 1990)

Watkin, David, ed., *Sir John Soane: Enlightenment Thought and the Royal Academy Lectures* (Cambridge: Cambridge University Press, 1996)

Weale, John, 'Squares', in *London Exhibited in 1851, Elucidating its Natural and Physical Characteristics, its Antiquity and Architecture* (s.l., 1851)

[Weir, William], 'The Squares of London', in *London*, vol. 6, ed. Charles Knight (London: Charles Knight & Co., 1844), 193–208; 2nd ed. (London: Henry G. Bohn, 1851)

Whately, Thomas, *Observations on Modern Gardening* (London: T. Payne, 1770)

Wheatley, Henry B., *Round about Piccadilly and Pall Mall* (London: Smith, Elder & Co., 1870)

Whipham, Thomas, *Montagu Square: An Account of its History and Development* (London: Olympic Press, 1990)

Williams, Laura, '"To recreate and refresh their dulled spirites in the sweet and wholesome ayre": Green Space and the Growth of the City', in *Imagining Early Modern London: Perceptions and Portrayals of the City from Stow to Strype, 1598–1720*, ed. J. F. Merritt (Cambridge: Cambridge University Press, 2001), 185–213

Williams, Michael, 'The Enclosure and Reclamation of Waste Land in England and Wales in the Eighteenth and Nineteenth Centuries', *Transactions of the Institute of British Geographers* 51 (November 1970): 55–69

Wood, John, the elder, *An Essay Towards a Description of the City of Bath*, 2 vols (s.l. [Bath]: W. Frederick, 1742)

Wordie, J. R., 'The Chronology of English Enclosure, 1500–1914', *Economic History Review* 36 (1983): 483–505

Zucker, Paul, *Town and Square: From the Agora to the Village Green* (Oxford: Oxford University Press, 1959)

Photograph Credits

Numbers refer to fig. references, unless stated

Photo by General Photographic Agency/Getty Images: pg. x; Reproduced by permission of Clare Hastings: 1; © The Trustees of the British Museum: 2, 10,11, 12, 18, 19, 20, 21, 22, 23, 24, 25, 31, 34, 35, 36, 38, 39, 42, 44, 46, 47, 48, 51, 59, 61, 62, 67, 68, 73, 74, 75, 78, 81, 87, 88, 89, 93, 95, 96, 100, 103, 115, 127, 131, 132, 137, 143, 157, 169, 191; Yale Center for British Art, New Haven, Connecticut: 3, 76, 92; Courtesy Sir John Soane's Museum: 4, 106, 107, 122, 144; English Heritage Photo Library. © English Heritage, National Monuments Record: 5, 15, 165; Photo Felix Man, Picture Post/Getty Images: 6; By permission of the Fitzroy Square Frontagers: 7; Courtesy Portman Estate Archives: 8, 80; Courtesy Hertfordshire Archives and Local Studies: 9; © Country Life: 13, 16, 256; Courtesy Lambeth Archives, Minet Library: 17, 251; City of London Corporation, London Metropolitan Archives: 27, 40, 85, 90, 99, 108, 120, 121, 133, 140, 141, 142, 146, 155, 166, 174, 252; Courtesy Pepys Library, Magdalene College, Cambridge: 28; By kind permission of the Duke of Bedford and the Trustees of the Bedford Estates: 29, 82, 114, 129, 187; © Ayuntamiento de Madrid. Museo de Historia: 32; © Collection of the Earl of Pembroke, Wilton House, Wiltshire / The Bridgeman Art Library: 33; The National Archives, Kew: 45, 124; © The British Library Board: 53, 70, 111, 126, 130, 135, 149, 150, 156, 184, 192; Royal Horticultural Society, Lindley Library: 55, 56, 170, 171, 172, 176, 177, 178; Private Collection / The Bridgeman Art Library: 57; Courtesy the Grosvenor Estate: 58; The Royal Collection © 2011 Her Majesty Queen Elizabeth II: 60; By kind permission of Soprintendenza alle Gallerie per le Provincie Firenze: 63, 64, 65; London Metropolitan Archives, courtesy Trustees of the Foundling Hospital: 83, 84; Stiftung Oskar Reinhart, Winterthur: 101; The Scarsdale Collection, © National Trust / Andrew Patterson: 102; © Museum of London: 104, 105; Courtesy City of Westminster Archives Centre: 112, 128, 236; Courtesy of Royal Academy of Arts Library, London: 116; © National Library of Scotland: 125; Courtesy Royal Borough of Kensington and Chelsea, Family and Children's Service: 136, 159, 161, 193, 207, 227; Islington Local History Centre: 138, 222, 253, 267; © V&A Images: 147, 258; Photo Otto Herschan, Getty Images: 164; © Illustrated London News Ltd / Mary Evans Picture Library: 168; Courtesy London Library: 179; © Grenville Collins Postcard Collection / Mary Evans Picture Library: 183, 201; Courtesy Tower Hamlets Local History Library and Archives, Bancroft Library: 185; Hammersmith and Fulham Archives and Local History Centre: 196; Topical Press Agency / Getty Images: 199, 200, 226, 242; Courtesy Robert Byng, Wrotham Park: 202; Courtesy Kautz Family: 203; Courtesy The London Society: 205, 268; Courtesy Gavin Stamp: 208, 209, 212, 215; © Tate, London: 211; Camden Local Studies and Archives Centre: 213, 234, 235; Photo H. F. Davis, Topical Press Agency / Getty Images: 214; Hulton Archive, General Photographic Agency / Getty Images: 217; Photo Herbert Felton, Hulton Archive / Getty Images: 219; Keystone / Getty Images: 220; Architectural Press Archive /RIBA Library Photographs Collection: 221, 224, 237, 238, 240, 244, 254, 255, 260, 264, 266, 269, 270; Hulton Archive / Getty Images: 223; Photo by Central Press / Getty Images: 225; Imperial War Museum: 228, 230, 231, 232; © City of Westminster Archives Centre, London / The Bridgeman Art Library: 229; Picture Post/Hulton Archive/Getty Images: pg. 234; PNA Rota / Getty Images: 239; Photo Kurt Hutton, Picture Post / Getty Images: 245; © J Paul Getty Trust: 246; Architectural Press Archive / RIBA Library Photographs Collection, © Estate of Gordon Cullen: 247, 248, 249, 250; RIBA Library Photographs Collection: 257; Henk Snoek / RIBA Library Photographs Collection: 259; RIBA Library Drawings and Archives Collection: 261, 262; Photo Peter Trulock, Fox Photos / Getty Images: 265; Courtesy Nick Wates (www.nickwates.co.uk): 271; Courtesy Neville Capil: 272; Photo Jim Gray, Keystone / Getty Images: 273; Photograph by Phil Gyford: pg. 274; Courtesy Martin Usborne (www.martinusborne.com): 277

Index

Note: Page numbers in *italics* refer to illustrations; references to end notes are given by page number followed by 'n' and the note number in parentheses, e.g. 296(n.74)